D1572037

CANADIAN
WARSHIP NAMES

CANADIAN
WARSHIP NAMES

LCdr David J. Freeman, CF (Ret'd)

Vanwell Publishing Limited
St. Catharines, Ontario

Vanwell Publishing acknowledges the financial support of the Government of Canada through the Book Publishing Industry Development Program for our publishing activities.

Design: Linda Moroz-Irvine

Vanwell Publishing Limited
1 Northrup Crescent
P.O. Box 2131
St. Catharines, Ontario L2R 7S2

Printed in Canada

Canadian Cataloguing in Publication Data

Freeman, David J., 1941-
      Canadian warship names

Includes bibliographical references and index.
ISBN 1-55125-048-9

1. Canada. Royal Canadian Navy – Lists of vessels. 2. Warships – Canada – Names. I. Title.

VA400.F73 2000   359.8'3'0971   C00-931650-7

To my father
3859E C2QR3 David H. Freeman, RCNVR & RCN
and to my uncle
3731E C2TI4 George (Gerry) Freeman, RCNVR & RCN
1919–1980
the real seamen in the family
and

to the men and women
who served, are serving, or will serve,
in the ships and establishments
in these pages.

Former warships in Bedwell Harbour on the west coast, early Dec 1947. From L to R, the former CHARLOTTETOWN (?), LONGUEUIL, WASKESIU, KOKANEE (?). Photo taken from quarterdeck of former DUNVER. (R Greene, Capital Iron, Victoria, BC)

And now the old ships and their men are gone;
the new ships and the new men, many of them
bearing the old auspicious names, have taken
up their watch on the stern and impartial sea...
Joseph Conrad, *The Mirror of the Sea*

Kingston class minesweepers at Esquimalt, December 1999. On the right of the formation: YELLOWKNIFE and to her left SASKATOON, NANAIMO, EDMONTON, BRANDON and WHITEHORSE. The masts of the former destroyer escorts RESTIGOUCHE and KOOTENAY can be seen behind the mast of NANAIMO. (660-00A, AC)

Table of Contents

Foreword

A warship's name; is it important? Should it have meaning? If so, what? Is there historical context to a name? Does a name honour a person, and if so, who? Is a place or a community to be linked to the ship through her name? Is there a process used to gain approval for a name? If there is, what is it and has it been followed? Who approves the names for new warships and auxiliary vessels belonging to the Department of National Defence? Where can one find answers to these questions?

In *Canadian Warship Names*, Dave Freeman provides an immediate answer to the last question. He has also done an admirable job at answering the remaining questions. Dave has turned a lifelong hobby and professional interest into a book that traces the history of how and why Canada's warships and Department of Defence auxiliary vessels have been named. He has traced that development of the process, with all its warts, through the ninety-year life of our Navy. He has compiled a comprehensive listing of names used in the RCN and the Canadian Navy, which will serve as an excellent reference for those interested in the names used in the 20th century. Those yet to come will have at their disposal a tool that was not available to those of us who had to struggle with the development of names for new ships. I can recall some tough discussions with the author as he helped to develop lists of names for new ships when we were both still in uniform.

In the final analysis, choosing a name for a ship or class of ships is much like picking the name for a child. The decision on an approved list will be influenced by many of the same factors; personality of military and civilian personal involved, the circumstances of the time and politics—be it within the Naval family, the Department of National Defence or the Government of the day. In today's context, all one can hope for is that the requirement to name new ships will be forever present for Canadian Naval Staffs. This book will be a great starting point for addressing the issue.

John R. Anderson
Admiral (Ret'd)
North Saanich, BC

Preface

Names of HMC Ships were not created out of thin air. Many are the reasons why a piece of steel or a plot of land, has received a particular name. This volume records those reasons for the years 1910–1999. With respect to the RCN and Maritime Command of the Canadian Forces, this volume contains the names of the following:

◆ commissioned warships;

◆ vessels designated as warships to which names were given or intended to be given;

◆ Canadian Naval Auxiliary Vessels and Canadian Forces Auxiliary Vessels;

◆ RCN shore establishments; and

◆ a few RN ships/establishments whose history has special connotations to Canadians. Some of these are AVALON III, NABOB, PUNCHER and SEABORN. Each RN name is clearly labeled "HMS."

Except for the six unnamed submarines, numbered vessels are not included.

In compiling this book, an unavoidable problem is deciding what names to exclude. One of my first ideas was to base the list on the vessels included in a standard work of reference. This approach possessed two major flaws:

1. shore establishments would not appear; but in the Navy a shore establishment was still a "ship"—the only difference between the two was that the latter floated and traveled about and up to 1972 Canadian seaman received their "tot;" and

2. standard works often include numbered vessels that had no name.

Another problem was whether or not to include all the small vessels such as tugs. But try to define "small." Thirty feet? Four hundred tons? An auxiliary? No matter the criteria, it seemed that some vessel of historical importance would be left out. The solution gradually appeared: include all possible names regardless of size, tonnage or purpose. Excluded from this sweeping list were:

◆ the Sailorette class sloops and other vessels of the RCN/CF Sailing Association;

◆ "shore" establishments of the Canadian Forces after 1965; and

◆ various RCASC and RCAF vessels (but some are included in Appendix M).

This book, therefore, incorporates within one volume a comprehensive list of the names of all known naval vessels and establishments, plus their dates in commission, and

- for each name, lists each time the name was given or intended to be given, to a ship;
- indicates the origin or purpose of the name and its meaning, where known;
- records stories on the background of and procedure for, the selection of those names;
- records information such as the reason for alternative names;
- lists the appropriate pennant numbers borne by the ship; and
- indicates whether or not an official badge was assigned to that name.

Acknowledgements

This information started as a card file compiled for my own purposes and grew out of all proportion. The inspiration came from *British Warship Names*, a dictionary containing the origin of many of the names borne by ships of the Royal Navy. The motivation came from a chance visit to the then Directorate of History, NDHQ, in the spring of 1983.

This book would not have been possible without the help of many people. In particular, the following must be thanked for replying to letters, listening with patience to ideas and explanations, digging into dusty files or racking their memories for long-neglected facts. For details on the Supplementary Radio System and Naval Radio Stations: Maj Ron Beal, NDHQ; Maj Catherine Eyre; Maj Charlie Hensby, CFS Newport Corner; and LCdr Al Young.

My thanks also to: Mr. Ron Perkin, Prince Rupert Chamber of Commerce, for locating CHATHAM, PORT EDWARD and MONTREAL CIRCLE; Cdr Tom Miller, for details on the unofficial names in the Training Group Pacific; Cdr Wally Turner, for information on the Halifax Class Frigates; Dr. J.G. Pike, RMC, for locating STONE FRIGATE; LCdr Ron Lysell for articles on VENTURE; Mr. Dave Kealy, NDHQ/D HIST, for advice, assistance, unlimited access and for having all the classified references downgraded; Mr. Roy York, NDHQ/D INFO, for searching his files; Mr. Dave Mulligan, NDHQ/DAV, for details on auxiliary vessels; Lt(N) Ray Stacey, CO of HMCS MIRAMICHI, for facts on the minesweepers; LCdr Mike Hodgson, for data on the Porte vessels; Mr. J.E. MacNelly, formerly SO STATS, for reading and approving selected sections of the manuscript; LCdr Bob Munday, who knew everyone I didn't know; Mr. Philip Chaplin, Cdr Fraser McKee, Capt (N) Bob Darlington, and Adm John Anderson, for reading the manuscript and making invaluable suggestions; for P1 Mike Grayson for comments regarding ceremonial matters; Ken Macpherson for assistance in sorting out the minor vessels; Dave Perkins for submarine information; Lt(N) M Lafleur, HMCS HURON, for organizing a photo session of the brow; LCdr Richard Gimblett, NDHQ/DHH, for insights, support and encouragement; Maj Paul Lansey, NDHQ/DHH, for assistance above valuation over the years and for answering all my questions, sometime even cheerfully; to various members of the naval community across this country who responded quickly and accurately to mail, telephone messages, faxes and email—VMT and BZ. My heartfelt thanks to my editor Angela Dobler, who always kept me on course. And to Marion, Lynne and Leigh, my wife and daughters, for their continuous support and encouragement during the last 16 years.

Finally, to Mrs. Sharon Hodkinson, Mrs. Debbie Labrie, Mrs. Merilyn Ekman, and Mrs. Jean Brooks, CFTSHQ Trenton 1983-86; Miss Bernadette Turgeon, Mr. Jim Lobban and Miss Louise Keenleyside, PMO TRUMP Ottawa, 1986; and LS Rosemarie Janzen, TRUMP Detachment Esquimalt 1994-96; for typing and updating the manuscript over the years and without whom this book would not have been possible.

Every effort has been made to check all available sources and to ensure that the information is as accurate and up to date as possible. All human endeavours come complete with mistakes and this book is no exception: I take credit for any and all mistakes, may they be few. Readers are requested to inform the author of errors, omissions or new information.*

David J. Freeman
Victoria, BC
April 2000

A Note About Photographs

For this book I have chosen to employ photographs of many different types of "ships," to show groups of ships as well as many of the smaller, lesser known vessels such as auxilliaries and some establishments. All photos used with permission.

The photographs were obtained from the following sources:
1. Ken Macpherson, Port Hope, Ontario. (KM Coll)
2. Lt Col F.H.D. Nelson, Esquimalt, BC, the CFB Esquimalt historian. (FDN Coll)
3. The British Columbia Provincial Archives. (BCPA)
4 Author's collection. (AC)
5. Naval Public Affairs. (NPA)

Where known, the source of the photograph, usually RCN or CF, plus the negative number have been included in each caption.

My special thanks to Ken Macpherson and Lt Col F.H.D. Nelson for unlimited access to their extensive photographic libraries; and LCdrs G. Arbuckle and R. Gimblett of NDHQ/CMS for obtaining the photograph of NIOBE used in Section N of the List of Ship Names.

---

*LCdr David J. Freeman, CF (Ret'd), 992 Karen Crescent, Victoria, BC, V8X 3C6.

Introduction

At first view, the subject of names for warships would seem to be a simple one. After all, a name is no more than a sound which in writing is represented by a collection of letters. Like other names, however, the one carried by a ship is much more than just a sound. It often has historical and geographical connotations and references. Depending on how the name was selected and when, the name may have political, social or propaganda purposes as well. The meaning or significance of the name affects the ship's badge, whether official or unofficial. Names, of course, also influence a ship's nickname and by its name a ship is linked to its class and often to its type. A ship's name is directly related to Battle Honours and the dates when the ship was in commission. Finally, to the ship's company, the name of their ship is the name of their home.

Since this book deals with over 900 names, each name can have only a brief mention. Consequently, much information on class and type is left out. The chapters at the beginning are an endeavour to add cohesion to these 900 names that cover a span of 89 years. Such a broad subject has been tackled by topics and each chapter is devoted to one or more related ideas. Within each chapter, topics are organized within three broad chronological areas: Early Days, 1910–1939; Second World War, 1939–1945; and Post War, 1945 to the present. Each topic is covered in depth but for ease of understanding and narrative flow, certain facts are briefly repeated in other topics and chapters.

By long standing tradition,[1] a commanding officer of a ship is known by the name of his vessel, e.g. "SAGUENAY."[2] To distinguish the ship from her CO, the ship is referred to as "the SAGUENAY," "the destroyer SAGUENAY," or "HMCS SAGUENAY."[3] In this work, many of the references are to the names and not to the ships themselves. Following the usage of Manning & Walker, therefore, the article "the" is usually not placed in front of a name except where direct reference to the ship is made or intended. Similarly, the title "HMCS" is used only where necessary for clarity. "HMS," however, is always used in front of RN names or when the name is being used in its RN connotation, e.g. HMS NABOB and HMS PATRICIAN.

The style followed with respect to capitalization of ships' names is that set out in BR 49, *The RCN Correspondence Manual*, CFAO 36-7 (1998-1995), and MAR-CORD 36-07(1995-1999), all of which state that the names of ships shall be typed in capitals. This follows the form seen on cap tallies, Kisbie rings and a ship's name board. To distinguish naval vessels from other vessels, the names of non naval vessels are noted in italics, e.g. *Queen Mary*. Town, city and place names are printed in normal type, e.g. Regina.

Unless otherwise stated, references are from sources in the Directorate of History and Heritage (DHH), National Defence Headquarters (NDHQ). As can be seen from the bibliography, the main source of information is taken from primary and secondary sources in DHH, supplemented by sources from the National Archives of Canada (NAC). Reference books were obtained from the author's collection as well as the library of the Royal Military College, Kingston, and the Department of National Defence (DND) Library in NDHQ, Ottawa.

Notes

1. A custom is a practice that a certain group follows, but a tradition is a custom that has been passed from one generation of that group to another.

2. For an example of this use, see Lamb, *The Corvette Navy*, p 96.

3. See "Nothing so Indefinite as the Definite Article," *The Crowsnest*, Dec 1955, p8. Unlike the phrase "the USS CONSTITUTION," the use of the article "the" in front of the title HMCS is grammatically incorrect: an article does not precede a pronoun.

Chapter One

In Commission

Prior to this work no single list existed of all vessels and establishments commissioned in the Canadian Navy. This book deals with the names borne by Canadian warships, auxiliaries and establishments in commission since 1910. As will be illustrated, documenting that a given ship commissioned on one specific date and paid off on another can be arduous. Even proving that a given ship actually commissioned can be difficult. Consequently, the clarification of certain terms, concepts and regulations—such as in commission, warship, establishment, auxiliary, and the white ensign—is necessary prior to any discussion on names. If the vessel was not commissioned or at least not intended to be, the name has no significance to this book.

Being a ship in commission does not entitle a vessel to a name. Trawlers in the First World War and Motor Launches in the Second were both commissioned warships but they received only numbers and not names. Further, recording such changes as did occur in terminology and regulations can explain why pieces of steel or a collection of buildings earned the right to be referred to as one of HMC Ships in commission; and why others with similar characteristics did not.

The principal regulations originally governing the RCN were *King's Regulations and Admiralty Instructions* (KR&AI) and the British *Naval Discipline Act* of 1866. These were modified as required by the *Naval Service Act* of 1910 and

The first NADEN (foreground), the first STADACONA (left rear) and GIVENCHY at Esquimalt circa 1919. (BCPA B-06809)

a few *Canadian Naval Orders*. A new *Naval Service Act* was enacted in 1944. This led to the first edition of *King's Regulations for the Government of His Majesty's Canadian Naval Service* (KRCN) in October 1945. In 1951, as a result of the *National Defence Act* of 1950, a new *King's Regulations and Orders for the RCN*, also called KRCN, came into force. And in 1968 with the unification of the three services, *Queen's Regulations and Orders* (QR&O) for the Canadian Forces became law.

One of the features that sets seamen apart from people who live and work ashore is their language. At the core of this language is a select number of terms and phrases which have been in constant use for generations, originating with the Royal Navy, used in the RCN and still in use in Maritime Command. On occasion, some of these terms have been applied either casually or inaccurately by some of the Naval community such as the term "decommission." Up to 1990 when this term first appeared in the concise Oxford Dictionary, there was no such word, the correct term being "to pay off." In other cases the Navy has continued to follow some practices whose original purpose has long been superseded—the daily issue of a tot of rum far outlived its original purpose—or whose governing regulation has been changed, e.g. see the use of the title HMCS for shore establishments later in this chapter.

The second VENTURE, date unknown but probably in the late 1930s. (RCN O-781-2, KM Coll.)

In Commission

The term "in commission" originated in the days of sail and referred to the captain being given a commission to take one of HM Ships and bring her into service. The captain on being appointed "to a ship laid up 'in ordinary' [that is not in commission], hired a boat, [and] had himself rowed out to the ship."[1] He then gathered whatever crew he could find, hoisted his pennant and the appropriate ensign,[2] and read aloud his commission. From that point on, the ship was said to be in commission.[3] By the end of the 19th century, this procedure had been modified somewhat. The captain still received a directive from the Admiralty but he now received a ship's company as well. In Canada, after 1910, the directive to place one of HMC Ships in commission came from MND through his naval staff. Such a procedure is still more or in less in effect.

Today, the commissioning ceremony is complete with general officers, a band, a guard, civic dignitaries, speeches, etc. In the past, some commissioning ceremonies were quite brief. As told by Lawrence, *Tales of the North Atlantic*, in the fall of 1937, VENTURE was due to be taken over from her Nova Scotian builder. Unknown to the navy, the builder of this wooden schooner had run into financial difficulties, the result being the nailing of a lien on her mast. This lien effectively prevented the commanding officer designate from placing his vessel in commission. Using his initiative and imagination, the CO duped the deputy sheriff who had served the lien into briefly absenting himself from the ship. While he was ashore, an armed sentry was immediately stationed at the brow and the Red Ensign hurriedly replaced by a White Ensign. Thus, in one of the shortest but most interesting commissioning ceremonies ever recorded, the second VENTURE commissioned.

The date a ship commissioned had several immediate effects. Up to 1970, on the day of commissioning, personnel dressed as seamen could wear the appropriate cap tally for the first time. This was also the date on which a person's service documents were annotated as having joined the newly commissioned ship. Immediately prior to the commissioning date, should a rating be charged for an offence, he was summarily tried by the commanding officer of the depot ship, or supporting establishment, and not by the designated CO of the about-to-be commissioned ship. Rum issue also started on the day of commission as did the rendering of honours and salutes. And on this date the ship could display her Kisbie (life saving) rings on which was painted her name and title, and her tally plate. She was now His/Her Majesty's Canadian Ship.

Paying Off

To bring a ship into service the commanding officer (CO) places her in commission. To take her out of service, the CO pays her off. By 1815 the term "paid off," which dates from at least 1698, meant that the seamen were paid up to date the wages owing them, then dispersed and the ensign and the captain's pennant hauled down. At this time, the only person who could haul down the pennant was the cook who held the rank of Warrant Officer. In fact, no officer could depart the vessel until the cook struck the pennant at sunset. It is recorded that once when HMS CALEDONIA was to pay off, the cook could not be located and the officers had to wait a day or so until he returned before they could depart.[4]

Paying off also meant the temporary or permanent end to a ship's ability to fight, and up to the 1990s that meaning still held true. Not only was the ship's company removed but so were such items as documents, ammunition and explosives, stores, and often some equipment or machinery.[5] Legally, the vessel has no right to use the title HMCS but seamen tended to overlook this technicality when the ship was just placed in reserve. Where weapons or major pieces of equipment were removed and she was reduced in status to that of a hulk, naval personnel usually tended to refer to her now as "the former SAGUENAY," or the hulk SAGUENAY. Custom and habit meant many seamen continued to refer to the ship as HMCS, even when the ship was being towed to the breakers, but this was incorrect. In recent years, the Artificial Reef Society on the west coast has purchased several former destroyers, sunk them in specific locations and turned them into reefs. On all occasions, the actual sinking has been heralded in local advertisements by phrases such as "Help Sink the [sic] HMCS CHAUDIERE." When a ship pays off, she no longer retains the title HMCS. But she can be referred to as "the former HMCS CHAUDIERE."

The terms "in commission" and "paid off," as well as related terms such as "commissioned," are applied by seamen to all manner of floating craft. With respect to a warship, these words have a special significance.

Characteristics of a Warship

In broad terms, a warship is any vessel either specifically designed or later modified to take offensive action during war and there are two basic characteristics that distinguish a warship from any other vessel. First, warships generally carry some form of armament although admittedly today, the armament on some cannot easily be seen. Like all generalizations, there are exceptions. LABRADOR carried no armament although she had provision for a forward mounting, and in 1995 neither CORMORANT nor PROVIDER carried armament. Further, in wartime some merchant vessels carry armament and even in peacetime some government and police vessels are armed.

Second, and almost universally, warships in peacetime in the 20th century are painted some shade of grey. Again, there are exceptions. Submarines are generally painted black but British boats have had a variety of colours, including blue and green, depending on their areas of operation. LABRADOR was painted white and HMS ENDURANCE, an ice patrol ship circa 1980, had her hull painted a vivid red. When a warship is taken out of commission, her armament is rarely removed and she is not painted another colour. By themselves, therefore, neither of these two characteristics are indicative that a specific vessel is a warship in commission.

Commissioned Warship

In all the various regulations that governed the Navy from 1910, only once was the term "commissioned ship" ever defined in writing and that was between 1945 and 1951. Thirty-five years after the start of the navy, a commissioned ship was finally defined in article 1.02 in KRCN 1945, as "a ship placed in service in His Majesty's Canadian Naval Service in accordance with a commissioning order issued by the minister." The authority to commission a ship resides only with the captain, a fact sometimes forgotten. A plaque at the entrance to SCOTIAN c. 1986 alleges that J. Michael Forrestal, MP, commissioned her in March 1985.

In a later edition of KRCN, Chapter 39 was allocated for regulations on commissioning but this chapter was never written. Even today, there is not one chapter or article in QR&O or Maritime Command Orders on the significance of commissioning. A ship is simply defined as "a unit that is a vessel of the Canadian Forces commissioned or ordered to be commissioned."[6] Even the latest version of the *Maritime Command Ceremonial Manual* states only the procedure for commissioning a ship. The significance of this act is not mentioned.

This decided lack of written regulations has made it very difficult to determine when a vessel was actually a commissioned ship in the Naval Service of Canada. By circumstantial evidence however, a warship in commission displays certain traits.

Characteristics of a Commissioned Warship

By the early 20th century, a commissioned vessel in the Royal Navy had these characteristics:

a. captain. The officer in command of a commissioned vessel was called the captain—under the 1950 National Defence Act, this officer became the Commanding Officer—and under the Naval Discipline Act and its successors, the captain had specific powers of punishment accorded no other Naval Officer of equal rank. Later, the captain of a commissioned warship received "command money," a special allowance accorded him as long as he held his appointment as captain;[7]

b. ship's company. Assigned to that vessel, these personnel had a uniform, were subject to the Naval Discipline Act, were authorized to be paid, and were entitled to a daily ration of rum. Even as late as 1959, RN ships and shore establishments had to be in commission before the men could be paid or the captain could exercise his disciplinary powers.[8] When cap ribbons were introduced as part of the seamen's uniform, ratings drafted to the ship were also entitled to wear the appropriate ribbon displaying the ship's name, from the day the vessel was placed in commission. During wartime, as a security measure, Canadian seamen wore only "H.M.C.S." on their cap tally;[9]

c. the right to be referred to as HMS/HMCS. The earliest definition that could be located was KR&AI (1938). The title was strictly confined to HM ships in commission flying the white ensign;

d. the right to fly a captain's (or commissioning) pennant. This pennant was hoisted on the day of commissioning and except when displaced by a Royal Standard or a distinguishing flag, was never struck until the ship paid off.[10] That a vessel wore a commissioning pennant, however, is not recorded in the documentation and because of the pennant's size, shape, colour and location, it is usually very difficult to see, especially in photographs;[11]

e. the right to fly the Union Flag as a jack. This right belonged only to British warships and not to merchant vessels.[12] Up to 1965, the RCN flew as a jack the blue ensign bearing in the fly the shield of the Canadian coat of arms;

f. the right to pipe the side and to have her quarterdeck saluted by personnel coming on board and departing;

g. the right to wear the white ensign; and

h. when in a foreign port, status as a warship. This meant that while in the port she respected but did not adhere to the laws of the other country and within the ship British law, later Canadian law, was sovereign.

This traditional scheme of things was either inherited by the RCN in 1910 or copied at a later date and remained more or less in force until the late 1960s.

Warships and the White Ensign

On 21 Nov 1910 the Governor General, Lord Grey, proposed to the minister "that the White ensign used by RCN ships be defaced with a green maple leaf on a white disc in the centre"[13] of the white ensign for use on RCN ships. In reply, the Admiralty "politely pointed out that the White Ensign was the King's Flag... [and] it would be unfortunate therefore if the White Ensign were not flown by Canadian warships, even if only to indicate their equality with British vessels."[14] So from 1910 to 1965, the RCN flew the naval ensign of another country and as probably was the intent, RCN ships looked like RN ships.

No serious consequences from such a policy could be found. But there could have been. On 3 Sep 1939, Britain and Germany were at war. As described by captain H N Lay, the Admiralty had sent their War Telegram to the RCN. Canada, not being then at war, had not sent one. Had one or more of our vessels been visiting Britain or Europe at that time, they could have been subject to attack by German forces.[15]

Such a lack of a Canadian identity likely led to the painting of a green maple leaf on the funnel as early as 1918.[16] After the Second World War, a red maple leaf symbol was officially adopted by the RCN and its size and shape standardized. This symbol though, is not the mark of a vessel in commission for the device remains on the funnel when the vessel is paid off. Further, since 1962, Coast Guard vessels have also had a red maple leaf on the funnel and although the term "in commission" could apply to them, they are neither a vessel of war nor an auxiliary.

Prior to the commissioning of NIOBE in October 1910, the designated CO, Cdr W B Macdonald, RN, had apparently been approached by a Canadian government official who wanted HMC Ships to fly the blue in lieu of the white ensign. "I short-circuited them by asking H.M. the Queen to present a white ensign to my ship. This she very graciously did, and the Canadian Navy has flown a white ensign ever since."[17] Since both NIOBE and RAINBOW first commissioned with a Canadian crew but for legal reasons as RN ships, it is a moot point that the RN would have allowed these ships to commission under the blue ensign which was apparently worn by all Canadian government vessels at that time.

The only record that could be located of a Canadian warship commissioning under the blue ensign was during the Second World War. AMBLER commissioned at Midland, Ontario in May 1940 and to permit her to pass through the Great Lakes to the sea without prior approval of the United States—in accordance with the

Rush-Bagot Agreement of 1817—NSHQ ordered her captain to wear the blue ensign "until 0800 on the day of arrival in Montréal, after which the White Ensign will be worn."[18]

In 1960, in a letter to NSHQ the Naval Officers' Association suggested that the RCN fly a white ensign with a Coat of Arms on it in the same position as on the red and blue ensign. The Naval Board stated:

> ... that to carry out its function, a flag must be easily distinguish-
> able from others and have a striking design. Small details of
> design such as a Coat of Arms are hard to distinguish.[19]

The Board did note that some Commonwealth navies had their own flag which was used in place of the white ensign but it agreed that until the country adopted a national flag, it would be premature to change or modify the flag flown by the RCN. Since 1965, all Canadian vessels—naval, government and civilian—have flown the Maple Leaf Flag and there has been no distinctive ensign denoting one of HMC Ships as being in commission.

For some fifty-five years, the RCN flew the white ensign and this one symbol is probably more closely linked to a British or Canadian warship in commission than any other. There were strict regulations on when and where this ensign could be flown and by whom, but contrary to popular notion, the white ensign could be also legally flown by certain other vessels that were not commissioned warships. For example, some vessels of the Royal Yacht Squadron in Britain are permitted to wear the white ensign. Captured and surrendered vessels also wore the white ensign, usually but not always, over their previous ensign. Further, by direction of the Admiralty, all warships

The launch of the second SAGUENAY, 30 Jul 1953, wearing a white ensign as required by regulations. (RCN DNS 10789. KM Coll.)

The yacht *Magedoma* prior to her entering naval service. (RCN O-1140. KM Coll.)

wore a white ensign on the day of their launch. The RCN also followed this practice. Apart from this, however, the white ensign was "on no account to be worn whether or not she (was) in commission, before her official acceptance."[22]

In one case the simple fact that a vessel had been wearing the white ensign proved to be of great importance, at least as far as the term "in commission" was concerned. In this instance the problem was money, a subject near and dear to the hearts of all seamen. The MAGEDOMA was a yacht taken over by the RCN on 14 July 1941. Two years later she was a tender to CATARAQUI. In August 1943, CATARAQUI queried NSHQ as to whether or not the MAGEDOMA was actually a commissioned ship and if so, should not her captain (a Sub-Lieutenant) receive command pay?[23] NSHQ replied that inasmuch as MAGE-DOMA had been flying the white ensign since being taken over, she should be considered as in commission from 14 July 1941.[24] Presumably, the captain got his command pay.

Generally speaking, therefore, a warship in commission had certain outward characteristics. It is relatively simple to determine that destroyers, submarines or aircraft carriers are warships but there are a host of other craft that might or might not be warships and in commission, depending on circumstances. Some of these vessels are known as auxiliaries.

Auxiliaries

A warship is a vessel that has been designed or modified for some type of offensive warfare. On the other hand, an auxiliary is a support vessel, one that supplies certain needs of the fleet. An auxiliary may be armed but such armament is defensive in nature. Since 1910, the term auxiliary has been used in several different ways.

First, the term has been applied to those civilian vessels which in time of war, are taken over, converted to a naval role and given some form of armament. The Second World War auxiliary cruiser PRINCE ROBERT is one example where such a vessel supplemented the fleet as an auxiliary warship.[25]

Second, all navies have support vessels of different sizes and shapes. Known as auxiliaries, support vessels like tugs, torpedo recovery vessels, etc., are classed differently by each navy. A glance at any edition of the *Jane's Fighting Ships* will show a great difference in the use of the term among the navies of Canada, Britain and the United States.

Third, some DND vessels were officially classed as Canadian Naval Auxiliary Vessels (CNAVs) starting about 1946.[26] Prior to this, the term used was "local craft." Since 1968, these vessels have been known as Canadian Forces Auxiliary Vessels (CFAVs).

Today, CFAVs are civilian-manned, carry no armament, and are generally smaller vessels. The approximate equivalent to our CFAVs in the RN is their local craft. In addition, the RN has Royal Fleet Auxiliary (RFA) and Royal Maritime Auxiliary Service (RMAS) vessels which are civilian-manned, wear the blue ensign, and are unarmed. In 1985, however, based on experience during the 1982 conflict in the Falklands, consideration was being given to arming some of the RFAs. The Canadian Navy currently has two ships (PRESERVER and PROTECTEUR) which are the

The auxiliary cruiser PRINCE ROBERT as an A/A ship, Taranto, Italy, March 1945. Note maple leaf on funnel. (KM Coll.)

equivalent of the RFA vessels except ours are commissioned warships. From time to time they are armed, e.g. in 1986, the 3/50 gun was removed from PROTECTEUR and PRESERVER but in 1990, in preparation for the Persian Gulf war, the former had her mounting—plus additional weapons—re-installed.

During the Second World War, almost all of the RCN support vessels and local craft wore the white ensign, were generally armed and had naval crews. After 1946, such vessels wore the blue ensign, carried no armament and were manned by civilians. The larger vessels, like the Saint class tugs, even had official badges assigned to them in the 1950s[27] and the expressions "placed in commission" and "paid off" were applied to them.

Employing some of the more common terms, an auxiliary could join the navy by being constructed specifically for, chartered, requisitioned, loaned to, or taken over by, the navy. Some vessels had all naval crews, some all civilian, and some a mix of the two. Since the term commissioned and the title HMCS were often applied indiscriminately by naval personnel of all ranks, the sole significant fact as to whether a given vessel was a combatant vessel or an auxiliary, appears to rest mainly on the wearing of a commissioning pennant. As already noted, such a pennant is not easy to see and other evidence can be inconclusive.

Correspondence now held in the National Archives indicates that during the First World War when it was intended to use a specific vessel as a fighting ship, she was commissioned and flew the white ensign. Other vessels were "simply auxiliaries, and (were) not to be considered in any way as fighting ships."[28] Here, the writer clearly differentiates between combatant and auxiliary vessels, stating that the former fly the white ensign and have naval crews.[29] Such a statement, however, tends to over-simplify a rather complicated area.

For example, SABLE I, PREMIER and DELIVERANCE were brought into naval service late in 1914. They were chartered but not on a bare boat basis, and hence their owners were responsible not only for providing the crew, but for paying and feeding them as well. In each case, the nominal CO was a naval officer but his authority seems to have been limited to ordering the general movement of the ship. These three are not isolated cases and at least four Fishery Protection vessels—CONSTANCE, CURLEW, GULNARE and PETREL—also appear to have retained their original ship's company during at least the early part of their naval service. Later, at least SABLE I was commissioned.[30]

A study of available photographs for First World War vessels shows some correlation between armament and the wearing of the white ensign by auxiliaries. For example, the contraband control vessel *Gulnare* was acquired in 1916. A signal was sent from Halifax 4 May 1916, to the Director of the Naval Service:

> IS GULNARE TO BE PUT UNDER THE WHITE ENSIGN; IF
> SO IS SHE TO BE ARMED?

The only reply was:

> GULNARE WILL NOT FLY WHITE ENSIGN.[31]

No mention was made of armament but it seems *Gulnare* never carried weapons and although she served over a period of three years, no records of her commissioning could be found. Apparently she never commissioned.

With respect to the ensign worn by auxiliaries, in August 1914 both CGS *Canada* and CGS *Margaret* were ordered to hoist the white ensign.[32] When *Margaret* entered naval service there was no change in her crew or their status as members of the Fisheries Protection Service. The only difference seems to be that NSHQ issued operational orders to her. It was not until early 1915 that *Margaret* formally commissioned with a new ship's company as HMCS MARGARET. CGS *Canada* was in a similar situation except her captain, Mr. C.T. Stuart, was a RNR Lieutenant and after a brief appointment to NIOBE, he returned to his ship and commissioned her HMCS CANADA on 25 January 1915.[33]

In a similar fashion in 1914, the owner of the yacht *Albacore*, Lt J.K. Ross, loaned her to the naval service. After the transfer, some of her crew retained their civilian status and were paid by Ross himself for several months. Learning of this, Admiral Kingsmill ordered her commissioned as one of DIANA's tenders. Although the crew appears to have been enlisted in the navy, her captain remained

The auxiliary MARGARET during the First World War. (KM Coll.)

a first officer in the Fishery Protection Service[34] but she is in the records as HMCS ALBACORE. In an earlier instance still, CGS *Earl Grey*, a freighter with ice breaking capabilities, was temporarily transferred to the navy in July 1912 and apparently commissioned under the white ensign for the sole purpose of taking the Governor General on a cruise from Québec City to the Maritimes. There is no record of the status of her crew. In October 1914, *Earl Grey* was taken over by and commissioned in the navy for transit to Archangel, where she was handed over to the Russian Navy. This time she had a naval crew.[35]

From 1911 to 1939 and the start of the Second World War, all Canadian Government Ships (CGS) and all naval auxiliaries wore the blue ensign.[36] In black & white photographs where a red ensign is difficult to identify from a blue ensign, it becomes all but impossible to distinguish between an auxiliary and a CGS during this period.

Instead of being loaned, some auxiliaries were chartered from civilian firms. Some of these vessels were later commissioned and in such cases "the officers invariably and the crew always were enlisted in the RNCVR class 2A, RNCVR or RCN (Temporary) and were carried on the books of a parent ship."[37] Although it cannot now be proven one way or the other, it was once the opinion of the naval historian that class 2A personnel were considered simply as merchant seamen or civilian government employees under naval discipline. They were not naval personnel.[38]

From such records as are available, it seems the policy was to subject crews to naval discipline wherever possible. For instance, Admiral Kingsmill instructed the Chief Hydrographer to obtain a list of the ship's company of CGS *Acadia* who would be willing to serve under naval discipline during the winter of 1915 when *Acadia* would be in naval service.[39]

Even as late as 1917, several chartered vessels used on examination duties had crews who were not subject to naval discipline. The Naval Control Officer (NCO) in the Halifax Dockyard complained to the captain superintendent that "it looks extremely bad when these tugs [M.W. WEATHERSPOON and DELBERT D] are going alongside Neutral vessels...to see the crews in all sorts of disreputable rigs."[40] In order for the Naval Officer on board to effect more control over the crews, the NCO wished to enrol the crew into the RNCVR and put them in uniform. Although NSHQ approved their enrolment, none of the crew was willing to become subject to the *Naval Discipline Act*.[41] The charter for M.W. WEATHERSPOON ended in June 1917 but DELBERT D may have been kept on until 1918.

The records kept during this period are so incomplete that even immediately after the war, NSHQ could not tell which auxiliaries it had acquired nor when they had served.[42] Further, some vessels had their status changed when some or all of their crews were enrolled into the RNCVR, or when the vessels were purchased. Because of the lack of documentation, it has not proven possible to record completely all these changes.

With respect to armament and the white ensign, the practice of the First World War seems not to have been followed in the Second as a comparison done for this period indicates that there was little if any correlation between mounting armament and flying the white ensign. For example, in the Auxiliary vessels' files in the Directorate of History and Heritage, there are several photographs of tugs from various classes, all flying the white ensign but with no visible armament, not even a Lewis gun.

In the Second World War as in the First, the navy chartered many vessels. The problems encountered in the First World War were largely overcome in the Second by acquiring the bare boat and adding armament, naval personnel and stores as required.

In both World Wars, some vessels were chartered complete with crew, for a single purpose and for a short, specific period. The cable layer *Lord Kelvin* is one example from the First World War. She apparently never flew the white ensign, nor was she armed. Vessels such as this were in the service of the navy but not in naval service. Chartered vessels from the First World War whose actual commissioning is in doubt are listed in Appendix R.

During the Second World War, the RCN had to compete with both the RCAF and RCASC for auxiliaries. There are several recorded instances where a requisition order was issued by one service for a particular vessel only to discover she had already been acquired by another service. In addition, vessels were transferred between the three services causing some confusion in the lists of naval local craft and auxiliaries. All known RCASC and RCAF vessels are listed in Appendix M.

Early in the Second World War, all private and merchant vessels that were entitled to fly the blue ensign, were ordered to cease this practice for the duration of hostilities. No reason was given.[43] Photographs taken in this period indicate that most RCN auxiliary vessels—regardless of size or status—flew the white ensign but a search of such photos shows a lack of a commissioning pennant in every case. But some COs could and did, demand "command money."

With the formation of the Canadian Navy Auxiliary Vessel (CNAV) Service right after the Second World War, the matter of who flew the blue ensign was resolved: CNAVs flew it at the stern while commissioned warships flew it at the stem as the jack. Incidentally, many of the CNAVs started life as warships. One example is SACKVILLE, but the second CORMORANT turned the procedure around. She was a CFAV for two years before being commissioned in 1978. This interesting occurrence was due to the circumstances of her acquisition.[44] LAYMORE added another twist. She became a CNAV in April 1946, re-commissioned as a warship that July to sail from Halifax to Esquimalt and at the end of August, she became a CNAV for the second time.

With termination of the use of the red, white and blue ensigns in the RCN in 1965 and the advent of unification in 1968, matters once again became cloudy. CNAVs became CFAVs and their status apparently deteriorated. For example, neither QUEST nor ENDEAVOUR have badges, unlike many smaller vessels such as ST CHARLES. If a CFAV is not now commissioned, what *condition* is she in? Similarly, by tradition HMC Ships are still commissioned, but what is the significance of this fact? What, for example, was the difference between CFAV CORMORANT in 1977 and HMCS CORMORANT in 1978? Because such questions remain unanswered, the problem has been side-stepped in this volume by stating that present ships—warships, CFAVs and reserve divisions like HURON, QUEST and NONSUCH—are "still in service" (SIS) as opposed to "still in commission."

A similar problem has arisen in the middle 1990s over the phrase "to pay off." With the laying up of TERRA NOVA, ANNAPOLIS and other "steamers," Maritime Command and Public Information staff refer to such vessels as being in "extended readiness" instead of in reserve or paid off. But there they sit alongside a jetty without a commanding officer, crew, ammunition, stores, and other materiel required of a fighting ship. When finally these vessels are sold or otherwise disposed of, they are then often referred to as "paid off." The author has chosen to continue to employ the traditional terminology but obtaining or defining accurate dates for paying off from about 1995 onwards has not always been possible.

Clearly, the CFAVs of today are not commissioned warships. But many of their predecessors were. To list some but not all is not logical. The author has, therefore, decided to include in this volume all named ships: warships, auxiliaries, shore establishments of all types, and naval divisions.

In summation, some commissioned ships did not possess all the characteristics of a warship in commission. On the other hand, many of the Second World War auxiliaries had most of the characteristics of a commissioned warship thereby fulfilling the spirit if not the actual requirement, of the regulations. A study of relevant photographs shows that auxiliary vessels appeared to lack only a commissioning pennant. With

An aerial view of HMCS NADEN about 1946. (FDN Coll.)

inadequate documentation, the question must then be raised: were the 1939–1946 auxiliaries actually in commission or did they fly the white ensign simply because they were in the navy? Regardless of type of crew, size or purpose of the vessel, or the armament carried, there is evidence that auxiliaries in this period were treated as warships in commission, and they are so noted in the list of ship names.[45]

Shore Establishments and Depot Ships

Up to the late 1800s the RN had few shore establishments. Older ships whose days at sea were ended filled their function. Called hulks, many of these vessels gave their names to present RN establishments such as HMS EXCELLENT. In fact, at least one hulk is known to be still in service with the RN: HMS CRESSY (ex UNICORN), Drill Ship of the Tay Division of the RNR.

Regardless of its size or location, a shore establishment was organized and established for only two reasons:

a. functional: where a need arose to control a particular naval activity in a specific location, then a base was set up. For example, NOICs were set up in ports such as Montréal early in the Second World War; and

b. training: where a need arose to set up some form of training such as at Debert or Deep Brook, NS.

Such establishments became commissioned for one or more of the following reasons:[46]

1. Administrative: until commissioned, a shore establishment did not carry its own personnel records. All personnel were carried on the books of some other independent command already in commission. For example, until the NRS at Churchill, Manitoba, commissioned in 1956, all her staff were carried on the books of GLOUCESTER, near Ottawa.

2. Pay and Accounting: until an establishment commissioned, its cash accounts and pay records had to be operated through another independent ship. To operate its own accounts and records, the establishment had to have its own supply officer.

3. Disciplinary: one of the reasons for commissioning the reserve divisions in 1941 and the radio stations in the late 1940s, was to give their COs adequate powers of punishment. Sometimes these powers were limited and in many cases the organization started as a tender to another establishment.

There was at least one other reason—command money. With respect to the commissioning of the naval divisions, NSHQ/DNP felt it was desirable that their captains receive command money, a monthly responsibility allowance given to commanding officers.[47] Other officers of equal rank but not holding appointments as a commanding officer, did not receive this allowance.

As the need for shore establishments grew in the Royal Navy, each consisted of a floating depot ship and some buildings on shore. Both were known by the same name. The reason for this practice is summed up in the following:

> In considering any questions dealing with shore establishments and their nominal depot ships afloat, during this period, it must be borne in mind that, in accordance with the traditional Admiralty interpretation of the Naval Discipline Act of 1866, an officer or man had, in order to be subject to that Act, to be borne on the books of a ship in commission, and this meant an actual vessel afloat. Hence any shore establishment, such as LANSDOWNE in Sydney or GUELPH in Halifax, was represented by a vessel afloat, on whose books were carried, in theory, all personnel serving in the shore establishment.[48]

If the problem of depot ships, bases and their dates of commission is confusing to us, it was often also confusing to those at the time. In July 1922, all officers and ratings attached to the schooner NADEN at Esquimalt were transferred to the books of GUELPH, the depot ship at Halifax, and the schooner paid off. This system, needless to say, did not prove satisfactory and the schooner officially re-commissioned in November 1922.[49]

A commissioning ceremony for NADEN is recorded having been held in Building 77 of the Dockyard on 3 Sep 1922[50] but it appears that the vessel herself was not re-commissioned until 1 Nov 1922. The first date, however, may have been selected for the sake of convenience. In fact, the Senior Naval Officer (SNO) in Esquimalt believed that NADEN was not in commission. On 27 Mar 1923, just five months later and probably due to a disciplinary concern, he wrote to the naval secretary in Ottawa:

> Submitted for consideration of the Department, that I may be informed whether Officers and Men borne on the books of H.M.C.S. "NADEN" can be legally tried by Court Martial, observing the said "NADEN" is not a ship in commission.
>
> Charles T. Beard
Lieutenant-Commander[51]

The reply from A. Woodhouse, the naval secretary, stated:

> ...H.M.C.S. "NADEN" is officially in commission as one of H.M.C. Ships, for the purpose of bearing complement of R.C.N. Barracks on her books.
>
> 2. The White Ensign and your Pendant should be flown in "NADEN."[52]

There must have been other correspondence now no longer in the files, for nineteen months later, the SNO wrote a very short letter to NSHQ which stated: "1st Nov 1922, date of commissioning of NADEN."[53]

Early in the Second World War, the RCN took over a craft named *Oracle* at Gaspé, Québec. A report on her sailing for Ottawa referred to her as HMCS and she flew the white ensign.[54] On arrival in Ottawa, she commissioned as BYTOWN but there is some doubt as to whether or not she ever actually commissioned as *Oracle*. On 15 Jan 1942, she became HC 128 (BYTOWN). By May of that year, she was being referred to as HC 128 (ex "BYTOWN") and later that same month she sailed for Trois-Riviéres, her connection with NSHQ severed.

The patrol vessel STADACONA circa 1918. (KM Coll.)

The interesting point is that until *Oracle* arrived at Ottawa and became BYTOWN on 1 Jun 1941, the entire staff of NSHQ Ottawa had been carried on the books of STADACONA, the depot ship in Halifax, several hundred miles to the east. In cases such as these, the phrase used for transferring officers—men were drafted—was "appointed to STADACONA, additional for NSHQ." Such phraseology died in the RCN with the advent of unification. But such phrases were still in use in the RN in 1974 when the author, while on exchange, was appointed to HMS VICTORY (Barracks) in Portsmouth, additional for the RN School of Education and Training Technology located in the Barracks.

In the Annual DND report ending 31 Mar 1941, on page 11 the following appears with respect to NADEN and STADACONA:

> The Barracks are commissioned as depot ships in order to comply
> with the regulation whereby all Naval personnel must be borne on
> the books of one of H.M. or H.M.C. Ships. The depots are actually
> ashore.

What was ignored in this statement was the requirement for each establishment to have a floating vessel attached to it. A similar sentence is to be found in the 1938 report but no such statement appears in either the 1940 or 1942 reports.

In August 1941, a Naval Order ended depot ships in the RCN. Worded with care, this brief order stated that:

> Canadian Naval Personnel who are borne on any official books,
> accounts or other records...shall be deemed to be borne on the
> books of one of His Majesty's Canadian Ships in Commission and
> accordingly subject to the Naval Discipline Act.[55]

The reasons for this order can be traced to the naval secretary who felt that during wartime, it would not always be practicable and might even be impossible to observe the requirement to have an actual floating craft for each establishment.[56] To guard against any awkward legalities, therefore, the above order was issued and in effect it did away with the need for an establishment to have an actual vessel, without once mentioning this fact.

The background for such concern is not well documented. Circumstantial evidence, however, points to AVALON, the establishment at St John's, as the source for the secretary's concern. Supposedly, this establishment was never formally commissioned but was set up at the end of May 1941 as an independent accounting establishment by signal.[57]

By July, AVALON contained about 900 personnel. Because she would have all the outward trappings of a commissioned establishment—white ensign, pennant, commanding officer, executive officer, etc.—it is fair to assume that some simple administrative problem was the reason that spurred the naval secretary to action. In the files are two messages from AVALON, on 11 and 15 July, one asking for directions on leave for ratings and the other on pay for RN personnel. Either one could have caused the naval secretary to send his memo to the Judge Advocate General, the result of which was the order quoted above.

Establishments commissioned before AVALON, such as BYTOWN, GIVENCHY, and PROVIDER are referred to in Naval Orders as depot ships. But by the time ST HYACINTHE was commissioned in October 1941, the term depot ship is no longer in the order.

The passing of depot ships led to the establishment of the Depot System by Naval Order 2223, on 15 Aug 1942 and the formation of Shore Branches later that same year. The term "depot" survived until 1948 when the term "RCN Barracks" was applied to Esquimalt and Halifax.

The idea of a depot ship did not die out immediately. In 1949 in a bit of naval farce recorded by Swain in *History of the Naval Reserve in Newfoundland,* "to conform with Naval tradition that there should be an actual vessel for any shore establishment bearing a ship's name, a ten-foot punt moored at Three Island Pond was ceremoniously christened and commissioned as HMCS CABOT, but the...Division itself was located at Buckmaster's Field, St John's."

What is now known as the Fleet Diving Unit (Atlantic) was originally located at the French Cable Wharf in Halifax. In 1953 the Diving Unit commissioned as GRANBY and consisted of the minesweeper of that name plus buildings ashore. The minesweeper paid off in 1966 and was replaced by the frigate VICTORIAV-ILLE. She was renamed and re-commissioned GRANBY. This seems to be the last use of a depot ship in the RCN.

In the Royal Navy, the requirement to have a nominal vessel for each shore establishment ceased in 1959 and their *Navy List* stopped listing such vessels in 1962.[58] But tradition, with all its momentum is sometimes difficult to stop. Up until the 1990s, HMS HOWARD in Ottawa had as its nominal ship a motor launch on Dow's Lake, and personnel at CARLETON, the local reserve unit, used this craft.

Because the Navy traditionally referred to all establishments as ships, the term "depot ship" came to be applied to the base as well as to the vessel. Often, one vessel replaced another without affecting the establishment; in some cases, the shore establishment paid off but the vessel remained; and in other cases, the shore establishment changed its name or its function with no effect on the vessel. Needless to say, with the passage of time and the loss of local knowledge, it has proven difficult to distinguish between the vessel and the base in situations such as these. There were further complications.

In 1939 NADEN is identified in the *Navy List* as a "motor vessel and depot ship," indicating that there was both a vessel and a base. So too is STADACONA. With the commissioning of other bases in 1939/40, the navy distinguished between some vessels and their base with the same name, by adding a suffix to the name of the base, e.g. CHALEUR, the vessel and CHALEUR II, the base.

When the requirement for the depot ship's nominal vessel ceased in 1941, the base dropped the suffix and became CHALEUR. She was so listed but the vessel, which continued to serve and to have a crew, was no longer even listed in the *Navy List*. When mentioned—but not listed in—subsequent *Navy Lists*, the Navy referred to the vessel as CHALEUR I, although her name plate still read CHALEUR. A similar process happened in CAPTOR. Even more changes happened to VENTURE: she served as a depot ship with several changes in name and suffix but uniquely, never appears to have had a distinct location ashore.

As the Second World War progressed and some shore establishments expanded to other sites, the Roman numeral suffix was used to denote another, separate establishment in the local area with the same name, e.g. STADACONA and STADACONA II; and GIVENCHY, GIVENCHY II and GIVENCHY III.

When required to distinguish between a shore establishment and her ship, therefore, the terms "base" and "vessel" have been used throughout this book rather than "depot ship."

Shore Establishments and the White Ensign

Both the white and the blue ensign were developed for use at sea and as a consequence, the Admiralty rigidly controlled their use on shore. At first, even the new shore establishments did not wear the white ensign as it was only to be worn by the depot ship. Gradually, its use ashore was condoned and it was flown over the barracks and other related buildings.

Both ensigns were also to be found on cenotaphs and laid up in churches but in both cases they are not being "worn." Even as late as 1931, it was not considered proper for the white ensign to be carried in processions or marches ashore.

With the introduction of the King's Colour to the RN in the 1920s, the white ensign was more and more seen ashore. By 1938, in accordance with article 117

Moresby House in 1944, Building 91 in Esquimalt and formerly, the Coach & Horses Inn.
(RCN E-6493-2. FDN Coll.)

of KRCN 1938, it could be used "on occasions of important ceremonial reviews...on shore outside the United Kingdom, at which the parading of the King's Colour was not authorized." Although in use in the RCN as early as 1927, King's Colours were not presented officially until King George VI did so in 1939. The last white ensign version of the subsequent Queen's Colour was replaced in 1979 by a maple leaf flag version, presented by HM The Queen Mother, the widow of King George VI.

Some organizations such as post Second World War RCN recruiting centres, often flew the white ensign even though none of them ever commissioned. During the Second World War, some NOICs and SNOICs also flew the white ensign over establishments, which were not in commission. For example, along with the other two service ensigns, the white ensign flew over Royal Roads military college until replaced by the Canadian Flag in 1965. All three ensigns also flew at RMC and at the Joint Air School, Rivers, Manitoba. And for one example of a non-commissioned establishment having all the rights and privileges of a commissioned one, see the story of HMS QUEBEC in Chapter 3.

The formation of WRCNS establishments—known as houses—in 1942 saw NSHQ authorize the wearing of the white ensign by these establishments.[59] Unlike their British cousins the WRNS, the WRCNS was an integral part of our Navy and a reading of the relevant regulations leads one to the conclusion that such an authorization was redundant. Regardless, only one WRCNS establishment ever commissioned—CONESTOGA—but all wore the white ensign.

In November 1984, the Maritime Commander sought approval to have the Naval Jack authorized as a Maritime Command Flag to fly over bases and stations and in HMC Ships as the Ensign.[60] CDS concurred with the first part of this idea and in the spring of 1985, the cabinet gave its approval for the Naval Jack to become the Maritime Command Flag.[61]

As for using the Naval Jack as the Ensign for HMC Ships, CDS noted that "the ensign is the principal flag in a warship's suit of colours" and as such "it is worn for the purpose of providing national identity on the International scene."[62] Of the devices on the Jack "neither the Naval Coronet nor the anchor and eagle... symbolize Canada. Therefore, it would not be appropriate to incorporate these devices on HMC ships' ensigns as symbols of the nation on the international stage. Because the nation does not possess a distinctively Canadian symbol which is universally recognizable, other than the maple leaf, the alternative to the proposed ensign would be one with a plain white fly, which would have little significance."[63]

Shore Establishments and the Title "HMCS"

As described earlier, shore establishments originally took both their name and the title HMCS from their depot ship. With the passing of the depot ship system in 1941 in the RCN, shore establishments continued to exist as ships.

When the new KRCN came into effect in 1945, the title HMCS was defined in article 1.02 as "a commissioned ship or fleet establishment flying the white ensign." It was at this time that "commissioned ship" was first defined and the definition of the term "ship" was altered somewhat to reflect the Canadian origin of these regulations.

Just five years later, the passage of the National Defence Act required a new edition of KRCN that saw two minor but very important changes. First, the definition of a commissioned ship was deleted and second, in article 1.02 the definition of HMCS became "any vessel of the Royal Canadian Navy commissioned as a vessel of war." In a later version of KRCN, chapter 39 was allocated to commissioning and perhaps relevant definitions were to be included there. This chapter was never written and so a shore establishment was a ship but not a vessel. Since there were no longer floating depot ships to qualify as vessels, establishments were effectively robbed of the legal entitlement to use the title HMCS. They could, however, still be commissioned as the definition of a fleet establishment in article 1.02 of both KRCN 1945 and 1951, included the phrase "commissioned by order of the minister."

Thus from 1951 to unification in 1968, fleet establishments, radio stations and naval divisions commissioned and paid off in accordance with long standing naval procedures but legally, under the *National Defence Act*, they were no longer authorized to use the title HMCS.[64] Legalities notwithstanding, all establishments continued to employ it.

In the mid 1960s, the *National Defence Act* was completely rewritten to reflect the unification of the three services. In the 1968 version of *Queen's Regulations and Orders*, the terms naval establishment, fleet establishment and Naval Division were not included. As legal entities, the shore establishments ceased to exist and became bases or stations in the Canadian Forces, and so they remain today. The only exceptions were the naval divisions.

About 1970, each Naval Division was officially styled a Naval Reserve Unit (NRU).[65] The title HMCS was dropped and for a short period a division became, for example, NRU HUNTER. By the early 1970s, however, the customs and traditions of the service prevailed and the last of the navy's numerous shore establishments officially returned to using the title HMCS and they were so annotated in CFP 133, CF Addresses, Issue 14, 23 Apr 1985.

Regardless of the size of the vessel or establishment, each one had official commissioning and paying off dates. These dates are recorded in Chapter Six.

Dates of Commission

In this volume, the dates following each name indicate the official commissioning and paying off dates as indicated by the records held in the Directorate of History and Heritage (DHH), the National Archives of Canada (NAC), or the former Directorate of Auxiliary Vessels (DAV). Most reference books only state the first commissioning date and the last paying off date. This can be misleading. Take the

The Battle class trawler ARRAS. She served in both World Wars. (RCN CN 3270. FDN Coll.)

CAP DE LA MADELEINE as an example. She was laid down in May 1943, launched one year later and in commission from 30 September 1944 to 25 Nov 1945. She was later sold only to be reacquired, modified, and returned to the reserve fleet. Her second commission was from 20 May 1959–15 May 1965. Since the dates 30 September 1944–15 May 1965 do not accurately reflect her career, each commissioning and paying off date has been included. For an even longer gap between periods of service, see the entries for ARRAS or ARLEUX that were in commission in both World Wars.

During the first forty years, the RCN took over many RN vessels. Even though Canadian-manned, many of these warships spent a period in RN commission before legally becoming part of the RCN. Details for the Second World War RN vessels are given elsewhere but the precedent for an RCN vessel first being commissioned as an RN vessel had been set with the very first warships, NIOBE and RAINBOW. In 1910, while being taken over by the RCN, both vessels ran into legal difficulties raised by the Admiralty. The legal question dealt with Canada's apparent inability to apply the 1866 *Naval Discipline Act* (British) to personnel in RCN warships outside Canadian territorial waters. This resulted in a legal deadlock, the solution to which was to commission both cruisers as RN vessels and to transfer them to the RCN on arrival in Canadian waters. This in fact happened so the normally stated commissioning dates (NIOBE, 6 Sep 1910; RAINBOW, 4 Aug 1910) are inaccurate as on these dates the two ships commissioned as RN vessels.

CANADA in 1918 in commission as one of HMC Ships. (KM Coll.)

SCATARI on the Great Lakes in the summer of 1959. (DND 5411. KM Coll.)

Legally, they started their Canadian commissions on 21 Oct and 7 Nov 1910, respectively, as it is on these dates that they first entered Canadian waters and became HMC ships.[66]

The paying off dates are the official dates that a vessel would have hauled down her commissioning pennant. Where the vessel was then immediately recommissioned with another name, the paying off date of the first would be the same as the commissioning date of the second. (See the entries for GRIFFIN and the second OTTAWA.)

In some cases, the paying off date given is the day the vessel was lost. In such cases as this, although lost, the ship was still technically in commission for the purposes of the (British) *Naval Discipline Act* of 1866. By Article 91, a ship that was lost, wrecked, destroyed or captured was not considered paid off until a court martial had been held to determine the cause of such loss. Although this Act was amended in 1922, this particular Article was not changed until the Act was rewritten in 1956 and therefore, the RCN came under its jurisdiction up until the (Canadian) *Naval Service Act* of 1944 was promulgated. How such a regulation affected the actual paying off date of a vessel such as LEVIS, sunk 19 Sep 1941, is not known. Information of that nature is not recorded in the individual ship files in NDHQ/DHH.

On the other hand, a sinking did not always determine the paying off date. HMCS ARMENTIERES sank September 1925, was re-floated 26 October and paid off into Dockyard hands 20 Nov 1925. The KINGSVILLE flooded and sank

3 April 1943 at St. John's. She was raised and returned to service without any effect on her dates of commission. Finally, on 18 Aug 1945, AUBURNVILLE capsized while moving the PRESTONIAN but she too remained in commission while being raised.

Some vessels were acquired and used by the Navy but not actually commissioned until a later date. During the First World War, the *Canada* was acquired 4 Aug 1914, flew the white ensign[67] and was referred to as HMCS when she was not actually in commission until 25 Jan 1915.[68] Similarly, the *Diana* was acquired 25 August 1911 and referred to as HMCS but not actually commissioned until some three years later.[69]

In addition, there is at least one instance of a vessel being put in commission before the navy actually and legally acquired her. The second BRAS D'OR commissioned 18 Jul 1965 and although she had all the normal characteristics of a Canadian warship in commission, De Havilland the builder still owned the vessel. It was not until after her pre-acceptance trials had completed in February 1972, more than six years after commissioning, that she became RCN property.[70]

During the Second World War, many civilian vessels were chartered, some complete with their crews. Such charters varied in length. Some of the vessels so employed were later purchased outright while others were returned to their owners. It is not known for certain which, if any, of these vessels were placed in commission but all wore the white ensign. For lack of sufficient details, the day they were placed in service was used as the date of commission unless other details were known. For example, the DOT tug *Helena* was requisitioned by the Navy in 1940 but immediately chartered to the Dominion Coal Corporation in Sydney to save the Navy having to pay $30,000 to refit her. The HELENA finally commissioned in 1945.[71]

Motor launches of the 1950s and 1960s (such as MOOSE) saw service in the Second World War but only as numbered vessels. They were nonetheless, commissioned. In this book, their commissioning dates refer only to when these vessels carried names. This policy on commissioning dates also applies to reserve divisions.

In both war and peace, many of the small craft employed on the St Lawrence River and the Great Lakes were only in commission during the spring and summer. Because of the ice, each winter they paid off and this practice continued well into the 1960s, if not longer. Where possible, dates have been noted for each commission but many files are incomplete. In the Québec City area during the Second World War some of the vessels involved in these annual rites were CHALEUR I, ANNA MILDRED, MADAWASKA, MARION 3, LIL II, MILLICETTE and

MACSIN. For the post Second World War period, most of the vessels used to train reservists on the Great Lakes, such as COUGAR and SCATARI, also commissioned and paid off each summer. The practice is still followed today by RCSC training establishments such as QUEBEC.

As for shore establishments, many were organized and functional long before being officially commissioned. For a good example, see the entry for KINGS. In addition, the specific duties of establishments on both coasts changed frequently especially during wartime, and the author deemed it beyond the scope of this book to attempt to chronicle such changes.

In Retrospect

With respect to warships, auxiliaries and shore establishments, evidence shows that the use of such terms as commissioned and paid off, the wearing of the white ensign and other characteristics of a commissioned warship, were often applied to all types of vessels and bases in what can only be called a flexible manner in both the RN and the RCN. Although defined in writing and in some cases even embedded in pieces of legislation, naval personnel often adapted such regulations when required, obviously following precedent set by Nelson and others. Such flexibility in the interpretation of regulations still applies today. The regulations governing piping the side and hand salutes, for example, clearly show that neither the prime minister nor MND are entitled to such marks of respect but these are commonly rendered by the crews of HMC Ships to the holders of each office.[72]

Another application of such flexibility centred around *Terra Nova*, Captain Robert Scott's vessel on his last voyage to the Antarctic from 1910 to 1912. *Terra Nova*, a merchant ship with a naval crew, wore the white ensign although she was not a commissioned warship. To make the wearing of the white ensign legal, she registered as a yacht in the Royal Yacht Squadron. To all intents and purposes, therefore, she looked like a commissioned warship in the Royal Navy, which was the intent.[73] Compare her to the later Royal Yacht, HMS BRITANNIA, which up to 1997 was a commissioned warship but didn't look like it.

Although the procedure for actually commissioning a ship is now laid down in the *Ceremonial Manual—HMC Ships*, the actual impact of such a ceremony has never been committed to paper. In addition, this commissioning ceremony is clearly written for new construction—there is no procedure for the re-commissioning of a vessel that has been paid off for a specific period. In fact, this oversight and the current practice of not paying off vessels when they enter a long refit, has led

BONAVENTURE flying her paying off pennant in 1970. She opted for a smaller, destroyer sized paying off pennant.

to the development of a Reactivation Ceremony, which is in effect a re-commissioning ceremony with an awkward name.[74]

Starting shortly after unification in 1968, the re-commissioning ceremony for HMC Ships fell into a state of neglect from which it has yet to revive. A good example is MIRAMICHI. In 1970 after finishing a refit at Yarrows Ltd. in Esquimalt, some unknown person on board MIRAMICHI assumed the security watch from the shipyard at 0730, 5 Jan 1970. Half an hour later, the navigator logged on board and at 0930 "Lt(N) J.B. O'Reilly joined from CFHQ and assumed command." Over the next several days, the log entries are few but on 22 January, MIRAMICHI slipped and proceeded to sea for exercises, obviously now a commissioned vessel.[75]

Finally there are now regulations governing when a vessel is to pay off.[76] When the four Restigouche class destroyer escorts were being converted in the late 1960s, however, three paid off but TERRA NOVA apparently did not.[77] The only ceremony now connected with paying off is the wearing of the traditional paying off pennant, often an unauthorized but traditional and lengthy version of her commissioning pennant. With the paying off of QU'APPELLE in 1992, the paying off pennant became standardized. There is now one length for all vessels, regardless of rate or class, and one paying off pennant is kept on each coast for use as required.

By 1975 most of the criteria that distinguished a commissioned warship from one in reserve or fitting out—the outward signs—had gone:

a. the White Ensign was replaced by the Maple Leaf Flag, 15 February 1965;

b. the legal implications had sunk—the CO's special powers of punishment were deleted in an amendment to the National Defence Act circa 1970;

c. command money disappeared shortly afterwards;

d. the maple leaf emblem on the funnel was worn by other than just naval vessels; and

e. technically, the ship's company became just another administrative "unit" in the Canadian Forces.

Towards the end of the period from 1968 to 1992, the characteristics of a commissioned Canadian warship stabilized: she was still light grey in colour and usually carried some form of armament. In addition, there were still a few distinctive characteristics that set her apart from her non-commissioned sisters:

a. the title HMCS: the title remained but it was only seen on correspondence and Kisbie rings, as there was no cap ribbon on which to wear the ship's name with this title;[78]

b. a crew in naval uniform. The Navy began changing back to a blue uniform 1 July 1985. Any colour uniform can be considered as Navy but historically and traditionally, naval uniforms throughout the world are either dark blue or black, and in summer or under tropical conditions, white (and sometimes khaki). Because all CF support trades are unified, both army and air force uniforms are seen in HMC Ships today;

c. the right to pipe the side[79] and to have personnel salute the quarterdeck when coming on board or going ashore;

d. the naval jack:[80] since 1985, also known as the Maritime Command flag, this jack is different from the one worn by Coast Guard and other Canadian Government vessels, and by CFAVs;

e. the commissioning pennant; and

f. in a foreign port, status as a warship within which Canadian law is sovereign.

The last characteristic is not visible. There is another non-visible characteristic. Prior to a ship first commissioning today, all accounts are held on a NDHQ suspense file until the date of commissioning when they are transferred to the ship.

While these characteristics easily distinguished a commissioned warship from a hulk, in the late 1990s there is little to differentiate between a Canadian warship and a Canadian warship in commission. Take the second ALGONQUIN as one example. In November 1990, after being updated under the TRUMP program but before being accepted by the navy, and while still in commission, she sailed from Lauzon to Halifax with a civilian crew on board and a few naval personnel in the operations and engine rooms. To all outward appearances, during this voyage she looked like a warship in commission and she was, but she was incapable of acting like one.

As a second example, during the early 1990s HALIFAX sailed in and out of Halifax for many months with a naval crew on board when she was not in commission. To all outward appearances during this time, HALIFAX looked like a commissioned warship when she was not, but she was capable of acting like one. This situation led the Commander of MarLant, RAdm L. Mason, to propose a change to the regulations.[81]

This proposal was accepted. In a message NOO-325, 192037Z Dec 1992 promulgated at the very end of 1992, Maritime Command changed some rules for vessels in commission. This message pointed out that for new construction vessels, commanding officers now assume "responsibility for custody of the ship...[and] once a ship is under the command of a naval officer and it [sic] is manned by a naval crew, it [sic] has certain inescapable obligations as a warship." For "the period between the Commanding Officer assuming custody and the commissioning, Canadian warships shall conduct and be accorded the same ceremonial procedures and honours as a commissioned ship...except the commissioning pennant shall not be flown until the ship is actually commissioned." No mention was made of vessels undergoing long modifications or refits where the crew is removed.

One of the results of the 1992 change can be seen when the new-construction vessels NANAIMO and EDMONTON completed a coast transfer by sailing from

The second ALGONQUIN still in contractor's hands early in 1991 at Dartmouth, near the end of her TRUMP conversion. (PMRC 91-392. AC)

Halifax to Esquimalt in late 1996 and early 1997 respectively. They looked like commissioned warships but they were not. When they did commission in the spring of 1997, the effect on the ships, their outward appearance and their effectiveness was virtually nil.

Once a CO assumes custody of a new-construction vessel, the outward signs noted in a. to f. above are assumed but such criteria no longer indicate a commissioned vessel. On commissioning, the only definitive outward sign is the commissioning pennant, this small and all-but-inconspicuous piece of nylon. And since it is flown on the mast above the funnel on the Iroquois and Halifax classes, it tends to turn dark very quickly. Against the black portions of the mast where it is normally flown on a gaff, it can be almost invisible.

In 1999, the term "in commission" in the Canadian Navy no longer appears to serve much purpose. A warship is what MND says is a warship and whether she is in commission or not, the Admiral says she can act like one. And when she should be paid off, she can remain in commission without any naval personnel, ammunition or materiel on board.

If the expression "a warship in commission" is to retain any significance in the Canadian Navy, other than sovereign status in a foreign harbour, a strong case can be made that our commissioned warships require a distinctive naval ensign.

Summary

Throughout the ninety-year history of the Navy, the naming and commissioning of HMC Ships has had a haphazard existence. In the middle of this period, our ships were finally allocated official badges, some thirty years after their RN counterparts. In certain instances, our warships have won distinctive Canadian Battle Honours that they can pass to the next astern but they can no longer use those from the common Commonwealth list. In some

The unofficial badge of the second NADEN.
(Freeman 661-34. AC)

periods, names were allocated in accordance with a pre-determined set of rules known as nomenclature, and history and the traditions of the service determined such naming. At the time of writing, however, after witnessing the names allocated to both the Kingston and Victoria classes, this no longer seems to hold true. The next four chapters look at other factors and implications that went with, as well as the history behind, the names held by commissioned warships, auxiliaries, shore establishments and naval divisions.

Notes to Chapter One

1. See "A Letter from the Queen," *The Crowsnest*, Oct 1964, p 15.
2. Up to 1864, ships of the RN wore either Red, White or Blue Ensigns, depending on their Squadron. After that date, only ships in commission wore the White Ensign. See *The Crowsnest*, Jul 1964, p 16, and the *Manual of Seamanship*, Vol. 1, Chap XIV (1951).
3. See "A Letter from the Queen," *The Crowsnest*, Oct 1964, p 15.
4. From the *Naval Chronicle*, quoted in "The Cook, a Mighty Man was He," by EC Russell, *The Crowsnest*, Jan 1960, p 19.
5. See MARCORD 40-1, AL 6/83, para 3.
6. QR&O (1968), Article 1.02.
7. See Naval Order 1086, 6 Nov 1940.
8. Manning & Walker, *British Warship Names*, p 10. In the post Second World War RCN, powers of punishment of the CO were limited by his rank and some COs could have none at all. For example, the CO of a Bird Class vessel in the late 1960s was a Chief Petty Officer 1st class who, because of his rank, had no powers of punishment.
9. But not from day one. As late as Sep 1940, sailors in RESTIGOUCHE were still wearing named cap tallies. See Lay, *Memoirs*, photo on p 119. And, the author has seen a cap tally for HMCS EYEBRIGHT.
10. *Manual of Seamanship*, Volume I, p 256.
11. One clear view of such a pennant can be seen in *Ships of Canada's Naval Forces 1910-85*, at the top of p 141. In the background is a Town class destroyer and from the top of her main mast above the white ensign, flies her commissioning pennant.
12. *Manual of Seamanship*, Volume I, p 256.
13. T. Thorgrimsson, Memo to N Hist on the "FLAG QUESTION," para 13, 16 Jul 1962. DHH 81/520/1460-3.
14. Ibid, para 14. See also Letter, E. C. Russell to the editor, *The Crowsnest*, Sep 1962. There was also discussion about Canadian warships wearing "the White Ensign, defaced with the Arms of Canada, and the pendant of St. George's Cross defaced in the same manner." Letter, D MND to Under Sec't of State for External Affairs, 26 Nov 1909, in NAC RG 24 D1 Vol. 5588, NSS 9-1-1.
15. See *Memories of a Mariner*, page 98.
16. See "Whence the Funnel's Maple Leaf?," *The Crowsnest*, Jun 1957, p 15-16.
17. *At Sea and by Land, The Reminiscences of W B Macdonald, RN*, edited by S. W. Jackman, page 96.
18. McKee, *The Armed Yachts of Canada*, p 84.
19. Naval Board Minutes 621-7, 25 May 1960.
20. The Naval Board Minutes use the term 'flag'.
21. *Manual of Seamanship*, Volume 1, p 255.
22. Naval Order 423, 3 Aug 1937.
23. Letter, CATARAQUI to NSHQ, 18 Jul 1943. NS 8000-480/8.
24. Letter, NSHQ/SO Ops to CATARAQUI, 20 Sep 1943. NS 8000-480/8.
25. The term auxiliary was not applied to Defensively Equipped Merchant Ships (DEMS) whose role did not change. In the early days of the Second World War, the naval staff applied the term auxiliary to corvettes. See Milner, *North Atlantic Run*, p 18/19.
26. See CB(CAN) 0808 and 0809 respectively.

27. See BRCN 150.
28. NAC RG 24 5661, NSS 58-45-1. Letter, Director of Stores to Québec Salvage & Wrecking Co., 29 Mar 1915.
29. As used in this section, the term naval crew relates to personnel subject to the *Naval Discipline Act*. In the case of auxiliary vessels, this often meant that the crew was enrolled as members of the RNCVR, class 2A, "for discipline only." Where the chartered vessel concerned was not in commission, the owner was still required both to pay and feed the crew. Needless to say, these fine points of the law were lost on the crew, many of whom later tried to claim some form of pension or compensation. See NAC 5660, NSS 58-41-1, Volume 2, Letter N Sec't to A/Sec't War Veteran Allowance Board, NSS 47-23-W-339, 3 Nov 1949.
30. "RCN Shore Establishments on the Canadian East Coast, 1910-1919," p 10, NDHQ/DHH.
31. Notes in NS 1057-4-18, "Movements of vessels on examination, patrol, etc.," GULNARE file, NDHQ/DHH.
32. Tucker, *The Naval Service of Canada*, Vol. I, p 214.
33. "RCN Shore Establishments on the Canadian East Coast, 1910-1919," p 9 - 11, NSHQ/DHH.
34. Ibid. p 9.
35. See the *Crowsnest*, August 1964, p 25.
36. This ensign was referred to in contemporary documents as the Canadian flag, the Canadian Blue Ensign, and the distinctive flag of the Dominion. T Thorgrimsson, Memo to N Hist on the "FLAG QUESTION," para 9, 16 July, 1962. DHH 81/520/1460-3.
37. Ibid. p 11.
38. Letter, N Hist, NS 8000-300 TD 2176, 28 Jun 1962. *Curlew* file, DHH.
39. NAC RG 24 5660, NS 58-39-1, 8 Nov 1915. Letter Adm Kingsmill to Chief Hydrographer of the Naval Service.
40. NAC RG 24 5658, NSS 58-13-13 Vol. 1, NCO to Captain Superintendent, 17 Apr 1917.
41. Ibid. Captain Superintendent to N Sec't, 5 May 1917.
42. See correspondence in NAC RG 24 5656, NSS 58-6-1, Vol. 1, concerning BERTHIER. In some of the files on individual vessels, the only material is a charter agreement and some of these are incomplete.
43. See Naval Order 675, 18 Nov 1939. It is known, however, that Inspection and RCASC vessels wore the blue ensign throughout the war.
44. See Memo, DMRS to DAV, NDHQ 1190-ASXL 20, 20 Jun 1955, and attached certificate 46.
45. For example, see Naval Staff Minutes 230-9, para 1, 20 Mar 1944; and NAC RG 24 5656, NSS 58-6-1, Vol. 1, Memo, Adm Kingsmill to Chief Accountant, stores, 3 May 1918.
46. For details, see the following Naval Orders: 1598, 11 Oct 1941; 2245, 29 Aug 1942; 2438, 12 Dec 1942; 3002, 21 Aug 1943; Naval Staff Minutes 469-2, 8 Nov 1949; and Naval Board Minutes 342-5, 11 Apr 1951.
47. See Naval Council Minutes 33-1, 29 Sep 1941 in NAC RG 24 4049, NS 1078-3-4, Vol. 1.
48. "RCN Shore Establishments on the Canadian East Coast, 1910-1919," p 21, note 3, DHH.
49. "Esquimalt Naval Base," 24 Mar 1960, p 13-14.
50. CFB Esquimalt Military Heritage, p 108. This may only have been a change of command ceremony as it was on this date that Lt Cdr Beard relieved Cdr Nixon. However, see Longstaff, *HMCS NADEN*, p 13.
51. Letter, SNO Esquimalt to N Sec't, 1-31-1, 27 Mar 1923.
52. Letter, N Sec't to SNO Esquimalt, 0-8-1, 10 Apr 1923.
53. Letter, SNO Esquimalt to NSHQ, 8000-441/77, 25 Sep 1924.
54. Report #37, NS 100-5-19, for 13-20 Sep 1941.
55. Naval Order 1518, 30 Aug 1941.
56. Memo, N Sec to JAG, NS 42-1-1, 25 Jul 1941. See also PC 44/6172. Both are contained in the Customs & Traditions file in DHH.
57. Tucker, *Naval Service of Canada*, Vol. II. p 197, note 33. The original document is in NAC RG 24 5637, NSS 40-21-2: Message, NSHQ/DNP to COAC & others, 1441Z/31, 31 May 1941.
58. Warlow, *Shore Establishments of the Royal Navy*, p 9.
59. See Naval Order 2267, 5 Sep 1942.
60. Letter, Commander Maritime Command to CDS, MARC:1150-9 (COMD).
61. Letter, SSO COM to MARCOM units, MARC:1110-1(SSO COMM),24 Jun 1985.
62. Letter, CDS to Commander MARCOM, NDHQ 1145-1, 5 Feb 1985.
63. Ibid.
64. See letter, D. LAW/A to DMRS, NDHQ 3136-5-2016, 30 May 1985.

65. See CFAO 2-8.
66. Information taken from "Brief History of HMCS RAINBOW," 24 Mar 1961 and "Brief History of HMCS NIOBE," 26 Oct 1961. These papers were prepared by the Naval Historical Section and are to be found in the respective ship's files, DHH. Further, on display in the wardroom of CFB Esquimalt is a silver urn. The inscription reads: "To the Commander and Officers of HMS RAINBOW/ A souvenir from Lord Strathcona/ on the occasion of the departure of the Rainbow/ from Portsmouth for British Columbia/ on 18th Aug 1910/ As a unit of the/ Canadian Navy." In fact, the Admiralty did not transfer both ships to the RCN until 12 Nov 1910, back dated to their entry into Canadian waters. See Thorgrimsson, memo to N Hist on the "FLAG QUESTION," para 12, 16 Jul 1962. DHH 81/520/1460-3.
67. Tucker, *The Naval Service of Canada*, Vol. I, p 215.
68. *The Ships of Canada's Naval Forces 1910–1981*, p 15. See also the CANADA file, DHH.
69. See the DIANA file, DHH.
70. Lynch, *The Flying 400*, p 69.
71. Memo, Superintendent Local Craft Section to ACNS, NS 20-52-1, 16 Nov 1943.
72. See the *Ceremonial Manual—HMC Ships*, Articles 242(c) and 413.
73. See Huntsford, *Scott and Amunsen*, p 281 & 284.
74. See CFB Esquimalt *Lookout*, 13 Jan 1993, page 1.
75. MIRAMICHI ship's Log for Jan 1972, NAC 24 9440. For the period from 1968 to 1980, many of these monthly logs are not in the files. Further, there are no entries in many of the surviving logs to indicate that the ship paid off. In fact, there are several instances where a ship is at sea when the log finishes for the month and no subsequent log is available. The logs for CHALEUR, for example, are missing for several months, e.g. Sep to Dec 1968; Aug to Dec 1969; Jan to Mar 1970; Jan Feb, May, Nov and Dec 1971; etc. See NAC RG 24 5493, 10354 and 9426 respectively.
76. See MARCORD 40-1, in effect from about 1982.
77. TERRA NOVA ship's logs 1967-68, NAC 24 5444 to 5446. LCdr R Wolicky confirmed this in a talk with the author on 30 Oct 1989. He served in her at that time and confirmed that she never paid off. Apparently, this was due to her conversion consisting of a series of short individual projects rather than one long project.
78. Up to 1984 the title HMCS had no meaning in the other official language. In the 1970's, following the official introduction of ship's companies whose daily (but not operational) language was French, the title HMCS became simply "Le," as in LE SKEENA. This followed the French naval practice. By 1983, however, NDHQ belatedly recognized that the use of this title as a French translation of HMCS was contrary to official language policy. Consequently, in 1984 NDHQ adopted the more suitable French title NCSM - Navire canadien de Sa Majesté. (Various correspondence in NDHQ 1000-5 from Oct 1983 to Feb 1984; and memo, Director Translation and Terminology Coordination, 1211-7-0, 24 Apr 1984.)
79. *Ceremonial Manual - HMC Ships*, article 413.
80. See CFP 200.
81. Letter, Commander MarLant to Commander MarCom, 20 Nov 1992.

Chapter Two

Badges, Battle Honours and Bells

Today, each named warship due for commissioning receives a badge, Battle Honours won by her predecessors, and the bell carried by her immediate predecessor or the first of name, where available.

Badges

RN Badges Pre-1920

A Badge is a heraldic device unique in design to that name and the ship that carries the name. In days of sail ships had figureheads and the first and only warship in the Canadian Navy to be so equipped was the first SHEARWATER. With the change to metal hulls and engines in the 19th century, the figurehead disappeared, being replaced by ornate scrolls on the stem and stern.

Within the scrolls were one or more emblems. Some COs, entitled to bear Arms, used an heraldic device from their Arms in the scroll. Towards the end of

The destroyers SKEENA and SAGUENAY at Halifax, 1 July 1931. (KM Coll.)

the 1900s, scrolls tended to be discontinued and in their place emblems or badges started to appear, often designed by one of the ship's officers. Needless to say there was considerable variety in the quality and style of these early badges. This diversity led to calls for standardization but plans were put on hold by the outbreak of the First World War in August 1914.

In 1916, the British Government established a museum—later to be known as the Imperial War Museum—to show various aspects of the ongoing "Great War." A noted expert on medieval armour and firearms, Charles ffoulkes, became the first curator. At the start of the war ffoulkes had joined the RNVR as a sub lieutenant but resigned his commission in March 1916 to devote his time to the museum. As a hobby, ffoulkes collected badges and emblems of HM Ships and in 1917 he was asked to design an unofficial badge for the destroyer HMS TOWER, then under construction on the Tyne at Swan Hunter. The request came from the CO designate, Lieutenant Harold Joyce, DSC, RN. As completed, this badge consisted of the four parts still seen today in our Navy: a circular rope frame enclosing the central device, topped by a rectangular tally plate, surmounted by the naval crown.

Swan Hunter then asked ffoulkes to design badges for other vessels being built in their yard. In all, he designed some twenty badges. In August 1918, to give him more authority in running the museum, ffoulkes was given a commission as an honourary Major in the Royal Marines.

At the end of the war, Major ffoulkes offered to design badges for all HM Ships, free. The Admiralty took up his generous offer and appointed him as their advisor on Heraldry. As one of his first steps Major ffoulkes set forth some criteria for the design of a ship's badge. The design of each ship's badge should:

1. illustrate the name;
2. be simple, striking and easy to paint; and
3. consider the historical association(s) of the ship.[1]

The bow of CHARNY sometime during the Second World War. Note scroll work and drying hammocks. (KM Coll.)

In December 1918, following the appointment of Major ffoulkes, the Admiralty issued Monthly Order 3943—Battle Honours, Badges and Mottoes for H.M. Ships. Paragraph 6 of this order read:

> In future the Badge and Motto will be combined with the Battle
> Honours for display on the Quarter Deck, the whole design
> becoming a naval counterpart of the military Regimental colour.[2]

Also in December, the Admiralty formed a Ships' Badges Committee, consisting of Major ffoulkes, the admiralty librarian and the director of naval equipment, a Commander RN. The committee had two immediate tasks: first to identify all the ships currently in service and those under construction that required badges; second, to standardize the size and shape for the badges. As described in Wilkinson, *et al*, this led to an experiment being conducted on the Thames near Westminster Bridge. A launch sailed up and down the river carrying various badge designs on her bridge while the committee members stood on the deck of the former U155, a surrendered German Navy merchant submarine. The committee decided to employ four different shapes, the shape being indicative of the type of ship: circular, for capital ships; pentagonal, for cruisers; shield, for destroyers; and diamond, for carriers, sloops, submarines, depot ships and all other vessels including establishments.[3]

In 1974, the Royal Navy reorganized their system of badges, reducing the number of shapes to three: circular, for ships, submarines and air squadrons; diamond, for shore establishments; pentagonal, for RFAs and other auxiliaries.[4]

It is thus possible to find a particular Royal Navy badge in a variety of shapes, depending on the type of ship to which the name has been assigned since 1920. And this explains the shape of most of the pre-1949 unofficial RCN badges.

Interestingly, the one ship in the RN without an official badge is HMS VICTORY. According to a story related to the author, with so many ships in commission in 1919, the Admiralty apparently decided to design and issue an official badge only to those ships about to

The bow of SHEARWATER during the First World War. Her figurehead is just visible. (KM Coll.)

commission or about to re-commission, something that happened more frequently in those days. Alone of all HM Ships since 1919, VICTORY has never paid off. She does have an unofficial badge.[5]

In March 1919, Major ffoulkes started designing the first badges. This task was a "secondary duty," a phrase well known to all seamen. The Committee estimated that it would take some two to three years to design, receive approval for, cast and distribute all the badges required. On hearing about the official RN badges, some RAN destroyers applied for badge designs and the Committee decided to treat them like RN ships.

On 9 Oct 1919, the Ships' Badges Committee decided that both the naval crown and tally plate would be deleted from boat badges. By 4 Aug 1921, some 243 badges for HM Ships had been designed and approved but not all had been cast.

The subject of "War Honours"—a task also given to the Ships' Badges Committee—was postponed until all the badges could be designed and issued. Whatever recommendations were made is not known but official Battle Honours had to wait until 1954.

The direct impact on Canadian ships was negligible. Neither RAINBOW, NIOBE, SHEARWATER nor ALGERINE had official RN Badges. It is also unlikely that AURORA, PATRIOT and PATRICIAN had official badges by the time they arrived in 1920.

RCN Badges 1910–1949

The Royal Canadian Navy did not follow the RN in designing badges until after the Second World War.[6] Prior to that, badges were unofficial and known as insignia, or more frequently but incorrectly, as crests. Many vessels had unofficial badges, most of the pre Second World War River class destroyers for example, and sometimes an establishment had one as well; the second PROTECTOR had an unofficial badge which consisted of a red cross on a shield imposed on a maple leaf. The naval secretary approved this "badge" on 29 Jul 1941.

The design of the pre-Second World War destroyer badges were of such good quality and they follow a standardized design that one is tempted to speculate that the Admiralty's Ships' Badges Committee got involved in the process but no evidence of this could be located.

Earlier, the naval secretary had no objection to the design of a 'crest' [sic] for the Halifax half company which would consist of a coat of arms of the city inside a shield "as this is the practice that has been followed by most of the companies of the R.C.N.V.R."[7]

The Second World War was only a few months old when ships' companies began seeking approval by and guidance from, NSHQ on badges. NSHQ formed an Insignia Committee headed by the naval historian, Dr G Tucker. Their task was to design badges for all HMC Ships but under wartime conditions and with the large number of new vessels expected, the only feasible policy was the one promulgated: commanding officers could devise their own unofficial designs, for now, but after the war official badges would be designed and issued. The captain of the port would be responsible for ensuring that no offensive designs were employed by individual vessels while the naval secretary would do the same for establishments. From this policy the unofficial wartime "badges" took two forms.

First, there were those badges designed to look official, like the ones for SACKVILLE, SIOUX, and CORNWALLIS. Second were the designs—insignia—painted on a ship's gun shield as shown in the book by Lynch, *Gunshield Graffiti*. One of the more notorious of the latter designs was worn by WETASKIWIN. The design consisted of a Queen of Hearts who, having slipped, was now seated in a puddle of water: a wet ass Queen. One of the better designs was worn by BADDECK: five playing cards, all aces, illustrating a bad deck of cards.

RCN Badges 1945–1999

In mid November 1945, the naval board approved funding to set up a permanent policy on RCN badges for the post war fleet. The Director of Plans, Captain HS Rayner, wanted the designs executed in Canada even if this meant a lack of some heraldic skill had to be accepted. To implement the policy, NSHQ formed the Ships' Badges Committee. This little known group staffed the production of a very high standard of badge for all the immediate post Second World War ships in commission, most of the badges being designed by Lt Cdr(SB) Alan B. Beddoe, RCN(R).

Before any designs were contemplated, Captain HF Pullen, Director of the Naval Reserves, requested that badges for all the reserve divisions employ the RN's circular design and according to Lt Cdr

The unofficial badge of SIOUX, c. 1945, cast in brass. (Freeman 661-25. AC)

Beddoe this design was consequently employed for all RCN ships and establishments. By early 1948, some fifty-two designs had been completed but the 18- by 24-inch bronze badges were apparently not issued to the Fleet until early in 1949.[8]

Some of our vessels have carried a name worn by previous vessels. In one or two instances, a ship was given the same name as a predecessor but for an entirely different reason. Take CAPE BRETON for example. The first vessel was given this name as an alternative one for the city of Sydney, NS. The name Cape Breton was probably taken from the island. The second vessel, however, was named for the cape in Nova Scotia.

For the purpose of the ship's badge, this is significant because the origin and purpose of the name—island or cape—influence the badge for each vessel. If both CAPE BRETONs had been entitled to a badge, technically speaking each badge should have been different. For an example of a name's influence on the design, see the badge of the second PRESERVER.

The badge for the third OTTAWA is also a good example of the way the name influences the badge design. The wavy bend in the background of the badge for OTTAWA signifies a river, from which the name originated for the first three ships.

An interesting use of the main device from a badge is seen on ORIOLE's spinnaker. This July 1978 photograph shows the back of the spinnaker, making it seem as if the Oriole is facing the wrong way.
(CF Photo by Cpl Max Johnston, IX78-196. FDN Coll.)

The badge, however, was designed only for the third vessel. But the name Ottawa could also be taken from a city, a valley or a native tribe. And with the last vessel of the Halifax class allocated the name OTTAWA in 1990, the name being for the city and not the river, it followed that her badge should change.

The then new Ships' Names Committee discussed this point at length in 1991. For such a scenario, there was little precedent to follow. With respect to this problem, the following decisions were made:

> an official badge should be designed for each of HMC Ships to which a name is allocated. Generally, the badge is to be based on the design of the origin of the ship's name. Once approved, the badge shall belong to the name and pass unchanged to successive ships.[9]

Thus the fourth OTTAWA retains and employs the badge designed for, and first worn by, the third ship of that name.

The reason why our ship's badges have not had to change is simple—with a few exceptions, we are still working through the first generation of badges for Canadian ships. There are few examples of badges having changed because the origin of the name changed. The badges worn by GLOUCESTER and QUEEN, for example, are not the same as those worn by their RN predecessors who used the same names. Further, BONAVENTURE, CRESCENT and CRUSADER all wore official Canadian versions of RN badges—which simply incorporated a maple leaf in their design—while WARRIOR reversed this procedure: the RN now use a badge for HMS WARRIOR, a shore establishment, which was first designed for and worn by, HMCS WARRIOR.[10]

A look at the vessels in the post Second World War period which had official badges shows that in the 1950s and early 1960s at least, it was the policy to have a badge for all ships, establishments, reserve divisions, radio stations, RCSC

The badge of HMCS WARRIOR. (RCN O-293-12. FDN Coll.)

The badges of GLOUCESTER and HMS DAEDALUS. The only major difference between RN and RCN circular badges is the three maple leaves at the bottom of the rope ring. (AC)

training establishments (ACADIA, QUADRA), and many CNAVs (CEDARWOOD, ST JOHN, etc).[11] That policy is no longer in effect as neither ENDEAVOUR nor QUEST, both of which were built in the 1960s, have official badges although the latter does sport an unofficial badge. After the Saint class, no further CNAVs or CFAVs received badges.

Regretfully, relatively few of the names in this book can claim official badges. Those that can are fairly well documented in either BRCN 150, CFP 267, or the library of the CF Photographic Unit in Ottawa. Other sources are the wardrooms in CFB Esquimalt (NADEN) and CFB Halifax (STADACONA), the War Museum in Ottawa, the Maritime Command Museum in Halifax, and the CFB Esquimalt Museum, where badges are on display.

The design of a badge usually starts sometime before the ship is completed and as a result, events can overtake the design. BLANDFORD for example, had a badge designed but her name was changed prior to commissioning.[12] SANDPIPER had a badge designed—approved by MND 28 Jan 1955—but NSHQ cancelled her and her three sister ships prior to construction ever starting.

The shape of Canadian badges closely follows the Royal Navy's circular pattern, with the addition of a sprig of three gold maple leaves in the centre bottom of the rope ring that surrounds the central device of the badge. A sample badge design from HMS DAEDALUS and one from GLOUCESTER are to be seen on this page. Badges for the RNZN are similar but with a large leaf or fern overlaying the bottom third of the rope ring. Badges for the RAN also follow the RN circular design but the tally plate at the top is larger and follows the curve of the rope ring.

In the 1980s, the Navy League of Canada began using badges of HMC Ships for Sea Cadet Corps, e.g. FRASER. For names with no badge, the Navy League designed its own, e.g. Stormont. They even used the same badge design complete with naval crown. The CF has no authority over the Navy League but after negotiations by the then Director of Ceremonial, Mr Vince Bezeau, two minor differences now distinguish a Sea Cadet badge from that for a warship of the same name. The badge of RCSCC Fraser differs from that of FRASER in that the three maple leaves are red not gold, and the name plate is always black on gold.

In the list of names later in this book, the letter B after the origin of the name indicates that the vessel was granted an official badge. Similarly 2. B indicates that the second of name was awarded a badge. As will be readily seen, most of the ships whose names are listed are not entitled to an official badge.

With badges, there is one known anomaly, REINDEER. A Fairmile ML in the 1950s, her five sisters all received a badge but she did not. Her short period in commission with a name is the probable reason.

One final point. The award of a badge has never been made in arrears. When discussing the first or second OTTAWA, the badge for the third ship can not be attributed to either of the first two. Neither badges nor Battle Honours can be made retroactive to previous vessels. For an example of where this has been done in error, see the badge supposedly worn by the first ACADIA in Arbuckle, *Badges of the Canadian Navy*. The badge shown was actually designed for the second ACADIA.

Battle Honours 1910–1954

Like badges, Battle Honours were developed by a committee in the RN which sat in the early months of 1954. The concept and selected awards subsequently passed to the RCN.

As described in both the Admiralty Fleet Order (AFO) and Naval General Order (NGO) 2.06, British-allocated Battle Honours were awards for successful war service by a specific commissioned warship. Successful war service included taking part in actions where the enemy was defeated or his intentions frustrated; that were inconclusive but well fought; and where outstanding efforts were made against overwhelming odds.

For a close convoy escort, a successful action could be considered the safe and timely arrival of the majority of the convoy after attack by the enemy, e.g. the convoys to Malta during the Second World War.

As noted in the AFO, Battle Honours were not awarded for inconclusive actions, those badly fought, or for "British defeats." There are of course, various ways to describe a defeat. HM Ships HOOD and PRINCE OF WALES, along with thirty-seven other British ships, hold the Battle Honour "Bismarck" 1941. This award is styled in the same manner as an individual ship action against another single vessel.

A vessel only need be present at an action—in the sense of under the control of an operational commander—to be awarded a Battle Honour such as NORMANDY 1944. Interestingly enough, the extent of her participation in the action concerned is immaterial. NGO 2.06/11, written in 1957, explained this as follows:

> In early actions, physical or visual contact with the enemy is a requirement. In modern actions, because communications allow patrols and scouting groups to operate effectively at great distances, the word "present" means presence at sea... under the direct orders of the senior officer controlling the operation. The award is therefore based on mention of the ship in the dispatch of the Commander-in-Chief, a Flag Officers' [sic] War Diary, a Battle Summary of the Naval Staff History ... the Report of Proceedings of the Commanding Officer, or the ship's log.

Such a concept is still in effect and a ship and her ship's company may never actually fire any of her weapons at the enemy and still be entitled to the award.

Actual service during a war, however, "does not necessarily make a ship's name eligible for a Battle Honour."[13] As with the award of individual medals and decorations, there are specific requirements laid down for each Battle Honour. For example, in the Second World War the Battle Honour ATLANTIC was awarded to, among others, all warships that formed part of a close convoy escort. Apparently, there is no minimum time requirement for such an award. Those vessels assigned only to a support group, even if the group sailed with a convoy, did not win this award until the group participated in a successful action, e.g. sank an enemy submarine, and then the award only went to the ships in that group actually present.[14] Neither FORT ERIE nor TORONTO, both of which have service in the Atlantic during wartime but with a support group only, were awarded a Battle Honour for such service. Appendix T contains details on area awards to Canadian warships.

The same reasoning applied to the one RN and 16 Canadian corvettes sent to the Mediterranean for Operation Torch in 1942/43. Of these corvettes, only LUNENBURG, PRESCOTT, REGINA, WEYBURN, and WOODSTOCK received Battle Honours for this war service: the first three received NORTH AFRICA and the latter two received MEDITERRANEAN, for successful attacks on submarines. Each award comes with the applicable years.

It follows, then that Battle Honours and a Record of War Service are two different concepts. The Admiralty Fleet Order 2565 distinguishes between them as follows:

> There is inevitably a tendency to regard Battle Honours in terms of general naval history and to include many actions and incidents which, meritorious in themselves, are not of sufficient importance to be ranked as Battle Honours. If awards are made too freely, they lose much of their value. Moreover, limitations of space prevent everything from being included on the (Battle Honours) scroll. A selection, therefore, has to be made—several incidents being often compressed into a single, short-titled Battle Honour—in a manner similar to that adopted when determining the Battle Honours which appear on a Regimental Colour.

The concern over the number of awards on any given scroll are important to the British where HMS AJAX has seventeen and HMS WARSPITE has twenty-five, the last fourteen won in the Second World War alone. The same problem does not concern Canadian ships at present but with the introduction of bilingual awards—see below—this problem will now arise far sooner that anticipated.

Battle Honours 1954–1987

Official Battle Honours have been awarded to the British Army since 1695 and to the Canadian Army since Confederation. Although displayed by various ships, up to 1954 Battle Honours for both the RN and RCN were unofficial and such awards as were displayed were often called "war service." In 1954, the Admiralty finally set to work to codify Naval Battle Honours, starting with the Spanish Armada of 1588. In October 1954 with the publication of the Admiralty Fleet Order on the subject, Battle Honours for the navies of the Commonwealth finally became official. In 1957, NSHQ published NGO 2.06/11 outlining Battle Honours for RCN ships and establishments.

From 1954 to 1987, within the Commonwealth there existed one standard list of Battle Honours—known as the common Commonwealth List. This list was both contributed to and used by, all Commonwealth navies. Under this system, individual vessels could earn Battle Honours for any one of six reasons:

   a. fleet or squadron actions;
   b. single ship actions;
   c. major bombardments;
   d. combined operations;

The Battle Honour board of HMCS HURON, 17 Jan 2000. (Freeman 661-1. AC)

   e. campaign awards; and

   f. area awards.[15]

While any individual vessel could be awarded one or more Battle Honours, such honours were allocated to a specific name and not to a particular hull.[16] When a vessel changed her name, she lost the Battle Honours associated with the old name. Consequently, when a name was revived for a new vessel, so too were the appropriate honours. It followed, therefore, that up to 1988 at any given moment there should have been only one vessel in service within the Commonwealth navies with a given name. This has not always been so as shown in Appendix D.

The purpose of reviving names of warships is not the same as that for awarding Battle Honours, and giving a new vessel an old name is not the justification for the award and display of Battle Honours. There are, it is true, many purposes served by reviving a name but generally, the ultimate reason "for repeating names of former HMC Ships is to honour the achievements of those ships"[17] and the personnel who sailed in them, a concept that in the 1990s tended to be forgotten by senior naval staff. For the first eighty years, the reason for the award of Battle Honours was somewhat different:

> The award of Battle Honours to Her Majesty's ships is intended to foster "esprit de corps" among their officers and ships' companies, who are thereby encouraged to take a personal interest in the wartime exploits not only of their present ship but also of those of the same name which distinguished themselves in the past.[18]

In the RCN during the Second World War, the award of unofficial Battle Honours had one more purpose. In a paper prepared in November 1943 by Paymaster Lt G. F. Todd to substantiate a large ship navy in the post-war era, he proposed that by acquiring such vessels now the navy would have "...an opportunity to win battle honours with them, and so greatly enhance the chances of their acceptance by public opinion as part of the post-war Canadian Navy."[19] That may have been the plan but only UGANDA and HMS PUNCHER earned such awards.

Up to the mid 1950s, RCN Battle Honours were treated quite differently from those for the Army and RCAF. Since the sovereign did not approve naval Battle Honours, they were unofficial and up to 1954, the selection of "war honours" to be displayed was left up to individual commanding officers.[20] Such a situation led to some confusion. In Manning & Walker's *British Warship Names*, the authors list war services and not Battle Honours. The number of war services they list for HM Ships MAGNIFICENT and BONAVENTURE differ from the Battle Honours listed for the same two vessels in BRCN 150.

Battle Honours held by HMC Ships now in commission have received official approval and are listed in the 1980 edition of CFP 200 and the forthcoming 2000 edition.[21] Because this publication is not widely available, an unofficial list of all awards to HMC Ships is to be found in Appendix S.

Although British vessels won the majority of Battle Honours previously awarded to HMC Ships, other Commonwealth vessels do wear Battle Honours won by Canadian warships. In 1960, for example, "some of these (were): HM Ships COLLINGWOOD, DUNDAS, LOCH ALVIE, MEON, NENE, RIBBLE and WHITBY: and HM Australian Ships HAWKSBURY and MELVILLE."[22] HMS COLLINGWOOD, incidentally, is a shore establishment near Portsmouth and she displays ATLANTIC 1941-44, the Battle Honour won by the Canadian corvette, even though they were both in commission at the same time.

Battle Honours 1987–1993

At a naval board meeting early in January 1987, the Director of Ceremonial at NDHQ, Mr Vince Bezeau, approached the naval board and suggested that perhaps it was time to repatriate the Battle Honours. He suggested three courses of action: first, retain the Commonwealth List as is; second, go to Canadian won Battle Honours only and leave the Commonwealth List forever; third, retain the List but display British won Battle Honours in another script, distinctive in either size or colour, or both. The naval board decided on the second option.[23]

The naval board also decided that those ships then in commission who held non-Canadian Battle Honours, could continue to display such honours for the length of their commission. When they paid off, non-Canadian Battle Honours would not pass to their successors. So CORMORANT continued to display Commonwealth won Battle Honours going back to 1759 but with her paying off in 1996, the right to such awards died and these will not pass to the next of name.[24] ORIOLE, in continuous commission since 1954, is still entitled to display her one British-won award, the last of HMC Ships in the regular force to do so.

The timing of this change also affected the Battle Honours awarded to the 2nd HALIFAX. In 1954 the name was awarded three honours, the first two of which were British. The third was for her Second World War service in the Atlantic. By the naval board's decision, the name Halifax lost the right to the first two awards.

Most of the British-won Battle Honours still on display by HMC Ships are carried by reserve divisions, one of which, UNICORN, has honours dating back to 1588. As stated in Appendix B, Chapter 3, of CFP 200, year 2000 edition, naval divisions and ORIOLE may display such awards "by right of continuous service." Once a division pays off, for whatever reason, she will lose the right to these awards. When a division changes location, she does not normally pay off so these awards should be on display for many years to come.

Also in this period, the Director of Ceremonial championed the establishment of two additional Second World War Battle Honours for the Canadian Navy: GULF OF ST LAWRENCE and ALEUTIANS.[25]

Battle Honours 1994–1999

This period saw the greatest change to naval Battle Honours since they were made official in 1954. Due to unification of the forces which commenced in the mid 1960s, and the Federal bilingual policy circa 1976, the Director of Ceremonial[26] issued a policy statement in 1994 which, for naval units at least, was not worded in a manner to catch their attention. No naval authority objected to the policy change that was to have a profound effect on future naval Battle Honour boards.[27] This effect would not yet have surfaced except for the 1991 Persian Gulf war.

By 1994, the war for Kuwait had resulted in the Battle Honour GULF AND KUWAIT GOLFE ET KUWAIT being awarded to ATHABASKAN, PROTECTEUR, and TERRA NOVA. Besides being the first Battle Honour won since Korea, this award is significant for three other reasons. First, this is the first CF Battle Honour. Second and third, by a NDHQ/DMTH ruling, this award is both bilingual and contains no year.

Of all the Battle Honours worn or won by HMC Ships, this will be the only one without a year date attached to the award. This is in keeping with a 1994 CF policy which broadly follows the previous army method of displaying Battle Honours where a year is noted only if the award covers more than one calendar year, or where a year is needed to distinguish one award from another. From a naval point of view this lack of a year makes the GULF AND KUWAIT award unique: it simply does not match previous Naval Battle Honours, all of which have a year attached. In the author's opinion, a tradition should be dispensed with whenever it impedes either effectiveness or efficiency. In this case, to sever a tradition simply to gain some form of CF commonality flies in the face of common sense.

As a CF Battle Honour, GULF AND KUWAIT GOLFE ET KUWAIT was won only by naval and air force units. While the army was certainly present in the Persian Gulf, individual battalions were represented only in company strength and that is not a large enough formation for the award of a Battle Honour to the whole battalion. Further, the air force will display this award in bilingual format. If the award had gone to an army unit, it would have been displayed in either French or English, depending on the language of the unit concerned.

The navy will display the bilingual version of the award. Although most ships are not bilingual "units" of the CF, the reason for employing the bilingual award apparently lies in the fact that all HMC Ships now have a bilingual title, e.g. HMCS/NCSM. Such a change in display policy is not retroactive but in a forthcoming publication on Heritage, an update of CFP 200, this policy and the loss of year dates is not clearly spelled out. It is the CF intention, however, that when a new Battle Honour board is prepared, regardless of the reason, all naval awards will be displayed in bilingual format, e.g. NORMANDY 1944 NORMANDIE.

For PROTECTEUR, with only this one Battle Honour, this is not a problem. For ATHABASKAN with three other awards, this means she should display GULF AND KUWAIT GOLFE ET KUWAIT immediately below KOREA 1950-53.

A check of the Fleet in December 1999 showed that ATHABASKAN and PROTECTEUR were using PERSIAN GULF 1991 on their respective boards in lieu of GULF AND KUWAIT. The Battle Honour board for TERRA NOVA, now in the MarCom Museum in Halifax, also uses Persian Gulf. No reason for this could be determined.

A similar check of the Battle Honour board for BRANDON, currently in service on the west coast, showed her awards to be rendered in the traditional manner, minus year dates for ATLANTIC. If she is typical of the Kingston class, then no ship presently in service is following the current policy for reasons not known.

Because Battle Honours are so closely associated with a name, Canadian-won honours are included in this book in Appendix S. They are not included with the actual names because most of the names listed are not entitled.

Regardless of which list was employed or at which time, Battle Honours can only pass to a successor warship if the latter had exactly the same name.

Spelling of a Ship's Name

For one ship to claim Battle Honours won by a predecessor, the spelling of the two names concerned must be identical. For example, the reserve division JOLLIET was named for the explorer who spelled his name differently from that given to the Second World War frigate, JOLIETTE. This latter name came from the town that in turn, took its name from one Barthélémy Joliette, siegneur de Lavaltrie. Since the two names are not spelled the same, the division can not claim the Battle Honours won by the frigate.

In the same way, in 1954 the reserve division GRIFFON could not claim the Battle Honours awarded to the name Griffin, even though both names are simply variations in spelling for the same creature in mythology.

The precise way in which a name is spelled, therefore, becomes of great importance. With the passage of time, the inaccuracy of records, and the loss of

The brow area of HURON, 18 Jan 00, showing from left to right her Battle Honour board, Kisbie ring, badge, tally plate and the Quartermaster, LS Brian Whitman. (Freeman 661-09. AC)

local knowledge, several names in this book have proven difficult to confirm their correct spelling. STONE TOWN is but one example.

The alternative for St Marys, Ontario, the name Stone Town was spelled both as two words and as one word, Stonetown. This occurred throughout the records in NSHQ/NDHQ. In such cases, the first thing to check would be the name plate, if one still existed. Otherwise, a photograph of the name plate would do. The ship's bell would also be acceptable evidence of correct name spelling. In this case, a visit was made in 1993 by the author to St Marys to see the bell in the town museum, and to confirm the spelling as STONE TOWN.

In the case of LA HAVE, *Jane's* spelt the name LE HAVE; the atlas used LaHave; the gazetteer and official road map of Nova Scotia had Lahave; and the file in the Directorate of History was labelled LA HAVE. No record of her bell or its disposition could be located. Fortunately, Directorate of History staff located a photograph of the ship showing her name painted on her bow: LA HAVE. Regardless of how the town or province wishes to spell the name, in order for lineage to be established, all future vessels will have to have their names spelled La Have.

In this regard, the source of the name is immaterial and can change from one ship to the next throughout its lineage. See the entries for CAPE BRETON and VANCOUVER as examples. But the spelling of the name can not change if lineage is to be claimed. Thus St John, St John's and Saint John are three different names given to three different ships.

Bells

The last item that one ship is supposed to inherit from her predecessors, is her bell. When the first of name is commissioned, she is presented with her bell, inscribed with her name. On paying off, the bell along with other assets like silverware, is returned to stores and is eventually placed in storage. When the next of name is commissioned, she is supposed to receive the bell of her predecessor. Originally, the second of name was to display and use the bell with the commissioning date of the first ship. Since the Second World War at least, Canadian warships have received a new bell when they first commission, along with the bell of their predecessor.[28] Of course, some ships are lost and go to the bottom with their bell. Some bells are lost while in, or en route to, storage. Some bells were, improperly, given away on paying off, usually to the namesake town. The bell for ROYALMOUNT, according to Cdr F McKee, went to the town of Mount Royal.

The bell used by both the 1st and 2nd QU'APPELLE. Note broad arrow indicating this is the back of the original bell. (Freeman 661-11. AC)

The original front side of QU'APPELLE's bell, showing the first vessel's origin as HMS FOXHOUND. The dates and names engraved on the bell are children baptized on board the 2nd QU'APPELLE. (Freeman 661-13. AC)

Most ship bells are made of brass but some receive chrome plating. A naval ship's bell should be inscribed with the title, name and year of commissioning but many do not include the year (See next page). Finally, the type, size and style of lettering varies greatly.

Sometime in the 1960s, the government began to loan out ship's bells to interested parties and special interest groups: the local branch of the Legion; Sea Cadet Corps; a museum; city hall, etc. In 1985 the bell of SAINT JOHN was in the Harbour's General Store Museum in downtown Saint John; and in 1990 WOODSTOCK's was in the naval club in Woodstock, Ontario. Wherever they wind up, the bells are supposedly only on loan.

Technically, each ship is only entitled to one bell with her name engraved on it but several ships have had two bells, e.g. ANTIGONISH, NEW WATERFORD, and ONTARIO. And at least two ships have had three: BEACON HILL and BONAVENTURE.[29]

Like the genealogy of a person, a name has a lineage. In the case of many names in the Royal Navy, such lineage extends back to the Armada of 1588. In Canada, we can now trace our ship's lineage no further back than 1910. Had the Provincial Marine of 1812 on the Great Lakes been a local initiative, we may have laid claim to lineage from certain ships like HMS CHIPPAWA, but this is not to be. Where a new ship had a Canadian predecessor with exactly the same name, she can claim the badge if any, the bell when available, and Battle Honours where applicable.

Notes to Chapter Two

1. After "History of Royal Navy Badges" in Wilkinson et al, *The A to Z of Royal Navy Badges*, Vol 1, p x.
2. Wilkinson, op cit, p xii.
3. Thomas, *A Companion to the Royal Navy*, p 49.
4. Defence Council Instructions (RN), S47/76, 12 Mar 1976.
5. Telephone conversation, author to MOD (Navy) Bath, circa 1976.
6. See BRCN 150.
7. Letter, N Sec't to CO Halifax Half Company, RCNVR, 116-2-1, 18 Feb 1930.
8. Memo, N Hist to N Sec't, NS 1460-1, 22 Feb 1955. See also, "Symbols and Ships," *The Crowsnest*, Aug 1961.
9. SNC Meeting No. 4, 15 Jan 1991. Up to 1998, CFAO 62-4 CF Badges had not been amended to reflect this policy.
10. See "Symbols and Ships," *The Crowsnest*, Aug 1961, p 7.
11. Naval Board Minutes 213-3, 16 Apr 1947.
12. Copy in author's possession. Undated. Source: CF Photo Unit Library, Ottawa.
13. Memo, N Hist to D Sea, NS 1460-23 SD 1676, 7 Jan 1960.
14. Admiralty Fleet Order 2565, 98/54, 1st October 1954.
15. After Weightman, *Heraldry in the Royal Navy*, p 22; Admiralty Fleet Order 2565/54, 1 Oct 1954; NGO 2.06/11, 1957. This list is still in effect in the 2000 version of CFP 200, Chapter 3.
16. Memo, N Hist to D Sea, NS 1460-23 SD 1676, 7 Jan 1960.
17. Ibid., para 6.
18. Admiralty Fleet Order 2565/54, para 1, 1 Oct 1954. See also ibid., para 2.
19. Douglas, "Conflict and Innovation in the Royal Canadian Navy," p 224; as quoted in Milner, *Canada's Navy, The First Century*, p 138.
20. *Flags, Ensigns, Colours, Pennants and Honours for the CF*, p 7–3. See also Naval Board Minutes 298-3, 28 Sep 1949.
21. CFP 200, *Flags, Ensigns, Colours, Pennants and Honours for the CF*. The 2000 edition will be known as *Honours, Flags and Heritage Structure of the CF*.
22. Memo, N Hist to D Sea, NS 1460-23 SD 1676, 7 Jan 1960.
23. NB Minutes 1/87, Item V, para 7.b., 7 Jan 1987.
24. Ibid.
25. CFSO 25/92 and 5/94 refer.
26. Since early in 1994, known as the Directorate of Military Tradition and Heritage, DMTH. On 1 Apr 1996, combined with D Hist to become the Directorate of History and Heritage, DHH.
27. Letter, NDHQ/DMTH to MARCOM/DComd & others, 1065-1 (DMTH 3), 29 Apr 1994.
28. List of Ship's Bells, NDHQ/DSRO4, Jun 1983.
29. Ibid. The reason for the extra bells is unclear but one explanation may be that once a bell is filled with the names of babies christened on board, the ship could demand another bell.

The bell of SWANSEA with no commissioning year. (Freeman 661-21. AC)

Chapter Three

Nomenclature

Warships are built generally in groups to standard patterns and each group is known as a "class." Vessels of a class should be identical one with the other but this is not always so, especially where different builders are involved or later modifications are made. All vessels of one class are referred to as sister ships.

A "type" of vessel on the other hand, refers to a category of ship whose purpose and general specifications are within some stated limits such as size or purpose, e.g. destroyers, submarines, and aircraft carriers. The type of vessel is often referred to as her rate, as HAIDA was rated a destroyer. Such limits are not fixed, however, and there are often differences in the use of type names from one navy to another.

The use of the term frigate in the 1960s is one example: our Prestonians (of 1600 tons) were given the same rate as the USN's Belknap (6500 tons), Leahy (5700 tons) and Coontz (4700 tons) classes. These USN frigates were later re-rated as Destroyer Leaders and even later still, as cruisers. A Second World War light cruiser such as the USS JUNEAU or HMS AJAX was about 6000 tons. The term frigate came back into

Halifax, circa October 1940. From left to right, the soon to commission PRINCE DAVID, and HMC Ships COLUM-BIA, ANNAPOLIS and RENARD. (PAC 105737. KM Coll.)

use in the navies of the world in 1941 following a suggestion by the CNS, VAdm P. Nelles. He was concerned that there were enough types of corvettes and to call the improved version a "twin screw corvette" would only add to the confusion. He suggested the term "frigate" in lieu and the Admiralty accepted this.[1]

A type of ship may last a long time but within each type a new class may be developed every few years. Within the class, the names of the sister ships generally conform to a pre-arranged pattern. These naming patterns vary from navy to navy.

Nomenclature is a system of names for things, in this case ships. The term refers not to the names themselves but to the system used for categorizing ships by classes and types and also to the method of naming warships by class within their types.

Within a given navy a warship's class and type is often recognizable from her name alone, e.g. ONTARIO (cruiser, 1950s), ALGONQUIN (destroyer, 1940s), and LOON (patrol craft, 1950s); USS LOS ANGELES (attack submarine, 1980s), USS ALABAMA (missile submarine, 1980s); HMS ILLUSTRIOUS (aircraft carrier, 1940s and 1980s), HMS RENOWN (battleship, 1930s, and submarine, 1980s), and HMS COSSACK (destroyer, 1940s).

Within any class, therefore, it follows that there should exist a "common thread" among the names, in other words all the names in that class are clearly linked one to the other by at least one factor. There are several methods for doing this. In the simplest case, the names all begin with one letter. Instead of a letter, a syllable may be used, e.g. dun as in Dundurn and Dundalk. The syllable may even be located at the back of the name such as the Ton class minesweepers in the RN and the Ville class tugs in our Navy. An extension of this idea is to employ a word common to each member of the class, e.g. Pine Lake, Birch Lake, etc.

Further, the names for warships in a given class can share one attribute by naming them after specific items such as geographical features (rivers, capes, bays); political divisions (provinces, cities, regions); historical or important people (prime ministers, explorers); creatures both real (animals, fish) and mythological (gods, legends); attributes (intrepid, fearless); or even be functional in nature (provider and preserver).

Where a nation chooses to name its warships after centres of population or political divisions, then the normal course is to have larger and more important vessels receive the names of large or important cities, states, provinces or regions. As vessels descend in size or significance, so too does the centre or area after which they are named.

Such naming practices have not been restricted solely to warships. Passenger vessels, freighters, ferries and tug boats, to name but a few, often have their own nomenclature. Early in the twentieth century vessels of the Cunard Line usually had names ending in "ia" like *Lusitania* while their rivals in the White Star Line had names ending in "ic" like *Titanic*.

With each new development in warships, the nomenclature of types changes. The latter half of the twentieth century has seen the complete demise of the battleship in every navy but the USN and the downgrading of the role of the destroyer in favour of frigates. And with the development of nuclear propulsion, submarines have taken a more important role. This is shown by the allocation of former battleship names to submarines in both the Royal and United States navies.

Early in 1940 the First Lord of the Admiralty, Winston Churchill, became concerned over nomenclature in the RN. A type of vessel of about 1000 tons was then being termed a Fast Escort Vessel. Churchill agreed with his First Sea Lord "about the needlessness of repeating the word vessel"[2] and their common wish was to simplify ship designators (rates) to one word. "I should like the word 'destroyer' to cover ships formerly described as 'fast escort vessels'. I do not like the word 'whaler' which is an entire misnomer as they are not going to catch whales and I should like some suggestions about this. What is, in fact, the distinction between an 'escorter', a 'patroller' and a 'whaler' as now specified[?]."[3] As a result of this, Escorters were designated Sloops, Fast Escort Vessels became the Hunt class of small destroyers (named after packs of foxhounds), and the Whalers became the Corvettes. In the RCN the term originally used for a corvette was whale catcher. It was not changed until July 1940.[4]

Life would be simple, indeed, if all vessels retained their assigned class and rate throughout their life. Some do but many change one or both. KAPUSKASING for example, started as a minesweeper, became a survey ship and ended up as an oceanographic research vessel. All the time she belonged to the Algerine class. BUCKINGHAM, on the other hand, was always a frigate but changed from River to Prestonian class in the 1950s.

These two simple examples do not do justice to changes in rate and class. Further, it has proved to be beyond the scope of this book to detail each subtle change such as the first IROQUOIS and her sisters changing their class from Tribal to Fleet Tribal in 1943, the differences between the River class destroyer and a Fleet River class destroyer of the Second World War,[5] or the various rates assigned to the St Laurent class during their long service from the 1950s to the 1990s.

As will be illustrated in this chapter, the idea of a common thread for our warship names within a given class, as well as simple and direct type and class names, has varied greatly during the first ninety years. For ease of illustration, the nomenclature story has been broken into three periods. Within each period, classes are discussed by types, the larger vessels being mentioned first.

Early Days: 1910–1939

For the first three decades, records are very scarce but from the evidence available, the former RN vessels in the navy retained their original class and nomenclature. Thus RAINBOW stayed an Apollo class cruiser, AURORA an Arethusa Class cruiser, SHEARWATER a Condor class sloop, and so on.

The first break with the RN classification came with the Battle class trawlers constructed in the closing days of the First World War. Apparently based on a British design called the Castle class but with a slightly larger tonnage, the Battles seem to be the first class with a distinct Canadian designation. No other would appear until the former RN destroyers taken over in the 1930s were eventually termed the River class and the Bassett minesweepers were re-classed as the Gaspé—or Fundy—class. But this would not occur until the Second World War.

According to reference books of the period, the VANCOUVER and CHAMPLAIN retained their RN classification as S class destroyers even though their names had been changed.

The first SHEARWATER under sail, date not known. (KM Coll.)

Second World War: 1939–1945

Like many other aspects of the Navy in this period, nomenclature was not high on the priority list and the first mention of the subject does not appear until June 1940 in Naval Orders 947 and 954. The RCN followed RN nomenclature procedures and the details promulgated in 1940 simply set out the type designator for corvettes, and the class names and type designators for minesweepers, auxiliary patrol vessels, and small craft. The subject of class nomenclature was then ignored for over three years.

Late in 1943 the naval staff pointed out that with all the various vessels "named after cities and towns, it is extremely difficult to distinguish between the various classes of Frigates and single screw Corvettes" and recommended that "as far as possible, the RN nomenclature for classes" be adopted.[6] This resulted in the following:

a. all A to I class destroyers converted to destroyer escorts to become River class destroyers, which is the first mention of this class name found in the documentation;

b. all A to I class destroyers fitted as fleet destroyers and named after Canadian rivers to become Fleet River class destroyers;

c. Tribal class destroyers to become Fleet Tribal class destroyers;

d. Town class destroyers;

e. Frigates to become River class frigates;

f. Revised frigates to become Loch class frigates;

g. Original Canadian Short Forecastle (SF) corvettes and those converted to Long Forecastle (LF) to become Flower class corvettes;

Originally a short foc'sle corvette, HMCS CHILLIWACK emerged from her 1943 refit with a long foc'sle.
(RCN ECP 68-271. FDN Coll.)

h. Corvettes built with extended forecastle with increased shear and flare to become Revised Flower class corvettes;

j. New corvettes built with LF and increased fuel stowage to become Long Endurance (the term changed to Increased Endurance early in 1944) Flower class corvettes;

k. Lengthened Single Screw corvettes to become Castle class corvettes;

l. Bangor class steam minesweepers;

m. Bangor class diesel minesweepers; and

n. Algerine escorts.[7]

By early 1944, the nomenclature drive had spread to the smaller classes of vessels. Various decisions led to the following classification:

a. Bassett minesweepers to become Fundy class m/s trawlers;

b. 105ft wooden minesweepers to become Motor minesweepers (105ft type) which became the Llewellyn class;

c. 126ft wooden minesweepers to become Motor minesweepers (126ft type) which became the Lake class;

d. Motor Launch (Fairmile B Type) to stay the same;

e. Base supply ships and depot ships to become Fairmile depot ships;

f. Auxiliary minesweepers to stay the same;

g. 112ft steel diesel and 100ft diesel tugs to become Norton class tugs;

h. 80ft steel diesel tugs to become Glen class steel tugs;

j. 80ft wooden diesel tugs to become Glen class wooden tugs;

k. 40ft steel diesel tugs to become Ville class tugs; and

m. 48ft, 8in harbour patrol craft to remain harbour patrol craft.[8]

As a general rule the RN practice of nomenclature was followed but there were both exceptions and variations.

Aircraft Carriers

Rated as escort carriers, HM Ships NABOB and PUNCHER are classed by authorities as either Smiter or Ruler class, depending on the authority cited. No definite or official classification could be located for these two vessels. From their names, however, it would appear that HMS NABOB was a Ruler class and HMS PUNCHER, a Smiter class carrier.

Cruisers

The two light cruisers ONTARIO and UGANDA were not, as is often reported, sister ships. UGANDA was the lead ship of, and thus provided the name for, her class. Confusion as to her class arose when after her transfer to the RCN, *Jane's* and other authorities started calling her RN sisters the Ceylon class. ONTARIO as HMS MINOTAUR had also given her name to her class but the class name was also changed when she was transferred to the RCN. The new RN class name became Swiftsure[9] and thus ONTARIO was often referred to as being in that class.

Three CNR passenger vessels were taken over by the Navy and converted to armed merchant cruisers. These were PRINCE DAVID, PRINCE HENRY and PRINCE ROBERT. All were modified during the war, two emerging as landing ships infantry and one as an auxiliary anti-aircraft ship. Although sister ships, no authority could be located stating their class name but one or two documents refer to them as Prince class vessels. Further, although most authorities class these vessels as a liner, they are not in the same league as the RMS *Queen Mary* and the author has chosen to refer to them as passenger vessels.

Destroyers

The River class was made up of former RN destroyers from several different classes and thus was not a true class in itself, and as noted earlier, the class was subdivided into Fleet River and River classes. Some of these vessels had been in the RCN since the 1930s and while it is possible that the term River class had been applied to them, the first official use of these terms did not appear until December 1943.[10] All ships of this class were given the names of rivers.

The Tribal, technically Fleet Tribal, class[11] took their class designator from the RN and like their RN and RAN sisters, were named for native peoples or native linguistic groups. The two Fleet V destroyers, ALGONQUIN and SIOUX, were

Halifax, circa 24 Sep 1940, Dartmouth in the background. Canadian personnel march on board six "four stackers" just prior to their commissioning in the RCN. Forward, inboard 175 former USS MACKENZIE (soon to be ANNAPOLIS); middle 162 THATCHER (NIAGARA); outboard 108 WILLIAMS (ST CLAIR). Aft, inboard, 252 McCOOK (ST CROIX); middle 256 BANCROFT (ST FRANCIS); outboard 183 HARADEN (COLUMBIA). (RCN H-255. FDN Coll.)

also given Tribal names, in part to deceive the enemy.[12] In the First World War, the RN used the name Crusader as a Tribal name.

The Town class was an RN designation suggested by Capt Tapprell Dorling, DSO, RN. It was his idea to give these former USN vessels the names of towns common to both Britain—and the Commonwealth—and the USA.[13] In the RCN, all received the names of rivers except two: BUXTON and HAMILTON, both of whom were first commissioned into the RN but due to technical problems, were offered to the RCN.

The River class frigate NEW GLASGOW in January 1944. (AC)

Frigates

Originally, frigates were intended to be another but larger class of corvette. In the RCN there were two classes, but three groups of frigates.

The first class was the River class. Having the same class designator as the destroyers must have led to some confusion. The class designator again came from the RN who named their frigates after their rivers. Seven of these served in the RCN, retaining their original river names, such as NENE. The second group in this, the Canadian-built frigates, continued to be given the names of towns and cities.

The third group of frigates was the Loch class, taking their class name from the RN. All three vessels retained their original RN names and were rated as revised frigates.[14]

Corvettes

"Whale catchers" came to be called corvettes in mid 1940. Originally designed as coastal escorts with a secondary function as a minesweeper, they were used almost from the start as ocean convoy escorts. Once more, the Flower class designator was taken from the RN but only the first ten received the names of flowers: the rest took the names of towns of moderate size.[15] Later, the names of towns and cities of all sizes were used for this class.

As the design of corvettes was modified to meet the demands of life as an ocean escort, five distinct classes of corvettes emerged:[16] Flower class, short foc'sle (SF); Flower class, long foc'sle (LF); Flower class; Long Endurance Flower class;[17] and Castle class.

Minesweepers

The pre-war minesweepers were originally termed the Bassett class following their RN sisters. In 1940, for reasons not explained, they were termed the Gaspé class.[18] During 1943 and 1944 this class was referred to by various titles, usually modified Bassets (Fundy) or Fundy class M/S trawlers.[19] Since FUNDY was the first to be commissioned, the class name more appropriately belongs to her than to GASPE.

NSHQ intended to name wartime minesweepers "after Canadian Bays,"[20] in the same manner as the Basset class. Originally, the first wartime class was designated as the Bay class in Naval Order 954, 20 July 1940. By late 1943, the director of naval construction considered "the best practice would be to adopt as far as possible the RN nomenclature" and the Bay class officially became the Bangors, subdivided into steam and diesel classes. Later vessels of this class were named for cities and towns.

The next class was the Algerines. Although technically minesweepers, the need for escort vessels proved so great that all of this class were used for escort work. This change of function affected their class designation and they were called Algerine escorts in Naval Order 954. Like the other minesweepers, the class designator came from the RN.

Because the Germans were using magnetic mines in large numbers, several classes of minesweepers were built of wood. The first of these, later to be known as the Llewellyn class, were known in this period simply as motor minesweepers (125ft type). Similarly, the later Lake class were originally termed motor minesweepers (105ft type). Although not very inspiring, these designators remained in effect until after the Second World War.

The motor minesweeper PINE LAKE. She and her sisters never saw commissioned service in the RCN. (KM Coll.)

The remaining minesweepers in this era were generally converted civilian vessels that retained their original names. Initially, in Naval Order 954 they were divided into three classes known as Auxiliary, Harbour or Magnetic minesweepers but late in the war they were all known as Auxiliary minesweepers.[21]

The "pup" tug MANVILLE circa 1947.

Tugs

Like the auxiliary minesweepers, the early tugs were generally former civilian craft that were used for a variety of purposes other than towing and originally they were not given a class name at all. In January 1942, with the coming of numbers in lieu of names, many were designated simply as harbour craft. (See below.)

With the arrival of tugs both designed and constructed to naval specifications, four classes were recognized and named. The Norton class, later called the Ton class, were large vessels of either 112 or 100 feet in length. The Glen class were all 80 feet in length but made from either wood or steel, dividing that class into two groups: Glen Class steel and Glen Class wooden tugs.[22] The last were the small Ville class, affectionately called the pup tugs by naval personnel and dockyard mateys alike, which performed a variety of tasks including being used as gate vessels.

Auxiliaries: Nenamook Class

In 1941, six seine trawlers were constructed on the west coast for the Fishermen's Reserve. No official class name was ever given these vessels so following the principle of first of class, the author has assigned them the class name Nenamook.

Animal Class Armed Yachts

These vessels were not a class of ships but rather a collection of civilian vessels from many sources. At the beginning of the Second World War, the RCN was rather desperate for ships of any type and thus yachts were purchased and armed. For an interesting account of how the pressures of wartime forced the government to bend a few of the rules on acquisition, readers are directed to the article by Keenlyside and the book by McKee. Most of the yachts thus acquired were given animal names but two, AMBLER and SANS PEUR, retained their original names. As in other cases, these two vessels apparently retained their name because they were chartered while the rest were purchased. But Cdr F McKee, *The Armed Yachts of Canada*, claims these two vessels retained their names because they were not from the USA: American-obtained vessels had to disguise their neutral origins.

Harbour Craft

As far as can be determined, the term "harbour" craft was first officially used in the RCN in late 1941 when NSHQ decided to allot numbers to some 200 vessels.[23] The term was applied to that mass of small vessels which came in an assortment of sizes and shapes, and whose original civilian purpose was often unrecorded.

The harbour craft HDC 21, formerly HMCS LUCINDA II, at Saint John circa 1944. (RCN DBO 548-2. KM Coll.)

By 1944, three distinct classes of purpose-built harbour craft were in service and like the minesweepers before them, two of the classes were indifferently known by their length: 46-foot and 72-foot Harbour Craft (HC).[24] The other class, 48 feet 6 inches in length, was called Harbour Patrol Craft (HPC). All carried numbers.

Postwar 1949–1999

Like the country it was designed to defend, the RCN evolved as a separate Navy rather than being created by a revolution. In this evolutionary process, one of the major changes occurred in 1949 when DN Com and DNPO at NSHQ suggested that it was essential that "HMC Ships be given a standard system of type designators, and ships' numbers which are clearly understood by, and do not conflict with the RN and USN."[25]

The system of nomenclature suggested by these officers closely followed once again the RN system but the pennant numbers[26] were modelled on the USN practice. These numbers were apparently phased in over a period of several months. No indication could be found as to why such a broken series of numbers—205 to 260—was selected for the St Laurent and Restigouche classes. Apparently, pennant numbers were not considered for the Vancouver class but the unnamed General Purpose Frigates were to start with the number 270. The Iroquois class started with the number 280 and the Halifax class originally was to commence at 290. This latter idea was cancelled when it was realized that if the program were expanded to include ten or more ships, then numbers commencing at 290 would run out. A series of numbers was required, therefore, which would be continuous, expandable, and not conflict with yard craft or other NATO vessels. The first series that met this requirement started at 330 and conformed to the custom that frigates had numbers in the 300s, as did the Prestonians.

Under this nomenclature, ONTARIO and QUEBEC were rated cruisers as opposed to light cruisers; the destroyers and frigates remained unchanged; the Algerines became Fleet Minesweepers and the Ton class tugs, having changed their class from Norton, became ocean tugs.

What was to become the St Laurent class of destroyer escorts was now on the drawing boards and several discussions took place concerning their designation. Various type names were suggested: destroyer escort, sloop, A/S vessel, A/S frigate, and hunter-killer destroyer. In July 1949, the naval board felt moved to consult the Admiralty "who planned to have similar ships in their Fleet."[27] Ultimately, the ships were rated as destroyer escorts.[28]

About this time, consideration was being given to the construction of a class of A/A frigates. In the various documents, reference is often made to the Vancouver class frigates, which would later be cancelled in favour of additional St Laurent class destroyer escorts.[29]

But before this occurred, another discussion took place on nomenclature. This resulted in the Tribals, Cs and Vs, and the new St Laurents being rated as Ocean Escorts 1st rate. The frigates became Ocean Escorts 2nd rate while the Algerines and Bangor minesweepers became Coastal Escorts.[30]

It was pointed out at the time that the RN, USN and RCN were discussing the standardization of type names and the naval staff suggested that such a re-rating be deferred, but it wasn't.[31] Even later, the fleet went to another reclassification and the St Laurents were rated as frigates.

The point of listing the changes noted above is to show the lack of direction prevalent in NSHQ on the subject of nomenclature. There are too many changes and they are too frequent to record completely in this book.

Postwar: Class Names

One decision of importance was that each class would be named after the first ship in that class.[32] Such a policy resulted in the class names for the destroyer escorts becoming St Laurent, Restigouche, Mackenzie and Annapolis respectively, and the modernized frigates became the Prestonian class. Later, the Provider, Protecteur, Iroquois, Halifax, Kingston and Victoria classes would also follow this rule.

Although such a rule did exist, there were many exceptions. Ignoring the older classes of vessels and concentrating solely on new construction, the Bay class minesweepers, Bird class patrol boats, Porte class gate vessels, and O class submarines, did not follow this rule, and neither did the various classes of tugs: Saints, Glens, Woods and Villes.[33]

Aircraft Carriers

All three carriers retained their original RN class names: WARRIOR was a Colossus class carrier while MAGNIFICENT and BONAVENTURE were both members of the Majestic class which in effect, made them sister ships although they were completed to different designs.

Cruisers

The cruisers, covered in the previous section, retained their original classifications. Rumours indicate that there were plans to replace these vessels with two 5,000-ton, 500-foot missile cruisers of the Manitoba class. No documentary evidence could be located.

Destroyers

Towards the end of the Second World War, the RN constructed a large number of destroyers to one basic design. All the vessels had names commencing with the letter C and consequently, they were known as the C Class although some authorities call them the C Group of four classes. This class consisted of four groups whose names started with Ca, Ch, Co and Cr. The latter group were the Crescents. All eight of these vessels were intended to be transferred to the RCN for use in the Pacific. With the end of the war coming earlier than expected, only the CRESCENT and the CRUSADER were transferred.[34]

The Fleet V destroyers were near sisters of the Crescent class and they retained their RN designation. When the ALGONQUIN and CRESCENT were modified in the 1950s, they plus their two sisters, SIOUX and CRUSADER, were officially redesignated as the Algonquin class.[35]

The Second World War Tribal class retained their class name throughout their service, the last one being discarded in the late 1960s. The introduction of the 280 class destroyers in the 1970s brought back four tribal names. For the purposes of nomenclature, however, this class was termed the Iroquois class[36] and this distinguished them from the different class of Tribals then serving in the RN. In the Fleet, however, these destroyers are referred to as 280s or Tribals. In the 1980s, a project began whereby these vessels were converted to a new AAW role. This was the Tribal class Update and Modernization Project, TRUMP, and as a class these vessels are now often referred to as TRUMPs.

With the construction of the destroyer escorts in the 1950s, the policy determined for class names was to employ the first of class name. These destroyer escorts were divided into four distinct classes—St Laurent, Restigouche, Mackenzie, and Annapolis. Technically, after their conversion to helicopter carriers, the first class was then titled the Improved St Laurent (ISL) class. After the conversion of four of the Restigouche class in the 1970s, a fifth class was formed known as the Improved Restigouche (IRE) class.

Originally, the Mackenzies were designated as the Saskatchewan class but the naval board "considered the name MACKENZIE preferable because the association of SASKATCHEWAN with the river rather than the province might not be evident."[37]

As for the Annapolis class, these two vessels were originally part of the "repeat Restigouche class," which were later designated as the Mackenzies. When the decision was made to finish them as helicopter carrying escorts, like the converted St Laurents rather than as standard destroyer escorts like the rest of the Mackenzies, the two vessels became a separate class.

Frigates

The Second World War frigates of the River class which were re-acquired after the war, retained their original designation until modernized in the 1950s. From this rebuilding, these ships were designated the Prestonian class after the first vessel so modified. Although the class name remained, the navy gave PRESTONIAN to the Royal Norwegian Navy shortly after her modernization in 1956, along with TORONTO and PENETANG.

A class of small frigates on the drawing boards in the early 1950s was known as the Vancouver class. Eventually, it was decided that construction of this class should not be undertaken as the design was not suitable for a large percentage of the required roles. In the late 1950s a larger class of vessels were proposed—to be called the Mackenzie class—but budget constraints put an end to them as well. Additional St Laurent class vessels were approved instead[39] and these also came to be called the Mackenzie class.

The general purpose frigates of the 1960s, also known as the 270 class, were apparently never given a class name. The names of towns and cities were proposed but later, CNS decided to continue using the tribal names.[40] These were cancelled.

The twelve patrol frigates (330 class) are known as the Halifax class and all are named for cities. The project that acquired these vessels was known as the Canadian Patrol Frigate (CPF) and that abbreviation was often applied to the class, as was the term City class. Originally, the class only had six ships but the intention was to build two additional batches of six ships each. The third batch were to be anti-air warfare ships with basically the same design but somewhat longer in length. When cost considerations dictated that only a total of twelve could be built, the staff recommended a repeat of the first six. The second batch was first designated as the Montréal class but since these vessels were now identical to the Halifax class, the separate class idea was dropped and all twelve vessels were allocated to the Halifax class in 1991.[41]

Minesweepers

The Bangor and Algerine classes retained their Second World War class titles but with the introduction of the new class of coastal minesweepers in the early 1950s, the RCN returned to its prewar system of naming these vessels after bays and other coastal formations. The term Bay was brought back for the class name.

Two civilian vessels were acquired in the 1980s to supplement the naval reserve as minesweepers and renamed ANTICOSTI and MORESBY, both new names. They were not allocated a class name until about 1996.

In the 1990s, the Maritime Coastal Defence Vessel (MCDV) project saw the construction of twelve vessels known as the Kingston class. Because of difficulties at the highest level with the choice of names for these vessels (see Chapter 4) they were for a time known as the Frontenac class.

An analysis of the names in the Kingston class show that five of these names were new, without Battle Honours or lineage; nine had never been recommended by the Ships' Names Committee; and, contrary to CFAO 36-7 then in force:

◆ five vessels shared the names of CF bases and stations;
◆ the names were not those of coastal geographic formations;
◆ some names were not appropriate to the type and size of ship, e.g. EDMONTON (when CALGARY—a smaller city—was a frigate, a larger class of vessel); and
◆ the names did not allow the class and type of vessel to be determined, e.g., are SASKATOON and REGINA both frigates?

Submarines

The two German U-boats taken over at the end of the Second World War were neither given a class designator nor names. The two former USN boats, however, were renamed but retained their USN class names: RAINBOW was a Tench class and GRILSE a converted or modified Balao class. The O class submarines took their class name from the first letter of their names. In the RN and RAN, their sister boats were known as the Oberon class.

In the late 1980s, the government proposed the construction of a class of up to twelve nuclear powered submarines. Among other ideas, consideration was given to using plans for either the British Trafalgar or the French Rubis class. Although the Ships' Names Committee proposed to name these boats after provinces and territories in the order which these joined the country, they also inappropriately designated them the Canada class.[42] While MND approved the title Canada class,[43] the government later cancelled this acquisition proposal.

In 1998, the government finally announced their intention to purchase four laid-up British submarines of the Upholder class. Due to commission in 2000/01, they will become the Victoria class.

Support Ships

The two support ships acquired after the war were given names of Capes and were known as the Cape class. It was intended that cape names also be given to the operation support ships (AORs), the first of which, the second PROVIDER, was laid down in 1961. She became the sole member of the Provider class, while her two later cousins are in the Protecteur class.[44]

Other Vessels

In the mid 1950s the six Fairmiles previously known only by numbers were given the names of animals, although the class retained its original designation of Fairmile. Similar vessels built at this time were called the Bird class.

The naval Constructor-in-Chief, Cmdre R Baker, proposed the designator for the Saint class of tugs. He noted in a memo that "these tugs are a development of the old British Admiralty Saint Class ... and although there may be advantages in naming the new Canadian Tugs after obscure villages in the bush, I would like to suggest that it would be better to name them after Canadian Saints."[45] The reference to the obscure villages in the bush most likely refers to the Ton, Ore, Glen and Ville class tugs, discussed elsewhere, as being probably named after dispersed villages and hamlets. In reply to his Constructor-in-Chief, the CNS, VAdm R Mainguy, wrote: "Apart from Saint John and St. John's, I think most Canadian Saints are 'obscure villages in the bush'."[46] In fact, these tugs were named after Jesuit martyrs.

LABRADOR was a Wind class icebreaker, the class name being taken from the US Coast Guard Wind class on which her design was based. As far as can be determined BRAS D'OR did not have an official class name, which was appropriate for an experimental prototype.

The Saint class tug CFAV SAINT ANTHONY, Sep 1971. (FDN Coll.)

The first CORMORANT, a Bird class patrol craft about 1960. (RCN DNS 290385. KM Coll.)

The designations for the Bird, Fairmile, Porte, Glen, Ville, Norton and Wood classes were formally approved in 1954.[47]

According to the former Directorate of Auxiliary Vessels (DAV) in NDHQ, the RCMP class names were retained for vessels acquired from that service in the late 1970s and early 1980s. STANDOFF and NICHOLSON as well as ACADIAN and her sisters, were all known as Detachment class although the first two are a different size and hence, technically, a different class. The other former RCMP vessel, FORT STEELE, was a Fort class vessel while the two former DOT vessels, RAPID and RALLY, were termed R class vessels.

The diving tender CORMORANT (second of name) and the yacht ORIOLE were never allocated class names.

The five gate vessels were officially termed the Porte class but were referred to either as gate vessels, or more colloquially, as pig boats.

While nomenclature should change as new types of ships are developed, some degree of permanence is required or else the policy dissolves as each succeeding staff attempts to mold the nomenclature to meet current political or staff feelings. Nomenclature, especially that of warships, is a matter of policy for the naval staff, one which not only meets the present and future requirements of the navy but one which also requires reflection on and consideration of the past.

Notes to Chapter Three

1.   See Tucker, *The Naval Service of Canada*, Vol. II, p 66.
2.   March, *British Destroyers*, p 475-8. The term was coined to avoid political feelings. See also Cunningham, p 194.
3.   Ibid.
4.   See Naval Staff Minutes 3, 4-2 and 8-1, plus Naval Order 947 and 954 (20 Jul 1940).

5. Nomenclature for classes of RCN ships, Naval Staff Minutes 215, 20 Dec 1943, NS 1057-1-56, Vol. 1.
6. Ibid.
7. Ibid. Appendix B.
8. Nomenclature for classes of RCN ships. Naval Staff Minute 228-1, 6 Mar 1944 (NS 1057-1-56, Vol. 1).
9. Confidential Canadian Naval Order (CCNO) 655, 3 Mar 1945 (NS 15370-240).
10. Naval Staff Minutes 215, 20 Dec 1943 (NS 1057-1-56, Vol. 1).
11. Ibid.
12. Tucker, *Naval Service of Canada*, Vol. 2, p 93, note 28.
13. Manning, *The British Destroyer*, p 20. Capt Dorling was an author who used the pseudonym of "Taffrail," a thinly disguised form of his first name.
14. Confidential Canadian Naval Order 266, 5 Feb 1944.
15. CNS weekly report to MND. NS 1000-5-7, 18 Jul 1940.
16. Naval Staff Minutes 215-10, Appendix B, 20 Dec 1943.
17. In Naval Staff Meeting 219-2, 10 Jan 1944 (NS 1057-1-56, Vol. 1), DN Construction pointed out that the term Increased Endurance would be more appropriate. So the term was changed and abbreviated I.E.
18. Naval Order 954, 20 Jul 1940.
19. See Naval Staff Minutes 206-11, 19 Oct 1943; Naval Staff Minutes 228, Appendix A, 6 Mar 1944; and Confidential Canadian Naval Order 304, 8 Apr 1944.
20. CNS Weekly Report to MND. NS 1000-5-7, 18 Jul 1940.
21. Naval Staff Minutes 228, Appendix A, 6 Mar 1944.
22. Ibid.
23. Memo, N Sec't to COAC and others, NS 40-1-6, 31 Dec 1941.
24. Naval Staff Minutes 228, Appendix A, 6 Mar 1944.
25. Naval Staff Minutes 442-3, 25 Jan 1949 (NSC 1305-300).
26. Ibid. Called a ship's number.
27. Naval Board Minutes 292-2, 6 Jul 1949.28.
28. CFAO 36-7, 15/81.
29. See Naval Board Minutes 446-1, 1 Jun 1955.
30. Naval Staff Minutes 505-8, 27 Dec 1950 - 15 Jan 1951.
31. Ibid.
32. Names for New Construction Vessels, NS 8000-5, 4 Nov 1959.
33. See NAC RG 96-87/167 Navy 3539, NSC 8000-5, Vol. 3. Memo, DNPO to VCNS, 25 Jun 1954.
34. Naval Board Minutes 163-4, 12 Feb 1945.
35. Naval General Order 2.06/8, circa 23 Apr 1953.
36. CFAO 36-7, Annex B.
37. Naval Board Minutes 507-1, 9 Oct 1956.
38. Naval Board Minutes 573-1, 17 Jul 1958.
39. Naval Board Minutes 608-3, 4 Nov 1959.
40. Letter, CMDO to author, NDHQ 11900-1, 5 Mar 1985.
41. CFSO 55/85 and CFSO 16/91 refer. Information on the third batch from Adm J. Anderson.
42. CFAO 36-7 required the lead ship to provide the class name. To reach the total of twelve names, the SNC included the rather long name of "North West Territories."
43. Minutes of Naval Board meeting 2/88, 13 Oct 1988, item 23. 1150-110/N48 (DGMDO/MPC), 26 Oct 1988.
44. CFAO 36-7, Annex B.
45. Memo, Constructor-in-Chief to CNS, NS 8200-489 (NCC), 28 Jan 1953.
46. See NS 8200-489 (NCC), 28 Jan 1953.
47. NAC RG 83-84/167 Navy 3539, NSC 8000-5, Vol. 3. Memo, DNPO to VCNS, 25 Jun 1954.

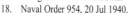

The bell of the second HURON showing her actual date of commission. (Freeman 661-02. AC).

Chapter Four

Naming Policies and Procedures

Introduction

Up to the 1950s, no written authority appears to define ships' naming policy. With the promulgation of NGOs 2.06 and 2.08/5, some structure was given to nomenclature and to policy. But after only a few years these two orders were cancelled and it was not until the revision of CFAO 36-7 in 1988 that the navy established a naming policy. From about 1990, such policy as was written down has tended to be ignored. MARCORD 36-07 (sometimes 37-07) replaced the CFAO early in 1995. In 1999, a new MARCORD 10-2 replaced 36-07, supposedly to reflect changes made by the closure of MarCom HQ in Halifax in 1997. But the staffing at NDHQ was such that all the references to MarCom HQ are still in the new order. (See Appendix U.)

Fishermen's Reserve vessels at Esquimalt, circa 1944. From left to right, VAN ISLE, VALDES, WESTERN MAID, CAPE BEALE and SAN TOMAS.

The records show that since 1910, the actual selection of a name has been made and approved at various levels ranging from the Sovereign and the minister, down to relatively junior staff officers. In many cases, the minutes of meetings indicate that the choosing of a name could be a long and protracted affair with various staff officers arguing for their favourites.

Use of Roman Numerals with a Ship's Name

No written order was located covering the policy of employing the use of roman numerals as a suffix to a ship's name, e.g. AVALON I and AVALON II. A study of names over the years indicated that in all such cases a suffix was only used to distinguish between ships with the same name in commission at the same time, e.g. NADEN I, NADEN II, and NADEN III; and SUDEROY I, SUDEROY II and SUDEROY III.

At no time in official correspondence was a suffix used to denote the second of name or to distinguish between the first and second of name. It follows therefore, that to use the format HURON I and HURON II to distinguish the first and second of name is incorrect. But this style is often seen with modern writers. The first time such a practice came to the author's attention was in the wonderful collection of historic ship photographs in the wardroom of CFB Halifax in the mid 1980s.

Policy: 1910–1939

Although documents on policy for the early period could not be located, a general policy can be inferred from a study of the names. Such a policy seemed to be to retain original names. There were, however, some new names in this period and even some renaming of former RN vessels—for example, all the destroyers from 1928 onward. Up to 1939, the cabinet approved the names of these destroyers.[1]

Policy: Second World War 1939–1945

The policy at the commencement of the war was to continue naming minesweepers after bays and destroyers after rivers. But after the introduction of new types of vessels had started, the policy changed to one of using the names of cities and towns. This change occurred when Cdr E.S. Brand, RN, at a NSHQ staff meeting where there was a discussion on naming policy for the new ships, spoke from experience: "One suggestion, in line with RN practice in both wars, was that they (the corvettes) might be named after Canadian flowers. Remembering the success in selling war bonds during the First World War as a result of the RN twin-screw minesweepers being named for towns, I said… 'Flowers do not knit socks.' This won the day...."[2] This naming policy was later modified to include the use of city and town names "in order of population" although an exception could be made where a smaller municipality had shown a high degree of patriotism.[3]

Names of the smaller centres of population were employed in two different ways: as names for harbour craft such as tugs; and as names for vessels built for the RN. To include as many small towns and villages as possible, the minister (Angus L MacDonald) proposed to the naval staff that the names of counties be used.[4] Although DOD agreed, in late 1941 no new ships were scheduled for launch for about half a year so except where used as an alternative name, this proposal was forgotten.

At one point the city of Charlottetown requested that a ship be named after that city. Such an innocent request eventually sparked a discussion among the naval staff on how best to employ the names of large cities and provincial capitals. The end result was that the names of the four largest cities—Montréal, Toronto, Vancouver and Winnipeg—were reserved for cruisers[5] while the names of the other cities were allocated to corvettes. This policy lasted about one year before the name Vancouver was allocated to a corvette, followed a few months later by the name Winnipeg going to a minesweeper. Montréal and Toronto were assigned to frigates in 1943, and cruisers eventually were given the names of provinces, probably on a suggestion by SO STATS, a staff officer at NSHQ.[6]

In this period, the RCN devised a naming policy unique among the navies of the world. As mentioned earlier, many of the names of our cities, towns and countries are common to Britain, France or the USA. Several of these common names such as London, Selkirk, and Richmond, were already in use in other navies and thus the Canadian communities would not be represented by one of our ships unless the names were duplicated. Further, some names like Salaberry-de-Valleyfield and Portage la Prairie were simply too long for use as a ship's name.

As a result, in the spring of 1942 DOD (Cdr H N Lay) and D Naval Info (Mr. Walter J. Gilhooley) introduced the idea of using an alternative name for such communities to involve the Canadian people more closely with the war effort. Names for HMC Ships are a sensitive topic at the best of times. Many Canadians, some of whom had never seen the ocean or a naval vessel, took a great interest in having the name of their town used for one of HMC Ships and where the actual name could not be employed, an alternative one would do just as well. As illustrated in the next chapter, alternative names generated a great deal of correspondence, so much so that less than two years after the policy began, MND conceded that it should never have been started. The politics surrounding the various alternative names apparently far outweighed any benefits, at least as far as MND was concerned.[7]

When the policy of naming vessels after towns and cities became known, one city wrote to NSHQ and offered to "furnish and equip" a corvette! Naturally, said corvette was to be called after the community, Kirkland Lake, and the "Kirkland Lake and District Salvage Committee" was prepared to part with five hundred dollars. After some discussion at the naval board level, it was confirmed that the $500 was meant for the purchase of comforts for the ship's company. While the naval board was not disposed to making a guarantee that any vessel would ever be named Kirkland Lake, they did decide early in 1942 that future offers of this sort should be accepted in kind but not in cash.[8] The frigate KIRKLAND LAKE commissioned in mid 1944.

This generous offer was the start of vessels being sponsored and eventually adopted by the communities after which they were named. By February 1943, the Director of Special Services was responsible for seeing that the adopting cities were given a list of permissible comforts and/or equipment that could be sent to the ships.[9] This adoption procedure was later expanded to include visits between the ship's company and the population concerned.[10] Such an obvious morale booster even led to vessels like ARROWHEAD, whose name came from the flower, being adopted by the town of Arrowhead, BC. But some vessels were never adopted, e.g. the Tribals.

In early 1943, based on a suggestion by VCNS, the Navy formulated a policy of "perpetuating the names of certain RCN Ships sunk due to enemy action, by using these names for RCN new construction."[11] At this time, the only names put forth were Charlottetown, Lévis, and Ottawa, all of which were subsequently used for new vessels. Later, the names Louisburg and Athabaskan were also reused.

There are several reasons why the names of other vessels lost during this period were not used again. First, there were two unwritten rules, seemingly imported from the RN: the names of vessels lost through neglect were not to be used again; and it was "not advisable to give the name of a ship lost or placed out of commission to a new ship for a considerable period"[12] in order to avoid confusion in pay accounts and other matters.

Second, the policy of employing a name a second time was not started until January 1943 and by that point only ten vessels had been lost: two from "neglect" (FRASER and MARGAREE); two had flower names contrary to the city and town policy then in effect; three were never replaced (BRAS D'OR, OTTER and RAC-

COON); and the other three names were used a second time as noted above. Of the fourteen vessels subsequently lost, only two had their names reused. This was due solely to a lack of vessels to attach the names to, for as early as the fall of 1943 the Navy was cancelling escort building contracts to concentrate on obtaining larger vessels for the postwar Navy, and a surplus of escort type names soon developed.

Postwar Period: 1945–1968

The end of the Second World War left the RCN with far too many vessels for its needs. Further, many of the names of those vessels did not readily indicate the class nor even the fact that the vessel was Canadian.

Shortly after the end of hostilities, therefore, consideration was given to a plan whereby most of the fleet would be renamed. This proposal was based on four factors: each name should, so far as possible, be immediately recognizable as Canadian; adequate cross-Canada geographical representation is desirable; each type of ships [sic] should be immediately distinguishable by its type of name; and some notice should be taken of established tradition.[13]

Basically, the proposal stated that WARRIOR should be renamed Nova Scotia, MAGNIFICENT renamed British Columbia, ONTARIO and the Tribals to remain unchanged, and UGANDA "if [a] decision [is] made to change, 'Quebec' [sic] would appear to be the logical choice."[14]

The "train buster" CRUSADER, probably in November 1953 en route to Korea. She was almost renamed Restigouche in 1945/6. (RCN E-24942. FDN Coll.)

It was also proposed that ALGONQUIN, SIOUX, CRESCENT and CRUSADER be called Assiniboine, Skeena, Saguenay and Restigouche respectively. Further some eighteen frigates were to be called "Vancouver, Victoria, Edmonton, Calgary, Regina, Saskatoon, Winnipeg, Brandon, Toronto, Hamilton, Montréal, Ville de Québec [sic], Charlottetown, Summerside, St. John [sic], Moncton, Halifax, Glace Bay."[15]

Lastly it was proposed that twelve Algerines be given lake names: "Okanagan, Kootenay, Wabamum, Katepia, Waskesiu, Winnipegosis, Nipigon, Nipissing, Temiskaming, Temiscouata, Grand Lake, Bras d'Or."[16]

Had such a renaming of the fleet taken place, the impact on, for example, the St Laurent class—yet to be proposed—would have been profound. And of course the postwar Navy would not have had both minesweepers and frigates named after a mixture of cities, towns, bays and geographic features such as glaciers.[17] The only renaming that actually took place involved the cruiser UGANDA.

The RAF had a policy of naming its air stations after the closest community. The RCAF also followed this policy, as did the RCN with regard to its radio stations. In late 1949, the first radio station to be commissioned was COVERDALE in New Brunswick. Within ten years, commissioned radio stations existed from coast to coast and in the Northwest Territories. A complete list of known radio stations is contained in Appendix K.

When unification occurred in 1968, all naval radio stations became CF stations, losing the word radio from the title. The new radio station south of Halifax was scheduled to commission as Blandford but by the time the station was ready, unification had taken place and Blandford became CFS Mill Cove instead. No reason was given.

In 1949, the government announced its intention to construct a class of A/S destroyer escorts. The first of what was to become a series of four classes were the St Laurents. All vessels in all four classes were named for rivers and most carried the names of vessels in the previous River and/or Town classes. Some new names were added to include Newfoundland and the Territories.

The entry of Newfoundland in 1949 as the tenth province had a direct bearing on naming policy. Not only did this result in the addition of two reserve divisions plus one regular force base,[18] but also it affected the allocation of river names to destroyer escorts. New names like Terra Nova and Yukon came into use at the expense of previous river names such as St Clair and St Francis.

Interestingly enough, with the ST LAURENT due to commission in 1955 and soon to be followed by her six sisters, it was as late as 1954 that the naval board first learned that precedent existed for giving warships the same name as contem-

porary merchant ships or former vessels lost by neglect.[19] Although not specifically mentioned, the names of Fraser, Margaree and Skeena spring to mind as possible candidates for concern under the "neglect" category.

Also in 1954, DNPO laid down a policy on naming auxiliary vessels which
stated that those vessels "employed solely on harbour duties will be referred to by
type designator and number only" while those "which may proceed to sea in the
course of their normal duties will be given names."[20]

By 1955, at least one staff officer complained that there was "no established
method laid down for the naming of ships."[21] The Naval General Order (2.08/5)
governing a naming policy had been cancelled in 1953. Further, there did not seem
to be any record remaining on the origins of such names as D'Iberville, Venture or
Bonaventure. Lastly, he pointed out that "it would appear that (the) naming of
ships has been 'acquired' by DNPO as the branch responsible for allotting type
designators and numbers to ships."[22]

Some name policies were set by one naval board and totally ignored by its successors. A classic example was the names for submarines. After a suggestion put
forth by Cmdre A.G. Boulton in September 1959, the naval board reviewed a list
of Inuit words for undersea creatures. When discussing this idea, the board noted
that a list of words for creatures of the sea had sufficient variety of choice of rea-
sonably pronounceable names to be workable.

Further, since the English names for undersea creatures had been widely used
in naming submarines in other navies, this choice would be an appropriate innovation. One of the names considered was Arlu (Killer Whale).[23] The board then
approved that Inuit "names which are readily pronounceable, be used in the naming of new construction submarines."[24] But just five years later, when considering
the names for three Oberon class submarines, CNS chose to have the names of
these vessels start with the letter O.[25]

Such a state of affairs was to continue all through this period. Without a stated
policy, the names of naval vessels continued to be subject to the whims and fancies of senior officers. Each change in membership in the naval board saw changes
in naming policy and procedure. That the Navy managed to choose good names in
this period can only be ascribed to the general level of historical knowledge of senior officers and to good luck, as in many cases, the naval historian was not even
consulted, or if he was, his advice was ignored.[26]

With the disappearance of the RCN in 1968, any remnants of the machinery that
formulated naval naming policy and procedure were swept aside. Until CFAO 36-7

was expanded and re-issued in 1988, no policy on ships' names existed and successive generations of staff officers were free to exercise their imagination. As late as 1979, RAdm R Yanow as CMDO in NDHQ was moved to write: "I understand that the pennant numbers and naming of ships is within my prerogative—particularly the numbers, and the names, only to be sanctioned by the MND in my rationale."[27]

Policy: 1968–1987

After unification, ship's names were unceremoniously lumped into one NDHQ file, 1000-5, entitled "Naming of Buildings, Units, Locations, Ships and Aircraft." Naming policy became unclear or at the very least, inconsistent. The CORMORANT, purchased in Italy, was renamed, but the RCMP Detachment class vessels acquired in the mid 1970s, such as NICHOLSON and SIDNEY, were not renamed. Similarly, when some of the Ville class tugs were given to reserve divisions, some were renamed: LAWRENCEVILLE became CREE; ADAMSVILLE became BURRARD; but others were not, e.g. PLAINSVILLE and YOUVILLE.

Naval Board meeting 1/87 authorized the formation of a Ships' Names Committee (SNC). The first committee meeting took place late in 1987. One of the first tasks of the newly formed committee was to revise CFAO 36-7 from covering NATO class and type indicators to include policy, attributes of a name, and nomenclature. A new CFAO was issued in the fall of 1988. This was the first written policy on nomenclature since the cancellation of the NGO over thirty years before. Basically, the order laid out the nomenclature for ships then in commission. Further, this order was carefully worded to ensure that commissioned naval shore establishments—the only ones left were the reserve divisions—retained historic rights and privileges accorded to their sisters afloat, such as piping the side.

Policy: 1987–1999

The revision of CFAO 36-7 in 1988 to include a policy on ships' names held much promise. Written in large part by three members of the future Ships' Names Committee, the order stipulated the duties and responsibilities of the SNC, listed the classes and names of the present fleet, laid down a nomenclature, formalized the name proposal and selection procedures, and established criteria for the names of HMC Ships. When actual cases were encountered, unfortunately, in almost every case the CFAO and the SNC suggestions were both largely ignored by the senior naval staff. In some instances, the Ships' Names Committee was not consulted at all.

The patrol frigates were not named by the SNC but because many of their names duplicated those used for CF bases, causing some administrative confusion, the updated CFAO 36-7 stated that the names of HMC Ships were to be easily distinguishable from the names of CF bases and stations. The Ships' Names Committee stuck to this rule but the naval board to whom it made recommendations, did not. Technically, the Ships' Names Committee did not name either the Kingston or Victoria classes.

Policy: Attributes in a Ship's Name

Over the years many staff officers have suggested desirable attributes for names. In the Second World War, due to the pressure of wartime and the large number of vessels requiring names, the Royal Navy formed a Ships'Names Committee[28] which among other things, set down several attributes for a good ship's name. No similar list could be discovered in Canadian sources but a look at our warships'names will show that something similar must have been in the back of the minds of many of the officers who selected or approved a name, at least most of the time.[29]

Basically, a ship's name should:

   a. sound pleasing to the ear (euphonious);
   b. be easy to pronounce in both official languages;
   c. be appropriate to the type and size of ship, and her purpose;
   d. not be liable to ridicule;[30]
   e. in both the written and spoken form, be easily and readily distinguishable from the names of other ships;
   f. where possible, have a historic or traditional past, or connotation;
   g. be relatively short; and
   h. wherever possible, be distinctly Canadian.[31]

When assessing names against the characteristics in the above list, readers should remember that it refers to original names rather than names of taken-over vessels.

Policy: Personal Names

Of the 900 names listed in this book, only eighteen can be said to have been named directly for individuals. (See Appendix O.) As summed up by SO STATS, the general policy was "to avoid any suggestion or reference to persons or family names."[32] In the Second World War, the only deliberate and intentional use of personal names was for BURRARD, CORNWALLIS and LAVALLEE. In the latter case, CNS directed that this name be used even though there was no incorporated city or town by that name.[33] As for POUNDMAKER and VIEL, NSHQ staff certainly knew these were names of men and as they were alternative names, the latter for Montréal North, this may have provided the excuse for going against policy.

After the war, personal names were used for the recruit training establishment in Québec City, D'IBERVILLE; the RCSC establishment at Comox, QUADRA; for the three Saint class tugs; and in the early 1990s for all the new reserve divisions in the province of Québec. Other than these exceptions, the policy of not using personal names was retained.

The names of explorers have been suggested for almost every postwar class and the naval historian even generated a list of such names in 1956.[34] At first it appeared that explorers names would be used for the proposed General Purpose Frigates of the 1960s but the naval board felt that such names were already widely commemorated throughout the nation and that these vessels should be named after towns and cities "as were our present frigates."[35]

With the advent of the Halifax class frigates in the 1980s, the names of explorers were once again considered but rejected on the grounds that DOT named their ships after explorers "and we should not follow suit."[36]

When the MND, M. Marcel Masse, ordered the formation of several new reserve divisions in Québec in the 1980s, NDHQ/DMOPR staff, instead of approaching the Directorate of History for suggested names as had been done in the past, wrote to the cities concerned and requested suggestions. In all cases, the suggested names were those of famous persons, contrary to the policy governing the previous divisions which received names of historical vessels. And so it came to pass that more personal names entered the *Navy List*, regrettably none of which had any Battle Honours and only two, CHAMPLAIN and D'IBERVILLE, could claim predecessors. The current MARCORD now states that "except for NRDs, names of persons or families are not to be used for HMC Ships..."[37]

When MND M. Marcel Masse rejected the first list of harbour names for the MCDVs, he suggested using the names of explorers instead. He did not accept the naval staff explanation that the Navy did not use personal names and so produced his own list of fourteen explorers, many of which proved to be already in service with the navy (e.g. CABOT), the Coast Guard, or DOT. As late as early 1999, the names of explorers were one of the final four groups of name suggestions for the Victoria class submarines.

Interestingly enough, some personal names have come full circle. Many of the towns, cities and counties in Canada were named for famous RN officers—Barrie,

Collingwood, Hallowell, etc. During the Second World War, many of the names of these towns, etc. were used as names for RCN warships and thus the name at least, went back to sea.

Naming Procedures: Introduction

Since the earliest days of the RN, the Sovereign's approval had to be obtained for all warship names and since 1913, the reigning monarch has usually taken a great interest in matters relating to ship's names.[39] This was certainly so in the Second World War and pertained to all the navies of the commonwealth. Since 1945, however, any such interest by the monarch has been reserved for the Royal Navy alone.

Naming Procedures: 1910–1939

Although no documents could be located on naming procedures up to 1939, circumstantial evidence shows that the names for the post-1935 destroyers were approved at cabinet level.[40]

Naming Procedures: 1939–1945

Up to the beginning of the Second World War, the Royal Navy apparently had no formal procedure for generating ships' names but the sudden demand for a large quantity of new names forced the formation of a Ships' Names Committee. Although this committee was disbanded at the end of the war, it formulated the rules for the selection of names, stated the attributes of a good name, and generated various lists from which names could be selected for different classes in the future.

Prior to 1987, no evidence could be discovered of any Canadian equivalent. The closest our Navy ever had to such a committee was the Second World War office of the Staff Officer Statistics (SO STATS) at NSHQ who, from December 1942 to October 1944, worked for the Director of the Operations Division (DOD). (For the organization of NSHQ at this time, see Tucker, *The Naval Service of Canada*, Volume 2.)

Lt(SB) J.E. MacNelly, RCNVR, arrived at NSHQ 1 Dec 1942 to take up the new position of SO STATS. His primary duties were to analyze convoy reports and to extract pertinent information from them, as well as to study each convoy log in an attempt to identify any trends or patterns in the German methods. One part of these duties was to give a verbal report on the naval situation to the joint chiefs of staff each weekday at 11:00 and as a secondary duty, SO STATS was responsible for coordinating ships' names.

At the outset of the war, names for ships apparently required the approval of the naval staff before being sent to CNS and MND. By late 1942, the "Naval Staff delegated authority to VCNS to approve the allocation of names approved by Admiralty to ships of new construction."[41]

Less than a month later, VCNS stated that "names were not a matter that required full discussions of staff" and he recommended that "DOD be authorized to prepare submissions direct to CNS and the minister."[42] A few months later, DOD received the authority to "select and approve names for new construction Local Craft without reference to higher authority."[43]

The procedure outlined above was not destined to be permanent and in mid 1943, SO STATS[44] was ordered to turn over his duties to the Director of Special Services. By that time, most names for Second World War vessels had already been allocated. But CNS did not approve the change and ordered SO STATS to assume full responsibility for the naming of ships. Thus it was SO STATS who suggested the name Athabaskan be revived for one of the last two Tribals under construction in Halifax.[45]

Approval authority for names was always held by his superiors but towards the end of the war, SO STATS had direct access to the minister and his recommendations for names were usually accepted, except where political considerations took precedent.[46]

When the Second World War started, it appears that the prewar procedure of assigning a hull a particular name and then seeking approval was followed for the first batch of names, which were promulgated in the summer of 1940.[47] Of these twelve names, ten were changed within the space of only five months. In this short period, nine of the names had been found to be in service with, designated for, or similar to, the names of other Commonwealth vessels.[48] The nine names were Banff, ex US cutter in RN service; Bathurst, RAN minesweeper; Burlington, RN depot ship; Campbellton, RN destroyer; Churchill, RN destroyer; Dalhousie; Esperanza; Jasper, RN trawler; and Selkirk, RN minesweeper. In an August 1940 message, the Admiralty stated that among others, the names Esperanza and Dalhousie had been allocated to other HM Ships serving or near completion. In fact, Dalhousie was the name of an establishment in India.[49]

The tenth name was Carlton and it was changed because it was not a town but a village with a population of about one hundred. When Carlton's true size was discovered, the vessel's name was changed to that of another larger, Saskatchewan town, Kamsack.[50] It was not a bad start but the next several months were noted for confusion and errors in the naming of HMC Ships.

Names were obtained from various sources. The twelve original medium-sized town names for the early corvettes and minesweepers had been picked by the simple expedient of selecting names that were printed in a particular size of type in an atlas![51] Next, NSHQ solicited names from the Boards of Trade in the provincial capitals as well as Dawson, Yukon.[52] When the number of names produced proved inadequate for the forecast requirement, NSHQ then turned to the census of 1931 and later 1941, creating lists in order of population.

By December 1941 "a comprehensive list showing all the cities…(and towns) with a population of over 3000, and which have not previously been used for naming HMC Ships"[53] had been prepared. Apparently based on the 1931 census, the list was somewhat dated, but it was the start for allocating city and town names to most frigates, corvettes and minesweepers during this period.

For a variety of reasons, the names of every city and town on this and subsequent lists could not be used. For example, the town of Bridgeburg, Ontario, population 3,521 showed up on a later list[54] but when the name came up and the town was contacted by NSHQ, the mayor of Fort Erie replied to say that Bridgeburg had become part of Fort Erie. Later lists were based on the "preliminary 1941 census returns."[55]

Names for rivers and First Nations tribes were usually first produced by the naval historian as were the third set of names suggested for naval divisions. Officers in various headquarters thought up other names.

Later in the war when SO STATS took charge of all names, he was responsible for comparing each suggested name with an up-to-date list of Allied vessels and for appending comments such as "man's name," "similar to USS _____ ," "RN Ship," or "too long." The names then passed to the naval staff where decisions were made and a final list prepared for submission to the naval board and MND.[56]

This final list of name proposals was then sent to the Admiralty in London so that they in turn could submit the names to the King for approval. At a later date, the list was sent via "Bomber Mail" to CCCS in London and even later, to the SCNO London.[57] When the list was finally approved, the names were assigned to the various hulls under construction across the country and published in Canadian Confidential Naval Orders (CCNOs). Any change in the name assigned to a vessel under construction also required the King's approval.

Originally, the Monarch approved the names for all vessels but sometime late in 1942, this procedure was applied only to vessels of corvette size or larger.[58]

Even though a naming procedure came into effect, such a simple act as the assignment of names to vessels being constructed throughout the country did not always proceed smoothly, due in many cases to the influence of politics. In July 1943, for example, authorities at Canadian Vickers Ltd. in Montréal sent a telegram to NSHQ requesting the name for hull CN 353 which was scheduled to be launched in just twelve days' time. NSHQ replied immediately: Stormont. This simple message started a complex chain of events.

Stormont is a county in Ontario and on the suggestion of the minister, the name became an alternative one for the City of Cornwall.[59] When they heard of STOR-MONT, the people in the adjacent county of Glengarry felt that they too should have a warship named for their county.

There is little information in the files but it is known that MND directed that a vessel be named Glengarry.[60] This was easier said than done. In late 1943 and early 1944, drastic cutbacks were occurring in the naval ship construction program and the few remaining vessels were fast approaching their launching dates. The only suitable hull was CN 565. Her assigned name, STONE TOWN, was an alternative one for St Marys in Ontario. The immediate problem was that the name Stone Town had already received the Monarch's approval.

When approached, the Admiralty advised NSHQ that the King would not approve a change of name for STONE TOWN unless a very good reason could be provided. The reason given by NSHQ was simple if not complete: the County of Glengarry should have a ship named after it. This reason completely ignored the feelings of the people in St Marys but on 31 March 1944 approval was received to change the name of CN 565 from STONE TOWN to Glengarry.

Earlier in the month, however, a representative of the shipyard had contacted NSHQ asking if CN 565 could be given a Québec name. He was assured this was not possible but at the same time he was also informed of CN 565's potential change of name to Glengarry. Further, NSHQ requested that CN 565 be launched without any ceremony. Maybe the shipyard representative was miffed that a local name was not used but in any event, "the word" was not passed. Instead, the president of the shipyard invited representatives of St Marys to the launching scheduled for 28 March 1943.

Among others, the mayor from St Marys arrived on that date, delivered a speech, had pictures taken and then they went home to arrange for home town clubs to provide amenities for "their" ship.

Upon learning these facts early in April, MND decided to retain the name Stone Town for CN 565. This decision resulted in yet another message being sent from NDHQ to the Admiralty, via SCNO(L), with a request to retain the original name. SCNO(L) proved to be a reluctant messenger: "After making strong representation to have the name of the ship changed once, I hesitate to reopen the matter with a further request to revert to the original name since this will entail yet another approach to His Majesty."[61] NSHQ replied, quite briefly, that CN 565 had been launched three days prior to the approval for the change of name being received. The King accepted this reason and approved the retention of the name Stone Town. Due to a lack of hulls, the name Glengarry was never used.

Naming Procedures: 1945–1968

Before the Second World War, CNS submitted the names of destroyers to the minister that eventually reached the cabinet, requesting that names be "selected." The pressure of wartime lowered Canadian approval levels from the cabinet to MND and the recommendation level from CNS to the naval board, then to DOD and finally to SO STATS himself.

The large shipbuilding program undertaken in the 1950s saw at least a partial return to the prewar procedure. Early in February 1953, for example, CNS (VAdm E.R. Mainguy) sent seven river names to the minister and requested approval of these names for the Restigouche class. MND forwarded these names to the cabinet who decided that the names Humber and St John should be used in place of Saskatchewan and St Croix. Unknown to the cabinet, ships were already using these names: HMS HUMBER and the tug ST JOHN. CNS therefore suggested a return to the original two names but this was not to be.

In May of that same year, the cabinet defence committee accepted the name St Croix but directed that a river name from Newfoundland should be selected by MND. MND and CNS discussed four possibilities—Gander, Exploits, Humber and Terra Nova. CNS preferred to use the name Hamilton, a small river in

HMCS OJIBWA. (FDN Coll.)

Labrador, because of its previous use as the name of a destroyer. His second choice was Humber followed by Terra Nova. The minister then canvassed various people and discovered that the name Terra Nova would be the most acceptable to people from Newfoundland.[62] The use of the name Saskatchewan was set aside and Terra Nova chosen instead. There were other problems.

When the letter listing the seven Restigouche class names was promulgated in August, the name for DE 256 was listed as SAINT JOHN. It was almost three weeks before a letter arrived from PNO Québec asking if the name of the tug was to be changed. The staff finally corrected the error and DE 256 became ST CROIX.

Some five months later, having learned a lesson from the several months of discussions over the previous destroyer names, CNS changed tactics when it came to the names for small craft and sent the following to the minister:

> The attached copy of Naval Board Minute 394-2 which approved allocation of names to three types of small naval vessels is forwarded for the information of the minister.[63]

By 1960 and with another CNS (VAdm H.S. Rayner), the renaming of the submarine USS BURRFISH was handled quite simply by CNS informing the minister of his intention to rename her GRILSE.[64]

In 1961, the same CNS handled the name of the first supply ship by sending a memo to the minister which stated in part, "after due consideration by the naval board it is intended to name the ship 'PROVIDER'."[65]

In 1963, when the question of names for the O class submarines was raised, VAdm Rayner informed MND that he had decided to name the first boat Ojibwa. The Honourable Paul Hellyer, MND, concurred.[66] A few months later, the second two names were sent to the minister in a similar fashion, ending with the words, "Your concurrence is requested."[67]

In 1965, with the start of what proved to be the complete unification of the Forces, the senior naval officer was required to pass such information through the senior armed forces officer, the Chief of the Defence Staff (CDS), Air Chief Marshall F.R. Miller. When the name of the hydrofoil was put forward, CDS asked MND to concur with the Navy's choice of a name, BRAS D'OR. The same procedure was followed for the names of PROTECTEUR and PRESERVER in May 1966.

The unification of the three services saw the end of the naval board, a collection of senior naval officers who among other things, reviewed and approved ships' names. About 1980, however, an unofficial naval board was reconstituted by RAdm A Fulton, then Commander of Maritime Command. Consisting of various senior naval officers, this group meets from time to time and selects and even invents, names for new-construction vessels. Since this board is unofficial, the minutes of its meetings are generally unavailable. Final approval of names for HMC Ships, however, still resides with the minister.

Naming Procedures: 1968–1987

Very few vessels were constructed during this period and the procedure followed, as closely as can be determined from the scarce documentation located, was that the senior naval staff, usually CMDO in NDHQ, forwarded name proposals to CDS who sent them, unchanged, to the minister.

The one major name requirement occurred when the government announced in 1987 the proposed acquisition of ten to twelve nuclear-powered submarines. The Ships' Names Committee was then only a proposal and to obtain name suggestions, the Maritime Commander issued a general message.[68] Replies flooded in from many units suggesting a variety of names. Among other categories were forts, towns, marine creatures and fish, rivers, stars, lakes, straits, mythical deities, Inuit settlements, historical vessels and animals. Several types of people were also suggested such as fathers of confederation, admirals, Victoria Cross winners, Governors General, and a quite popular suggestion, explorers. The most popular suggestion, however, outnumbering explorers three to one, was for using the names of provinces and territories. In fact, members of the Maritime Commanders staff[69] suggested the submarines be called the Canada class, a suggestion later accepted by the newly formed Ships' Names Committee, forgetting the principle of having the lead ship give her name to the class. Regardless, this class was destined not to go forward.

Naming Procedures: 1988–1999

One minor vessel was named early in this period and Chief of the Defence Staff Gen P.D. Manson sent her name to the minister (Bill McKnight) as follows: "The following name has been selected for consideration: RIVERTON. I concur with this proposal and recommend your approval."[70]

There were three major naming requirements in this period. The first was for the auxiliary minesweeping vessels acquired from civilian service. These two vessels received the names of islands, one on each coast. Instead of employing new names, the use of two historic names from vessels that did yeoman service during the Second World War may have been more appropriate. As it was, a trend for new names seems to have started here.

The second requirement was for the Maritime Coastal Defence Vessels (MCDVs) which eventually became the Kingston class minesweepers. This is a convoluted story that spans seven years and four ministers. The tale includes both political interference and the senior naval staff's disregard of regulations and their apparent concern more for the navy's public image than its heritage.[71] And even worse, this story seems to show the degree to which senior officers have come to politicize their offices since the unification of the forces in 1968.

On request and before knowing the rate of the vessels—minesweepers or patrol craft—the new Ships' Names Committee (SNC) sent three lists of possible names for the MCDVs to the naval board in July 1988. For this meeting, the SNC had forgotten to notify their advisor and thus were without guidance on this and other naming matters. These three lists included animals, forts and guardians such as Sentinel, Lookout and Defender. All suggestions were rejected. At a subsequent meeting of the naval board on 13 Oct 1988, the board directed that this class be named for towns. By February 1989, several groups were championing names. A list from COND contained the names of communities, two of which were already in use and six of which were clearly the names of cities similar to those being assigned to the Halifax class frigates, often incorrectly being referred to at this time as the "city" class.

By March 1990, a meeting of the SNC—with the advisor present—noted both the naval board's rejection (at meeting 2/88) of previous suggested names and its decision to identify this class as towns. After some discussion, the SNC Chairman (Cdr J.A.C. Gauthier) pointed out that the English words "city" and "town" both translated as "ville" in French, making the designated class name difficult to distinguish from the frigates, as well as contravening CFAO 36-7, the regulation then governing the naming of HMC Ships. Earlier, the advisor to the SNC had pointed out that the word "town" had no official status with Statistics Canada and its use varied from province to province. Both Charlottetown, population 15,776, and Rossland, BC (3,377) are cities. Cobourg, Ontario (13,197) is a town and Chilliwack (41,000) is a district municipality. Notwithstanding these points, the SNC then generated a list of twenty "town" names, most previously used for ships, and forwarded these to the naval board for review. For reasons not discovered, staffing of these names was never completed.

In October, the Maritime Commander sent a letter to the Commander Canadian Fleet and the naval reserves asking for name suggestions for the MCDVs.[72] Attached to this letter was a set of guidelines taken from CFAO 36-7. Suggestions were required by late November.

In January, the MCDVs were formally declared to be minesweepers and not patrol craft. The SNC considered all suggestions at its fourth meeting on 15 Jan 1991 and produced a fourth list of names for the MCDVs. In accordance with CFAO 36-7, these consisted of twenty-three harbour names, most of which had been used before for HMC Ships. As a result of using harbour names, neither Saskatchewan, Alberta nor the Yukon was represented. On receipt of these names, the naval board was too busy to deal with this subject at their meeting that May and delegated authority to CMDO (RAdm J. Anderson) to choose the required twelve names. In June 1991, he picked Alberni, Bonavista, Churchill, Dawson, Gaspé, Lunenburg, Malpeque, Oshawa, Penetang, Shediac, Sorel and Tuktoyaktuk. RAdm J. Anderson had altered the SNC list, adding the names Dawson and Tuktoyaktuk.

Later that year, COND (Capt (N) P. Yans) successfully pushed for the inclusion of Red Deer and Melville "in order that all provinces and territories be represented."[73] These two names were added and Penetang and Shediac dropped. Neither Dawson, Red Deer nor Melville are harbours and so the list had no common thread. Further, the SNC had not approved these three names and in all likelihood would never have recommended the fourth name, Tuktoyaktuk, for one of HMC Ships as the name could be open to ridicule, contrary to the requirements of CFAO 36-7.

In September, the SNC advisor put his objections in writing to the naming procedures being followed. He was joined in this protest by the Director of History, Dr. W.A.B. Douglas, himself a former naval officer, to no avail.[74]

Around December 1991, CMDO (Cmdre G. Garnett) apparently sent or took a list of eleven names—apparently no one noticed the name Dawson was missing—to MND, M. Marcel Masse. MND queried the whole rationale for naming naval vessels. When told, he proposed a "better" rationale: explorers; and he produced a list of twelve explorer names. Of these twelve names, seven were already in use as warships, CF stations, reserve divisions or Coast Guard vessels. When apprised of this, MND next suggested using the names of famous Canadians—no one could define who would qualify under this designation—and late in March 1992, after the SNC agreed that such a list could be produced, CMDO (Cmdre G. Garnett) personally tasked the SNC advisor to create the list. Suggestions from the advisor that such a policy could open the navy to pressure from every interest group in the country were discounted.

Shortly thereafter, the naval board formally requested two lists for MND, both of persons. The first list would be of famous Canadians; the second would be a list of city and town names—which were named for persons—acceptable to the Navy. With a weather eye on Nelson and his successors, the advisor delayed producing the first list. For the second, he took his own catalogue of all previous naval vessels and compared the names to those contained in a dictionary of Canadians. Where two names matched, he recorded the name. In an attempt to prevent the naval board from calling the vessels the Town class, the advisor recommended the class name be Frontenac. As was known to the advisor there is no city or town in the country with this name but it is the name of a county in Ontario, and as such was the alternative name for Kingston in the Second World War.

In June 1992, the advisor forwarded to NDHQ/DMOPR 2 the following list of twenty-two personal and town names, all of which had seen previous service and none of which were similar in sound or spelling to vessels then in service: Bayfield*, Beauharnois, Blairmore*, Brant*, Buckingham, Cartier*, Chambly, Frontenac, Galt*, Hallowell, Jonquière, La Salle*, Lauzon, Lévis*, Lindsay*, Melville*, Mulgrave*, Poundmaker, Prescott, Quesnel*, Sherbrooke* and Timmins. All the names except Cartier were entitled to Battle Honours. (*Names later recommended by the CDS.)

Time passed. The downsizing of NDHQ continued and in June 1992, the DMOPR organization disbanded and the responsibility for ships' names was transferred to Maritime Command Headquarters, EA/COS Ops in Halifax. Chairmanship of the names committee went to SSO Fleet Replacement Coordinator (FRC), N39-1.

On 2 Oct 1992, MND announced the construction of the twelve MCDVs. Five days later, Cmdre Garnett made a telephone request to the Directorate of History for name suggestions and the reply came back the same day. Included were names of battles such as Loos and Givenchy, and the names of distinguished former British and Canadian naval officers such as Cook, Brodeur, Hose and Pullen. On 16 October 1992, CDS (Gen de Chastelain) sent a letter to the minister in French with twelve recommended names from the advisor's list of famous Canadians. CDS, however, attributed these names to the Directorate of History. The names he recommended are indicated above. The other ten names were included for consideration. No class name was recommended. In his letter, CDS noted that our naval "customs and traditions ...state that the names chosen should preferably reflect those ships which won battle honours.... As I have already mentioned to you on numerous occasions, I also happen to feel that it is important to maintain the customs and traditions of the navy."[75]

From this list, M. Masse apparently selected twelve names. These became the Frontenac class. Exactly which names were chosen could not be discovered.

NDHQ gave PMO MCDV (Capt (N) R. Buck) permission to refer to the class by that name but not to release the names at this time. Eventually, the class name appeared in print and became known to the city of Kingston for which Frontenac was once an alternative ship's name.

For reasons not clear, the names were never promulgated, there being one delay after another. At one point, days before the names were once to be announced, a serial killer apparently resurfaced in one of the cities and the Public Information Office did not want the navy to be seen naming a ship after a city in which this event was on-going. The announcement was delayed again. Eventually, such delays became the list's death sentence. Ms Kim Campbell then replaced M. Masse as MND.

Over a year later, about December 1993, the naval board was given a brief on these names. Here it was stated that some of the staff felt there were reasons to start the name selection process again. Basically the current list failed to include large communities which could sponsor and promote the vessel and, more to the point, the geographic distribution of the names left a lot to be desired from the view of improving the navy's image with the public. Further, CDS (Adm J. Anderson) would accept another list recommended by Maritime Command. The naval board decided to re-open the list and the SNC was, once again, called upon to produce a list with Frontenac as the class name.

Consequently, in the spring of 1994 the chairman summoned the SNC members to MarCom Headquarters in Halifax. There the latest members were asked to produce two lists of names for the MCDVs: one in accordance with CFAO 36-7 and one of town names, both with Frontenac as the lead ship. Using once again the names of harbours but redefining the term "harbour" to include any body of water large enough to float a marina, the SNC managed to produce a list of fourteen harbour names which were also the names of towns. From a heritage point of view, many of these names had been used before. All provinces and territories were included along with three alternate names. As for the list of pure town names, the SNC had difficulty producing such a list as it contravened the CFAO, but they managed. The meeting ended, the names on both lists being forwarded to the naval board.

The names on the first list were: Battleford, Churchill, Glace Bay, Iqualuit, Malpeque, Nanaimo, Oshawa, Red Deer, Rimouski, Shediac, Whitehorse, and Wabana, plus the three alternates. Although some members of the SNC wanted the name Frontenac, it was not included in either listing.

Unknown to the SNC, the naval board arbitrarily changed this list. One year later on 1 May 1995, the minister (now David Collenette) held a conference call

The second GLACE BAY about 1998.

on the telephone with the twelve mayors of the communities whose names had been chosen for the MCDVs.[76] This occurred only weeks before the lead ship was scheduled for launch. As promulgated by the public information office, the twelve ships were BRANDON, EDMONTON, GLACE BAY, GOOSE BAY, KINGSTON, MONCTON, NANAIMO, SASKATOON, SHAWINIGAN, SUM-MERSIDE, WHITEHORSE, and YELLOWKNIFE.

These names are a mixture of town and city names with no common thread, contrary to the very basis of nomenclature. Of the fifteen names recommended by the SNC, only three remained. Of the other nine, five names were new to the Navy, without lineage or Battle Honours and chosen within their respective provinces apparently on the basis of population or other considerations, the sole Québec name, for example, being in the riding of the prime minister. Five ships were even to share their names with existing CF bases and stations, again contrary to CFAO 36-7.

When the SNC advisor pointed out in writing to the chairman that these names went against several aspects of the policy laid down in the CFAO and further, an unofficial naval board appeared to lack the authority to counter a CFAO, Maritime Command subsequently had the CFAO cancelled and later in 1995, this CFAO was replaced word for word with MARCORD 36-07, a lower level regulation under the direct control of the Commander of Maritime Command.

The justification for such a naming policy for the MCDVs is summed up here: "The enormously positive response on the part of the Canadian public indicates that the best interests of the Navy have been served by the adoption of municipal names for the HALIFAX [sic] class. In view of the political and budgetary realities of our times, it is very unlikely that this situation will be any different when the names of other classes of ships are chosen in the future. The eventual selection of city and town names for the MCDVs certainly supports this conclusion."[77] This letter produced no proof in support of these assertions.

If the city and town names had a common source, e.g. were taken from towns of similar size, and all the names selected had seen previous use as proposed by the SNC on several occasions, such logic would be justified. New names are required to honour Newfoundland and the territories but employing five new names out of twelve is excessive.

The third requirement for names in this period were for submarines, originally termed the 876, and later the Victoria class.[78] These four boats were relatively new vessels, surplus to requirements in the Royal Navy and formerly the only four in their U class. The government showed interest in acquiring these submarines as early as 1995 but little action was taken on names until September 1997. Then a proposal was made to use the names of provinces; former vessels, e.g. Rainbow; marine mammals, e.g. Orca; or bodies of water whose names were the same as those of former vessels, e.g. Nootka. Over the next few months suggestions included explorers, battles, native leaders, water sheds, sea life, port cities, and cities whose names started with Ch, e.g. Chilliwack, Chicoutimi, Churchill, and Chatham.

In NDHQ on 26 May 98, Cdr D. Harper wrote a memo for his boss DMPPD, Capt(N) D. Murphy—who had taken over the chair of the aptly titled Submarine Naming Committee—in which he incorrectly outlined the process for selecting a ship's name. Unaware of the provisions of the relevant MARCORD, he stated that the process "is a rather simple one but may be time consuming if a badge…does not already exist…There is no requirement to select a name from among those used previously…." And finally, "there are many instances in our naval history of a warship being named to honour a …community." Instead of tying these facts together to suggest using previous ship names, he paved the way for the use of new names for this class by suggesting four possible class names: port cities; community names related to arctic islands; regional names, e.g. Acadia; or a fort class. At no time was the subject of Battle Honours raised.

Between then and the late summer, other interested parties wrote in. Memos and e-mails were sent back and forth. By mid August, proposed city names included Victoria, Iqaluit, Sault Ste Marie & Corner Brook. In September, the Naval Officers' Association of Windsor wrote a letter suggesting the use of city and town names. The writer correctly noted that BORDER CITIES had once been named for their city but instead of asking that her name be reused he pushed for Windsor, a name not hitherto considered for this class.

Although some names starting with the letter U were suggested, by November 1998 the focus was clearly on the names of cities and towns. Just before Christmas, CMS wrote a memo to CDS recommending the names Resolute, Victoria, Windsor and Corner Brook. Included were other city names such as Sault Ste Marie, Cornwall and Hamilton, plus three optional groups: marine mammals, arctic islands and explorers—contrary to the provisions of the MARCORD. The response to this proposal apparently was not favourable for on 5 Feb 99 CMS sent an almost identical memo to CDS. These four city names—Chicoutimi, Corner Brook, Victoria and Windsor—were now listed with no options. Still included were the three other groups of names.

On 30 March 1999, the Federal MP, David Anderson, announced the four names in his riding, Victoria. Later, MND (Art Eggleton) was quoted in a DND Public Affairs press release: "We decided to continue a Canadian naval tradition by naming the submarines after Canadian communities." From DND's perspective, these submarines received the names of port cities and towns—to which the boats could actually sail—representing various regions of the country. Technically, however, all four communities are cities and these are the first submarines so named.

Regretfully, with so many wonderful and historical ship names of towns and cities to choose from, the four names of the Victoria class are a disparate collection surpassing even the Kingston class for diversity. Only Chicoutimi has any lineage. The 800 series pennant numbers allocated to this class were to conform to a new policy to have all vessels possess three-digit numbers and the first available series, 600, could lead to confusion with the USN's Los Angeles (688) class of submarines. A nod to tradition started the series at 876 where the last two-digit number for earlier submarines, 75, ended.

Significantly, no meeting of the Ships' Names Committee was held to discuss, vet and recommend these names. Despite provision for such a committee in MARCORD 36-07, the committee now appears to exist on paper only. Since the SNC and its advisor were redundant, and in protest over both the names selected and the procedures followed, the advisor resigned in June 1999.

From 1988 to 1999, eighteen names were chosen for new vessels. Eleven (60%) of these names had seen no previous service. The selection of names for the Anticosti, Kingston and Victoria classes shows a disregard for the service and sacrifice of previous ships' companies in a quest for an unproven degree of public support by a limited and short-lived group of people such as mayors, reeves and other local politicians. In this period, it is certainly ironic to note an army officer,

General de Chastelain, arguing for the retention of naval customs and traditions such as Battle Honours while the senior naval staff appear to trade traditions for a limited degree of public support.

Ships' Names Committee Procedure 1987–1995

The procedure outlined here uses the Kingston class as an example of how the naming system was designed to work. The first step in the naming procedure was for a section of NDHQ/DMOPR to assign the proposed vessel a rate, e.g. minesweeper, the rate for the Maritime Coastal Defence Vessels (MCDVs). Another section of DMOPR told the committee the number of vessels to be acquired. From that point on, the SNC could determine after what features the vessels could be named. For instance, by the nomenclature in CFAO 36-7, minesweepers were to be named after coastal geographic formations such as bays, estuaries, harbours, etc.

A general message requested input from units and interested personnel. Suggested names rolled in but in most cases the persons submitting them had failed to read CFAO 36-7. In the case of the MCDVs, since the names of bays were already in use, another coastal formation was required, one that was large enough to produce a suitable number of potential names. The only category that fit was harbours.

Remembering that a given name can represent many items, all previously used harbour names were checked for possible consideration. The list was then checked against the names of present ships and reserve divisions, CF Bases, and other Canadian vessels, to avoid names that were similar or identical in either spelling or sound; e.g. Halifax is a harbour and so is Esquimalt. Both are excellent names and unfortunately, they were already in use. Proposed names were then divided up geographically. Depending on the number of names required, this could be done by province and territory, or by region. To each proposed name was added its historical connotation, e.g. previous ships, badge availability, Battle Honours, etc.

In the case of Newfoundland and the territories, where there is a scarcity of previously used warship names, consideration was given to employing a previously used name but ascribing it to a new location. For example, there is a community in Newfoundland named Valleyfield. The Second World War frigate of that name was called after Salaberry-de-Valleyfield in Québec but once a name is used, it can be allocated to any other feature or community without problem, as long as the spelling is not changed. Where this was not possible, new names would be employed. Harbour Grace in Newfoundland, for example, was once a candidate for the lead ship name for the Kingston class minesweepers.

A list of possible names was then compiled. If more than one name is available by province or region, the names are put in order of recommendation. All other points being equal, first of place was usually given to the name which had the most Battle Honours. How the naval board made its decisions is not known but reading between the lines, one assumes that public relations had a major impact, to the detriment of naval traditions.

In Retrospect

The purpose of a ships' names committee is to maintain the guidelines for the selection of ship names, produce lists of cleared and acceptable names for the senior naval staff to select from, and maintain files for the guidance of those who are next astern. While this latter activity was done up to 1995, files are only of use to those that read them and learn from the errors and successes of their predecessors. There may be other problems to overcome: in the move of Maritime Command from Halifax to Ottawa circa 1997, all the SNC files were lost.

The naming policy in effect in the late 1980s and 1990s has led to several anomalies, all of which directly contravene the very regulation that was designed to prevent such problems: in the fleet there were two minesweepers named for islands, a category allocated to aircraft carriers; two different classes of Glen tugs; a frigate named for a provincial capital, Regina; a minesweeper named for a larger city and provincial capital, Edmonton; and a submarine also named for a provincial capital, Victoria; several ships that carry the same name as CF bases and stations, e.g. KINGSTON, GOOSE BAY, MONTREAL, and YELLOWKNIFE; and several recent ships with new names like JOLLIET, WINDSOR, WHITEHORSE and KINGSTON which can claim no lineage or Battle Honours. Such a policy does not reflect well on those who implement it.

Notes to Chapter Four

1. NAC RG 24 3988, NSC 1957-1-5, Memo CNS to DMNS, 19 Jul 1940.
2. See *Salty Dips*, Vol 3, p 81. No date but probable spring/summer 1940.
3. See Naval Staff Minutes 136-3, 3 Dec 1942.
4. NAC RG 3988, NSC 1057-1-5, Vol 2. Memo, MND to DOD, 6 Nov 1941.
5. NAC RD 24, 3988, NSC 1057-1-5, VOL 1. Memo, DOD to CNS, 27 Mar 1941.
6. Interview, SO STATS, 27 May 1985.
7. See Memo SO STATS (unsigned) to MND's Sec't, 12 Apr 1944. DHH, *Naming of Ships* Vol 5.
8. Naval Board Minutes 1-9, 12 Feb 1942.
9. Naval Order 2595, 27 Feb 1943.
10. Ibid. See Naval Orders 3292, 14 Dec 1943, and 3563, 15 Apr 1944.
11. NAC RD 24 3988, NS 1057-1-5. Minute sheet, D Sec Staff to DG and CNP, 6 Jan 1943; see also Naval Staff Minutes 144-3, 9 Jan 1943.
12. NAC RG 24 3988, NS 1057-1-5, Vol 2. Letter, A/D/MNS to city clerk, Lévis, Québec, 27 Nov 1941.

13. Memo, DN Inf to A/CNS, 1886-147/1, 7 Dec 1945.
14. Ibid.
15. Ibid.
16. Ibid.
17. e.g. WINNIPEG, DIGBY, FORTUNE, and LLEWELLYN.
18. CABOT, CARIBOU and AVALON.
19. Memo, N Hist to N Sec't, 12 Feb 1954. DHH 8000-5, Vol 1.
20. NAC RG 83-84/167 Navy 3539, NSC 8000-5, Vol 3. Memo DNPO to VCNS, 25 Jun 1954.
21. Memo, Sec't Ships Badges Committee to N Sec't, ND 1460-1, 22 Feb 1955.
22. Ibid.
23. Ibid. In DHH, 8000-5, Vol 2, is a two-page paper with no title, file number or date. It is a summation of the proposal for using Inuit names. Attached are various lists. A note at the bottom of the first page states: "Ted: Information as promised. Eskimo names will be used for all submarines, not only new construction. Ed." It is believed these persons are Ted Russell, N Hist, and Cdr Ed Gigg.
24. Naval Board Minutes 608-1, 4 Nov 1959; and Names for New Construction Vessels, NS 8000-5, 4 Nov 1959.
25. NAC RG 83-83/167 Navy 3539, NSC 8000-5, Vol 3. Memo, CNS to MND, 21 Nov 1963. In this list of Inuit words (to be found in DHH 8000-5, Vol 2), there were no words that started with the letter O.
26. Interview, D. Kealy, D Hist, 4 May 1984.
27. Minute, CMDO to DGMDO and DMOPR, 6 Dec 1979. No file number.
28. Manning & Walker, *British Warship Names*, p 12-13 and Chap 4.
29. See Memo, DMOPR to CMDO, 1000-5, 13 Nov 1979; and Memo, N Hist to V/CNS, NSC 8000-5, Vol 3, 8 Apr 1959.
30. Compare the poem "Weepers Jeepers! Lookit the Names They Give Our Sweepers," *The Crowsnest*, Mar 1958, p 8, with the story of HMS WESTON-SUPER-MARE in Manning & Walker, *British Warship Names*, p 18.
31. After Manning & Walker, op cit, p 18; and Sayer, "The Naming of H.M. Ships," p 200. This list was originally written in 1983 and the listing in CFAO 36-7 (now MARCORD 10-2) was based on it.
32. Letter, NSHQ to Town of Montréal West, NS 1057-1-5 F.D. 391, 23 Jul 1943.
33. See Minute Sheet 117-134 General, 10 Feb 1943, and Memo, DOD to CNS and MNS, NSC 1057-1-5, Vol 3, 11 Feb 1943.
34. Memo, N Hist to Cdr Johnston, NSC 8000-5, Vol 3.
35. Naval Board Minutes 608-3, 4 Nov 1959.
36. Memo, DMOPR to CMDO, 1000-5, 13 Nov 1979.
37. MARCORD 10-2, Annex B, para 5, 16 Nov 1999.
38. Letter, E.C. Russell(?) to RAdm H.F. Pullen, 12 Jan 1961. No file number, unsigned. DHH.
39. Sayer, "The Naming of H.M. Ships," p 198. Since 1945, the highest approving authority for the names of HMC Ships has been the cabinet.
40. NAC RG 24 3988, NSC 1057-1-5, Vol 1. Memo, CNS to DMND, 19 Jul 1940.
41. Naval Staff Minutes 133-3, 12 Nov 1942.
42. Naval Staff Minutes 136-3, 3 Dec 1942.
43. Naval Staff Minutes 162-4, 18 Mar 1943.
44. Memo, SO STATS to DSS, NS 1057-1-5, 8 Jun 1943; and memo, ACNS to CNP, NSC 1057-1-5, 30 Jun 1943.
45. See Naval Staff Minutes 244-5, 20 Jun 1944.
46. Interview with Mr. J. MacNelly (former SO STATS), 27 May 1985.
47. See Naval Order 962, 27 Jul 1940.
48. See Naval Order 1080, 2 Nov 1940. See NAC RG 24 3988, NS 1057-1-5, Vol 1; message, Admiralty to NSHQ 602, 2037/25, 25 Aug 1940.
49. The last list of names approved by the naval staff contained ten alternative names. See Naval Staff Minutes 126-3, 13 Oct 1942.
50. NAC RG 24 3988, NSC 1057-1-5. Memo, DOD to CNS, 23 Apr 1941.
51. Ibid.
52. Ibid.

The first GATINEAU during the Second World War. She appears to have a skull & crossbones on her after funnel. (RCN Photo. FDN Coll.)

53. Memo, DOD to DCNS and MND, NS 114-1-56, 5 Dec 1941. See also Naval Council Minutes 41-7, 8 Dec 1941. NAC RG 24 4044, NSS 1078-3-4.
54. "Names of Canadian Cities and Towns of over 2,800 Populations Not Allocated to RCN Ships." DHH, Ships' Names File, undated but circa late 1944.
55. "List of Names of Cities and Towns (over 3000 population) of Dominion which are not yet used for Naming HMC Ships." This list was based on preliminary figures of the 1941 census. Ops Div, NSHQ, 19 Aug 1942.
56. See Memo, SO STATS to DSS, NS 1057-1-5, 8 Jun 1943. See also Naval Order 2595, 27 Feb 1943, and Minutes of meeting held in office of DOD, 11:30, 31 Dec 1942, 450-11-1 FD 12, 31 Dec 1942.
57. Message, High Commissioner London to NDHQ, 1030B/24 24 Jun 1942, and 1030/8, 8 Aug 1942.
58. Memo, SO STATS to DSS, NS 1057-1-5, 8 Jun 1943.
59. NAC RG 24 3988, NSC 1057-1-5, Vol 2. Memo, MND to DOD, 6 Nov 1941.
60. Information from documents in DHH file, Naming HMC Ships, Vol 5.
61. Message, SCNO(L) to NSHQ, 171810B, 18 Apr 1944.
62. NAC RG 83-83/167 Navy 3539, NSC 8000-5, Vol 3. The information was taken from various correspondence in this file.
63. Ibid. Memo, N Sec't to MND, 21 Dec 1953. The vessels were Fairmiles, Bird class and BLUETHROAT.
64. Ibid. Memo, CNS to MND, 8 Aug 1960.
65. Ibid. Memo, CNS to MND, 21 Feb 1961.
66. Ibid. Memo, CNS to MND, 20 Dec 1963.
67. Ibid. Memo, CNS to MND, 17 Apr 1964.
68. MARGEN 0075/88 COS 067 161700Z Jun 88.
69. Message MARC DCOS P&T 2043 2320000Z Jun 88.
70. Memo, CDS to MND, 12 Apr 1989.
71. Information taken from the Minutes of the SNC; the author's own notes; the 1000-5 files in TRUMP Detachment Toronto and NDHQ/DMTH; and the 1153-110/S132 file from NDHQ/DMOPR.
72. Letter, MARC: 11900-NRMP (COS) 24 Oct 1990.
73. Letter, COND to MarCom/COS Pers, 11900-1 (COND), 15 Jul 1991.
74. Memo, D Hist to DMOPR, 1150-110/S132, 10 Oct 1991.
75. Letter, CDS to MND, no file number, 16 Oct 1992. Translated by the author.
76. Email. Capt(N) R Westwood to various addressees.
77. Letter, MarCom HQ/FRC to SNC Advisor & others, MARC 3250-1 (N39 FRC), 22 June 1995.
78. Information on this class was obtained from 320 pages from the NDHQ 1000-1 file obtained in Nov 1999 under the Access to Information Act.

Chapter Five

Introduction

The sources from which HMC Ships have derived their names are many and varied. The first attempt at nomenclature did not appear until the 1950s and lasted only a few years. With no nomenclature to guide them, senior naval officers were free to exercise their imagination and fancies. After 1988, even with a nomenclature, little thought was given to lineage and more often than not new names were generated at the expense of the older, honourable names, ones with Battle Honours and lineage. And as usual, politics often played a part.

In general, the names of HMC Ships form a diverse collection which is easiest to look at when divided into periods—Early Days, Second World War, Postwar—and within each period, by rate and by class.

From left to right, HMC Ships U889, U190, JOLIETTE, THETFORD MINES, and ST CATHARINES at Halifax, 23 Sep 1945. (KM Coll.)

Early Days: 1910–1939

For the first twenty-nine years, the source of ships' names can be divided into three categories:

a. former RN vessels loaned, turned over to, or purchased by the RCN and which retained their original names, e.g. AURORA;

b. former CGS or civilian vessels taken over by the RCN and which retained their original names, e.g. NADEN; and

c. original names (allocated to new or acquired vessels), e.g. CHAMPLAIN.

Of the vessels acquired from the RN, most retained their original names, the exceptions being the destroyers acquired after 1927. Incidentally, when it came time in 1928 to rename HMS TOREADOR, the RCN wished to use the name Vancouver for her. The RN then kindly changed the name of their other destroyer, HMS VANCOUVER, to HMS VIMY, to permit this to happen. Readers who know their military history will agree that the choice of Vimy could only have been intended as a compliment to Canada.

There is one well known name from this period that has been used only once: Aurora, and this name almost failed to become part of the RCN at all. At the end of the war, the Admiralty decided to offer the ten-year-old cruiser HMS GLAS-GOW plus the four-year-old destroyers, HM Ships PATRIOT and PATRICIAN, to the RCN. Although the minister had already accepted this gift, Captain Walter Hose—about to become director of the naval service—did not want HMS GLAS-GOW because she was a coal burner. Captain Hose travelled to the Admiralty but

The first GRILSE during the First World War. (KM Coll.)

found their Lordships had no intention of giving a modern oil burning cruiser to the RCN. Hose then drafted a letter in which he stated Canada's willingness to assist the RN but regretted that our repair and supply establishments would not be too useful to oil burning RN vessels as such facilities would be fitted out to support only coal burning vessels. The Admiralty got the point and agreed to part with a modern oil burning cruiser, HMS AURORA.[1]

Many of the early RCN vessels were acquired from other government departments and simply retained their names. Some examples are CANADA, FLORENCE, LADY EVELYN, NEWINGTON, and RESTLESS.

In the category of original names the honour of having the first original name apparently belongs to DIANA, ex *Advocate*. She was acquired in 1911 and seems to have been named after the daughter of the first CNS, Admiral Kingsmill. The next two original names were TUNA, ex *Tarantula*, and GRILSE, ex *Winchester*. Lt J.K.L. Ross, RNCVR, with his own money purchased these two yachts, and it was he who apparently gave them their names. TUNA commissioned 5 Dec 1914 and GRILSE followed a few months later.

These vessels were followed by the Battle class trawlers[2] of 1918, all of whom received names of First World War land battles in which components of the Canadian Army took part. Many of these vessels also served in the Second World War but five of them exchanged their names for numbers in 1942: ST ELOI, LOOS, ARRAS, ARLEUX and FESTUBERT became Gate Vessels 12, 14, 15, 16 and 27 respectively.[3] YPRES became Gate Vessel 1 in 1938 while VIMY went to the Department of Marine and Fisheries, becoming Lightship No. 5.

But three other names almost beat out these contenders for first place in the original name category. In 1912, two years after its formation, debate still raged as to the size and shape of the Navy. In fact, in September 1912 our prime minister was negotiating with the British government over whether or not Canada would contribute "$35M for the construction of three modern battleships to form part of the Royal Navy."[43] The names slated for these RN vessels were Acadia, Ontario and Québec and it was intended that the vessels eventually would become part of the RCN had not the *Naval Aid Bill*—which would have provided the necessary funds and authority—been defeated in the senate on 29 May 1913.

Such speculation on names can be endless. For example, prior to the formation of the naval service, the government considered various plans for obtaining vessels for the navy and by coincidence, somewhere in each plan was the requirement for some RN River class destroyers. Since it was proposed to build these vessels in Canadian shipyards, they would probably have received the names of rivers, one full generation ahead of the first SKEENA and her sisters. (See Tucker, *The Naval Service of Canada*, Vol 1.)

The next instance of original names occurs with the renaming of HM Ships TORBAY and TOREADOR as CHAMPLAIN and VANCOUVER. SKEENA and SAGUENAY plus other "Rivers" followed and all were renamed RN destroyers of various classes. The term River class was only a convenient label for vessels of closely related design and apparently, as noted in Chapter 3, it was not authorized until 1943. Prior to this, SKEENA and her sister were called either A, Acasta, or Skeena Class destroyers.

In 1936, when it came time to replace CHAMPLAIN and VANCOUVER with new destroyers, some eighteen names were considered. These names included those of cities, men and rivers but in the latter case, MNS, I.A. Mackenzie, deliberately excluded the name Mackenzie for reasons that were personal to him. The minister himself selected the river names Fraser and St Laurent. CNS then allocated the first name to HMS CYGNET and the second to HMS CRESCENT. Something, however, made him change his mind and he reversed the allocation.[5]

For the renaming of HMS KEMPENFELT in 1939, CNS suggested the names of thirteen rivers, noting that the naval staff favoured the name Margaree. The minister strongly recommended to the cabinet the name Assiniboine as being euphonious as well as giving recognition to the prairie provinces because so far they had been passed over when ships were named. The cabinet approved Assiniboine, not Margaree.[6]

Another example of original names in this period is found in the four Bassett class minesweepers. The class designation originated with the RN but all four vessels were named for Canadian bays or other coastal formations. The last example of an original name in this era was the second VENTURE, a schooner built at Meteghan, NS. CNS chose the name and in spite of some opposition by MND who wanted a river or historical/geographical Nova Scotia name, Venture was approved.

It was during the First World War that the first shore establishments made their appearance as named entities. In every case, their names were taken from the vessel that was assigned to them as their depot ship. For examples, see the entries for LANSDOWNE and GUELPH. It was in this manner that the names NADEN and STADACONA made their way to their respective establishments. STADACONA, however, had a more circuitous introduction than did her sister.

The name Stadacona first appeared in the *Navy List* with the commissioning of the former American yacht *Columbia* as a patrol vessel on 13 Aug 1915. A few years later, when the OIC of naval patrols was authorized to establish a depot, he took STADACONA as his depot ship. As explained in Chapter 1, in these days the depot ship was a vessel, often with a shore establishment attached, that held and controlled a seaman's documents. In this case, STADACONA became the depot ship to the naval patrols on 21 Mar 1918. NIOBE continued to be the depot ship for all other personnel in the Halifax area.

On 1 May 1918, the trawler CD 20 was renamed GUELPH and took over the depot ship duties. About this time the vessel STADACONA sailed to the west coast in company with GIVENCHY and ARMENTIERES.

The reason for the selection of the name Guelph for CD 20 has not been established but she remained the naval patrols depot ship until she in turn paid off 31 Jan 1919. Shortly thereafter, some disciplinary problem arose in Halifax that called for a court martial. By the regulations then in effect, a court martial could only be held if two vessels, "not being tenders," were in commission at one place at the same time. This ensured that the officers on the court martial did not come from the ship concerned.[8] At this time, only one vessel was in commission: NIOBE.

Consequently, NSHQ directed SNO Halifax to select and commission a second vessel and to do so urgently. The next day, 8 Mar 1919, GUELPH (ex CD 20) was recommissioned "for disciplinary purposes only," as her books were kept in NIOBE.[9] GUELPH was again paid off 31 May 1920. On that date, however, the trawler CD 23 was also paid off and immediately recommissioned as GUELPH (2nd). She took over duties as the depot ship.

Late in September 1922, GUELPH (2nd) was paid off and her civilian crew informed that their services would no longer be required.[10] What occurred next is not entirely clear. The vessel had been put up for sale as early as May of that year. After several false starts, GUELPH (2nd) was eventually sold around September 1923 but she was not actually moved away from the Dockyard until 21 Nov 1923. In the meantime and contrary to naval regulations, her shore based depot had apparently continued to function. While there is no direct evidence of this, there are two pieces of circumstantial evidence.

First, on 2 May 1923, the Accounts Officer of GUELPH wrote to the manager of the local Bank of Montréal to inform him that the name of the bank account would be changing from GUELPH to STADACONA (3rd) effective 1 Jul 1923.[11]

Second, in a message dated 12 Mar 1923, Commander Jarrain, SNO Halifax, pointed out to the naval secretary that the trawler GUELPH "having been disposed of there is now no ship (vessel) with this name." This would not have been a concern if the shore establishment had gone. In the same letter Cdr Jarrain stated that he also felt that the name of the depot should be changed from Guelph, a name of German origins, to a "more suitable British name."[12]

The next day, obviously after receipt of the letter from SNO Halifax, the Director of the Naval Service, Captain Hose, wrote a memo to the minister suggesting that both the names of the present naval depots, GUELPH and NADEN, "be changed for others having a greater historical interest to Canada." He suggested the names Stadacona and Nootka, and he quoted at length from a book of reference showing that the name Nootka was known around the world.[13]

The minister agreed to change the name of GUELPH to Stadacona but he did not like the name Nootka. To the minister, Naden seemed a better name and so it stayed. But on Dominion Day as it was then called, 1 July 1923, motor boat HC 131 was commissioned as STADACONA and took over from AURORA the duties of the depot ship in Halifax. It was "a near run thing" for she in turn would pass her name to the shore establishment. But for Cdr Jarrain's suggestion, the name Stadacona may never have appeared again. As it was, generations of seamen were to pass through and know "Stad" in the years to come.

The reason for the loss of Guelph as a name at this time was probably due to a residue of the anti-German phobia that reached its height during the latter part of the First World War. In June 1917, the Royal Family was forced to change its name to Windsor. The former First Sea Lord, Admiral Battenberg, was then asked by his cousin the King to Anglicize his family name to something like Battenhill or Mountbatten. The Admiral chose the latter. Consequently, he lost the title Prince Louis of Battenberg but as partial compensation, the King made him Marquis of Milford Haven, a title later inherited by his son Louis. (See Lambton, *The Mountbattens*, p 222-3.)

Names: Second World War 1939–1945

Similar to the previous period, names for the vessels in this period can be classified as:

a. former RN vessels which retained their original names, e.g. ANNAN;
b. former government or civilian vessels, which retained their original names, e.g. ADVANCE, BC LADY, PRINCE HENRY, and SANS PEUR;
c. original (and alternative names) for new construction or vessels taken over from other navies, e.g. EDMUNDSTON, and STETTLER; and
d. shore establishments, e.g. CORNWALLIS, NONSUCH and ST HYACINTHE.

Second World War: RN Names

Throughout the Second World War, the RCN took over and commissioned various RN ships. Some of these changed their names:
- the cruiser HMS MINOTAUR became ONTARIO;
- the Fleet destroyers such as HM Ships EXPRESS and VIXEN became GATINEAU and SIOUX; and
- the Castle class corvettes such as HMS NORHAM CASTLE became HUMBERSTONE.

Others did not change their names:
- the three Loch class frigates such as LOCH ALVIE;
- the ten original flower-named Flower class corvettes such as SNOWBERRY;
- the seven River class frigates such as MONNOW;
- three of the Town class destroyers, ANNAPOLIS, HAMILTON and BUXTON;
- the two C class destroyers, CRESCENT and CRUSADER;
- the two aircraft carriers, WARRIOR and MAGNIFICENT; and
- the cruiser UGANDA.

The available documentation does not provide reasons as to why this is so. It is known, though, that all the hulls of the Flower class corvettes with flower names (e.g. MAYFLOWER) belonged to the RN but were on "permanent loan" to the RCN. This may have been a factor in not changing their name. But one such case is well documented, that of the name Uganda.

During the Second World War, the British Government accepted donations from various countries or groups toward the construction of certain vessels. In turn, many of these vessels were given names in recognition of the donors. For example, when HMS GURKHA (2nd) was sunk in 1940, each man in the Gurkha regiments donated a day's pay toward another vessel. Rather than construct a new Tribal class destroyer, HMS LARNE was renamed.[14]

When the time came to turn over two cruisers to the RCN, the two available were HM Ships MINOTAUR and UGANDA.[15] There was no problem in changing the name Minotaur to Ontario but in the case of Uganda, the name Québec was not available. As it turned out, this was fortunate for the British. As the Admiralty informed the CNS, "representations have been received from the Colonial Office that the Government and people of Uganda have taken a great interest in the ship.... They have also subscribed substantial sums for her equipment."[16] Their Lordships went on to say that a difficult position would be created for the British if the name

UGANDA was to be changed. They even quoted the precedent of HMS GAMBIA when she became HMNZS GAMBIA.[17]

When the Admiralty's request was put before him, the CNS recommended that the name Uganda be retained. "Other things being equal sailors do not like changing a ship's name."[18] He then went on to say that this decision would also let NSHQ out of the difficult position of having to choose the name of a second province, other than Ontario and Québec.

With respect to the dates of commissioning of former RN vessels, each group had separate and often distinct terms of agreement concluded with the Admiralty. Such arrangements affected all vessels "purchased, commissioned, manned or on loan for special purposes."[19] Besides monetary considerations, each agreement was an involved procedure dealing with such items as which Navy was liable and for what, from what date the liability commenced, the title to the vessel, the terms of acquisition, and so forth. Such arrangements are best left to lawyers, accountants and supply officers.

With respect to the flower-named Flower class corvettes, all ten originally commissioned as RN vessels but with Canadian crews. This occurred because in 1940/41 the RN had experienced difficulty in transporting personnel to Canada to man these vessels. Consequently, the RCN provided crews for these vessels but they were all initially commissioned as HM Ships, not HMC Ships.[20] "Subsequently it was found that this arrangement was leading to unnecessary administrative confusion. Accordingly arrangements were made for the transfer of these vessels on loan to the RCN for the duration of the war, effective 15 May 1941. Under these arrangements the vessels became HMC Ships,"[21] at least in the eyes of the RCN. Some five weeks earlier NSHQ, in a reply to an Admiralty message, had stated that the RCN would be pleased to continue manning the "flowers" on the condition that "they shall be referred to as HMC Ships."[22]

When looking through various British reference books of this period, readers will notice that many vessels thought to be Canadian in the Second World War are referred to as HM Ships. With respect to the Fleet Vs, the three Loch class frigates, the ten Flower corvettes, the seven River frigates, plus BAYFIELD, the L.C.I.(L)s and the M.T.B.s, these "ships were referred to by Canadian Naval Authorities as HMC Ships since they are manned by Canadian personnel. When the first ten Flower class corvettes were taken over NSHQ declared that this would be their practice. However, until quite recently, Admiralty have usually referred to ships which they own but which are manned by Canadians as HM Ships, so in signals for British Authorities either (HMS or HMCS) may be found."[23]

Such a statement must be compared with a detailed study by the naval comptroller in mid 1944. Here NABOB and PUNCHER are correctly noted as being
HM Ships while the two cruisers, the two Fleet Vs, the River named destroyers and
the Towns, are noted as "transferred at no cost to the RCN," "Canadian owned"
and "commissioned as HMC Ships." On the other hand, the three Loch class
frigates, the River-named frigates, and the flower-named corvettes are noted as
"Loaned at no cost to RCN," "RN owned," but "in commission as HMC Ships."[24]

In this study, the six Bangors—BAYFIELD, CANSO, CARAQUET, GUYS-
BOROUGH, INGONISH, and LOCKEPORT—are noted as loaned to the RCN. First
commissioned as HM Ships but manned by RCN personnel, it was not until sometime after June 1942 that they transferred to RCN commission. This study by the
comptroller is complete with policy file references and is probably very accurate. The
dates of the RCN commission, however, were never determined.[25] From a study of the
logs of the six vessels concerned, it is apparent that some commanding officers and
ship's companies felt their ship was Canadian from the start.

It does appear that a few captains knew that their vessels started out belonging
to the RN and not the RCN. In the MAYFLOWER file in NDHQ/DHH, for example, is a monthly Report of Proceedings dated 3 Mar 1941 and signed by GH
Stephen, Lt Cdr, RCNVR, CO, HMS MAYFLOWER.

In the case of the British, however, the confusion continued throughout the
war: in 1944 the CinC Plymouth sent a signal to HM Ships CANSO, CARAQUET,
GUYSBOROUGH and others, and to HMC Ships COWICHAN, FORT
WILLIAM, MALPEQUE, MINAS, and others.[26] All seven were HMC Ships.

In February 1942, the Admiralty placed orders with British shipyards for six
destroyers and five weeks later they placed an additional order for two more of the
same class. The names originally assigned to these vessels were a mixed bag "and
subsequently it was decided to restart a C class as the four [sic] vessels so designated had been transferred to the RCN before the War."[27]

As a class, they were unique in that there were four flotillas built, these being
known as the Ca, Ch, Co, and Cr groups from the first two letters in each name.
The names were taken from a variety of backgrounds and even included one former Tribal name: Cossack. According to Tucker, in January 1945 the Admiralty
made an offer to loan one flotilla of eight destroyers to the RCN.[28] These vessels
were the Cr group (14th Flotilla). Eventually, two out of the eight did arrive—
CRESCENT and CRUSADER—and a third, CROZIERS, actually had an RCN
officer appointed to her.[29] The end of the war against Japan cancelled any plans to

acquire the rest of the flotilla. Thus the RN ships CREOLE, CRISPIN (ex CRAC-CHER), CROMWELL (ex CRETAN), CROWN, and CRYSTAL never appeared in our *Navy List*.[30]

With respect to CRESCENT and CRUSADER, in the summer of 1945 there was some discussion on renaming them with two of four possible names: Cartier, Champlain, Cunard or Currie, the names of persons. Although personal names are rarely employed, none of these names were used probably because both vessels were only on loan at this time. They were purchased in 1951.

Actually, neither CRESCENT nor CRUSADER nor their near-sisters ALGO-NQUIN and SIOUX, were part of the proposed plans for the postwar RCN. At one time plans called for the disposal of all four, it being the intention to retain only the Tribals and to acquire three Darings.[31] If these Darings had been acquired, it is interesting to speculate as to what their names might have been.

RN Ships

As shown above, during the Second World War, the distinction between RCN and RN vessels was a bit blurred. Precedence for this extends back to the First World War and the RN sloops ALGERINE and SHEARWATER. These vessels were

The second CRUSADER, dressed overall, probably in 1958. Note reviewing stand behind B gun. (FDN Coll.)

apparently leased to the RCN for the duration of the war and referred to as HMC Ships by Canadian authorities.

There have been many "Canadian" names that have seen previous use in the RN. One was HMS IROQUOIS whose name derived from a horse that won an annual race called the Derby. Others were HM ships CANADA, a First World War battleship; DOMINION, a pre-First World War battleship; HURON and CRESCENT.

One of the more interesting examples of Canadian names in the RN occurred with the Western Isles class of trawlers. On 9 Dec 1941, VAdm Evans of the British Admiralty Technical Mission (BATM) in Ottawa, wrote to MND advising him that the Admiralty wished to name the sixteen Isles class trawlers being built in Canada for the RN, after small Canadian islands. Further, the Admiralty preferred that Canadian authorities select the names for these ships and requested a choice of twenty or more names.[32] Early in 1942, thirty-three names were forwarded. From these names, the RN chose the following:

Name	Place
Anticosti	island in the Gulf of St. Lawrence
Baffin	island in the Arctic
Cailiff	after the rocks off the NB coast
Ironbound	Island off La Have, NS
Liscomb	island off the coast of NS
Magdalen	islands in the Gulf of St. Lawrence
Manitoulin	island in Lake Huron
Miscou	island at the head of Chaleur Bay

To say the least, not all of these islands are exactly small. Regardless, all eight of the class were built in Canada for the RN. They were manned by RN crews but were under RCN operational control. Because they were built in Canada and named after Canadian islands, the RN classified them as Western Isles class trawlers while their sister ships in Britain were known as Isles class trawlers.

Somewhat earlier, the Admiralty had requested that NSHQ recommend twenty names of seaports or coastal towns from which a selection could be made for the RN minesweepers being constructed in this country.[33] DOD made up an assortment of names, picking smaller towns and villages which he figured we would not need. This list included names like Ucluelet (BC) to which CNS added a minute: "not recommended—a tongue twister which would drive the average Cockney crazy."[34] The following twenty names were forwarded late in March 1941: Arichat, Barrington, Bayfield, Canso, Caraquet, Chemainus, Guysborough, Ingonish,

Ladysmith, Lockeporte, Maitland, Métis, Mingan, Montmagny, Mulgrave, Parrsboro, Qualicum, Shippigan, Tadoussac, and Wedgeport.[35]

The following became RN ships: PARRSBORO, QUALICUM, SHIPPIGAN, TADOUSSAC, and WEDGEPORT. The name Mingan was also assigned but she became FORT YORK at the request of the President of the Toronto Exhibition when the BATM paid a visit. The names Bayfield, Canso, Caraquet, Guysborough, Ingonish and Lockeport were allocated to RN vessels but the ships were taken over by the RCN instead. Since these particular six names are derived from both towns and coastal formations, they provided an unintentional transition from the bay to the town names for the minesweepers.

Later in the Second World War, the RCN wanted to obtain escort carriers for use with convoys. These types of vessels were then being constructed for the RN in the US. American legislation did not permit their sale so the RN leased them. For political reasons, Canada did not accept lend-lease at any time during the Second World War and the government decided that these vessels, and the later L.C.I.(L)s, were not to be exceptions to this policy.[36] The only option then left to the RCN was to man vessels that were leased to the RN.

On several occasions in late 1943 and early 1944, the cabinet refused to accept even this proposal despite the fact that HMS NABOB already had a Canadian crew.[37] But the RN was having difficulty in manning its vessels and in a renewed request for manning assistance in November 1943, the Admiralty had specifically mentioned HMS NABOB. Eventually it came about that the RCN manned two RN-owned carriers with RN aircraft and air complement, HM Ships NABOB and PUNCHER.[38]

Lastly, the RCN had a chance to impose Canadian names on every ship built in Canada for the RN. They did not grasp the chance. On 9 Dec 1941, while writing to the minister concerning the names for Western Isles class trawlers, VAdm A.E. Evans, RN, included the following paragraph:

> The Admiralty also inform me that they propose to select the names for corvettes and minesweepers building and projected in Canada for the Royal Navy unless any reason to the contrary is seen. Would you be good enough ... to inform me if you have any objection to this procedure.[39]

No reply was located but from other evidence, the RN generally selected their own names.

Second World War: Original Names

The term "original" can have either of two meanings depending on context. First, an original name was one never previously used which was assigned to a taken-over or a newly constructed vessel. In a few cases, the name assigned to a taken-over vessel may have been used in the First World War but these exceptions are rare. Second, a vessel taken over could retain its "original" name.

The easiest way to examine such names is by looking at each rate of vessel from the largest to the smallest and by discussing each class within that rate.

Cruisers

The only vessel of this rate that received an original name was ONTARIO, ex HMS MINOTAUR. QUEBEC did not receive her name until after the Second World War.

Destroyers: River Class

The River class consisted of former RN vessels of prewar construction and various classes. The seven original vessels acquired during the 1930s had been given the names of rivers, as had the first wartime acquisition, MARGAREE. She was acquired to replace FRASER who had been rammed and sunk by HMS CALCUTTA. Early in 1943, the RCN was due to take over four more Fleet destroyers from the RN and this acquisition started a debate at NSHQ as to whether or not these vessels would receive original Canadian names as had their sisters.

Apparently, one of the deciding factors was the name of the first of these destroyers to be taken over, HMS GRIFFIN. Due to be acquired in mid-March 1943, it was not until 7 March that SO STATS pointed out that her name was too similar to GRIFFON, the RCNVR Division in Port Arthur, now Thunder Bay. Accordingly, he recommended that four river names, listed in order of river length, be used for the new acquisitions: Saskatchewan, Peace, Fraser and Ottawa. These were the first four names on a list of seventy-seven river names whose length exceeded 200 miles.[40] On the attached minute sheet he wrote: "If it is not desired to use FRASER in view of the unfortunate end of the previous ship of that name, recommend 'KOOTENAY' in lieu." Two days later on 9 Mar 1943, MNS approved the names Ottawa, Kootenay, Saskatchewan and Gatineau, in that order.

On the same day, a message was sent to the Admiralty and CinC Portsmouth among others, but not to HMS GRIFFIN, mentioning the four names, requesting approval of these names by His Majesty, and asking that arrangements be made for HM Ships GRIFFIN and DECOY (the second destroyer) to be renamed.[41]

Cdr H.F. Pullen RCN assumed command of HMS GRIFFIN on 15 Mar 1943 and sent a signal to that effect.[42] Probably thinking Cdr Pullen had commissioned his vessel HMCS GRIFFIN, NSHQ replied the next day restating their intention that HMS GRIFFIN become HMCS OTTAWA and asking for a report on the present position. Cdr Pullen replied the very next day, 16 Mar 1943:

> In view of the war service of (HMS GRIFFIN) with present name
> and the long and distinguished record of her 10 predecessors since
> 1588, most strongly recommend that the original name be retained
> on commissioning for service in RCN. Details of service are being
> forwarded.[43]

One of his men later recalled that the CO "asked the ship's company to search their memories for any river, stream, or brook that bore the name Griffin in Canada, so that he could use this in influencing Canadian Naval authorities to retain the name."[44]

The Admiralty replied on the 18th that Cdr Pullen had been appointed to HMS GRIFFIN and had joined. Further, "because King's approval is required Admiralty is waiting for all four names, before submitting them."[45] Since the Admiralty already had the four Canadian names, this curious statement can only mean that all four RN ships had not yet been chosen. NSHQ mulled this matter over for four days and replied, obviously before the "details of service" sent by Cdr Pullen could possibly arrive:

> The information contained in (your signal) appreciated at NSHQ.
> The minister for Naval Services had however decided that the ships
> transferred from the RN to the RCN will continue to be renamed
> after Canadian rivers as has been the practice for some years.
>
> II. Request, therefore early action may be taken.[46]

From this message, NSHQ appears to believe that the vessel was still HMS GRIFFIN. In point of fact, Cdr Pullen, perhaps feeling that strong action was called for, commissioned her HMCS GRIFFIN on 20 March.[47] Whether or not the commissioning message reached the appropriate authorities in NSHQ before the above message was sent is not known. Despite further protests by Cdr Pullen and his senior officers, however, in a message to NSHQ on 7 April the Admiralty promulgated the King's approval for the name Ottawa. And on 10 Apr 1943 HMCS GRIFFIN was renamed OTTAWA. In his monthly Report of Proceedings for April, Cdr Pullen made no mention of the change of name of his ship. The final twist occurred when NSHQ made the name Ottawa retroactive to 20 March 1943, officially wiping the name Griffin from the files. [48]

Destroyers: Town Class

The Town class consisted of former USN First World War vessels. They were delivered to Halifax where the RN had set up a separate base, HMS SEABORN II, especially to handle the takeover. However, "the British were rather hard put to find crews for so many ships at once, and at their urging the Canadians agreed to take first four, then two more of them."[49] Eventually, eight of this class served in the Navy.

On a suggestion by DOD, the first five Towns were given the names of rivers that either formed or crossed the Canada/USA border.[50] COLUMBIA was almost given back when it was discovered that her main machinery was different from her sisters. But in the end, future logistics problems were accepted in lieu of waiting for another vessel.[51] Years later, "on 25 Feb 1944 (she) found herself out of position in heavy fog with her radar acting up. The next minute, she ran head-on into a cliff in Motion Bay, Newfoundland. Since she never touched bottom, this unusual accident may not have been a grounding, but her bow was thoroughly smashed just the same."[52] This finished her active career and she ended her days as a commissioned hulk in Liverpool, NS.

The sixth Town was ANNAPOLIS who according to some, was named after Annapolis Royal, NS and Annapolis, Maryland.[53] The RN gave their Towns the names of towns common to Britain (and the Commonwealth) and the USA[54] and it appears that the RN had chosen and applied the name before the RCN took her over. From the records, however, it is clear that the RCN intended the name Annapolis as a river name.[55]

The last two Towns arrived in the RCN literally by accident. Before leaving Halifax for the first time, HMS HAMILTON collided with HMS GEORGETOWN and had to be taken in hand for repairs. These were completed in Saint John but when coming out of dock, she grounded, necessitating an extended refit. Meanwhile her RN crew went to another Town and HMS HAMILTON was temporarily taken over by the RCN. Later, this takeover became permanent. HAMIL-

The Town class destroyer HAMILTON. (RCN H-2236 FDN Coll.)

TON had received her name from the RN and the name was not connected with the city in Ontario. DOD suggested her name be changed to a river name—Okanagan, Kootenay, St. John or Yukon. CNS asked MND for his preference and he selected Kootenay, but no action was ever taken.[56]

The sixth Town was HMS BUXTON. For her entire service with the RN she suffered from machinery problems which two trips to Boston for repairs could not correct for very long. In 1943, at St John's, she was "considered unfit to remain in Escort Service, and as passage to the U.K. (could) not be made without extensive and unjustified repairs,"[57] she was offered to the RCN for training purposes and became HMCS BUXTON.

Destroyers: Tribal Class

Unlike the Towns, the names of the Tribals followed their class designator and they were named for native peoples or their language groups. DOD appears to have pushed strongly for the use of tribal instead of river names, "as this is a different class of ship."[58] The naval historian produced a list of seven names and the first two names recommended by CNS were Okanagan and Athabaskan.[59] After a discussion between the minister and CNS, they agreed on the names Iroquois and Athabaskan. IROQUOIS was lead ship but while still on the builder's ways, she was damaged during an air raid. This meant she would now be completed after her sister. To avoid this, the two exchanged names. Incidentally, IROQUOIS is supposed to be the Tribal featured on the dollar stamp issued in 1942. The stamp design was based on a photograph of HMS COSSACK and the design included her pennant number. To the displeasure of NSHQ the artist added black funnel smoke. In 1998 SHAWINIGAN (2nd) and SACKVILLE were pictured on stamps.

After the names Haida and Huron had been selected in 1942, the naval staff asked DOD to communicate with the Dominion archivist and obtain a list of tribal names showing their relative importance. This was done and early in 1943 the names selected as being the next in importance were Nootka and Micmac.[60] After these names had been assigned to their respective hulls but before they had been made public, the general manager of the Halifax shipyard wrote and suggested the names be exchanged. NOOTKA was lead ship but this person had done some research and according to him, the Micmac were far more important than the Nootka, especially to a shipyard in Nova Scotia. Eventually, the matter reached CNS who directed that the names be switched.[61] The construction of these two destroyers took so long that sailors in Halifax called these vessels Methuselah and Moses.[62]

Although there were to be eight in this class, only seven names were used, the name Athabaskan being used twice at the suggestion of SO STATS.[63] The names for CAYUGA and the second ATHABASKAN were taken from a list prepared by SO STATS and which was submitted to A/CNS in mid 1944. Apparently, CNS himself selected the names. Interestingly enough, the three tribal names used for the postwar O class submarines were included on this list.

Destroyers: Fleet Vs

The former RN Fleet V destroyers, ALGONQUIN and SIOUX, were renamed with tribal names, in part to fool the enemy.[64] It is interesting to note that these names were used even though they were already in use for a US Coast Guard cutter and an USN fleet tug, respectively.

Destroyers: Crescent Class

The names of these vessels are RN in origin and are covered under an earlier section.

Frigates: Loch Class ex RN

The three ships in this class—LOCH ACHANALT, LOCH ALVIE and LOCH MORLICH—were all on loan from the RN and named for Scottish Lakes. They retained these names while serving in the RCN.

Frigates: River Class ex RN

The British named these frigates after rivers in Britain and the seven vessels loaned from the RN retained their River names—ANNAN, ETTRICK, MEON, MONNOW, NENE, RIBBLE and TEME. HMCS TEME was noted for the Tudor Rose superimposed on the maple leaf worn on her funnel.[65]

Frigates: River Class Canadian

Because the River class destroyers were named for rivers, the River class frigates had to turn elsewhere for names. Following the lead of the corvettes, therefore, these frigates were named for cities and towns across the nation. The corvettes had first been allocated names of medium sized towns with the intent of reserving the names of provincial capitals and large cities for larger ships. This intent was not carried out. One of the first provincial capital names to go to a corvette was VILLE DE QUEBEC and her story is told elsewhere in this chapter. Of the other eight capital cities, only four names (or their alternatives) were used for frigates, three were used for corvettes, and one for a minesweeper.

Corvettes: Flower Class

The first corvettes were built for the RN under an agreement whereby we would build corvettes in exchange for Tribal class destroyers. The rate of exchange was five corvettes for one destroyer. With typical British courtesy, nine of these ten corvettes were given the names of Canadian wildflowers: ARROWHEAD, BITTERSWEET, EYEBRIGHT, HEPATICA, MAYFLOWER, SNOWBERRY, SPIKENARD, TRILLIUM and WINDFLOWER, with FENNEL being the exception—fennel is a herb, the name coming from its yellow flower. Before any exchange could take place, the agreement fell through. Although RN ships, they were manned by the RCN from the start but it was not until 15 May 1941, that they were officially loaned to and commissioned in the RCN.[66]

Because of Cdr Brand's comments (noted earlier) about flowers being unable to knit socks, the remainder of the Flower class corvettes were named for cities and towns of various sizes. Later in the war twelve Castle and four Flower class corvettes were taken over from the RN and renamed. In exchange, the RN received Algerine minesweepers from the RCN. The sixteen names originally assigned to these Algerines were then assigned to the corvettes.[67] There were actually seventeen Algerines involved and the name of the seventeenth, Toronto, was given to the frigate GIFFARD.

Minesweepers: Bangors and Algerines

As noted in Chapter 3, it was the original intent to continue naming the Bangor class after bays and other coastal formations. In fact, the first eighteen ordered were so named.[68] The RN had allocated names to the next six vessels, BAYFIELD, CANSO, CARAQUET, GUYSBOROUGH, INGONISH and LOCKEPORT from names of small Canadian coastal towns. Then, as related elsewhere, these vessels were taken over by the RCN. After this, Bangors in the RCN were named after cities and towns and so were all the Algerines. Like the corvettes and frigates, the minesweeper names varied from large cities—Winnipeg—to small towns like Digby.

Llewellyn Class (Motor Minesweepers, 125-Foot Type)

According to Macpherson and Burgess, the names of this class of vessel were to "reflect the fact that they were equipped with 'double L' magnetic minesweeping gear, but ingenuity seems to have failed when it came to naming the rest of the class."[69] It is interesting to note, however, that the first two vessels of this class, LLEWELLYN and LLOYD GEORGE , were ordered in the spring of 1941 and both commissioned 24 Aug 1942. The remainder of the class were not even

The badges of the first two 125-foot motor minesweepers. (RCN O-793-49 and 50. FDN Coll.)

laid down until January 1943 and by this time, the policy of naming all minesweepers after towns and cities was well established. Further, a list of towns and cities in order of population had been drawn up as early as April 1942, and was now being used to select names for frigates, corvettes and minesweepers.[70] This is the probable reason for not continuing with names including a double L which are not so rare that eight additional names could not have been located. Names of small communities like Bella Coola or Mallaig might have been used but may have been confused with vessels like the corvette BELLEVILLE or the frigate BEACON HILL. But names like Lladner, Llanberis, Llanfair, Llangorse, Llanover, Lloy or Llysfram, or others taken from a gazetteer, would have made for a unique class of names.

Fairmile Depot Ships

There were several types of names suggested for these vessels but in early 1941, DOD suggested the names Companion and Provider. DCNS liked both names but CNS approved only the latter.[71] The only clue as to the origin of the names for the next two vessels comes in a reply to the Department of Munitions and Supply where the statement was made that "it's Naval custom to name depot and repair ships after the work in which they will be employed." This statement was fine as far as it went but the logic was somewhat impaired by the concluding part of the sentence that stated, "or other suitable names such as Tyne, Medway, etc."[72] Regardless of alleged RN policy, RCN depot ships received descriptive or functional names.

Lake Class (105-Foot Type Minesweepers)

Most of this class of small minesweepers were never completed and originally were to have been named for trees. This however, would have led to a great deal of duplication with other names in other navies so a "lake" was added to each name. In common with other small vessels, it seems these were named after small communities, not actual lakes.

Western Isles Class Minesweepers

Based on the RN Isles class trawlers, the Western Isles class were built in Canada for the RN, manned by the RN and named by the RN for small Canadian Islands.[73] The islands of Anticosti and Baffin, however, are hardly small. On the other end of the scale, Miscou is only a rock. The fault lies not with the RN, but with NSHQ who forwarded the list from which the Admiralty made its choice.

Fairmile Motor Launches

As early as the summer of 1941, "it was decided that Fairmiles should only be given numbers, not names."[74] Names for these vessels had to wait thirteen years.

Tugs and Smaller Vessels

With the exception of the post-Second World War Saint class of tugs mentioned in BRCN 150, no documents could be located on the naming of various classes of small vessels such as the Wood, Ton, Dun, Ore, Ville, etc., classes. All these classes had names with a common last syllable such as NORTON. The names for the Glen class tugs and the Dun class oilers had a common first syllable, as in DUNDURN.

It first appeared that many of these names were invented, e.g. GLENVALLEY, but a search through various gazetteers revealed at least one community for each name. Most of these communities were either hamlet size or dispersed communities and circumstantial evidence in the records indicates these names were used because of the small size of the community. Thus the names were a most appropriate choice but when it came to indicating the origin of the name, a problem arose. Take GLENWOOD as an example. In NS, there are four communities named Glenwood plus one each in New Brunswick and Alberta. Which Glenwood is the one after which the vessel was named? Perhaps it was all of them. Lacking documentary evidence and/or guidance, the origin of place names for all vessels in the above classes, has not been indicated. ATWOOD is the only Wood class tug whose source for a name is documented and she was named after a hamlet located near Listowel, Ontario.

Animal Class Armed Yachts

This rather strange "class" of vessels consisted mainly of former American yachts purchased early in the war. Except for SANS PEUR and AMBLER, which retained original names, all these vessels were given the names of animals native to this country such as VISON.

Nenamook Class

The Fishermen's Reserve was a group of west coast fishermen who with their vessels, became a part of the naval reserve in the 1930s to assist in patrolling the coastal waters of BC. Mobilized at the beginning of the war, these vessels resound with the names of the BC coast: BARKLEY SOUND, TAKLA, CAPELLA, VANISLE, etc. For a complete list, see Appendix O. But little known are six vessels which were purpose built for the Fisherman's Reserve: EHKOLI, KUITAN, LEELO, MOOLOCK, NENAMOOK and TALAPUS.

The first vessel was NENAMOOK. She was a seine trawler under construction on the west coast when she was requisitioned in January and purchased outright in March 1941. Her five sisters were built for the Navy.

All took their names from animals or fish in the Chinook Jargon, a pidgin that became the medium of communication among many west coast native people. These names were submitted by COPC to NSHQ and approved without change.[75]

The harbour craft MELVIN SWARTOUT, 17 Sep 1943. (RCN E5218. KM Coll.)

Miscellaneous Craft

Of the remainder of the small craft most were given numbers. Some retained their original name thus bringing into the navy such colourful titles as SALTPETRE, COMBAT, KWABEETA, MELVIN SWARTOUT, MOBY DICK, WEETIEBUD and ZOARCES. The author of the poem about "the names they give our sweepers" would have been pleased.[76] There were also some small craft whose names were changed.

By 1941, the growth in the number and variety of harbour craft was apparently causing some problems about names.[77] On the last day of that year, NSHQ issued an order that effective 15 January 1942, all harbour craft were to be numbered and lose their names. Thus many of the entries in Chapter 6 are annotated in this manner: "15 Jan 1942 became HC (harbour craft) number 19."

There were some exceptions to the order. All harbour craft that carried the names of bases or depots were to continue to carry their names but numbers were also allocated to them. Just how these vessels were to be addressed was not made clear. Further, the order does not seem to have been strictly enforced. As late as 1945 some harbour craft, like LIL II and JEFFYJAN, were still being referred to by name even in official documents.

All the harbour craft names are original in that they were used "as is." The next batch of names could well be called "original substitutes" for it was not always possible to use the proper name of a town or city, or to retain a vessel's original name.

Second World War Vessels: Alternative Names

During the Second World War, the names of cities and towns with a population of over 2800 were used to name most frigates, corvettes, and minesweepers. But many of the names for these centres of population could not be used. Basically, there were three reasons for this: the name, or a similar one, was already in use in the RCN, RN, USN or an other allied navy, e.g. Yarmouth, Nova Scotia; the name was too long, e.g. Penetanguishene, Ontario; or the name was inappropriate, e.g. Hanover, Ontario.

Thus a warship would not have represented many of our cities and towns if NSHQ had not devised what apparently is a uniquely Canadian solution: the alternative name for a city or town. Nowhere, for example, will there be found a Canadian naval vessel which to date has been named London, Dartmouth or Hull. But in the Second World War, we do find vessels named MIDDLESEX, WENTWORTH, and LA HULLOISE, the alternative names chosen for these cities. This program affected some 100 cities and towns. (Appendices A, B and C provide details.)

Since many Canadian and American cities and towns are named after British places, people or geographical features, the number of common names is large. To honour the town, on request by NSHQ the mayor or town council devised alternative names. Such names were supposed to refer to geographical features in or around the town. As SO STATS of NSHQ described in a letter to one town, the available choices received to date "have included rivers or streams, land marks of various type, name of county, contractions of the full name or an interchange of syllables." In addition an attempt was made "to retain the identity of the municipality and to avoid any suggestion or reference to persons or family names."[78] Since the significance of alternative names was not generally mentioned in the correspondence, only those who reside in that town know their meaning. In many cases, the correspondence itself is missing and only rough summaries remain.

The development of an alternative name could be quite time-consuming. The name Newmarket for example, was first rejected in August 1942. A letter was sent to the Ontario town, a reply received, alternatives considered and rejected, more letters written. By July 1944, when the requirement for more names ceased, no suitable alternative name had been found.

Other places had other problems, the town of Verdun for example. Since the RN already had a destroyer with that name, NSHQ wrote to the city in early November 1942. The mayor forwarded three alternative names. Only one proved feasible and that was Dunver, derived from a simple transposition of the syllables in the town's name.[79]

Hull CN 344 was launched shortly thereafter but Admiralty approval for the use of the name Dunver for this hull was not received until after the event. In fact, the name was not promulgated until the summer of 1943. Meanwhile, some opposition to the name had caused the MP for the region to visit MNS on several occasions to complain about the name. In July 1943, the MP wrote to suggest a substitute: a double name headed by Verdun and followed by the words Canada, Québec or Lasalle, e.g. Verdun Canada.

This caused an overreaction in NSHQ: SO STATS sent a letter to the Admiralty via SCNO stating that "quite urgent representations have been made on behalf of the town to have the name 'DUNVER' withdrawn and replaced by one which would show the name...in its proper form."[80] Four alternative names were included with this letter: the three suggested above plus Ville de Verdun.

Before London could reply, a second letter arrived at NSHQ from the MP, this time suggesting the name Argoulets be used instead of Dunver. Besides being similar to names already in use by several Allied vessels, the name was rejected by SO STATS because in the vernacular of the day, "argoulets" implied a person of bad character. In his letter to the secretary of MND, SO STATS wrote in by hand: "Personally, and quite off the record, I feel we are paying too much attention altogether to the MP." [81]

Meanwhile, the Admiralty had replied and suggested that there would be less chance of confusion if the name Verdun of Canada were used. Assuming this name to be acceptable, the Admiralty had passed it to the King who had given the name his approval. Having put themselves in a corner, in early September 1943 NSHQ sent a signal to NOIC Québec asking him to inform Morton Engineering Ltd. that the name of CN 344 had been changed from Dunver to Verdun of Canada. The very next day, 10 Sep 1943, NOIC Québec replied that the ship's officers were quite disturbed because at great expense to themselves, they had crests, plate and stationery prepared in the name of DUNVER. Further, according to NOIC, the name had been accepted by the citizens of Verdun. The very next day, in true naval tradition, the captain commissioned hull CN 344 as DUNVER.

The early commissioning was a development not apparently foreseen by NSHQ. Late that same month, NSHQ dispatched a letter to the ship asking if the reasons for the objection still applied and also if there were any further reasons why the name should not now be changed to Verdun of Canada. Back came a short reply, eventually endorsed by the Commander in Chief of the Canadian North West Atlantic, stating that "it is the very strong feeling of every man borne in the 'DUN-VER' that the ship's name on no account be changed." [82] The name stayed.

Another alternative name that caused problems was the one for Québec City. [83] The Commando Training Centre (CTC) was formed at Inverary, Scotland, about September 1940. This was a combined operations base and it was given the name HMS QUEBEC, probably in recognition of the "combined op" in 1759. Many Canadians served in HMS QUEBEC. Approval of the Admiralty to use the name, however, was neither sought nor received.

In late January 1942, an officer from HMS QUEBEC, Lt W.S. Brooke RCNVR, was visiting the Admiralty in an attempt to obtain a badge for his base. By chance he met Mr. C. Loughton, the Admiralty librarian, who was also a member of the RN Ships' Names Committee. When he learned where the officer came from the Librarian was most disturbed for the King had just granted his approval for the names of the next class of destroyers: the Q or Québec class. In short order, the problem compounded when the Admiralty remembered that the name Québec had received their approval for use by the RCN some ten months earlier. [84]

To retain the name for the base, Commodore Lord Louis Mountbatten (head of Combined Operations) and the CO of HMS QUEBEC prepared some persuasive arguments. To win, Lord Louis was quite prepared to use his influence with persons in high places (including our Governor General, The Earl of Athlone—a cousin of his)[85] but this apparently was not necessary. In the end the base won and the ships lost. The deciding factor in favour of the base was the fact that the documents of some 4,000 men would have to be altered if the name of the base were changed. The CTC remained in operation as HMS QUEBEC until 1946 so the name was not even available for UGANDA in 1944.

Instead of the Québec class, the RN destroyers became the Quilliam class. The destroyer, the former HMS QUEBEC, became HMS QUEENBOROUGH. After a decision by the naval board, the corvette became VILLE DE QUEBEC, this alternative name having been suggested by Vincent Massey, the High Commissioner in London, and the mayor of Québec City was so informed.[86] All this could have been avoided had someone recalled an October 1940 agreement that permitted a shore establishment in one Allied navy to share her name with a vessel in a second Allied navy.

The question of alternative names first arose as early as 1941 and the subject was still being discussed in 1942. In September of that year, the Admiralty pointed out that the use of duplicate or similar names among Allied vessels could lead to awkward situations. Further, in cases where the name in question was borne by small British craft, these could alter their names.[87] Such a generous offer was completely ignored. Take the case of HMS VICTORIA, a target vessel. The RCN had intended to use the name Victoria—for the city—for a frigate but once they learned of this target vessel, NSHQ decided not to pursue this option and the alternative name of Beacon Hill was employed instead. From the viewpoint of many years later, this shows a willingness to defer to the RN especially where this was neither necessary nor expected.

The mistake of assigning names already in use by other navies was not confined only to this side of the Atlantic. On one occasion, the Admiralty misread their lists and tried to employ the name Lindsay. Upon hearing of the proposed RN vessel, NSHQ politely inquired if HMCS LINDSAY should change her name. The Admiralty, tacitly admitting that the RCN had prior claim, simply changed the name of their captain class frigate, K564, to HMS PASLEY in late 1943.[88]

There were several other mistakes as well. When the town's name could not be used, Dalhousie, NB, sent in three alternatives. One of these was Baie des Chaleurs.

The name was considered too long. DOD suggested a shorter version, Chaleur, and dispatched a reply to that effect. A few days later it was pointed out that the navy already had a minesweeper named CHALEUR and NSHQ hastily wrote to the town retracting their offer. The alternative name Inch Arran was finally selected.

When the town of Trenton, Ontario, sent in three alternative names in November 1942, their first choice was Trentonia. NSHQ accepted this name but when it was placed on a long list, it was typed in immediately below the name Prestonian. The name thus typed became Trentonian and so it remained. The town never objected.

Early the next year, SO STATS wrote to his superior, DOD, noting that there were now two escort carriers which carried the names of two of the reserve divisions, HUNTER and QUEEN. He posed an "either or" question to his superior: "do you feel that we can allow these names to stand...or do you feel that we should set about to rename (the divisions) now?"[89] In a handwritten reply, DOD responded with: "Yes for the present. These names were chosen by CNP without our advice."[90] This was not exactly a useful answer but since no action was taken, it can be assumed that SO STATS interpreted his orders as to leave well enough alone. Apparently, SO STATS was not aware of the agreement concluded with the Admiralty earlier in the war concerning HMCS/HMS COLLINGWOOD.[91]

Finally, the RN even managed to misread their lists such that they named one vessel HMS PINCHER and another HMS PUNCHER, the latter being one of the two escort carriers manned by the RCN. Such a similarity of name made for confusion, especially with the distribution of correspondence.[92]

One of the frigates from this era, which served well into the postwar period, was STETTLER. In several wartime lists of alternative names, this name is listed as the alternative for Edmonton. In 1941, the time came to use the names of provincial capitals. NSHQ then discovered that the name Edmonton was too similar to EDMUNDSTON whose name had been assigned in July of the previous year by Naval Order 962. When asked by NSHQ to suggest another name, the city was less than pleased that a small town should take precedence over a provincial capital. Reluctantly, they suggested two alternatives: City of Edmonton (too long) and Fort Edmonton (name of a merchant ship). When informed that neither was acceptable, the city council suggested that the city honour the "nearby" town of Stettler by letting the Navy name the ship for that town.[93] This was perhaps the most unusual choice for an alternative name. The name Edmonton was not to appear in the Navy until 1996.

Second World War Vessels: Long Names

One of the reasons for using an alternative name was the length of the names of some towns and cities. One of the characteristics required of a ship's name is that it be relatively short, for several reasons. First, a long name is a stumbling block in most forms of communication, be it by semaphore, morse, voice, or in writing. Secondly, in the days when a sailor wore a cap fitted with a cap ribbon or tally, the standard size letter spaces made long names impossible. Thirdly, in harbour our ships display a large mahogany nameplate with the ship's name attached in large chrome plated letters. Similarly, the name often appears on decorated Kisbie rings and as anyone who has ever tried to paint a sign will quickly tell you, short names are preferable.

But some long names did enter service. Only one instance could be located which said how many letters in a name were too many, and excluding H.M.C.S., that number was thirteen.[94] The longest ships' name was Cap-de-la-Madeleine with eighteen letters and spaces but the longest known tally was ROYAL CANADIAN FLEET RESERVE. Although not well documented, the story is that the navy wished to shorten the name to either Madeleine or Cap Madeleine but when the townspeople learned of this, some unpleasant letters were apparently written to MNS. So acidic were some of these letters that an unknown staff officer, on a list of prospective names, was moved to add the following note beside the name Cap-de-la-Madeleine: "In view of numerous rude communications received from organization insisting on full name, minister is inclined to leave this name off the list."[95] Eventually, the name was accepted but the mayor of the City was informed that only the name Madeleine would appear on cap ribbons in peacetime.[96] But, as any member of her postwar ship's company can affirm, the full name was used on the tally. For a man with a small cap size, this meant that the name and title commenced well on the starboard quarter of his cap.

Cap-de-la-Madeleine of course, was not the only

A long name on a Kisbie ring. To fit the name in, the painter had to reduce in size the middle two words. (Freeman 661-23. AC)

name that was deemed to be too long. Penetanguishene was shortened to Penetang; Carleton Place, which is a shorter name than Cap-de-la-Madeleine, became Carlplace; La Ville de Matane became Matane; Portage La Prairie, Portage; and Salaberry-de-Valleyfield, Valleyfield.

Some cities were informed that their name was too long only to have NSHQ reverse its decision. Such reversal occurred after NSHQ accepted the name of Cap-de-la-Madeleine.[97] Thetford Mines, Rivière du Loup and Victoriaville fall into this category. So too did Sault Ste Marie whose name, with the mayor's blessing, had actually changed to The Soo. The citizens, however, disagreed with their mayor and succeeded in making the Navy change the name back again.

One other long name that came into service at this time was the alternative name for Chatham, NB: Northumberland. After the Second World War, two other ships challenged CAP DE LA MADELEINE for the longest name. These were the PORTE SAINT LOUIS and PORTE DE LA REINE.

Second World War Vessels: Names Chosen but Never Assigned

Some names of towns and cities were selected for use as names for HMC Ships but for one reason or another, the names were not used. Some, like La Tuque, were actually assigned to a hull only to have the name changed later to Fort Erie. Other names fell by the wayside when the hulls to which they were assigned were cancelled. And some names, like Chatkenada and Ste Rose were ready for approval when the requirement for more names ceased.

Because this latter group of names was never assigned to any vessel, they do not appear in Chapter 6 but they are listed in Appendix E.

Similarly, alternative names like Live Oak and New Toro, which were never assigned to a vessel and which are not in the list of names, are to be found in Appendices A and B.

Second World War Vessels: Requested Names

When ships started to be named after cities and towns, it did not take long before many places were requesting the name of their town be used. In fact, such letters started arriving in early 1940.

As pointed out earlier, even though NSHQ went eventually to selecting names from a list of towns in descending order of population, if a city or town drew attention to itself (by a letter for example), then it stood a much better chance of having a ship named after it. In one case, in June 1942, a Mr. Thomas Hussey suggested the name Glace Bay be used as it was then the country's largest town. The town itself wrote in on 23 Oct 1943.

One town really got itself organized in this respect: Kapuskasing. In 1942, letters flowed into NSHQ from the Board of Trade, Volunteer Civil Guard, Brotherhood of Electrical Workers, the Catholic Women's League, and the Girl Guides, among others, moving DOD to suggest that the Town of Kapuskasing really needed a file all its own.[98]

Individuals, unconnected with any organization, also wrote. A Miss Millie Midler wrote and suggested the name of her town—Erieau, Ontario—as a name for a warship.[99] Politics also played a part. MP Gordon B. Isnor, representing Halifax, suggested Dartmouth and Bedford but the RN already had ships with the same or similar names. The minister of Labour, H. Mitchell, suggested Welland. R.W. Gladstone MP, suggested Guelph and Fergus.[100]

Sometimes, even small towns and villages could find their names being used for a ship. Charny, Québec, for example, had requested its name be used but it was too small to merit consideration until CARTIER had to give up its name to a reserve division, and the name Charny was picked as a replacement. Similarly, a Saskatchewan MP suggested the name of Qu'appelle but with a population of only 600, the minister regretted the name probably would not be used.[101] Yet just a few months later, that very name was selected from a long list of rivers for the destroyer QU'APPELLE. Coincidence?

The corvette VANCOUVER was built in the Victoria area and launched 26 Aug 1941. Originally, she was slated to become KITCHENER but the hulls exchanged names. Was it this change that prompted the mayor of Victoria, R.N. Mayhew, to request MNS to have a ship named Victoria built in his city? In a note to NSHQ, MNS approved the request by the mayor provided there was no conflict. There was: see BEACON HILL. Ironically, the name Victoria had been submitted for approval first but when NSHQ learned of HMS VICTORIA, they substituted the name Vancouver![102]

Second World War: Duplicate Names

If, in the Commonwealth navies, it holds that a ship with a given name is entitled to display the Battle Honours won by its predecessors of the same name, then it is logical to assume that at any given time, no two vessels or bases would hold the same name. Furthermore, as a deliberate policy during the Second World War NSHQ did not allocate names which were duplicated by or similar to, other vessels in Allied navies.[103] Appendix D lists some twenty instances of duplication in names, most of which occurred during the War.

One of the first names to be duplicated was BURLINGTON. After being informed of HMS BURLINGTON, the RCN changed the name of its vessel to ST ANN. This change was rendered useless for through an oversight, ST ANN was launched and christened as BURLINGTON! Although NSHQ would have changed the name if the Admiralty had objected, the latter solved the problem of two BURLINGTONs by changing the name of their minesweeper to HMS FAIR-FAX.[104]

Hard on the heels of this was the problem of two COLLINGWOODs, the solution to which allowed for some duplication of names. The Admiralty felt that as a general principle, similar or identical names should be avoided but this principle should only apply to vessels. Accordingly, it was considered acceptable to have an RCN corvette and an RN establishment, both named COLLINGWOOD.[105] This principle was later confirmed when the RN used the names HUNTER and QUEEN for two escort carriers, even though two reserve divisions employed these names. By the time this latter incident occurred in 1943, however, personnel in NSHQ appear to have forgotten this principle.

Duplicate names of another sort also caused a few problems. Early in the war, an agreement was made that no RCN ships were to have names starting with Fort as the Wartime Merchant Shipping Board had a class of such vessels. Exceptions were made when the board agreed to let the navy use the names Fort Frances and Fort William but when it came to the name Fort Erie, another problem arose. In the spring of 1943, the shipping board had a vessel already named Fort Erie, which was nearing completion in the USA. The town of Fort Erie, Ontario, would not accept a merchant vessel being named for the town. The town wanted a warship and would accept nothing less. The shipping board did not wish to change the name of their vessel because to do so at this stage would only cause considerable confusion.

The Navy was caught in the middle but DOD provided the solution when he recalled the case of the battleship HMS QUEEN ELIZABETH and the liner RMS *Queen Elizabeth*, both of which were currently in service. He recommended that in addition to the merchant ship, a warship be named Fort Erie and the town was so informed.[106] The name was first assigned to a frigate, subsequently cancelled, but a second frigate FORT ERIE commissioned late in 1944. In the 1960s, she was senior ship of the 7th Escort Squadron in Halifax.

Second World War Vessels: Name Exchanges

During this period, an exchange of names between two vessels under construction was not a rare occurrence. The following are typical:

FERGUS and FORT FRANCES	ROYALMOUNT and BUCKINGHAM
GLACE BAY and LAUZON	STORMONT and MONTREAL
KITCHENER and VANCOUVER	STORMONT and MATANE
PENETANG and RIVERSIDE	TORONTO and GIFFARD
ROYALMOUNT and ALWINGTON	GUELPH and SEA CLIFF

The first exchange of which a record was discovered was between SHEDIAC and AMHERST in mid 1940.[107]

The precise reasons for such exchanges are not always clear but in the case of FERGUS and FORT FRANCES, PENETANG and RIVERSIDE, these are well documented.[108] In these two cases, the names were exchanged simply to permit the construction of the vessels to be as close as possible to the centres of population for which they were named. The minister himself had suggested just such an action when he pointed out that representatives of each town should attend the launching of each ship.[109]

Such exchanges were not without their side effects, one of which has already been dealt with (see VANCOUVER earlier in this chapter). Another effect was that in each case the King's approval had to be sought and received. At least, this was the view of NSHQ. Messages were duly sent[110] but whether or not the King actually saw the requests is not known since any reply always came from the Admiralty through the senior Canadian naval officer (SCNO) in London.

As a result of the request by MND to exchange the names of FERGUS and FORT FRANCES,[111] SO STATS wrote to A/CNS in July 1943 and explained the reasons for the signal he was about to send the Admiralty on this subject. He suggested that instead of having to send a signal each time, perhaps NSHQ could seek more discretionary powers for the exchange of names. He went on to explain that if such approval could be obtained, then NSHQ:

> could more readily comply with changes requested by the minister
> from time to time and merely advise Admiralty as each case crops
> up. However, I personally feel that making a request of this type
> places us in a rather weak position in the eyes of Admiralty who,
> undoubtedly, would wonder just what we are trying to do and
> would feel that we could have no pre-arranged plan. Further if the
> present arrangement is continued, whereby individual cases must

be submitted to Admiralty for their approval when any change is requested, it would perhaps deter the minister's Department, or any others desiring changes, from putting forth requests indiscriminately. I think you agree that changes to names already published by Canadian Confidential Naval Order should be held down to the very minimum and anything that can be done in the reduction of the number of amendments or alterations is worthy of our best consideration.[112]

In a note scribbled on the bottom of this memo, A/CNS wrote "Inform Admiralty we intend doing this." Although further documents are not available this seems to mark the first successful break the RCN took in evolving a totally separate naming policy.

The comments by SO STATS, worried about the Admiralty thinking that NSHQ had no pre-arranged plan, are interesting. Although he does not specifically say this, the documents seem to suggest that at this time the plan, if any, was still evolving. If there had been a plan, all this exchange of names would have not been necessary, as the proper names could have been allocated to the geographically correct shipyard in the first place. After all, by this time, such name trading had been going on for two years.

The number of such changes even affected the name allocation procedure. In the fall of 1943, the navy admitted that its policy now was not to promulgate the names of new construction vessels until the first of the month prior to the month in which the launch was to occur "because of the changes that are often made in the names."[113]

Second World War: Name Changes

Similar to but distinct from the exchange of names between two vessels, is the subject of changing the name of a specific vessel, examples of which are mentioned elsewhere. Some reasons for a change are clear. For example, THREE RIVERS became TROIS RIVIERES on the request of the citizens of the city; MALBAIE became LA MALBAIE, the correct name for the town; the RCMP vessel Acadian became INVADER to distinguish her from the other ACADIAN then wearing the white ensign; and the vessel CARTIER became CHARNY so the former's name could not be confused with the Reserve Division in Montréal. One of the best known name changes was when the minesweeper NOOTKA became NANOOSE so her name could be used for the destroyer.

When the name Campbellton conflicted with the destroyer HMS CAMPBEL-TOWN in 1940, NSHQ sought another town name from the Province of New Brunswick. The names considered were Richibucto, Moncton, St. Stephen, Grand Falls, Dorchester, Caraquet and Fredericton.[114] Of these, four would eventually be used with Moncton chosen to substitute for Campbellton. Later in the war, the alternative name Atholl was chosen to represent the Town of Campbellton but in 1940, alternative names were still one year in the future.

As with other aspects of names, politics also intruded. In August 1944, the vice president of the Port Carling Boat Works wrote to NSHQ and asked if the name of the minesweeper BEECH LAKE then building there, could be changed to something that could be identified with that area of Ontario. He suggested the names Port Carling, Honey Harbour or Muskoka.[115] The official reply said that these names could not be used without compromising the other names in that class, all of which were names of trees.

Shortly thereafter, the MP for the region wrote to MND suggesting the name Muskoka be used instead of BEECH LAKE. The matter was settled eventually by having the name changed to PINE LAKE as the Muskoka region was noted for pine, and additionally, there was a Pine Lake in the district. A minesweeper named BEECH LAKE was constructed in Vancouver but the records are not clear whether the two vessels actually exchanged names or not.

INVADER, October 1939, the former RCMP *Acadian*. She is still wearing a Kisbie ring with her original name. (KM Coll.)

On 1 May 1942, four of the Battle class trawlers—ST ELOI, LOOS, ARRAS, ARLEUX and FESTUBERT—were given numbers in lieu of names: GV 12, 14, 15, 16 and 17 respectively.[116] Some of these vessels, however, were still referred to by their names throughout the war.

One class of vessels that had their names changed were the armed yachts, which with two exceptions, received the names of animals native to this country. The yacht *Oracle* had her name changed to BYTOWN and finally, the little tug *Restico* was renamed ASSISTANT, probably to avoid confusion with RESTIGOUCHE.

Most of the former civilian vessels retained their original names but as early as the summer of 1940, COAC had suggested renaming SUDEROY I and her sisters, as well as REO II, MARLIS, and ROSS NORMAN. COAC suggested using the names of insects such as Ant, Fly and Bee.[117] No reply to this letter could be located but in any event, many insect names were already in use by the RN for Coastal Forces bases like HMS HORNET.

On the west coast, the large number of taken-over fishing boats for the Fishermen's Reserve resulted in several duplicate names like LOYAL I and LOYAL II, or CHATHAM S. Vessels such as these were given new names related to the water through which they sailed: FOAM, SEA WAVE, RIPPLE, SPRAY, etc.

One curious incident occurred with respect to the shore establishments in Esquimalt. In November 1942, a proposal was put forward by COPC to reorganize Esquimalt, the result of which would be a new name for the training section of NADEN. The suggested name was Camousun but in discussing the matter, the naval

Gate Vessel 12, the former ST ELOI, circa 1944. (RCN 2699. KM Coll.)

staff recommended either Rainbow or Swiftsure. These two names were passed to the Admiralty who approved Swiftsure. The name Rainbow was turned down but the staff could not recall why.[118] Other suggestions submitted by COPC included Nasqui, Malacca, Saanich, Tweedsmuir, Constance, and Queen Charlotte. By April of the following year, COPC wrote to say that because of the long delay in granting approval for a change in name, no further action should now be taken as GIVENCHY was now well known and to change her name would only add to the confusion!

The origin of the name for the reserve division in Montréal, DONNACONA, is not documented but its change from the original name Montréal is well covered. As early as June 1943, the name Montréal was assigned to a frigate under construction in that city.[119] A letter from CORD to NSHQ followed this move, the former suggesting the name of the division be changed from Montréal to Wolfe.[120] This was a good choice as HMS MONTREAL in 1813 was the former Wolfe. Unfortunately this name conflicted with both HMS WOLFE and HMCS WOLF.[121]

In June, the name Montréal was officially assigned to hull CN 352.[122] Late in September 1943, NSHQ apparently wrote to the CO of MONTREAL stating that they wished to use that name for a ship and he therefore should suggest alternative names for his division. The CO replied with four suggestions. The naval board objected to these four as follows:

Name	Objection
Drummond	DRUMMONDVILLE & DRUMHELLER, and Argentine minesweeper DRUMMOND
Dorchester	HMS DORCHESTER (no such vessel)
Laurentian	DOT Vessel *Laurentian*
St Lawrence (after a vessel built on the Great Lakes during the War of 1812.)	ST LAURENT, HMIS LAWRENCE

SO STATS had suggested the name Mountain, probably after the street on which the Division was then located but this name did not find favour with DOD.

The pressure on NSHQ now increased as the commissioning date for the frigate MONTREAL was fast approaching. In fact, the ship commissioned 12 Nov 1943 but the name of the Division was not changed to DONNACONA until nine days later.

At least on one occasion, the introduction of a series of names in one class caused other vessels to change their names. In 1944, after five of the Glen class tugs had been commissioned, NSHQ realized that there were two other small vessels whose names could mislead one into thinking that they were also Glen class tugs. So after the fact, GLENCAIRN and GLENDALE became CAIRN and DALEHURST respectively.[123] But the name of a chartered tug, GLENCLOVA, went unchanged, as did an RCSC training vessel, GLENFRUIN, which served at Gananoque.

Second World War: Names of Establishments

As noted in Chapter 1, the name of an establishment initially came from the vessel assigned to it as a depot ship. Thus, in the 1910-1939 period vessels like NADEN, LANSDOWNE and STADACONA were acquired.

In the early part of the Second World War the depot ship requirement still existed and so establishments such as CAPTOR, CHALEUR, GIVENCHY, HOCHELAGA, PROTECTOR, SAMBRO and VENTURE took their names from the small vessels assigned to the base. One exception to this rule was BYTOWN, which took the first name of the site now known as Ottawa. Her name was preordained and as described, *Oracle* had her name changed to match the intended name for the depot. At one time, however, the new reserve division CARLETON also shared the same quarters as BYTOWN. In 1942, BYTOWN moved to The Navy Building, later to be known as A Block, Cartier Square, and a decision was made to retain the name BYTOWN at the expense of CARLETON and so the latter paid off.[124]

With the passing of the requirement for depot ships,[125] NSHQ was at liberty to indulge in some innovative naming for shore establishments. Of the names generated for these establishments, some could be easily distinguished from the town- and city-named ships and a few could be called innovative. Overall, however, there was no pattern. The names of these establishments were drawn from two areas: geography and history. The geographic names are AVALON, CHATHAM, CONESTOGA, FORT RAMSAY, KINGS, MULGRAVE, ROYAL ROADS, SHELBURNE, SOMERS ISLES and STONE FRIGATE. The names taken from history are BURRARD, CORNWALLIS, DOMINION, and NIOBE. A complete list of establishments is contained in Appendix H.

The Kisbie ring and unofficial badge of ROYAL ROADS, as displayed in the CFB Esquimalt Museum. (Freeman 661- 30. AC)

The origin of two shore establishment names, PEREGRINE and GANNET, is not known. Since a Peregrine is a type of falcon, and since the name was applied to the ex RCAF depot in Halifax, would it be safe to assume the name was somehow related to the Air Force?[126] But what then of the origin of GANNET? Her name only lasted six days because the name was considered undesirable.[127]

Once an establishment received its name, it was not normally changed. There were exceptions: DOMINION, located in Britain, became NIOBE to avoid confusion with the High Commissioner whose cable address was "Dominion London,"[128] and MONTREAL, the reserve division in Montréal, to free the name for use by a frigate, became DONNACONA. Because personnel often confused the two establishments, HOCHELAGA I and II both located in Montréal, naval authorities tried on several occasions to have one of them renamed Maisonneuve. Not only did NSHQ refuse permission for this change, they made it more difficult by stating no reason for the refusal.[129]

The practice of creating additional shore establishments without creating new names seems to have originated with the Royal Navy. As early as the First World War, the practice was also in use in the RCN.[130] In the Second World War, there are recorded examples of HMS DRAKE IV, HMS VICTORY VI, HMC Ships GIVENCHY III, NADEN III, AVALON II, and STADACONA II.[131] Such a practice can be understood for a large navy such as the RN where the scarcity of good names for shore establishments must be considered. In 1975, for example, there were twelve commissioned shore establishments in the Portsmouth, England area alone.[132] In the RCN, with a much smaller navy, there seems to be little excuse for such a practice other than to "follow father." Even then, this practice of extending the original name was not followed consistently.

When the function of the ship or establishment changed, the name often changed. One has only to attempt to trace the history of five related ships—GANNET, VENTURE, VENTURE II, SAMBRO and SAMBRO II—in the Halifax area during the Second World War to realize the difficulties some seamen must have had after a short absence from Halifax.

Most shore establishments were situated in one location, at most two, or else within specific boundaries. Thus in the list of names, an address is given or a location described. Nothing has been noted for AVALON for the simple reason that a few words in a limited space could not begin to describe the size, location and complexity of the various components that constituted this establishment.[133]

Sometimes, however, the component parts of an establishment had an effect on the name. As related earlier, until the Navy commissioned BYTOWN in Ottawa during the Second World War, all personnel in the city were borne on the books of the Halifax depot ship STADACONA. With the enormous expansion of NSHQ during this period, the Ottawa organization required its own depot ship and so BYTOWN commissioned in June 1941. Regulations of that time required such a stone frigate to have a nominal vessel actually afloat. In the case of BYTOWN, it seems this requirement was not fulfilled until October when *Oracle* was renamed and became the naval reserve depot ship, HMCS BYTOWN. The naval reserve part of this title seems misleading for the name BYTOWN is usually associated only with NDHQ. An explanation is required.

As mentioned earlier, the requirement for an actual vessel for each shore establishment had been legislated out of existence in August 1941. From her first commissioning, however, BYTOWN included the Ottawa reserve division. Thus the good ship *Oracle*, renamed BYTOWN, became the depot ship for a naval reserve division, NSHQ and other Ottawa units. Like other reserve divisions, the Ottawa division commissioned one month later under the name CARLETON. Both ships, however, continued to share the same Slater Street site.

With the move of BYTOWN to Cartier Square in May 1942, CARLETON paid off and her personnel once again found themselves on the books of BYTOWN. Among others, Cdr HN Lay (DOD, NSHQ, and the CO of BYTOWN) felt this combined organization was "extremely impractical and dangerous," especially in view of the proposed move of the reserves to a new site at Dow's Lake.[134] On 23 Nov 1942, therefore, BYTOWN paid off but recommissioned immediately as the depot ship for NDHQ. On the same day, CARLETON commissioned as a separate reserve division, and the motor yacht HC 128 became the NSHQ depot ship.[135]

About the same time, the name BYTOWN also had an association with the WRCNS at Galt, Ontario. The establishment there became BYTOWN II, the name being promulgated in Naval Orders.[136] The *Navy Lists* of the period, however, show this base as a WRCNS Training Establishment on a par with other WRCNS establishments in Ottawa and elsewhere, and not commissioned.

Early in 1943, the Director of Wren Services, Chief Officer D. Isherwood, suggested that the Galt establishment should first be commissioned, and second, bear a name associated with its location. The choice of both the WRCNS and the town was CONESTOGA, a name which had been brought to the Galt area by the

Mennonites around 1800 and which in 1942, was considered "a link between Canada's courageous present and her pioneer past."[137]

Several writers, among them Tucker,[138] imply that the name Conestoga had been associated with the establishment at Galt from the very beginning but in fact the name did not arrive until June 1943. The first WRCNS course commenced in Ottawa in August 1942 and the second course started in Galt on 15 October. Second Officer Isabel Macneil, the training officer, had opened the base earlier in the month. The establishment commissioned as CONESTOGA in June 1943, some eight months after its initial opening, under the command of First Officer (later Cdr) Macneil, and paid off in March 1945. For the first few months of their existence, WRCNS used WRNS ranks. Thus a chief officer was equivalent to a commander, a first officer to a lieutenant commander, a second officer to a lieutenant, a third officer to a sublieutenant.

In 1942, the naval board contemplated moving CORNWALLIS away from Halifax. Among the sites considered were Dartmouth, Shelburne, St. Andrews (NB), La Have and Mahone Bay, as well as Deep Brook. When the latter location was chosen, the Department of Mines & Resources wanted the base called the Annapolis Naval Academy! This was rejected by the naval board first because it wasn't an academy, and second because of possible confusion with the USN Academy, Annapolis, Maryland.[139]

In 1944, the naval staff recommended that a separate sea training command be organized at Bermuda and proposed taking over the RN base, HMS MALABAR, which was located on Ireland Island. The Admiralty approved this proposal but a subsequent decision saw the base located at the opposite end of Bermuda. The list of suggested names for this base consisted of Preceptor, Rainbow, St George, Saunders and Somers. Personnel in Bermuda suggested the name for the base, SOMERS ILES.[140]

The dropping of two atomic bombs in August 1945 terminated the war in the Pacific and precluded the proposed RCN base in Sydney. By that date, however, names had not even been considered.[141]

Finally, there were several shore establishments that were not commissioned. The ones known to this writer were located at Mulgrave, Port Hawkesbury, and Louisburg in Nova Scotia, and Botwood, Corner Brook, Wabana and Harbour Grace in Newfoundland. Mulgrave once had a commissioned establishment that paid off on an unknown date, probably in 1942.

Second World War: Reserve Divisions

The first attempt to devise names for the divisions occurred in the spring of 1941. DNP prepared a list of names based on the earliest warships built in Canada, most of which were constructed on the Great Lakes. When these were presented to the minister, he agreed that the names for those divisions near the Great Lakes were satisfactory but for others and especially those in the Maritimes, he directed that names having some local historical significance be used. Two months later, after a second meeting had produced no progress, MND directed that the matter be given to the naval historian.[142]

The names for the initial reserve divisions were selected from a list compiled by the naval historian and forwarded to the naval council in the summer of 1941. In this report, N Hist stated:

> It is fully realized that the names chosen at this time will probably be permanent ones, and that a suitable and worthy name will be a valuable asset to the RCNVR Division concerned.[143]

The names suggested by the naval historian were based on four considerations:
1. The name is that of a formerly existing ship.
2. The name, as such, would seem to be convenient and suitable, and is not included in the current British or Dominions' *Navy Lists*.
3. The ship, in the great majority of cases, was connected with, and exercised an influence upon the general area in which the Division lies.
4. A distinguished and important ship has been chosen whenever possible.[144]

There followed a list of eighteen cities. Eleven cities had only one choice of name, the rest two. One of the cities listed, however, was Cartier and the name recommended for the division was Emerillon. *Emerillon* was one of Cartier's vessels but the reference to the "city" of Cartier is not known. The name Cartier was used for one of the divisions in Montréal but the origin of the name is not known.

Many of the names chosen are the well known ones of today, with a few exceptions. Originally, the French speaking division in Montréal was named CARTIER, the English speaking division MONTREAL. Eventually, both divisions became DONNACONA. (For the disappearance of these names, see the list of names.) MNS accepted neither the name Lady Prevost nor Little Belt for London, Ontario, even though the naval historian had written of Little Belt: "The name is a very good one, and would cease to annoy the officers and ratings after the first week."[145] She became PREVOST instead. MNS did not consider Royal George to be suitable for Toronto; nor Calgarian acceptable for Calgary; nor Churchill or Pioneer acceptable for Regina.

The naval historian had noted that should any of the names fail to prove satisfactory, then others could be provided but in that case, "names other than those of actual ships would have to be used."[146]

Some twenty years later, the naval historian noted that the list was revised in a form not now available and further, that MND approved this new list on 29 September 1941 with the exception of those names for Hamilton, Calgary and Regina "to which further consideration is to be given."[147]

It was not until mid October that the names for the divisions in the last three cities were finally approved: Brant, Tecumseh, and Queen. But somewhere between then and 1 Nov 1941, the name Brant became STAR. Surviving documents, however, fail to provide either a date or a reason.[148]

It is known that the divisions in both Toronto and London were named after vessels, as were the divisions in Hamilton and Calgary. Two of the postwar divisions, CARIBOU and CHATHAM were also named for vessels. The rest of this fascinating documentation is, unfortunately, missing and as a result documentary evidence of the origin of the names for these six reserve divisions is presently unknown or at best uncertain: CARTIER, DONNACONA, HALIGONIAN, MALAHAT, QUEEN and SCOTIAN.

The documentation on these names is scarce. In the RCN magazine *The Crowsnest*, the "word" Malahat is stated as being derived from the name of a Coast Salish First Nations village on Vancouver Island. Nothing however, is mentioned of the "name."[149] In another article, it was stated that the name Queen is simply the English translation of the name of the city in which it is located, Regina.[150] Finally, because of the problems of finding a suitable replacement name for the reserve division in Montréal, MONTREAL, it is possible that the division took the name Donnacona from the First Nations chief who met Cartier. This would be logical because of the name of the other Montréal division, CARTIER, and DONNACONA's badge, the main device of which consists of two hands, one native, one white.

The lack of documentary evidence, however, has led to the source of these names being listed as "probably from" rather than being more definite. Addresses for the reserve divisions given with each vessel in the main list are correct but not necessarily complete. Further, records consulted varied as to the actual dates of moves thus the dates provided should not be considered exact.

Postwar Names: 1946–1985

For this period, the sources of ships' names can be categorized as follows:

1. vessels from other navies which retained their original names, e.g. MAGNIFICENT and U889;

2. former RCMP, DOT and RCAF vessels, taken over by the Navy, and which retained their original names, e.g. FORT STEELE, RALLY and WOOD-COCK;

3. original names for new construction, taken-over vessels, reserve divisions and radio stations, e.g. YUKON, SERVICE, CABOT and INU-VIK; and

4. repeated names for new construction, taken-over vessels, and reserve divisions, e.g. ASSINIBOINE, RAINBOW, and CARIBOU.

Retained Names

Unlike the previous wartime period, there are only six ships in the first category: CRESCENT, CRUSADER, MAGNIFICENT, WARRIOR, U190 and U889. The first two names have been discussed earlier. Although from two different classes, the two carriers WARRIOR and MAGNIFICENT, were only on loan and probably retained their names for that reason. Of interest is the fact that the badge for WARRIOR was designed by a Canadian naval officer[151] for RCN use and is now the badge used by HMS WARRIOR, a Headquarters unit located near the northwestern outskirts of London, England.

The wartime idea of having two carriers in the Navy was reconsidered in the 1950s. With BONAVENTURE due to commission, serious consideration was given to the retention of MAGNIFICENT and the paying off of QUEBEC.[152] For reasons not discovered, MAGNIFICENT was not retained.

The two German U-Boats, U190 and U889, were not renamed when commissioned into the RCN. In 1941, the RN had captured a German submarine, renamed her HMS GRAPH and sent her back to sea where she acquired three Battle Honours. At the end of the war, the RN took over a German destroyer, Z-38, which they renamed HMS NONSUCH. By the Potsdam agreement, however, all surrendered U-boats were to be destroyed and to our Soviet allies, it would have appeared suspicious if the boats had been renamed. Further, as trophies of war, their original designators were preferable.[153]

After the war and to assist the RCN with A/S exercises, the RN established the Sixth Submarine Squadron in Halifax and kept it supplied with A class submarines. At one time, there was a proposal to establish an RN support base named HMS WOLFE. Since this name would have conflicted with one of the Fairmiles, NSHQ suggested the name Shannon but the records do not indicate the final result.[154]

Taken-Over Names

In the second category, the Navy has been most reluctant to rename vessels taken over from other government departments. Thus vessels like FORT STEELE have retained their original names. Such a process did not work in reverse. On transfer to the RCMP in the 1950s, five Bangors—BROCKVILLE, MELVILLE, NORANDA, TRANSCONA and TROIS RIVIERES—were all renamed becoming *Macleod*, *Cygnus*, *Irvine*, *French* and *MacBrien* respectively. Similarly, when BLUE HERON was given to the RCMP in 1956 she was renamed *Victoria*. But LABRADOR, on loan to DOT, retained her name.

Original and Repeated Names: Aircraft Carrier

By 1952, the search for a name for the new aircraft carrier was underway. Both the names of First Nations Chieftains (Crowfoot, Donnacona, Maquinna, Pontiac, Poundmaker, Tecumseh and Thayendanega) and famous explorers (such as Baffin, Brulé, Cabot, Hudson, LaSalle, Thompson & Vancouver) were considered.[155] CNS himself, VAdm E.R. Mainguy, picked the name Bonaventure apparently after a suggestion by a supply officer whose hobby was bird watching. The idea that Bonaventure Island, like the carrier, was a sanctuary for sea birds appealed to CNS. Further, the name was chosen as a "compliment to the great French speaking and early Canadian Explorer-seamen on whose charts this island is shown."[156]

Original and Repeated Names: Cruisers

The only new name for a cruiser occurred with the renaming of the UGANDA. As related earlier, the name Québec was not available until 1946. A suggestion had been put forward as early as 1945 to change the name of UGANDA to QUEBEC but such a move had to await events. The exact date of renaming is not recorded but it is thought to have taken place immediately upon the paying off of the UGANDA in August 1947. In fact, one of the notes in her file states that the UGANDA "paid off 1 August (after commissioning as the QUEBEC)."[157] It is known that the cruiser was referred to as the QUEBEC as early as 1948 even though at her recommissioning in 1952, there was an official renaming ceremony.[158]

Original and Repeated Names: Destroyers, Tribal Class

As related in the Second World War section, the last four Tribals were named MICMAC, NOOTKA, CAYUGA and ATHABASKAN.

The Improved Restigouche (IRE) class GATINEAU in 1971. (CF ET-71-672.)

Destroyers: St. Laurent, Restigouche, Mackenzie and Annapolis Classes

If not actually sister ships, the vessels in these four classes are definitely cousins and for the purposes of names, can be treated as one large group. Leaning heavily on destroyer names from the Second World War, these twenty vessels all took the names of rivers. The decision to employ river names for this class was taken as early as 1950 and the proposal included the name Mackenzie.[159] The purpose of using river names was originally to perpetuate the names of Second World War vessels which is probably why the name Mackenzie, not employed in the war, took so long to be used in this period.[160]

Very little documentation could be located on the St Laurent class itself but all seven names were borne by Second World War destroyers. In February 1953, CNS proposed seven names to MND for the next group, the Restigouche class.[161] As already related in Chapter 4, the cabinet kept this list in turmoil and it was not until some four months later that the matter was settled and the seven names were finally promulgated in August.

Following the St Laurent and Restigouche classes, DNPO considered the names for the next seven vessels, but only six were authorized and built. A DNPO paper proposed "that the same type of name be used for any succeeding new construction escorts which retain the basic St Laurent characteristics."[162] This paper noted the geographical representation of the previous two classes and proposed eight names be used as a basis for selection:

River	Province	River	Province
Saskatchewan	SK	St. Clair	ON
Qu'Appelle	SK	Hamilton	NF
MacKenzie [sic]	NWT	Haldimand	PE
St. Francis	QC	Annapolis	NS[163]

The second IROQUOIS in 1972. (CF PCN 72-253. KM Coll.)

The naval staff concurred with the proposal to use river names but only chose two names—Mackenzie and Saskatchewan—at that time. By 1957, the naval board had recommended and CNS had approved the names Qu'Appelle and Yukon for the third and fourth ships of this class.[164] That brought two new river names into the fleet at the expense of two historic names.

When it came time to choose the fifth and sixth names of what was then still the Mackenzie class, ACNS(P) suggested the names Annapolis and Hamilton but the government's Policy and Projects Coordinating Committee (PPCC) felt that the Newfoundland river was not well known and might be mistaken for the city of Hamilton so the recommended names were Annapolis and Rideau. The naval board agreed on the first name "but considered that the name Rideau was in such general use that a ship of that name would not clearly be associated with the river. As an alternative Ontario river, the name Nipigon was considered," and accepted.[165] These two ships became the Annapolis class. Interestingly, Nipigon had a lineage whereas Rideau did not.

Destroyers: Iroquois Class

About 1963, the CNS (VAdm H.S. Rayner) decided to employ tribal names for the General Purpose Frigates, some seven of which were requested.[166] The class, however, did not receive approval and was cancelled.

When the 280 class was proposed, the list of possible names included such diverse subjects as provinces, animals, explorers, battles, headlands, Arctic islands and floral emblems. For a time, city names were the front runner but as no consensus could be formed, Cmdre H.A. Porter (DGMF) appointed a committee— consisting of Cdr J. Rodocanachi, Lcdr AP Campbell and Lcdr I Webster—to make recommendations. Charged with suggesting distinctive Canadian names that incorporated geographical representation, ethnic heritage, maritime association and appropriateness, the committee's unanimous choice was tribal names. Assuming, correctly as it turned out, that HAIDA would continue as a museum and that the second ATHABASKAN would be shortly paid off, the committee recommended the names Huron, Iroquois, Sioux and Athabaskan. Cmdre Porter apparently objected to Sioux as not being distinctively Canadian and on reflection, the committee chose Algonquin. As was pointed out, however, Iroquois could be objected to on the same grounds as Sioux. Further, the name Algonquin holds fewer Battle Honours than do the other four names. Regardless, Sioux was not on the list sent to MND for his approval in late November 1967.[167]

Frigates: Vancouver Class

This class actually made it to the drawing board and received a class name. Following the precedent set by the River class frigates in the Second World War, it seems they would have been named for large cities but they were cancelled in 1955.

Frigates: General Purpose (GPF)

These 270 class frigates were first intended to be named for explorers but the naval board felt that such names were already widely commemorated and so opted to use the names of towns and cities like the then current Prestonian class.[168] VCNS suggested using tribal names but CNS (VAdm H.G. DeWolf) squashed that idea by saying "I think the 'Tribal' (names) should be given a rest. I like the explorers."[169] By 1964, however, another CNS (VAdm H.S. Rayner) decided to use the tribal names but the class was cancelled by the new MND, Paul Hellyer.

Frigates: Prestonian Class

Shortly after the Second World War, most of the frigates were sold but twenty-one were eventually reacquired and returned to the *Navy List*. Of these, three (the ST CATHARINES, ST STEPHEN and STONE TOWN) were eventually loaned to DOT and served out their days as weather ships on Station Papa off the west coast. Although the class was renamed from River to Prestonian, the ships kept their names.

The second TORONTO in 1994. (CF IMC 94-9-32. NPA)

Patrol Frigates: Halifax Class

After the Iroquois class DDHs commissioned in the late 1960s and early 1970s, only one major vessel was acquired by the Navy up to 1985, CORMORANT. The next vessel was the first of the frigates, the project for acquiring them being known as CPF, the Canadian Patrol Frigate project. After spending considerable time doing trials, the lead ship HALIFAX commissioned in 1991. The search for names for these vessels commenced as early as 1979. In a memo, DMOPR suggested that names for these vessels should have a pleasing sound; be appropriate to the ship type; be easy to pronounce; and not be liable to ridicule.[170]

Further, explorer names were ruled out as an option for the following reasons: it is difficult and controversial to arrange explorers in some order of priority; and DOT has already established the precedent of naming its vessels after persons, among them explorers.[171]

In the late 1950s, the names of explorers had been suggested for the general purpose frigates but the naval board concluded that such names were already commemorated enough by rivers, lakes, towns, etc. But the main thrust of DMOPR's memo lies in this statement:

> If these ships are to be frigates and assigned frigate pennant numbers [in the 300 series], why not follow our own historical precedent...and rejuvenate our old frigate names?[172]

A letter followed this memo from the Commander Maritime Command to CMDO suggesting that the eighteen names required—for three classes of six each—could be taken from the list of cities in which reserve divisions now exist.[173] Included was a list of the present eighteen divisions. But some fourteen months later, the final list of names had not been arrived at and DGMDO wrote a memo asking for consideration to be given to the use of old destroyer names such as those of rivers.[174] Several other senior officers put pen to paper to champion the names of their choice but early in 1982, the list sent to the minister read: Halifax, Calgary, Vancouver, Ville de Québec, Toronto, Regina. And the names were announced by CMDO early in April of that year.[175] The names were chosen for three reasons: they represented the larger cities with the selection balanced among the provinces, and the names commemorated previous vessels whose achievements were notable.[176] No one listed criteria to qualify the term "notable" and no mention was made of Battle Honours. The name Ville de Québec is the only alternative name to be used in the postwar era.

Patrol Frigates: Montréal Class

In mid 1985, MND approved six names for the second class of patrol frigates. In the original list sent forward by the naval board in 1981, Esquimalt was the name recommended for number 341. In the first announcement, the name Esquimalt was in the English section of CFSO 40-85 while the name Ottawa was in the French section. This was corrected in CFSO 55/85.

According to Adm J. Anderson, when the list had reached the CDS, Gen Theriault, he raised the question of why the city of Ottawa—the nation's capital— had been excluded. The list was then changed to delete Esquimalt and add Ottawa before being sent on to MND. This is one of the few instances in history where a vessel still in commission—the third OTTAWA—has had her successor in name announced. It is also the only known instance of an Canadian army officer picking a name for a naval vessel.

The other names were Charlottetown, Fredericton, Montréal, St John's and Winnipeg. All these names but St John's have been employed before.

Originally, this class was to be a lengthened version of the Halifax class. Since these six ships were built to the same specifications, however, early in 1991 NDHQ announced that they would form part of the Halifax class.[177]

Minesweepers: Bay Class

The 1950s saw a return to the use of geographical names associated with shore-lines—such as bays, sounds, inlets, etc.—for the minesweepers of the appropriately named Bay class.[178] Some of the names employed (Fortune, Resolute and Trinity) were used for the first time while others (Gaspé, Thunder and Ungava) were names used before for earlier minesweepers. Other names considered were Belle Isle, Canso and Chantry. Normally, the type of geographical feature was not employed in the name but there was one exception: JAMES BAY. Why she was singled out is not known. Had she been named simply James, she would have inherited four Battle Honours, all British, as the name dates from 1222.

Shortly after being placed in commission, six vessels of this class were given to the French Navy. Six new construction vessels bearing the same names but not the same pennant numbers replaced them.[179] In 1958, four vessels of this class were also given to Turkey.[180]

Minesweepers: Kingston Class

Intended to be named for harbours, instead the twelve vessels of this class were named for a curious mixture of large and small communities—from populations varying between 7,000 and 600,000—and thus lacked a common thread to their names. KINGSTON was lead ship.

Minesweeper: Auxiliaries

Former civilian vessels, ANTICOSTI and MORESBY were named for islands, although CFAO 36-7 then in effect clearly stated that aircraft carriers are usually named for islands.

Escort Maintenance Ships: Cape Class

Originally constructed as Fort class cargo vessels, both served in the RN and were named for headlands. On coming to the RCN, they were given the names of capes, initial suggestions being Cape Beale and Cape Scott. Probably for reasons of better geographical representation—both proposed capes are on Vancouver Island—the minister, the Honourable Brooke Claxton, directed that the name Cape Breton be used in lieu of Cape Beale, thus missing a chance to revive a name from the Fishermen's Reserve.

Operational Support Ships: Provider and Protecteur Class

The naval board agreed in late 1959 that support ships should be named for capes and they had further agreed that tanker supply ships or other specialized support ships could perpetuate the names borne by earlier RCN ships, such as Aurora and Rainbow.[181] Shortly thereafter, DNPO recommended the name Rainbow be used but VCNS wanted this name retained for the next submarine. Further, VCNS recommended the names Provider, Preserver and Protector for the "tankers," as these vessels were then termed. CNS, on the other hand, wished to employ the names of capes. But in late 1960, for the first vessel the naval board settled on the name Provider, going back to the Fairmile depot ship of the Second World War for the name.[182]

A few years later, when the next two support ships required names, the naval historian raised the idea of going back to cape names. In a submission, he attached a list of forty-seven such names noting that his choices were Cape Tormentine and Cap d'Espoir.[183] In this memo, he also included information on the names Distributor and Investigator.

The idea of employing a French name seems to have originated with Captain Fotheringham.[184] Although he was preoccupied with the problems of the impending unification of the three services, much thought and many words went into the selection of the names Protecteur and Preserver. It is not clear from the records just who made the actual decision on their use but the names were recommended by DCOps in April 1966 and approved by the minister early that May.[185] The name Protecteur was the French version of the name for the Second World War depot ship. The English version of this name, Protector, first entered the Navy as an ex RCMP patrol craft and the name was later used for the base at Sydney, NS, and still later as the name for the RCSC training establishment at Point Edward, NS.

The third support ship took her name from the other Fairmile depot ship in the Second World War, PRESERVER, thus giving cohesion to the names by having each commence with the letter P.

In 1970 after PROTECTEUR commissioned in Halifax and PROVIDER transferred to the west coast, PRESERVER was delayed at the builders. PROTECTEUR then had problems with her shaft bearings, necessitating a return to her builder in late 1969. An operational support ship was required on the east coast so the about-to-be paid off BONAVENTURE was given a lease on life through to the spring of 1970 and became a support ship, minus her aircraft and air complement. It was from this service that the Bonnie acquired her other nickname, Pretender.

Icebreaker: Wind Class

The initial discussions on the name for the icebreaker, or Arctic patrol craft, saw a decision deferred on employing the name Hudson Bay.[186] Some fifteen months later, the majority of the naval staff favoured the name Labrador and CNS (VAdm H.T. Grant) approved their recommendation to use that name.[187] The probable cause of the change was the ease with which the name Hudson Bay could have been mistaken for a Bay class minesweeper.

While under the command of Capt T.C. Pullen, all the personnel and much of the equipment on board the LABRADOR were given the names of cartoon characters of the day. The CO was known as Top Hat and one of the ship's boats became known as Pogo after Walt Kelly's lovable possum. As POGO, this vessel later became a tender to CARLETON.

The Arctic patrol ship LABRADOR, December 1955. She displays her badge below her bridge. (RCN LAB 148. FDN Coll.)

Hydrofoil

When the hydrofoil was under construction in the 1960s, no one could tell if this vessel was to be a single ship or the forerunner of a large family. For that reason, the naval historian suggested bird names even though such names were already in use for the patrol boats. He suggested the names Kingfisher, Storm Petrel, Black Skimmer or Thunderbird.[188] The name Thunderbird also was suggested by DCOPR but DOPS noted that "the Ford Motor Company have pre-empted us. Please try again."[189] The name Peregrine was suggested—it was a bird name and had historical connections but DGMF settled the issue: "the logical name for the first hydrofoil is BRAS D'OR"[190] after the Cape Breton lakes where Alexander Graham Bell and Casey Baldwin conducted their hydrofoil experiments. The VCDS concurred with this suggestion but because DRB's prototype of the hydrofoil had the same name, VCDS sought and received their permission to use the name Bras d'Or.[191]

Diving Support Vessel

The first diving support vessel was the old minesweeper GRANBY. The frigate VICTORIAVILLE was renamed and replaced her, and this simple change led to two ministerial inquires. Apparently the two towns are rivals and the Navy had to explain to Victoriaville the reason behind the change.[192] When it came time to replace her, a vessel capable of going to sea was required and an Italian vessel was purchased. She was renamed CORMORANT because Cormorants "are excellent divers, at home in both salt and fresh water, found in both the MAR-LAND [sic] and MARPAC areas and [are] known for their wariness and alertness to danger."[193]

Patrol Craft: Bird Class

Early in the 1950s, NSHQ gave consideration to construction of seaward defence patrol craft. It was estimated that in wartime some ninety vessels of this type would be required and it was further considered that there were "an adequate number of Canadian birds to choose from" in order to find the ninety names.[194] The initial plan called for eight—Loon, Cormorant, Blue Heron, Mallard, Arctic Tern, Sandpiper, Herring Gull and Kingfisher. The last four were cancelled in 1956.

Fairmile: Animal Names

At the same time as the naval board decided on bird names for patrol craft, the Second World War Fairmiles which up to this point had always been known by numbers, were given animal names.[195] Thus were revived the names of some of the armed yachts of the Second World War—BEAVER, COUGAR, ELK, etc.

Submarines

When the time came in 1960 to discuss the name for the first Canadian-owned submarine in this period, VCNS felt that notwithstanding the earlier agreement on the use of Inuit names, it would be more suitable to employ the names of native fish such as Steelhead, Rainbow, Pike or Chinook, among others. CNS (VAdm H.G. De Wolf) agreed and selected the name Rainbow but VCNS suggested Coho or Tyee instead. CNS had the last word: "I favour Grilse—which is in keeping with USN system and has RCN background."[196]

Late in 1960, while discussing names for the new supply ships, VCNS recommended that the name Rainbow be saved for the next submarine and exactly eight years later, it was so used.

Submarines: O Class

As related earlier in Chapter 4, the naval board had decided as early as 1959 to name new construction submarines using Inuit names. Barely five years later, with the impending purchase of three British-built Oberon class submarines, CNS (VAdm H.S. Rayner) wanted to employ names that started with the letter O. The naval historian responded to a request for O names with the information that none of the Inuit names started with an O and therefore he suggested using place names like Oak Bay, or names from previous vessels such as Orillia or Otter. Lastly, he suggested the possibility of using names having First Nations tribal backgrounds such as Odanak, Ojibwa, Okanagan, Oneida, Onondaga, or Owikeno.[197] A few days later, the naval historian added sixteen O names of First Nations bands as opposed to the tribal names suggested earlier.[198]

Little progress was made in the selection of names until DG Ships noted in November 1963 that Chatham dockyard was due to launch ONYX on 29 February 1964, no Canadian name had been allocated, and perhaps she should retain her original name. On his own, DG Ships had asked a gem shop to list the names of common minerals that began with the letter O. These he suggested as possible names for the two sister boats of ONYX.

When CNS proposed retaining the name Onyx but using community or Inuit names for the later two vessels, MND stated that "the name ONYX doesn't inspire me! Couldn't you get a Canadian name for the first one as well?"[199]

In the ensuing discussion, VCNS suggested using the tribal names and picked Okanagan, Ojibwa and Onondaga. CNS agreed and informed MND that the first submarine would be called Ojibwa. Although all three had a common thread, such tribal names were already in use and all three were new names without heritage.

Submarines: Victoria Class

With the O class boats more than ready for replacement, the government announced their intention to purchase four relatively new British boats that had been paid off by the RN. One class name considered but later rejected was Resolute. Named for four port cities that each boat can actually visit, these boats will commission in 2000/01.

Gate Vessels: Porte Class

With all the lead time available in peacetime, rushed decisions on names should not occur. But in November 1950, with only fourteen days remaining until the launching of the first gate vessel, names had still not been assigned. The five names were quickly approved but an unknown staff officer wrote on the minutes: "Someone should check names of other gates and not limit our choice to the five above."[200] Notwithstanding this dissension, the selection of names was most appropriate, except perhaps for the length of some of the names.

Research Vessels

With the requirement for purpose-built research vessels to replace or at least augment the various vessels converted to this task, came a requirement for specific names. The naval historian first suggested the names Enterprise or Investigator. Later, he suggested using the names of flowers, particularly those of the flower-named corvettes from the Second World War. Dr. Zimmerman, the chairman of the Defence Research Board (DRB), however, picked the name selected—Endeavour.[201] Senior naval staff, however, felt that the name should honour a scientist like Banting, or an explorer like Cook, and on several occasions the chairman of DRB was asked to reconsider his choice. He would not and did not.

No records could be located on the selection of the name Quest, the name of the second research vessel, but in all likelihood this functional name was also picked by the chairman of DRB.

Training Ketch

The ORIOLE, one of the best known naval vessels on the west coast, started her naval career as an RCSC training vessel on Lake Ontario. At that time her name was *Oriole IV*. In 1950 and again in 1952, the Navy chartered her as ORIOLE IV from the Navy League. In July 1954 she became ORIOLE and in 1957 she was purchased by the RCN.

Shortly after she lost the "IV," a senior naval officer wrote suggesting her name be changed to Rainbow for the reason that the name Oriole lacked both appeal and imagination. But both CNP and DNPO felt the name should be kept and that the name Rainbow be retained for a more suitable ship.[202]

Small Craft: Saint Class Tugs

The idea for naming these three vessels after Canadian saints originated with Commodore R. Baker in 1952. The chaplain of the fleet suggested the names of seven Canadian martyrs amongst other names, and DNPO, worried about the length of the full names, recommended that only the first name be used. Further, he chose the names for these vessels: ST ANTHONY, ST CHARLES, and ST JOHN.[204]

Small Craft: Glen and Ville Class Tugs

In the 1960s and 70s some of the Ville and Glen class tugs were replaced with vessels of new design and construction but retaining old names. See for example, the entries for GLENBROOK and MERRICKVILLE.

Small Craft: Miscellaneous

When it came time in 1948 to rename the newly acquired RCASC vessel *General Schmidlin*, the staff officer operations in NSHQ recommended she be given "a name more in keeping with naval auxiliary vessels of the same [sic] class, such as" Oakwood. He suggested the name Dogwood but the naval staff opted for Cedarwood.[205] In the early 1950s, an USN minesweeper was acquired and like her cousins she was given the name of a bay. Instead of the historic name of Nanoose, however, the new name Cordova was selected.

In 1955, there was a requirement to produce a name for a second mine planter and the decision to name her BLUETHROAT was taken solely to identify her with a ship of similar size and function, WHITETHROAT.

The forty-first anniversary of the founding of the RCAF saw the Navy take over various Air Force vessels which were being used as crash rescue boats for air stations located near large bodies of water. The RCAF had given these small craft bird names and these were retained. The navy also retained this naming practice for new vessels like BLACK DUCK and ALBATROSS when completing their acceptance trials in the spring of 1985.

In 1978 the reserve divisions acquired various small craft as tenders. Some vessels were renamed. ADAMSVILLE, for instance, became BURRARD. Others like STANDOFF and YOUVILLE retained their original names. Still others like YMU 116 did not possess a name but after an eloquent plea by Cdr(R) K.B. Towers, the CO of HUNTER, the division to which she was attached, she became CROSS-BOW, after the main device in HUNTER's badge.[206]

For almost twenty years reserve divisions had a collection of tenders which had no pattern to their names, a point noted in 1979 by the then Commander of Maritime Command, VAdm A.L. Collier. The admiral recommended to NDHQ that future tenders for these divisions should receive an appropriate series of names.[207]

In 1990 four torpedo recovery vessels were under construction when their names came up for consideration by the Ships' Names Committee. It was proposed that the names all start with one letter and that the names of smaller centres be employed. Because these four vessels were to be based on the west coast at

Nanoose, the committee decided that using only west coast names was suitable. Of several suggestions, four S names were chosen: SECHELT, SIKANNI, SOOKE, and STIKINE. Half a decade later with the paying off of CORMORANT without replacement and the retirement of YDT 8 and 9, a decision was made to convert two of the S class to yard diving tenders. SECHELT and SOOKE were modified in 1996/97 and transferred to the east coast.

Postwar: Requested Names

Only two instances could be located of people or municipalities requesting a name be used for a warship. When the city of Edmonton was not included in the names used for the Halifax class frigates, the mayor Laurence Decore—a former naval reserve officer—wrote to complain and ask that the name of his city be given consideration in the future. And as noted under the Victoria class, the Naval Officers' Association in Windsor wrote requesting the name of their city be used for a submarine. As shown in the Second World War, letter writers generally have an impact out of all proportion to their numbers.

Postwar: Changes in Names

In the fall of 1945, ACNS directed that consideration be given to the renaming of the postwar fleet. This proposal, outlined in Chapter 4, would have affected every ship in the fleet except ONTARIO and the Tribals. For reasons not written down, the only part of this proposal to be accepted was the change of UGANDA to QUEBEC circa 1948.

In 1947, the RCN decided to reinstate reserve divisions in Victoria and Halifax but instead of bringing back the original name, the Halifax Division was given the name SCOTIAN. Reasons were not recorded.[208]

ORIOLE IV, VICTORIAVILLE and some CFAVs were also renamed in this period. Their stories are told elsewhere in this book.

The last example is another proposal that was made but never carried out. In 1950, FOAC requested that the name of the frigate LA HULLOISE be changed to that of her namesake city, Hull. No reason was stated for this proposal and the naval board did not accept the idea.[209]

Postwar: Establishments

If any pattern can be seen for naming shore establishments in this period, it is the use of former ships' names. Perhaps the most significant acquisition was SHEAR-WATER. This base started life as an RCAF station to which an RNAS unit was added in September 1939. This unit commissioned as HMS SEABORN in

December 1943, paid off in January 1946 and its buildings and equipment were taken over by the RCN and known as the RCN Air Section Dartmouth.[210] A name was chosen for the air section as a result of COAC recommending "that a suitable ship's badge be approved" for this unit.[211] When approached, the head of the Ship's Badge Committee suggested that a badge could only be designed when based on a name, and this unit didn't have one. Further, he suggested the names of several sea birds for use as a name. In deciding on a ship's name for this base, the naval staff considered four different categories:

a. employ some local historical association such as Acadia;
b. use the name of a sea bird, a practice already in use by the RN and USN;
c. revive an old RCN name like Rainbow; or
d. adopt a name from Canadian aeronautical history such as McCurdy.[212]

Category b was not initially a front runner but "after considerable discussion Naval Staff agreed that 'SHEARWATER' was most appropriate,"[213] bringing in as it did elements of both category b and c. The establishment was finally commissioned under that name in December 1948.

A few months later, the name CORNWALLIS once again appeared in the *Navy List* as the base recommissioned. Similarly SHELBURNE, paid off in 1946, recommissioned in 1955. One year later, the commanding officer naval divisions, co-located in Hamilton with STAR, commissioned as PATRIOT, named after the former destroyer.

Apparently, at one point in 1946 the naval staff even considered paying off BYTOWN but it was pointed out that a large number of personnel were borne on her books: HQ staff, staff in Washington, DC and staff of four W/T stations—Churchill, Gloucester, Chelsea and Ottawa. So BYTOWN remained in commission.[214]

The two naval establishments in other countries were also placed in commission in the late 1940s. The one in London resumed the name of her wartime predecessor, NIOBE, while the one in Washington, DC, took her name from HMS NIAGARA, a vessel that had served on the Great Lakes in the 1830s. The design of the badge however, seems to imply some connection to the Niagara River. The naval staff had proposed the names Champlain, Patrician, Patriot and Rainbow[215] but the name Niagara came from the RCN staff in Washington.

With the entry of Newfoundland into Confederation in 1949, the RCN re-established a presence there. Within two years, difficulties with additional accounting duties combined with the fact that all pay accounts were held in STADACONA, led to the commissioning of AVALON in 1951 as the base in St John's.

Only one other base was commissioned in this period and that was NIOBE II. She was established in Belfast, Northern Ireland, to assist in the commissioning of the BONAVENTURE.

After the unification of the armed forces in 1968, all surviving establishments became either a CF base or part of a CF base. With the exception of CORNWALLIS and SHELBURNE, all lost their names. See below.

In 1994, plans were underway to close CFS Shelburne, formerly HMCS SHELBURNE, and to construct a new unit within CFB Halifax. The intention was to name the new Integrated Undersea Surveillance System (IUSS) Centre, HMCS TRINITY [sic]. RAdm G. Garnett, Commander of MarLant, gave his blessing to this proposal.[216] The request bounced around NDHQ before DMTH replied that "the need to commission naval shore establishments ceased upon unification" and the IUSS Centre did not fit the specific circumstances of the naval reserve divisions. There was, however, no objection to the centre including the name Trinity in its title, but the centre could neither be commissioned nor be awarded the title HMCS.[217] Therefore, like NOTC Venture in Esquimalt, the centre was called CF Integrated Undersea Surveillance Centre Trinity.

Postwar: Reserve Divisions

During the war, the reserve divisions across the land did a yeoman job of recruiting and giving basic seamanship training to tens of thousands of personnel. The Japanese surrender was less than two months old when the commanding officer naval divisions (COND) suggested that each division be renamed after the city in which it was located, if and when the vessel of that name paid off.[218] This idea was given short shrift by the naval staff and never implemented.

Both MALAHAT and HALIGONIAN paid off after the war only to recommission again in April 1947. But this time, the Halifax division took the name formerly employed by the Commodore Superintendent of the Dockyard, SCOTIAN.

In the same year, a division was established in Prince Rupert, CHATHAM, the name coming from the previous wartime establishment.

Shortly after Newfoundland became part of this country, a division was formed in St John's. Her name, CABOT, was apparently taken from an American vessel captured during the American Revolutionary War. Four years later, a division was formed at Corner Brook, CARIBOU. She took her name from a Newfoundland government ferry that was torpedoed and sunk during the Second World War.

COND moved to Hamilton in 1953 and his organization was commissioned as PATRIOT early in 1956. Although not a division as such, PATRIOT was the headquarters for all the divisions and housed COND and his staff. When paid off in 1966, the ship ceased to be but the organization moved to Ottawa and then to Halifax (South Street). In the process, it was renamed—Director of Naval Reserves (D Nav Res)—and became part of the staff of the maritime commander. Here it stayed until 25 July 1983, when the organization was moved to Québec City. The title COND is now used for the Senior Officer Naval Reserves and stands for Commander Naval Reserve Divisions. One of his staff is known as D Nav Res.

In 1964, five divisions paid off—CHATHAM, NONSUCH, PREVOST, QUEEN and QUEEN CHARLOTTE. Since CARIBOU paid off in 1958, only sixteen divisions remained across the country. In 1975, however, NONSUCH and QUEEN were recommissioned bringing the total back to eighteen.

In 1984, NDHQ proposed to establish new divisions in Québec at Chicoutimi, Rimouski and Trois-Riviéres. There were eight names proposed for these divisions: Cartier, Champlain, D'Iberville, Jonquière, Frontenac, Joliett, Vauquelin, and Vaudreuil.[219] Former ships had carried all but the last three names. Later, a new division was established at Sept-Iles. Thus CHAMPLAIN (Chicoutimi) and D'IBERVILLE (Rimouski) re-entered the list of commissioned ships, followed soon after by JOLIETT (Trois Riviéres, technically in Cap-de-la-Madeleine), not to be confused with a similar name, JOLIETTE, a frigate in the Second World War. All were the names of people, and thus did not match the historical ship names for other divisions.

Remembering their history, the city of Rimouski asked that RIMOUSKI be used but Capt(N) J Steele in Naval Reserve HQ pointed out that it was "not naval practice to name a Division after its host community."[220]

In February 1993, MND announced the pending formation of a new division in Salaberry-de-Valleyfield.[221] Ignoring the Second World War frigate VALLEYFIELD, the name chosen for the division was Salaberry, contrary to reasons given to the city of Rimouski just a few years before. NDHQ consulted on the name with MarCom and the city, but not with the now existing Ships' Names Committee. Although staff were posted in, Salaberry closed prior to being placed in commission.[222]

Postwar: Naval Radio Stations

A tender was originally a small vessel employed to attend to a larger vessel for duties such as ferrying personnel and stores, or for training. She was under the direct command of her parent ship but was not to be confused with the ship's boats—she was too big to hoist in. In later days, shore establishments had small craft attached to them as tenders. Further, some administrative units ashore were referred to as tenders. For example, the University Naval Training Divisions

The Fairmile MOOSE in the Rideau Canal, 1951. (RCN O-2023-3. KM Coll.)

(UNTDs) were tenders to a reserve division. In this case, the tenders were supported by the parent unit in much the same ways as their harbour-going counterparts were supported by a ship.

Basically, up to 1949, Naval Radio Stations (NRS) were tenders to parent establishments. When the NRS near Moncton, NB, was being reorganized in late 1949, it was pointed out that under the present regulations, the following difficulties could not be overcome:[223] all drafts and appointments had to be to STADACONA in Halifax; only limited powers of punishments could be delegated by the CO of STADACONA; and both the cash account and the pay records would have to be kept by STADACONA and this would cause more work than it would be worth.

Since no ship's name was required, there was no objection to commissioning Coverdale as "HMC Radio Station Coverdale."[224] CNS wrote to MND stating that due to increases in personnel, it was preferable to operate Coverdale, Gloucester and

Churchill as Fleet Establishments and requested permission to do so.[225] But only Coverdale and Gloucester were commissioned that year; Churchill had to wait.

The discussion on the establishment, organization and commissioning of NRS can be traced back to late 1944.[226] By 1947, Gloucester and Churchill were tenders to BYTOWN.

In the beginning some of the NRS were relatively small affairs. In December 1947, for example Coverdale, Aldergrove and Albro Lake were commanded by officers; a chief petty officer was in charge in Gloucester; and Montréal Circle in Prince Rupert had an operator-in-charge.[227]

As the size of a NRS grew, so too did the administrative problems caused by being a tender. In NSHQ, DS Div recommended that Coverdale should no longer require direct supervision from BYTOWN and that it be commissioned as Bytown II.[228] DGFA disagreed. He felt that the NRS should be kept clear of BYTOWN and if Coverdale must be commissioned, then it could be named Monkton [sic] or Coverdale, not Bytown II. Further, he recommended that a Central Command be set up to look after the NRS.[229] Ten days later DS Div recommended Coverdale be commissioned as an independent command and eventually this led to the events described above. With the commissioning of these NRS, the cap tally HMC RADIO STATION came into being.[230] In 1962, GLOUCESTER became the depot for all Radio Supplemental personnel.[231]

NRS MONTREAL CIRCLE, Prince Rupert, in June 1958. (FDN Coll.)

By 1955, COVERDALE, GLOUCESTER and ALDERGROVE were in commission as Fleet Establishments while the rest of the NRS were tenders: Albro Lake and Newport Corners were tenders to STADACONA, the rest were tenders to GLOUCESTER. It was at this time that DN Com requested that the commissioned NRS be upgraded to HMCS and the tenders be named "HMC NRS."

There is no record of a reply and early in 1956, DN Com repeated his request.[232] This led to naval board approval and on 1 Jul 1956 all NRS were redesignated in accordance with the wishes of DN Com.[233]

NRS took their names for the geographical location in which they were located. Generally, these were the names of the closest communities but in the case of ALDERGROVE, there was a suggestion to have her named Vancouver. In the case of GLOUCESTER, there was no local community and so she took the name of the township. Taking their names from the local community had a Second World War precedent in that the signal school in St Hyacinthe was called after the town in which it was located.

Only Prince Rupert had the honour of having two NRS: PORT EDWARD and MONTREAL CIRCLE. The former was named for the small community to the south of Prince Rupert in which the station was located. The latter took its name from a street in Prince Rupert that encircles the water tower. This NRS was located in a former RCN Second World War building on that street. Still standing in 1985, this building is now known as Applethwaite Hall.[234]

The last NRS was to be named Blandford. This was the replacement for ALBRO LAKE. Under construction when unification occurred, Blandford's name was changed and she was put in service as CFS Mill Cove. A rather striking badge had already been designed for Blandford whose name came from the peninsula since there was no community nearby.

RCSC Establishments

In 1956, in order to simplify a division of responsibility for sea cadet camps, NSHQ decided to commission the two camps at Comox and Point Edward as Fleet Establishments for the duration of each summer.[235] Several names were considered, among them Aurora and Protector. DNPO felt that the name Aurora is "frequently used by the Royal Navy, and has no particular Canadian Affiliation[!]"[236] Further, the name Protector was already in use in the RN and regardless, "should be reserved for use by the Point Edward Naval Base, if and when it becomes a fleet establishment."[237]

After considering these names plus Rainbow, Courtenay, Georgia, Bras d'Or, and Louisburg, the naval historian recommended Quadra and Acadia as being of similar significance on each coast.[238] These names were accepted. In 1964, when the Coast Guard took over the Point Edward Naval Base, ACADIA moved to CORNWALLIS.

In 1982, VAdm J. Allan, VCDS, granted permission for three RCSC camps to be commissioned as HMC Ships MICMAC, ONTARIO and QUEBEC, joining QUADRA and ACADIA.[239] One exception to this policy was Tillicum, the camp near North Bay, Ontario. About the same time, RCSC camps had their title changed from camps to training establishments.

Paying Off of Establishments

With the exception of the sea cadet camps and the reserve divisions, all other establishments were paid off in one form or another between 1965 and 1968. NADEN became part of CFB Esquimalt; STADACONA became part of CFB Halifax; CORNWALLIS became CFB Cornwallis; NIOBE and NIAGARA became parts of the Canadian Defence Liaison Staffs in London and Washington respectively; and HOCHELAGA, after becoming part of CFB Montréal, eventually disappeared altogether.

Since most of these establishments kept functioning albeit under a new name, few had paying off ceremonies. For example, on 7 Dec 1964, all the personnel on the books of BYTOWN in Ottawa were transferred to the ledgers of the Administration Unit for CFHQ. On that same date, the office of Commanding Officer, HMCS BYTOWN, simply ceased to exist.[240] As late as the fall of 1966, however, and probably much later, BYTOWN cap tallies were still being issued to ratings. Today, the naval officers' mess on Lisgar Street uses the name Bytown.

All the naval radio stations were taken over and each became a CFS. At one point, reserve divisions were actually called Naval Reserve Units (NRU) but even though some were co-located with militia units, their title HMCS still survives. (See Chapter 1.)

Unofficial Names

Nicknames are expressions of affection or derision given by seamen to some vessel or establishment. "Slackers" is still the term for Halifax while Esquimalt was once known as "Squibbley." Unofficial names, on the other hand, are official-sounding names given to a vessel in lieu of some other title or designation.

Unofficial names known to the author are listed in Appendix G while nick-names known to the author are listed in Appendix N.

Summation

A great variety of names have appeared in our Navy over the years. Many names show thought and historical connotation behind their selection. Others clearly show favouritism by both naval officers and those civilians who could influence, or attempt to influence, the choice of a name. And some names came into the Navy simply because the vessel concerned already carried that name and officials either did not care or could not be bothered to change her name.

Whatever the source of the name and regardless of the selection criteria, some 900 names are listed in the next chapter. These names are ours to reflect upon, reuse or ignore, as policy and personal feeling dictates.

Notes to Chapter Five

1. See Tucker, *The Naval Service of Canada*, Vol 1, p 318-9; Ogle, "The Politics of Walter Hose," p 9; and Eayrs, *In Defence of Canada*, Vol 1, p 165.
2. Although there seems to be a difference in tonnage, College, in *Ships of the Royal Navy*, Vol 2, lists them as Castle class trawlers.
3. Message, NSHQ to COAC 487, NS 40-1-3, 1947Z/28, 28 Apr 1942.
4. Cdr RA Grosskurth, "A Navy for Canada," *The Crowsnest*, May-Jun 1960, p 29. See also Tucker, *The Naval Service of Canada*, Vol 1, Chap 8.
5. See NAC RG 24 3988, NS 1057-1-5. Various memos, Dec 1936 to Jan 1937.
6. Ibid. Memo, CNS to DMND, 3 Jul 1939.
7. NAC RG 24, 5666. Telegram, NSHQ to Navyard Halifax, 17 Mar 1919, NSS 58-143-1, Vol 1.
8. Interview, Lt Cdr R Notley, RN (Ret'd), 9 Sep 1995.
9. NAC RG 24 5696. Memo, DNS to Heads of Branches, 10 Mar 1919. NSS 58-143-1, Vol 1.
10. NAC RG 24 5696. Letter, OIC Dockyard Halifax to Sec't DNS, NSS 842-3-3, 18 Sep 1922.
11. NAC RG 24 5666, Vol 1. Letter, NSS 58-143-1.
12. Letter, SNO Halifax to Sec't of Naval Service Ottawa, 95-1-1, 13 Mar 1923.
13. Memo, DNS to MND, 95-1-1, 13 Mar 1923.
14. Manning, *The British Destroyer*, p 19.
15. Originally, the cruiser was to have been HMS SUPERB, not UGANDA. See Tucker, *The Naval Service of Canada*, Vol 2, p 94, and Naval Staff Minutes 226-3, 24 Feb 1944. At a later date, the Admiralty also offered HMS ENTERPRISE, a damaged cruiser, as a training vessel "for the duration only (,) at no cost to the RCN." See Naval Board Minutes 160-8, 21 Aug 1944.
16. Letter, Admiralty to NSHQ, 30 May 1944.
17. Ibid.
18. Minute, CNS to MND (no file no.), 16 Jun 1944. When the CO wished to retain the name of his ship in lieu of naming her Ottawa in March 1943, the same CNS did not raise this point.
19. Memo, Comptroller to (not stated), 5 Jul 1944, NSS 18020-2, Vol 1.
20. Memo, DMND to Deputy Finance Minister, 16 Apr 1945, NSS 8020-500/RR, Vol 2.
21. Ibid.
22. NAC RG 23 4044, NSS 1078-3-4, Vol 1. Naval Council Minutes 14-1, 8 Apr 1941.
23. "RN Ships on loan to RCN." NSHQ 8020-147/25. Unsigned and undated, but written in late 1944. Further, even in NSHQ, many typists wrote HMS for HMCS, and vice versa.
24. Comptroller, "Terms of Acquisition for Ships Obtained by Arrangement with Admiralty." NSS 18020-2, Vol 1, 5 Jul 1944.

25. See letter, DMND to Deputy Finance Minister, NSS 18020-2 and others, 16 Apr 1945.
26. Quoted in message 110256Z/5/44, 11 May 1944, SCNO(L) to NSHQ, NSS 1028-4-1, Vol 22.
27. March, *British Destroyers*, p 281. Counting the leader HMS KEMPENFELT, there were five vessels remaining in the pre-war 'C' class and all were transferred to the RCN.
28. Tucker, *The Naval Service of Canada*, Vol 2, p 103. This question of acquiring eight more destroyers can be traced back to a NSHQ suggestion in late 1943 (see Memo, D. of P. to ACNS, NSHQ 8020-1(2), 16 Mar 1944) and involved much polite wrangling at high levels. See "History of Negotiations in London for Acquisition of Light Fleet Aircraft Carriers and Flotilla of Fleet Destroyers." NS 8020-147/25, 12 May 1945.
29. See *Navy List*, Jul 1945.
30. But all eight original Cr names are listed in BRCN 201, *Naval Service File Directory and Manual*, p 216 and 216a. The naval staff had recommended that suitable names be selected for them when they were acquired. See Naval Staff Minutes 276, 5 Feb 1945.
31. Naval Board Minute 292-10, 16 Jul 1949.
32. Letter, VAdm AE Evans to the Honourable Angus L MacDonald, MNS, 9 Dec 1941.
33. NAC RG 24 3988, NS 1057-1-5, Vol 1. Message, Admiralty 0414/15, 15 Mar 1941.
34. Ibid. Minute sheet, 24 Mar 41.
35. Ibid. Letter to BATM, 26 Mar 41.
36. Tucker, *The Naval Service of Canada*, Vol 2, p 97.
37. See Ogle, "The Creation of Canadian Naval Aviation in the Second World War," p 25-8. HMS NABOB commissioned 7 Sep 1943 and was manned by RCN personnel from 15 Oct 1943.
38. See Tucker, op cit, p 97-9.
39. Letter, VAdm AE Evans to The Honourable Angus L MacDonald, MNS, 9 Dec 1941.
40. There were two other destroyers acquired later, QU'APPELLE and CHAUDIERE, whose names were much further down on the list. Apparently, SO STATS based his list on one prepared by the N Hist which contained 126 river names, 24 of which N Hist had checked in pencil as being particularly eligible.
41. Message, NSHQ to Admiralty and others, 1700Z/9, 9 Mar 1943.
42. Message, HMS GRIFFIN to NSHQ and others, 1824A/15, 15 Mar 1943.
43. Message, HMS GRIFFIN to NSHQ 1446A/17, 17 Mar 1943. Two merchant ships of this name fought against the Armada in 1588 but the name was not used for one of HM Ships until 1656.
44. Cliff Aston, in Lynch, *Fading Memories*, p 101.
45. Message, NSHQ to Admiralty and others (but not HMS GRIFFIN), 1445Z/16, 16 Mar 1943.
46. Message, NSHQ to HMS GRIFFIN, Admiralty and others, 1623Z/22, 22 Mar 1943.
47. Message, FOIC Southampton to NSHQ, etc., NS 1057-1-21, Vol 2, 1132, 20 Mar 1943. See also NAC RG 24 3990, NSC 1057-1-5, Vol 5, Letter, OTTAWA to Capt(D) Newfoundland, OTT-1-1, 16 May 1943.
48. See naval secretary's letter to the Halifax Maritime Museum, Jan 1953, in NS 8000-353/28 (NHS).
49. Alden, *Flush Decks and Four Pipes*, p 23.
50. NAC RG 24 3988, NS 1057-1-5. Memo, DOD to DCNS and CNS, 13 Sep 1940.
51. Alden, op cit.
52. Ibid, p 26.
53. Ibid, plus undated and unnumbered RCN press release, "How Our Warships Get Their Names."
54. Manning, *The British Destroyer*, p 20.
55. NAC RG 24 3988, NS 1057-1-5. Message, NDHQ to Admiralty and others, 1206/16, 16 Sep 1940.
56. NAC RG 24 3988, NS 1057-1-5. Memo, DOD to CNS, 16 Dec 1940.
57. Naval Staff Minutes 199-8, 8 Sep 1943.
58. NAC RG 24 3988, NS 1057-1-5, Vol 1. Memo, DOD to DCNS and CNS, 21 May 1941.
59. Ibid, CNS Minute, 28 May 1941.
60. NAC RG 24 3989, NS 1057-1-5, Vol 3. Naval Staff Minutes 85-7, 27 Apr 1942; See also memo, DOD to DNS and MNS, NSC 1057-1-5, 19 Jan 1943, DHH.
61. Ibid, 3990 Vol 5. Various correspondence in Mar/Apr 1943.
62. Lamb, *The Corvette Navy*, p 8.
63. Memo, SO STATS to A/CNS, 1057-1-5, F.D. 284, 5 Jun 1944.
64. Tucker, *The Naval Service of Canada*, Vol 2, p 93, note 28.
65. See "Funnel Markings," *The Crowsnest*, Mar 1956.
66. Memo, DMNS to Deputy Minister of Finance, NSS 8020-500/RR, Vol 2, 16 Apr 1945.

67. Memo, SO STATS to DSS, NS 1057-1-5, 8 Jun 1943. For the reasons behind the exchange of vessels, see Tucker, *The Naval Service of Canada*, Vol 2, p 77/8.

68. Weekly report, CNS to MNS, NS 1000-5-7, 18 Jul 1940.

69. Macpherson & Burgess, *Ships of Canada's Naval Forces, 1910-1980*, p 134.

70. List of Names of Cities (over 3,000 population) of Dominion which have not been used previously for naming Corvettes and Minesweepers. Ops Div, NSHQ, 9 Apr 1942.

71. NAC RG 24 3988, NS 1057-1-5, Vol 1. Memo, DOD to DCNS and CNS, 31 Jan 1941.

72. Ibid, Vol 2. Letter, DIO to Dept of Munitions and Supply, 11 Dec 1941. HMS TYNE and her sisters were apparently named for rivers with large estuaries.

73. Letter, VAdm Evans to The Honourable Angus L. MacDonald, MNS, 9 Dec 1941.

74. Naval Staff Minutes 53-12, 14 Aug 1941.

75. Letter, COPC to N Sec't, P.C. 374, 29 Apr 1941.

76. See "Weepers Jeepers! Lookit the Names They Give Our Sweepers," *The Crowsnest*, Mar 1956, p 8.

77. Memo, N Sec't to COAC and others, NS 40-1-6 (and other numbers), 31 Dec 1941.

78. Ibid.

79. Information taken from the file on Naming of HMC Ships, Vol 5, DHH.

80. Letter, NSHQ to SCNO (L), NSC 1057-1-5, 19 Jul 1945.

81. Memo, SO STATS to Miss Bentley, 5 Aug 1943.

82. Letter, DUNVER to Capt(D), 5 Oct 1943.

83. The information for this story is taken from various British and Canadian papers located in the VILLE DE QUEBEC file, DHH. Cdr Wally Turner drew my attention to this story.

84. Message, Admiralty to NSHQ 847, 2217/25, 25 Apr 1941. The name QUEBEC was promulgated in Naval Order 1357, 17 May 1941.

85. Letter, Lord Louis to Sir Henry V Markham: Combined Ops HQ, S.18/1, 9 Feb 1942.

86. Naval Board Minutes 16-1, 2 Apr 1942; letter, NSHQ to Mayor, NS 1057-1-5, ED 241, 10 Apr 1942.

87. Message, (Cdn) High Commissioner London to NSHQ Ottawa, 779, 1130/26, 26 Sep 1942.

88. 14 Dec 1943. Message, Admiralty to various addressees, 131658Z, Dec 1943.

89. Memo, SO STATS to DOD, no file number, 9 Feb 1943.

90. Ibid. The reference to HUNTER was inaccurate. Her name was one of the originals proposed by D Hist in a report submitted to the Naval Council, 25 Jul 1941. See file 8000-5, DHH. But these remarks may explain how the name Queen came to be used for the division in Regina.

91. See the story of VILLE DE QUEBEC earlier in this chapter.

92. See AFO 625/45, reprinted as Naval Order 4668, 7 Apr 1945.

93. NAC RG 24 3988, NS 1075-1-5, various correspondence circa Oct 1942. Stettler is some 160 kms south of Edmonton.

94. NAC RG 24 3988, NS 1057-1-5.

95. Undated list of Names of Ships, File 3 (circa late 1942). The School Board, Historical Society, and the local Jean Baptiste Society wrote to MNS. None of these letters were rude but the one from the Junior Chamber of Commerce "insisted" on the use of the full name. NAC RG 24 3988, NS 1057-1-5, Vol 3, letter 29 Sep 1942.

96. Letter, Sec't Naval Board to Mayor, NSS 1057-1-5 FD DOD, 14 Dec 1942.

97. Memo, SO(N) to DOD, NS 1957-1-5, 14 Dec 1942.

98. NAC RG 24 3988, NS 1057-1-5. Minute, DOD to N/Inf, 14 Dec 1941.

99. NS 1057-1-5, FD 551, 30 Apr 1943.

100. Information taken from notes and extracts in Naming of HMC Ships file, Vol 1, DHH.

101. NAC RG 24 3988, NS 1057-1-5. Letter, MND to Mr. EE Perley, 14 Jul 1943.

102. Message, Admiralty to NSHQ Ottawa 847, 2217/25, 25 Apr 1941.

103. Memo, SO STATS to Director of Special Services, NS 1057-1-5, 8 Jun 1943.

104. NAC RG 24 3988, NSC 1057-1-5, Vol 1. See Memo, CNS to MND, 19 Dec 1940, and Message, NSHQ to COAC 193, 1204/4, 4 Jan 1941. See also Naval Orders 1080, 2 Nov 1940, and 1910, 28 Feb 1942.

105. NAC RG 24 3988, NSC 1057-1-5, Vol 1. Letter, Admiralty to NSHQ, 10 Oct 1940. See Chapter 2.

106. NAC RG 24 3990, NS 1057-1-5, Vol 5. Various correspondence between 15 Mar and 26 May 1943.

107. NAC RG 24 3988, NS 1047-1-5, Vol 1. Memo to DOD, 24 Jul 1940. See Naval Order 962.

108. Memo, Doris L. Bentley to SO STATS, 22 Jun 1943. And Memo, Doris L. Bentley to Lt McNelly [sic], 27 Jul 1943. Doris Bentley was private sec't to MND.

109. NAC RG 24 3988, NS 1057-1-5, Vol 2. Memo, MND to DOD, 20 Jul 1941.
110. For example, SO STATS to SCNO, 091417Z, 9 Jul 1943, NS 1057-1-5. And SCNO to NSHQ 291320Z, 12 Jul 1943, NS 1057-1-5.
111. Memo, DL Bentley to SO STATS, 22 Jul 1943.
112. Memo, SO STATS to A/CNS. NS 1057-1-5, 8 Jul 1943.
113. NAC RG 24 3988, NS 1057-1-5, Vol 6. Letter, Sec't Naval Board to Canadian Vickers, 13 Sep 1943.
114. NAC RG 24 3988, NS 1057-1-5, Vol 1. Minute on a memo, DOD to DCNS, 8 Oct 1940.
115. Letter, Port Carling Boat Works to NSHQ, 4 Aug 1944, Naming of Ships, Vol 1, DHH. There are several letters on this subject.
116. Message, NSHQ to COAC and (R)NO i/c Sydney, 1947 Z/28, NS 40-1-5, 28 Apr 1942.
117. NAC RG 24 3988, NS 1057-1-5. Message, COAC to NSHQ 635, 1058/1, 1 Aug 1940.
118. See Memo, SO STATS to DOD, NS 1-54-4 F.D. 1639, 27 Feb 1943. HMS RAINBOW, a submarine, was sunk in 1940 and it is likely the RN wished to use the name again.
119. Memo, DOD to N Sec't, NS 1057-1-5, 21 Jun 1943.
120. Letter, CORD to NSHQ, 23 Jun 1943. This letter is referred to in a second letter, Sec't Naval Board to CORD, NS 1057-1-5, FD 852, 7 Jul 1943.
121. See Appendix D, Duplicate Names.
122. CCNO 208, 14 Aug 1943.
123. Naval Staff Minutes 230-9, 20 Mar 1944.
124. Naval Board Minutes 16-6, 2 Apr 1942.
125. See Chapter 1.
126. This is speculation. She commissioned in Oct 1944.
127. In the spring of 1943, GANNET became the depot ship for Capt(ML). See messages in Ships' Names file, Vol 3, DHH, circa May 1943.
128. Tucker, *The Naval Service of Canada*, Vol 2, p 450.
129. See various messages, circa Mar/Apr 1944 in HOCHELAGA file, DHH.
130. See the entry for SHEARWATER II.
131. See Naval Orders 2438, 12 Dec 1942, and 3002, 21 Aug 1943. According to one source, these two STADACONAs were separate establishments but all pay accounts, etc. were kept in STADACONA (I). Compare the previous two Naval Orders with #2323, 10 Oct 1942. A/Capt Alfred C Wurtele, as CO of STADACONA in 1944, stated in 1998 that STADACONA II was a separate establishment over which he had no authority.
132. HM Ships CENTURION, COLLINGWOOD, DAEDALUS, DOLPHIN, DRYAD, EXCELLENT, MERCURY, NELSON, PHOENIX, SULTAN, TEMERAIRE and VERNON. In addition, there were at least six non-commissioned establishments.
133. For details, see Tucker, *The Naval Service of Canada*, Vol 2, Plate VI, opposite p 203.
134. Memo, DOD to DNP and VCNS, NS 117-1-1, 22 Oct 1942. BYTOWN file, DHH.
135. HC 128 (ex BYTOWN, ex ORACLE) had first received her number in Jan 1942 and was then known as 'BYTOWN (HC 128)', later as 'HC 128 (BYTOWN)', and still later as 'HC 128 (ex BYTOWN). By mid 1942, she was being referred to simply by her number.
136. Naval Order 2323. 10 Oct 1941.
137. Whyard, "His Majesty's Canadian Ship CONESTOGA," p 176.
138. See *The Naval Service of Canada*, Vol 2, p 321.
139. See Naval Board Minutes 24-1, 30 Apr 1942, and 44-10, 27 Jul 1942.
140. Naval Staff Minutes 244-22, 26 Jun 1944. It is interesting to see Rainbow appear once again on a suggested list of names. Rainbow also appeared on a list of "weather condition" name suggestions for destroyers. Unofficially, the name was apparently applied to the RCN base in Bermuda circa 1 May to 15 Jul 1944. See the article by Milner, p 44-5.
141. Naval Staff Minutes 261-2, 23 Oct 1944.
142. NAC RG 24 4044, NSS 1078-3-4, Vol 1. Naval Council Minutes 20-1, 8 Apr 1941 and 26-5, 7 Jul 1941.
143. Report and Recommendations on Names for RCNVR Divisional Headquarters, 25 Jul 1941, no file number. A cover sheet with file 8000-5 is attached, but this is a post Second World War file number.
144. Ibid.
145. Ibid.

146. Ibid.
147. Letter, EC Russell to RCN Benevolent Fund, 10 Feb 1960. RCNR Divisions file, DHH.
148. NAC RG 24 4044, NSS 1078-3-4, Vol 1. Naval Council Minutes 35-1, 14 Oct 1941.
149. *The Crowsnest*, Nov 1949, p 35.
150. *The Crowsnest*, Feb 1949, p 32. See also p 23.
151. See Beddoe, "Symbols and Ships," *The Crowsnest*, Aug 1961, pages 5-9.
152. Naval Staff Minutes 10/55-2, 15 Mar 1955.
153. Letter, Philip Chaplin (former D Hist staff) to author, 10 Jul 1985. See also Johnston, "Canadian U-Boat Commander," p 199.
154. Naval Staff Minutes 9/55-3, 8 Mar 1955.
155. Memo, N Hist to Cdr Elcock, NS 8000-5, 9 Sep 1952.
156. "HMCS BONAVENTURE Joins the FLEET," *The Crowsnest*, Feb 1957.
157. QUEBEC file, DHH.
158. Thorton, *The Big 'U'*, p 40.
159. Naval Staff Minutes 505-1, 31 Oct - 6 Nov 1950.
160. Naval Staff Minutes 335-1, 8 Nov 1950.
161. NAC RG 83-84/167 Navy 3539, NSC 8000-5, Vol 3. Memo, CNS to MND, 6 Feb 1953.
162. Naval Board Minutes 507-1, para 1, 9 Oct 1956.
163. Ibid, para 2.
164. Naval Board Minutes 551-3, 21 Oct 1957.
165. Naval Board Minutes 573-5, 17 Jul 1958.
166. Telephone conversation with RAdm RP Welland, RCN Ret'd, 15 Jul 1985.
167. Information taken from various correspondence in NDHQ 1000-5, Apr-Nov 1967, and confirmed by RAdm Rodocanachi, 2 Oct 1985.
168. Naval Board Minutes 608-3, 4 Nov 1959.
169. NAC RG 83-84/167 Navy 3539, NSC 8000-5, Vol 3. CNS Minute on Memo, VCNS to CNS, 28 Feb 1959.
170. Memo, DMOPR to CMDO, 1000-5 (DMOPR), 13 Nov 1979.
171. Ibid. See also Naval Board Minutes 608-3, 4 Nov 1959.
172. Ibid, para 11.
173. Demi-official letter, Comd MARCOM to CMDO, 6 Dec 1979. See also Arbuckle, *Customs & Traditions* p 67-8.
174. Memo, DGMDO to CMDO, 11900-CPF-910 (DGMDO), 23 Feb 1981.
175. Letter, CMDO to Comd MARCOM & others, 850-3 (DMOPR 2-3), 8 Apr 1982.
176. Letter, CMDO to author, 11900-1, 15 Mar 1985.
177. CFSO 16/91, 15 mar 1991.
178. See Naval Staff Minutes 501-5, 31 Oct - 6 Nov 1950.
179. *Jane's*, 1957/58, p 91. See also NAC RG 83-83/167 Navy 3539, NSC 8000-5, Vol 3. Minute Sheet, DNPO to ACNTS(5), 29 Apr 1953.
180. See *Jane's* 1966/67, p 41.
181. Naval Board Minutes 608-3, 4 Nov 1959.
182. Naval Board Minutes 640-3, 21 Dec 1960.
183. Memo, N Hist to DSCS, 8000-5 TD 5244, 17 Sep 1965.
184. NAC RG 83-83/167 Navy 3539, NSC 8000-5, Vol 3. Minute sheet, Capt Fotheringham to DGMF, 7 Jan 1966. N Hist felt there were too many French names already but Mr. Philip Chaplin of his staff compiled a list to prove this was not so.
185. Ibid, Memo, DCOps to VCDS and CDS, 15 Apr 1966.
186. See Naval Staff Minutes 480-1, 7 Mar 1950, and Naval Board Minutes 318-1, 22 Mar 1950.
187. Naval Staff Minutes 516-9, 15 Jun 1951.
188. Memo, N Hist to DOPS(M), NSC 8000-5, Vol 4, 18 Jun 1965.
189. NAC RG 83-84/167 Navy 3539, NSC 8000-5, Vol 3. Minute 2, Memo, DOPS to A/COPR, Jun 1965.
190. Ibid, Memo, DGMF to A/COPR, 22 Sep 1965.
191. Ibid, Letter, VCDS to CDRB, 18 Oct 1965. Reply, 25 Oct 1965. In 1918, Dr. Bell donated his motor launch *Kia Ora* to the RCN. He used her to tow experimental hydroplanes on the Bras d'Or lakes.
192. Various correspondence, NDHQ 1000-5, Jan - Mar 1967.
193. Memo, CMO to CDS, NDHQ 1000-5, 20 Apr 1976.

NRS PORT EDWARD near Prince Rupert in Nov 1963. (FDN Coll.)

194. Naval Board Minutes 394-2, 9 Dec 1953.
195. Naval Board Minutes 394-2, 9 Dec 1953.
196. NAC RG 83-83/167 Navy 3539, NSC 8000-5, Vol 3. Minute on a memo, VCNS to CNS, 20 May 1960. The name Grilse was not on the original VCNS list.
197. Memo, N Hist to A/DN Ops, NSC 8000-5, 1 Apr 1964.
198. Ibid, 6 Apr 1964.
199. NAC RG 83-83/167 Navy 3539, NSC 8000-5, Vol 3. On a memo, CNS to MND, 21 Nov 1963.
200. Naval Board Minutes 335-1, 8 Nov 1950. The first vessel was the PORTE SAINT JEAN.
201. NAC RG 83-84/167 Navy 3539, NSC 8000-5, Vol 3. Letter, C DRB to CNS, 23 May 1963.
202. NAC RG 86-87/167 Navy 3539, NSC 8000-5, Vol 3. See memos dated 27 and 28 Jul, and 10 Sep 1954.
203. Memo, N Constructor-in-Chief to N Sec't, NSS 8200-489 (NCC), 9 Dec 1953.
204. Memo, NDPO to Heraldic Adviser, NSS 8200-489 (STAFF), 15 Jan 1952.
205. See Naval Staff Minutes 399-3, 17 Jan 1948. CEDARWOOD was neither a sister nor a near cousin, to the Wood class tugs.
206. Letter, HUNTER to MARCOM, 11900-2, 24 Nov 1978, in NDHQ 1000-5. CHIPPAWA also wrote suggesting the names Service, Ambler or Sans Peur for her tender. See the entry under SERVICE. See also NDHQ 1000-5, 13 Mar 1979.
207. Letter, Comd MARCOM to NDHQ/DNAV & others, 11900-1, 4 Apr 1979, in NDHQ file 1000-5.
208. Naval Staff Minutes 300-3, 27 Jan 1948.
209. Naval Board Minutes 314-1, 9 Feb 1950.
210. Naval Board Minutes 234-2, 10 Jan 1948.
211. Naval Staff Minutes 402-4, 17 Feb 1948.
212. Ibid. The RN practice includes the use of names of other than sea birds for their air stations, e.g. HMS DAEDALUS. McCurdy was the first Canadian to fly.
213. Ibid.
214. Naval Staff Minutes 355-3, 2 Dec 1946. No further information could be located on W/T station Chelsea.
215. Naval Board Minutes 342-5, 11 Apr 1951.
216. MARC 1110-1 (N00 Comd) 11 Oct 94. See also Maritime Command *Trident*, 15 Dec 1994, p 5.
217. Letter, NDHQ 1000-5 (DMTH 3), 13 Jan 1995.
218. Naval Staff Minutes 311-4, 15 Oct 1945.
219. Demi-official letter, Capt(N) J. Anderson to author, 22 Mar 1985.
220. Letter, Nav Res HQ to MARCOM, 1901-1537 ©-, 15 Mar 1987.
221. Letter, NDHQ 1150-110-M2631 (DGMD) 15 Feb 1993.
222. Message, NDHQ DGFD 1038 111700Z Jun 93.
223. Naval Staff Minutes 469, 8 Nov 1949, NS 1924-189/166.

224. Ibid.
225. Memo, CNS to MND, NSC 1700-189, Vol 21, 17 May 1950.
226. See NSC 1700-189, 8 Nov 1944.
227. Letter, DS Div to various OICs, NSC 1700-189,5 Dec 1947.
228. Memo, DS Div to CN Pete (?), NSC 1700-189, 8 Jan 1948.
229. Memo, DGFA to DS Div, NSC 1700-189, 10 Feb 1950.
230. Memo, N Sec to D Vict, NSC 1700-189, 23 May 1950.
231. Naval Board Minutes 680-2, 6 Jan 1962.
232. Memo, DN Com to ACNS(W), NSC 1700-189, 23 Sep 1955.
233. CANGEN 133/56, 291424A May 1956.
234. Bowman, *The City of Rainbows*, p 74.
235. Memo, CNS to MND, NS 1700-173, Vol 4, 17 Feb 1956.
236. Memo, DNPO to DN ORG, NS 1700-172, Vol 4, 14 Feb 1956.
237. Ibid.
238. Memo, D Hist to DNPO, NS 1700-172 (N/Hist), 10 Fe 1956.
239. Message, NDHQ to CENTREGHQ Trenton and others, DCDS 106 131200Z Jul 1981; Letter, DGRC to RCO Cadets and others, 1088-11, 8 Dec 1977.
240. Note by N Historian, 14 Apr 1965, BYTOWN file, DHH.

The Kisbie ring and badge of the 2nd HURON as displayed on her brow in January 2000. (Freeman 661-03. AC)

Chapter Six

List of Names

A typical entry in the List of Names will consist of the following information:

1. The official name of the ship, correctly spelled, is followed (in brackets) by variants where used officially. Warship names are set in capitals—BARRIE or LAURIER—while the town, person or non naval vessel appears as *Barrie* or *Laurier* and the town or person is written as Barrie and Laurier.

2. In brackets following the name, the name's origin or meaning, supplemented by a note. Where a number precedes the origin of the name, this indicates a change from one use of the name to the next. The first CAPE BRETON, for example, was probably named for the island; the second was named for the cape. N* indicates that the vessel kept her original name on entering naval service.

3. B denotes this name had an official RCN badge after 1949. 2B means the badge was first granted to the second ship of the name.

4. Under the name, each use or intended use of the name, is numbered serially. Sub-paragraphs indicate changes to the hull bearing that name, e.g.: a. in class; b. in type; c. in status (e.g., became a CNAV), d. disposed of, and later reacquired.

West Coast ships 2 May 1966. Front row, left to right: ANTIGONISH, QU'APPELLE, YUKON and SUSSEXVALE. Rear row, left to right, JONQUIERE, GRILSE, and STETTLER. (CF E-83339. FDN Coll.)

5. For vessels, class type and pennant number(s). For establishments: exact addresses or building numbers. The function of a shore establishment often changed and it was deemed beyond the scope of this book to attempt to record each change or to list the schools and organizations contained within a given establishment.

6. Actual dates of each commissioning, each paying off, or loss. These dates may bear little resemblance to the dates the vessel was actually in the Navy. Where exact dates are not known or open to doubt the term "circa" indicates an approximate date.

Where authorities differ in their dates:

a. when one authority is clearly wrong, I so state;

b. when one authority disagrees with a primary source, this is included as a note;

c. when one authority disagrees with another and no corroborating evidence could be found, placed in brackets with a question mark, e.g. (3?) 5 August 1941; and

d. when there is only one authority but evidence suggests an incorrect date, a question mark in brackets follows that part of the date in question, e.g. 5(?) August 1941.

7. A note amplifies the information immediately above it, except notes concerning the origin of the names are generally at the bottom of the entry. See BURRARD.

8. Entries are in strict letter-by-letter alphabetical order; thus ROLLIN E MASON will be under R, not M.

Battle Honours and Badges

Battle Honours and Badges should have been included with each name. They have not been for reasons noted in Chapter 2. Appendix S contains a list of unofficial Battle Honours.

Pennant Numbers*

To avoid any confusion, up to 1949 pennant numbers worn by HMC Ships followed and were part of, the RN System. For a list by class and pennant number, readers are referred to books by Macpherson and Burgess.

---

* Some authorities such as Macpherson and Burgess use the term "pendant" in lieu of pennant. The author follows the style shown in Vol II, Plate 200, *Manual of Seamanship* (1951); CFP 200; and *Jane's Fighting Ships* 1957/58.

As always, however, there were exceptions to the numbering system. During the Second World War, pennant numbers of the S and Z Flag superior, for example, were locally assigned and thus many numbers were worn simultaneously by vessels on both coasts. See REINDEER and RIPPLE for just one example. Some RCASC vessels also wore Z Flag superior numbers. Further, many of the armed yachts changed numbers at various times. See HUSKY. Such changes in a pennant number appear to be more frequent in the First World War and the 1920s than in the Second World War. See PATRICIAN as an example.

During the period 1949-1952, the system of pennant numbers in the RCN changed from a letter plus two or three digits to the two- and three-digit system. In the mid 1990s all vessels were assigned three-digit numbers. Regrettably, only in rare cases are exact dates listed for any changes in pennant numbers.

Meaning of Names

Many of the names included are geographical. While the origin of the name is included, the meaning of the geographical name itself is outside the scope of this book. For such information, readers are directed to a good gazetteer of place names for the pertinent region.

Abbreviations

To save space, many abbreviations common to naval personnel have been employed. For those not so lucky to have been in the Navy and for those former Navy personnel whose memories may be a bit rusty, a glossary of these abbreviations has been included at the end of the book.

Caution

The listing that follows shows the historic uses of warship names. Readers should not confuse this with a listing of ship's lineage. The difference is significant. Take the entry for SUSSEXVALE as an example. The name was first assigned to a River class frigate under construction in 1941. Before commissioning, however, in December 1941 the vessel was cancelled. The name was next assigned to a second River class frigate that commissioned in 1944. For the purposes of lineage, Battle Honours, etc., the next SUSSEXVALE can claim descent only from the second use of the name, the frigate commissioned in 1944.

A

A.B. WINCHESTER (N*)

1. Tug. Acquired Sep 1917(?) Purchased 1918(?) and sold 1920(?).

ACADIA (1. N* 2. Geog. for the old French region of eastern Canada. 3. For 2) 2. B

1. a. Patrol vessel. 16 Jan 1917–Mar 1919. Acquired Apr 1915(?).
   b. Auxiliary patrol and later, training vessel, Z00/S00. 2 Oct 1939–3 Nov 1945. ex hydrographic survey ship *Acadia*. Circa 1984 became a floating museum in Halifax.
2. Sea Cadet training establishment, Point Edward, NS. 15 May 1956–?; 9 Jun 1961–?; 4 Jun–7 Sep 1962; 3 Jun–2 Sep 1963; see PROTECTOR II.
3. Sea Cadet training centre, Cornwallis, NS. 1964–1994. Commissioned each summer.
4. Sea Cadet training centre, Shearwater, NS. 1995–SIS. Commissions each summer.

ACADIAN (N*)

1. Detachment class patrol craft, 194. Circa 17 Mar 1976–circa Jun 1996. ex RCMP *Acadian*.

ACTIVE (N*)

1. Harbour craft, HC26. Feb 1942–? Known as HC26 for entire commission. SIS 1 Apr 1945.

ADAMSVILLE

1. a. Ville class tug, pd no N/K. 12 Jan 1944–1946?
   b. CNAV/CFAV, Ville class tug, 582. Circa 1946–circa 1975/6. Became BURRARD.

ADELAIDE (N*)

1. Motor launch. Circa Nov 1914–Jul 1919.

ADMIRAL'S LADY

1. Harbour launch, Esquimalt, YFL100. Aug 84–circa 1991. ex QUEEN BEE. Reverted to QUEEN BEE?

ADUR (see NADUR)

ADVANCE (N*)

1. Harbour craft, HC27. 1 Dec 1939–15 Jan 1942. Became HC27. ex RCMP *Advance*.

HMCS AVALON II at St. John's, Nfld, with HM S/M P554 alongside. (RCN NF 2147. KM Coll.)

ADVERSUS (1 and 2. N*)
1. Auxiliary patrol craft, J17. (3?)7 Sep 1939–(19?) 20 Dec 1941, went aground on McNutt's Island, near Shelburne, NS and was lost. ex RCMP *Adversus*.
2. Detachment class patrol craft, 191. 17 Mar 1976–circa 1996. ex RCMP *Adversus*.

AGASSIZ (Geog, for the town in BC)
1. Flower class corvette, K129. 23 Jan 1941–14 Jun 1945.

AKLAVIK (Geog, for the town in the NWT)
1. Naval radio station, Aklavik, NWT.
   a. established by Aug 1949.
   b. HMC NRS circa 1953–12 Mar 1961. Tender to GLOUCESTER. Moved to a new site and became INUVIK.
Note: A new site was considered as early as Nov 1954. By 26 May 1958, this site was called Aklavik East Three; it became INUVIK.

ALACHASSE (N*)
1. Auxiliary patrol craft, Z18/J18. 3 Sep 1939–28 Nov 1945. ex RCMP *Alachasse*.

ALASE (N*)
1. Motor yacht. 15 Jun 1917–Jul 1919.

ALASKA (N*)
1. Tug. Chartered Jul–Nov 1915; Apr–25 Nov 1916; Apr–Nov 1917; 15 Apr–Nov 1918. ex Sincennes-McNaughton Co tug.

ALBACORE (N*)
1. Patrol boat, Halifax. 10 Aug(?) 1914–9 Jun 1915. Tender to DIANA. ex yacht *Albacore*.

ALBATROSS (bird)
1. Crash boat, 661. 1985–SIS.

ALBERNI (Geog, for Alberni, BC; name later associated with both Alberni and Port Alberni, BC)
1. Flower class corvette, K103. 4 Feb 1941–21 Aug 1944, torpedoed and sunk by U 480 SE of the Isle of Wight, Great Britain.

ALBERTON
1. Norton class tug, W48. 10 Jan (2 Oct?) 1944–circa 1946.

ALBRO LAKE (Geog, for the lake near Dartmouth, NS) B
1. Naval radio station, Dartmouth, NS.
   a. established 1942.
   b. NRS circa 1953–1 Jul 1956.
   c. HMC NRS 1 Jul 1956–18(?) Sep 1967. Moved to a new site and became CFS Mill Cove.
The cut over from ALBRO LAKE to Mill Cove occurred between 31 Aug–18 Sep 1967.
See also BLANDFORD.

ALDER LAKE
1. Lake class minesweeper, J 480. Completed 22 Sep 1945. Never commissioned.

ALDERGROVE (Geog, for town in BC) B
1. Naval radio station, Aldergrove, BC.
   a. late 1943–1 Jun 1955. In operation as early as 29 Nov 1943. Site for SUMAS (later MATSQUI) taken over from Dec 1942–Dec 1945. Name Vancouver was also suggested.
   b. HMC NRS. 1 Jun 1955–1 Jul 1956.
   c. HMCS. 1 Jul 1956–10 Aug 1967. Became CFS Aldergrove.

ALEXANDRIA (Geog, for the town in ON)
1. River class frigate. Cancelled Dec 1943.

ALGERINE (N*, a native of Algeria)
1. Phoenix class sloop, loaned to RCN 1917–circa 1919. ex HMS ALGERINE.

ALGIE
1. Patrol vessel, pd no N/K. Second World War. Date, type and source not known.

ALGOMA (Geog, for the town of Algoma Mills, ON)
1. Flower class corvette, K127. 11 Jul 1941–6 Jul 1945.

ALGONQUIN (1. for the First Nations Tribe. 2. for 1) 1. B
1. a. V class destroyer, R17/D117/224. 17 Feb 1944–6 Feb 1946. ex HMS VALENTINE.
   b. Algonquin class destroyer escort, 224. 25 Feb 1953–14 Apr 1960;
      12 Jan 1961–1 Apr 1970.
2. Iroquois class helicopter destroyer, 283. 3 Nov 1973–SIS.

ALLAVERDY (N*)
1. Auxiliary, Fy 06. 19 Nov 1940–Nov 1944. ex fish packer *Allaverdy*.

ALVA AND MAY (ALWA and/or MAE?) (N*)
1. Motor launch. 19 May 1917–Mar 1919.

ALWINGTON (alternative for Portsmouth, ON, now part of Kingston. Name taken from Alwington House, the most historic in the city)
1. River class frigate. Became ROYAL MOUNT 5 Apr 1944.

AMBLER (N*)
1. Armed yacht, Q11/Z32. 6 May 1940–?; 14 Jun 1940–20 Jul 1945. ex *Ambler*, ex *Cynthia*.

AMHERST (Geog, for the town in NS)
1. Flower class corvette, K148. 5 Aug 1941–11 Jul 1945. ex SHEDIAC.

AMOS B (N*)
1. Motor launch. Circa Jun 1917–Mar 1919.

ANASHENE
1. Auxiliary? Date, type and source not known, Second World War.

ANDAMARA
1. Patrol vessel, Z22 (P). 24 Jul 1941–Jan 1946.

ANDREE DUPRE (N*)
1. Examination vessel, Z03/W03. 10 Oct (30 Dec?) 1939–Jul 1945. ex tug *Andrée Dupré*, ex *Napoleon L.*, ex TR class naval trawler.
Note: A charter agreement dated 25 Jun 1940 recommended return to owners 9 Jan 1945. Returned 9 (17?) Aug 1945. No commissioning dates recorded.

ANDREW LEE (N*)
1. Auxiliary. Chartered 1 Jan 1944–1 Apr 1945. ex MV *Andrew Lee*.

ANDY (N*)
1. Tug, W13. 2 Dec 1941–11 May 1942; 24 Nov 1942–23 May 1943.

ANNA MILDRED (N*)
1. Patrol vessel, Fy 87/Z12(A). 6 Jun 1940–14 Sep 1945? ex motor launch.

ANNAN (N*, for a river in Dumfries & Galloway, Scotland)
1. River class frigate, K404. 13 Jan 1944–20 Jun 1945. ex HMS ANNAN, K297.

ANNAPOLIS (1. As HMS, for the town of Annapolis Royal, NS and Annapolis, Maryland; as HMCS, for the river in NS. 2. Geog, for the river in NS) 2. B
1. Town class destroyer, I 04. 24 Sep 1940–4 Jun 1945. ex HMS ANNAPOLIS, ex USS MACKENZIE.
2. Annapolis class destroyer, helicopter carrier, 265. 19 Dec 1964–1 Jul 1998. Note: put into a zero manned "state of readiness" in Dec 1996.

ANTICOSTI (Geog, for the island) B
1. Anticosti class minesweeping auxiliary vessel, 112. 7 May 1989–21 Mar 2000. ex *Jean Tide*, ex *Lady Jean*.

ANTIGONISH (Geog, for the town in NS) B
1. a. River class frigate, K661/F61. 4 Jul 1944–5 Feb 1946; 26 Apr 1947–15 Jan 1954.
   b. Prestonian class frigate, 301. 12 Oct 1957–30 Nov 1966.

AQCHARAZA (AQUHARAZA?) (N*)
1. Store & water boat, HC28. 22 Sep 1941–15 Jan 1942. Became HC28. SIS 1 Apr 1945.

ARASHIO (N*)
1. Patrol vessel, pd. no N/K. 4–9 Feb 1942. ex fishing vessel *Arashio*. Became SURF.

ARCADIA (1. N*)
1. Auxiliary. 21 Aug–Dec 1918. ex Hendry Ltd steam lighter.
2. Harbour craft, HC73 (ML10). 13 Nov 1940–15 Jan 1942?

ARCTIC TERN (bird)
1. Name allocated to a Bird class patrol vessel which was cancelled 1956.

ARISTOCRAT (N*)
1. Auxiliary, Z46. Circa Apr 1944–Jul 1946. Acquired 12 Feb 1944. ex RCAF vessel *Aristocrat*, B113. Used as a WT calibration vessel.

ARLEUX (after a First World War land battle)
1. a. Battle class trawler. 5 Jun 1918–30 Jun 1922.
   b. Minesweeper, Z55/J14. 13 Sep 1939–1 May 1942. Became Gate Vessel 16 and served to Sep 1945.

ARMENTIERES (after a First World War land battle)
1. a. Battle class trawler, 5 Jun 1918–28 Oct 1919.
   b. 1 Apr 1923–20 Nov 1925. 2 Sep 1925, sunk in Pipestem Inlet, BC. Refloated 26 Oct, and paid off into dockyard hands 20 Nov 1925.
   c. Training ship 16 Jul 1926–8 Feb 1946. Became an examination vessel at Prince Rupert circa 1939 with pd no J29.
Note: Also carried the pt nos U02 & N29 at some point in her career.

ARNPRIOR (1&2. Geog, for the town in ON)
1. Name assigned to Algerine class minesweeper but never promulgated. Ship turned over to RN o/c as HMS COURIER, J349.
2. Castle class corvette, K494. 8 Jun 1944–14 Mar 1946. ex HMS RISING CASTLE, K398.

ARRAS (after a First World War land battle)
1. a. Battle class trawler, Z55/J15. 8 Jul 1918–1 Apr 1926.
   b. Patrol craft, Z52. 11 Sep 1939–1 Apr 1941. Became GV 15 and served to 1946.

ARROW (N*)
1. Harbour craft, Q18/HC29. 3 Sep 1939–15 Jan 1942. Became HC29. ex RCMP *Arrow*.

ARROWHEAD (a flower; name later associated with the town in BC)
1. Flower class corvette, K145. 15 May 1941–27 Jun 1945. In commission as RN vessel 22 Nov 1940–15 May 1941.

ARTHUR (N*)
1. Schooner. Sep–7 Oct 1918, sank off Labrador coast. ex Sincennes–McNaughton schooner.

ARTHUR W. (N*)
1. Schooner. Circa 1914–7 Sep 1915. Became DIANA (2nd). Never com'd. Obtained from Customs Service, ex prize *Arthur W.*

ARVIDA (Geog, for the city in QC)
1. Flower class corvette, K113. 22 May 1941–14 Jun 1945.

ASBESTOS (Geog, for the town in QC)
1. Revised Flower class corvette, K358. 16 Jun 1944–8 Jul 1945.

ASH LAKE
1. Lake class minesweeper, J481. Completed 1945 (as Dept of Mines ship *Cartier*) but never commissioned.

ASSINIBOINE (1&2. Geog, for the river in MB) 1. B
1. C/River class destroyer, D18/I18/I80. 19 Oct 1939–8 Aug 1945. ex HMS KEMPENFELT, ex HMS VALENTINE.
2. a. St Laurent class destroyer escort, 234. 16 Aug 1956–15 Jun 1962.
   b. Improved St Laurent class destroyer escort, helicopter carrier, 234.
      28 Jun 1963–14 Dec 1988. Became a harbour training vessel in Halifax.

ASSISTANT
1. Tug, HC32. 1 Jul (10 Sep?) 1941–15 Jan 1942. Became HC32. ex Restigouche Company tug *Restico.*

ATHABASKAN (1. for the First Nations language group. 2. For 1. 3. For 1 & 2) 2. B
1. Tribal class destroyer, G07. 3 Feb 1943–29 Apr 1944, torpedoed by German destroyer T29 and sank in Bay of Biscay off Isle de Bas. ex IROQUOIS. For note on name change, see IROQUOIS.
2. a. Tribal class destroyer, D04/R79/219. 20 Jan 1948–15 Feb 1954. Pt no changed Jan 1950 to 219.
   b. Tribal class destroyer escort, 219. 25 Oct 1954–21 Apr 1966.
3. Iroquois class destroyer, helicopter carrier, 282. 30 Sep 1972–SIS.

ATHOLL (alternative name for Campbellton, NB)
1. Revised Flower class corvette, K15. 14 Oct 1943–17 Jul 1945.

ATLANTIC (ATLANTA?) (N*)
1. Motor launch. Circa Jul 1917–Mar 1918.

ATTABOY (N*)
1. Training vessel. 1 Oct 1941–?; 1 Jun 1943–3 Sep 1943. ex schooner *Attaboy.*

ATTENDANT
1. Harbour craft, HC33. 29 Jul 1940–15 Jan 1942. Became HC33.

ATTENTIVE
1. Harbour craft, Fy 90/HC34/Z05. Circa Jul 1940–15 Jan 1942. Became HC34. ex MV *Dundee.*

ATWOOD (For the village near Listowel, ON)
1. Wood class tug, Z47. 20 May 1944–46.

AUBURNVILLE
1. Ville class tug, W50. 24 Jan 1944–Jan 1946.

AURORA (N*, for the Roman goddess of the dawn)
1. Arethusa class cruiser. 1 Nov 1920–1 Jul 1922. ex HMS AURORA.

AUTUMN LEAF
1. Former name for harbour craft, HC191. 10 May 1943–circa 1945.

AVALON (1. Geog, for peninsula in NF. 2 & 3. N/K. 4. For 1. 5. For 1 & 4.) 4. B
1. a. HQ Flag Officer, St John's NF. 31 May 1941–17 Sep 1941; Oct 1944?–31 Jul 1946. Located at Buckmaster's Field, an area bounded by Prince of Wales St, Le Marchant Rd, Munday's Pond Rd, and Colt St. For location, see *Naval Service of Canada*, Vol II, Plate VI. Became AVALON I.

Note: Supposedly, AVALON never formally commissioned. She was set up as an independent accounting establishment by signal. *Naval Service of Canada*, Vol II, p 197, note 33.

    b. as AVALON I. 17 Sep 1941–Oct? 1944.
2. Harbour craft, HC30. 1941–1942. ex *Alberta*. Became HC30.
3. Harbour craft, HC70 (ML7). 18 Jun 1940–15 Jan 1942?
4. SNOIC, St John's, NF. 1 May 1951–9 Apr 1964.

Note: Newfoundland joined Canada 31 Mar 1949 and the RCN returned as early as 5 Apr 1949. Originally located at Buckmasters Field, AVALON moved to former US base at Pepperrell, Quidi Vidi Lake, 10 Dec 1962.
5. Sea Cadet training centre, Long Pond, St John's, NF. 1985-SIS. Commissions each summer.

AVALON II
1. Floating barracks, St John's, NF. 23 Sep 1941–late Oct 1944. ex Lakeway Lines steamer *Georgian*.

AVALON III, HMS
1. Harbour craft, HC31. 23 Sep 1941 (?)–1946. Declared surplus by 1 Apr 1945. ex HMCS ZIG ZAG. Became HC31 (15 Jan 1942?). This was a Canadian vessel loaned to the RN.
2. RN accounting establishment, St John's, NF. Apr? 1941–30 Jun 1946?

Note: Before the establishment of HMS AVALON III, the term "Fort William" was used to designate the RN Officers' quarters. This name was used because it was the site of a fort by that name dating from 1618. There is recorded evidence of confusion in the post office between Fort William and FORT WILLIAM.

B

BADDECK (Geog, for the town in NS)
1. Flower class corvette, K147. 18 May 1941–4 Jul 1945.

BALEINE (N*)
1. Patrol vessel. 1 Feb 1915–2 Feb 1918. ex Lockeport Cold Storage Co steam trawler *Baleine*.

BALLY (N*)
1. Tug, Fy 88. 30 Nov 39–13 Aug 1942.

BANFF (Geog, for the town in AB)
1. Flower class corvette. Circa 1940. Before commissioning, became WETASKIWIN.

The second BRAS D'OR about 1971. (De Havilland photo by R Corlett, #32571. KM Coll.)

BANTIE (N*)
1. Patrol vessel, W04. Circa 1941–26 Jan 1945. ex fishing vessel.

BARKERVILLE
1. Ville class tug, Z19. Circa Jan 1945–17 Dec 1945, capsized and sank at entrance to Bedwell Bay, Vancouver, while towing HESPELER to her moorings.

BARKLEY SOUND (BARCLAY SOUND?) (N*)
1. Patrol vessel, Fy 23. 27 Jan 1942–Jul 1945? ex fishing vessel.

BARMAR (N*)
1. Patrol vessel, Fy 10/Z115. Second World War. ex fishing vessel *Barmar*.

BARRIE (Geog, for the town in ON)
1. Flower class corvette, K138. 12 May 1941–26 Jun 1945.

BARRINGTON
1. Tug? circa Jan–Oct 1918. Ex tug.

BARTLETT (N*)
1. Patrol vessel. Chartered 1 May–1 Dec 1915. ex Montréal Transportation Co ocean-going tug *Bartlett*.
Note: There is also a record of an ex Québec Salvage & Wrecking Co tug of this name in naval service May–Dec 1915.

BATHURST (probably for the town in NB)
1. Flower class corvette. Circa 1940. Before commissioning, became BUCTOUCHE.

BATTLEFORD (Geog, for the town in SK)
1. Flower class corvette, K165. 31 Jul 1941–18 Jul 1945.

BAYFIELD (1. N*. 2. Geog, for the town in NS)
1. Auxiliary patrol vessel. Circa Feb–Jul 1917. ex hydrographic service vessel *Bayfield*, ex *Lord Stanley*.
2. Bangor class minesweeper, J08. 1 Jul(?) 1942–24 Sep 1945. In commission as RN vessel 26 Feb–1 Jul(?) 1942.

B.C. CLIPPER
1. Auxiliary? Dates, type and source not known, Second World War.

B.C. LADY (N*)
1. Patrol vessel, Fy 07. 4 Jan 1941–May 1944. ex fishing vessel.

B.C. PILOT BOAT #1
1. Auxiliary? Dates, type and source not known, Second World War.

BEACON HILL (Geog, alternative name for Victoria, BC) B
1. a. River class frigate, K407/F407/303. 16 May 1944–6 Feb 1946;
   16 May 1949–15 Sep 1949; 15 Apr 1950–4 Jan 1954.
   b. Prestonian class frigate, 303. 21 Dec 1957–15 Sep 1967.

BEAMSVILLE
1. a. Ville class tug, Z61. 29 Jan 1944–21 Apr 1944.
   b. CNAV/CFAV, Ville class tug, 583. Circa 1949–Jun 1994?

BEAUHARNOIS (1 & 2. Geog, for the town in QC)
1. River class frigate. ex BUCKINGHAM 3 Mar 1944. Before commissioning, became PRESTONIAN.
2. Revised Flower class corvette, K540. 25 Sep 1944–12 Jul 1945.

BEAVER (1 & 2. animal) 2. B
1. Armed yacht, S10/Z10. 30 Sep 1940–17 Oct 1944. ex *Aztec*.
2. Fairmile B Type. 18 May 1954–13 Nov 1957. ex PTC706, ML106, Q106.
Note: Ship com'd and pd off each summer for several years.

BEAVERTON
1. Norton class tug, W23. 27 May 1944–Dec 1945. ?–? 1946, sank after collision with a freighter in the St Lawrence River off Cape Goose.

BECANCOEUR (N*)
1. Tug. Aug–Oct 1918. ex Dept of Marine & Fisheries tug.

BEECH LAKE
1. Lake class minesweeper, J482. completed 8 Feb 1946 but never commissioned.

BELLECHASSE (1. N* 2. Geog, for county in Québec; alternative name for St Charles, QC?)
1. Auxiliary. May–Nov 1914. ex CGS *Bellechasse*.
2. Bangor class minesweeper, J170. 13 Dec 1941–23 Oct 1945.

BELLEVILLE (Geog, for the city in ON)
1. Revised Flower class corvette, K332. 19 Oct 1944–5 Jul 1945.

BERMUDA (Geog, for the islands in the Atlantic Ocean)
1. Naval radio station, Daniel's Head, Ireland Island, Bermuda. 3 Jul 1963–10 Jul 1966. Located on site of an 11-acre former RN H.F.D.F. site.

BERSIMIS (N*)
1. Tug, W05. Circa 1941–24 Sep 1945. ex DPW tug *Bersimis*.

BERTHIER (N*)
1. Examination vessel. Taken over 15 May 1917–circa Dec 1918. Became a tender to GULNARE. Never com'd. ex Dept of Marine vessel *Berthier*.

BEULAH
1. Harbour craft, HC35. ?–14 Jan 1942. Became HC35. SIS 1 Apr 1945.

BILLOW (N*)
1. Patrol vessel, Fy 25. 25 Mar 1942–?; 9 Dec 1946–Jul 1950? ex seiner *Billow*, ex *Kuraisho*, #171790. Became YSF200?

BIRCH LAKE
1. Lake class minesweeper, J483. Completed as MV *Aspy III*. Never com'd.

BIRCHTON
1. Ton class tug, W35. 4 Nov 1944–Dec 1945.

BITTERSWEET (a flower)
1. Flower class corvette, K182. 15 May 1941–22 Jun 1945. In commission as RN vessel 23 Jan–15 May 1941.

BLACK DUCK (1. N*. 2. after 1.)
1. Crash boat, 872. 1 Apr 1965–1985. ex RCAF *Black Duck.*
2. Crash boat, 660. 1985–SIS.

BLAIRMORE (Geog, for the town in AB)
1. Bangor class minesweeper, J314. 17 Nov 1942–16 Oct 1945. Reacquired Jul 1951, pd. no. 193, but never re com'd. Transferred to Turkish Navy 29 Mar 1958 as BEYCOZ.

BLANDFORD (Geog, for the peninsula in NS)
1. Naval radio station, Lunenburg Co, NS. HMC NRS 1965–11 Jul 1966.
Note:Name in use as early as Sep 1965. During unification and before becoming operational, this NRS became CFS Mill Cove.

BLARNEY II (N*)
1. Patrol craft, Corner Brook, NF. ?–15 Jan 1942. ex Bowaters Ltd *Blarney II.* Became HC142.

BLIGH ISLAND
1. Auxiliary? Dates, type and source not known, Second World War.

BLISSVILLE
1. Ville class tug, W56. 18 Mar–Nov 1944.

BLUE BIRD (N*)
1. Motor launch. Sep 1918–1919.

BLUE HERON (bird) B
1. Bird class seaward defence patrol craft, 782. 30 Jul 56–19 Nov 56.
Note: On loan to RCMP as the *Victoria* from 28 Feb 57 until 6 May 1968. Disposed 1 Apr 70.

BLUENOSE (N*)
1. Patrol vessel, Fy 44/HC340. 21 May 1942–circa 1944, ex fishing vessel.

BLUETHROAT (bird) B
1. CNAV, harbour mineplanter, 114. 28 Nov 1955–circa 1990.

BLUE WING (N*)
1. Motor launch. Circa 1917–1920. Became RCMP vessel?

BOBBIE BURNS (N*)
1. Lighter and tug. 14 Apr 1917–26 Apr 1919. Former tug.

BONAVENTURE (Geog, for the island in St Lawrence River) B
1. Modified Majestic class light fleet aircraft carrier, 22. 17 Jan 1957–1 Jul 1970. ex HMS POWERFUL.

BONNYVILLE
1. Ville class tug. (8 Nov 1944) 7 Feb–Oct 1945.

BORDER CITIES (alternative name representing East Windsor, Walkerville, Windsor and Sandwich, which amalgamated into Windsor, ON, in 1935.)
1. Algerine class minesweeper, J344. 18 May 1944–15 Jan 1946.

BOWMANVILLE (1& 2. Geog, for the town in ON)
1. Name assigned to an Algerine class minesweeper but never promulgated. Ship turned over to RN o/c as HMS COQUETTE, J350.
2. Castle class corvette, K493. 28 Sep 1944–15 Feb 1946. ex HMS NUNNERY CASTLE, K446.

BRAMPTON (Geog, for the town in ON)
1. Revised Flower class corvette. Cancelled Dec 1943.

BRANDON (1 & 2. Geog, for the city in MB) 2. B
1. Flower class corvette, K149. 22 Jul 1941–22 Jun 1945.
2. Kingston class mine warfare vessel, 710. 5 Jun 1999–SIS.

BRANT (N*)
1. Auxiliary. 16 Dec 1914–4 Jan 1915; 11-28 Feb 1915; Mar–Apr 1915. ex Dept of Marine & Fisheries vessel.

BRANTFORD (2. Geog, for the city in ON)
1. Flower class corvette, K218. 15 May 1942–17 Aug 1945. ex MIDLAND.

BRAS D'OR (1. N/K 2. Geog, for the saltwater lakes in Cape Breton, NS) 2. B
1. Trawler, auxiliary minesweeper, TR 18/J06. 9 Oct 1939–19 Oct 1940, disappeared in the Gulf of St Lawrence. ex LV25, ex *Edouard Houle*.
2. Fast hydrofoil, experimental, 400. 19 Jul 1968–1 May 1972. Became a static exhibit, Musée Bernier, L'Islet sur Mer, Québec, 1983 to present day.

BRENTWOOD
1. Wood class tug, Z48. 28 Aug 1944–1947?

BROCKVILLE (Geog, for the city in ON) B
1. a. Bangor class minesweeper, J270. 19 Sep 1942–28 Aug 1945. Became RCMP *Macleod*.
   b. Reacquired by RCN, 178. 5 Apr 1951–13 Jan 1953; 22 Apr 1954–12 Dec 1956; 29 Aug 1958–31 Oct 1958.

BRUNSWICKER (for a provincial government vessel which served against American privateers in the War of 1812.) B
1. Naval reserve division, Saint John, NB.
   a. 1 Nov 1941–1 Sep 1942. Tender to CAPTOR II.
   b. 1 Sep 1942–SIS.
Originally located at 221-223 Prince William St and in 1945, moved to D.E.M.S. Training Centre (old NOIC Bldg) on Saint James Street. On paying off of CAPTOR II, moved to Reed's Point. Moved back to 221-223 Prince William Street, Jan 1958(?). The move to Bldg 36, Barracks Green Armouries, 60 Broadview Ave, was completed 22 Apr 1966. Moved to 160 Chesley Drive, 6 May 1995.

BUCKINGHAM (Geog, for the town in QC) B
1. a. River class frigate, K685. 2 Nov 1944–16 Nov 1945. Name changed from ROYALMOUNT 5 Apr 1944.
   b. Prestonian class frigate, 314. 25 Jun 1954–30 Sep 1957; 6 May 1958–23 Mar 1965.

BUCTOUCHE (Geog, for Bathurst, NB and Buctoche, NB)
1. Flower class corvette, K179. 5 Jun 1941–15 Jun 1945. ex BATHURST.

BURLINGTON (Geog, for the bay on Lake Ontario)
1. Bangor class minesweeper, J250. 6 Sep 1941–30 Oct 1945. ex ST ANN, ex BURLINGTON.

BURMA (N*)

1. Harbour craft, HC36. 3 Sep 1939–15 Jan 1942. Became HC36. ex RCMP *Burma*.

BURRARD (Geog, for the inlet. See note)

1. NOIC, 408 Marine Bldg, Vancouver, BC. Est'd 1 Sep 39, com'd May(?) 1942–15 Aug 1942.

Note: Burrard Inlet was named after Sir Harry Burrard Neale, RN, Admiral of the Fleet who died 7 Feb 1840. He was captain of one of Vancouver's ships on a west coast voyage circa 1792. Sir Harry assumed the name Neale in 1795.

2. Vessel, type not known; NOIC and depot "ship." 15 Aug 1942–28 Feb 1946.
3. Ville class tug, 582. Circa 1974–circa 1991. ex ADAMSVILLE.

BUXTON (N*, for two towns in England and one in the USA)

1. Town class destroyer, H96. 4 Nov 1943–2 Jun 1945. ex HMS BUXTON, ex USS EDWARDS. Only used as a stationary training ship.

BYTOWN (Geog, for the village, predecessor of the city of Ottawa) 2. B

1. a. Depot ship for NSHQ and reserve division, Alymer Bldg, Slater St, Ottawa. 1 Jun 1941–23 Nov 1942. The reserve division became CARLETON 1 Nov 1941 and apparently remained on site until Dec 1941.
   b. Depot ship for NSHQ and reserve personnel, Alymer Bldg, Slater St, Ottawa. 21 May 1942–23 Nov 1942. CARLETON paid off 21 May 1942 and recom'd 23 Nov 1942.
   c. Depot ship for NSHQ, The Navy Bldg, Cartier Square, Ottawa. 23 Nov 1942–7 Dec 1964. About 1950, The Navy Bldg was redesignated as A Bldg and NSHQ moved to B Bldg, opposite the present Bytown mess on Lisgar St.
2. a. Depot ship, naval reserve. 9 Oct 1941–23 Nov 1942. Became HC128 about June 1942. ex ORACLE.
   b. Depot ship for NSHQ, Ottawa. HC128. 23 Nov 1942–13 Oct 1945.

Note: The name is still used by the Naval Officers' Mess, 78 Lisgar St, Ottawa.

BYTOWN II

1. WRCNS training establishment, Galt, ON circa Oct 1942–1 Jun 1943. Became CONESTOGA.

Note: Never apparently commissioned. The second course of WRCNS commenced training there, 15 Oct 1942. The training officer, Second Officer Isabel Macneil, was in charge. Officially termed "WRCNS Training Establishment Galt", BYTOWN II was treated and termed the same as all other WRCNS training establishments until commissioned as CONESTOGA 1 Jun 1943 under the command of First Officer Isabel Macneil.

C

CABOT (probably after a prize taken from the Americans in 1777) B

1. Naval reserve division, St John's, NF. 20 Sep 1949–SIS. Originally located at Buckmaster's Field. Moved in Jun 1963 to Bldg 314, Pleasantville (which is the site of the ex US base at Fort Pepperrell). And in Nov 1999, moved to Pier 27 in the harbour of St John's.

CACHALOT (N*)

1. Tug, St John's, NF, W00. 19 Jul 1943–31 Dec 1944. Ex Victory Transport & Salvage Co tug *Cachalot*.

CAIRN

1. Auxiliary training vessel. 1 May 1944–Jul 1946? ex schooner GLENCAIRN.

CALGARY (1 & 2. Geog, for the city in AB) 2. B
1. Revised Flower class corvette, K231. 16 Dec 1941–19 Jun 1945.
2. Halifax class frigate, 335. 12 May 1995–SIS.

CAMENITA (N*)
1. Patrol vessel, Fy 41. 27 Apr 1942–16 Nov 1944. ex fishing vessel *Camenita*.

CAMPBELLTON (Geog, for the town in NB)
1. Flower class corvette. Circa 1940. Became MONCTON.

CAMROSE (Geog, for the town in AB)
1. Flower class corvette, K154. 30 Jun 1941–18 Jul 1945.

CANADA (N*)
1. Patrol vessel. 25 Jan 1915–Nov 1919. ex Dept of Marine & Fisheries patrol vessel *Canada*. Note: According to the *Naval Service of Canada*, Vol 1, p 215, CGS *Canada* was ordered to hoist the White Ensign on 4 Aug 1914 but she was not officially com'd until 25 Jan 1915.

CANCOLIM (N*)
1. Patrol vessel, P10/Z10 (P). Circa Jan 1940–Sep 1945. ex American Can Co vessel *Cancolim*.

CANFISCO (N*)
1. Patrol vessel, Fy 17. Circa 1943–Mar 1944. ex Canadian Fishing Co fishing vessel *Canfisco*.

CANSO (1. N* 2. Geog, for the town in NS)
1. Tug. 28 Dec 1917?–1 May 1919? ex DPW tug.
2. Bangor class minesweeper, M21/J21. 1 Jul(?) 1942–24 Sep 1945. In commission as RN vessel 5 Mar–1 Jul(?) 1942.

CAP DE LA MADELEINE (Geog, for the town in QC) B
1. a. River class frigate, K633. 30 Sep 1944–25 Nov 1945.
   b. Prestonian class frigate, 317. 20 May 1959–15 May 1965.

CAPE BEALE (N*)
1. Auxiliary minesweeper, Fy 26. Circa Oct 1939–Feb 1944. ex fish-packer *Cape Beale*.

HMCS CRESCENT on the Yangtze River of China in 1949.
(Negative number believed to be RCN EC 58-262. FDN Coll.)

CAPE BRETON (1. Island in NS. Alternative name for Sydney, NS. 2. for the Cape in NS.) 2. B
1. River class frigate, K350. 25 Oct 1943–26 Jan 1946.
2. a. Cape class escort maintenance ship, 100. 31 Jan 1953–25 Aug 1958; 16 Nov 1959–10 Feb 1964. In reserve 1964–1972.
   b. Hulk, 1972–1993. Used as a home for Fleet Maintenance Group (Pacific) and known as Building 100. In 1993, replaced by a building named "Cape Breton."

CAPE SCOTT (Geog, for the cape on Vancouver Island, BC) B
1. Cape class escort maintenance ship, 101. 28 Jan 1959–1 Jul 1970. ex HMS BEACHY HEAD, ex RNethN VULKAAN, ex HMS BEACHY HEAD. In reserve until circa 1975.

CAPELLA (CAPELLA 1) (N*)
1. Patrol vessel, Fy 31. 17 Sep 1939? (16 Aug 1940?)–Feb 1944. ex fishing vessel *Capella*.

CAPILANO (alternative name for the city of North Vancouver, BC)
1. River class frigate, K409. 25 Aug 1944–24 Nov 1945.

CAPTOR (1. N/K. 2. N*. 3. N*)
1. Naval Officer-in-charge, 250 Prince William St, Saint John, NB. 18 Sep 1939–circa 1942.
2. Harbour craft, HC37. 3 Sep 1939–15 Jan 1942. Became HC37. ex RCMP *Captor*. Referred to as CAPTOR I, 21? Apr 1945.
3. Detachment class patrol craft, 193. 17 Mar 1976–circa 1993. ex RCMP *Captor*.

CAPTOR II
1. Depot ship and accommodation vessel, Saint John, NB. Oct 1939–8 Sep 1942. ex DOT vessel PWD dredge No. 1.
2. Depot ship for accounting purposes and NOIC, Reed's Point, Saint John, NB. 1 Apr 1941–30 Sep 1944.
Note: The duties of this base were transferred to BRUNSWICKER from Sep 1944 until the position of NOIC Saint John was abolished, 1 Jan 1946.

CARAQUET (Geog, for the town in NB)
1. Bangor class minesweeper, J38. 1 Jul(?) 1942–26 Sep 1945. In commission as RN vessel 31 Mar (2 Apr?)–1 Jul(?) 1942.

CARIBOU (1. for the Animal. 2. after the Newfoundland Government ferry which was torpedoed and sunk Oct 1942. 3. N/K) 2. B
1. Armed yacht, S12/Z25. 27 May 1940–?; 9 Oct 1941–20 Jul 1945. ex *Elfreda*.
2. Naval reserve division, Corner Brook, NF. 28 Aug 1953–31 Mar 1958. Located in a portion of a Bowaters Co warehouse.
3. Diving tender, YDT 2. Circa 1982–circa 1992. Name used without authority for several years and officially authorized 1982.

CARLETON (after a schooner at Battle of Valcour Island, 11 Oct 1776) B
1. a. Naval reserve division, Ottawa, ON. 1 Nov 1941–21 May 1942. Tender to BYTOWN. Originally co-located with BYTOWN, moved to ex school at 453 Rideau St circa 11 Dec 1941.
   b. Naval reserve division, Ottawa. 23 Nov 1942–SIS. Located at 453 Rideau St but moved to Dow's Lake effective 20 Sep 1943, officially 17 Dec 1943.

CARLTON (Geog, for the village in SK)
1. Flower class corvette. Before commissioning, became KAMSACK circa Apr 1941.

CARLPLACE (alternative name for Carleton Place, ON)
1. River class frigate, K664. 13 Dec 1944–13 Nov 1945.

CARTIER (1. N*. 2. N/K)
1. a. Auxiliary patrol vessel. Sep 1914 (spring 1917)–circa Dec 1918. ex hydrographic survey ship *Cartier*.
    b. Training ship, Z02. 18 Sep 1939–9 Dec 1941. Became CHARNY to avoid confusion with reserve division.
2. Naval reserve division, 1057 and later 1464 Mountain St, Montréal, QC. This English-speaking division amalgamated with the French-speaking division DONNACONA, 9 Jun 1944, and moved to 1475 Drummond St. Still listed c/w officers as late as 1 Jan 1946, *Navy List*.
    a. 1 Nov 1941–1 Sep 1942. Tender to HOCHELAGA II.
    b. 1 Sep 1942–15 Sep 1945.

CASCAPEDIA
1. Tug. Circa 1943–44. ex ST ANNE.

CASTOR (N*)
1. Harbour craft, HC38. 3 Sep 1939–15 Jan 1942. Became HC38. ex RCMP *Castor*.

CATARAQUI (after a small vessel built at Fort Frontenac (Kingston) circa 1678 in the time of La Salle) B
1. Naval reserve division, Kingston, ON.
    a. 1 Nov 1941–1 Sep 1942. Tender to STADACONA. Located on the waterfront at the very bottom of Princess St.
    b. 1 Sep 1942–SIS. Moved to 453 Rideau St circa 1943, then to 47 Wellington St; then the Richardson Bldg on Princess St; then to the Athletic Centre, RMC; in 1972 to the PWOR Armouries, 100 Montréal St; and from 21 Nov 1993 to new facilities at Bldg 67, CFB Kingston.

CAVALIER
1. Ville class tug, 578. Circa 1974–circa 1991. ex LISTERVILLE. Tender to DONNACONA.

CAYUGA (For the First Nations tribe on the Six Nations Reserve, ON. One of the five original tribes of the Iroquois Confederacy in New York State, some of them moved to Ontario at the end of the American Revolutionary War) B
1. a. Tribal class destroyer, R04/D104/218. 20 Oct 1947–1 Jan 1949; 25 Sep 1949–14 Jul 1952. (Pt no. changed Nov 1949)
    b. Tribal class destroyer escort, 218. 23 Feb 1953–27 Feb 1964.

The depot ship CAPTOR II at Saint John, NB, May 1940. (KM Coll.)

C1, later **CC1**

1. Submarine, Electric Boat Co design 19E. Purchased by BC gov't directly from Seattle, Wash., shipyard and resold to RCN. ex Chilean IQUIQUE.
   a. C1, 7 Aug 1914–6 Oct 1914. Renamed CC1. The extra letter C stood for "Canadian" to distinguish her from the RN's C1.
   b. CC1, 6 Oct 1914–13 Dec 1918.

C2, later **CC2**

1. Submarine. Electric Boat Co design 19B. Purchased by BC gov't directly from Seattle, Wash., shipyard and resold to RCN. ex Chilean ANTOFAGASTA.
   a. C2, 7 Aug 1914–6 Oct 1914. Renamed CC2. The extra letter C stood for "Canadian" to distinguish her from the RN's C2.
   b. CC2, 6 Oct 1914–13 Dec 1918.

C.E. TANNER (N*)

1. Tug. Circa Oct 1918.

CECILIA (N*)

1. Motor boat. Chartered 10 Aug 1918–?

CEDAR LAKE

1. Lake class minesweeper, J484. Completed 4 Nov 1945 but never com'd.

CEDARWOOD (for the tree) B

1. Survey vessel, 530. 22 Sep 1948–19 Oct 1956. ex RCASC *General Schmidlin*, ex MV *J.E. Kinney*.

CH 14

1. H class submarine.1 Apr 1921–30 Jun 1922. ex HM Submarine H14. As RN boat, in reserve Dec 1915; com'd Feb & Aug 1918. Pd off Dec 1918 in Bermuda. Sailed to Halifax with Canadian steaming crew Feb 1919 & placed in reserve. *Naval Service of Canada* states com'd Jun 1919 but no evidence located for this.

CH 15

1. H class submarine.1 Apr 1921–30 Jun 1922. ex HM Submarine H15. As RN boat, in reserve Dec 1915; com'd Aug 1918. Pd off Dec 1918 in Bermuda. Sailed to Halifax with Canadian Steaming crew Feb 1919 & placed in reserve. *Naval Service of Canada* states com'd Jun 1919 but no evidence located for this.

CHALEUR (1. N* 2. N/K. 3. & 4. Geog, for the bay in Gulf of St Lawrence) 4. B

1. Patrol vessel, Z20/J20. Sep 1939–15 Jun 1945. ex RCMP motorboat *Chaleur*. Referred to as CHALEUR I.
2. NOIC, Customs House Bldg, Québec City. Est'd Sep 1939. Com'd 27 Apr 1940–21 Oct 1945.
3. Bay class minesweeper, 144. 18 Jun–30 Sep 1954. Transferred to French navy as LA DIEPPOISE.
4. Bay class minesweeper, 164. 12 Sep 1957–19 Feb 1964; 15 Apr–30 Sep 1967; 31 Mar 1969–(12?)18 Dec 1998.

CHALEUR II

1. Depot ship for pay and accounting purposes, Naval Office Bldg, Pointe à Carey, Québec City. 1 Apr 1941 to 21 Oct 1945.

CHAMBLY (Geog, for the city in QC)

1. Flower class corvette, K116. 18 Dec 1940–20 Jun 1945.

CHAMISS BAY (N*)
1. Patrol vessel, Fy 39/F50. 28 Mar 1942–15 Mar 1945. ex fishing vessel *Chamiss Bay*, 154926.

CHAMPLAIN (1 & 2. for the explorer Samuel de Champlain) 2. B
1. S class destroyer, ex HMS TORBAY, D17/H24/H25/F50. 1 Mar 1928–25 Nov 1936.
2. Naval reserve division, Gealerius Racine, 141 Racine East, Chicoutimi, QC.16 Aug 1986–SIS.

CHARLES H CATES V
1. Auxiliary? Dates, type and source not known, Second World War. Ex motor launch, 134415?

CHARLOTTETOWN (1, 2 & 3. Geog, for the city in PEI) 3. B
1. Revised Flower class corvette, K244. 13 Dec 1941–11 Sep 1942, torpedoed and sunk by U517 in the St Lawrence River near Cap Chat, QC.
2. River class frigate, K244. 28 Apr 1944–25 Mar 1947.
3. Halifax class frigate, 339. 9 Sep 1995–SIS.

CHARNY (Geog, for the town in QC)
1. Training ship, S02/Z02/Z26. 9 Dec 1941–12 Dec 1945. ex CARTIER.

CHATHAM (1. see note. 2. after HMS CHATHAM, one of the ships of the explorer Capt George Vancouver) 2. B
1. NOIC, 51 McBride St, Prince Rupert, BC. Established Jun 1940. Com'd 1 Apr 1942–circa late 1945. ex Fisheries Experimental Station.
2. Naval reserve division, Prince Rupert, BC. 21 Oct 1946–31 Mar 1964. Located at 51 McBride St, in a bldg now called Chatham House.
Note: Chatham is a local name used quite often in the Prince Rupert area for various geographical features. It is quite probable that the name of the first establishment was chosen for that reason.

CHATHAM S (N*)
1. Patrol vessel, Fy 47. May–13 Jun 1942. Became SEA WAVE.

CHAUDIERE (1 & 2. Geog, for the river in QC) 2. B
1. H/River class destroyer, H99. 15 Nov 1943–17 Aug 1945. ex HMS HERO.
2. Restigouche class destroyer escort, 235. 14 Nov 1959–23 May 1974. Lay alongside in Esquimalt until fall 1991 when sold for $1.00 to Artificial Reef Society and sunk near Whaleboat Island, Nanaimo, BC.

CHEBOGUE (alternative name for Yarmouth, NS)
1. River class frigate, K317. 22 Feb 1944–25 Sep 1945.

CHEDABUCTO (Geog, for a bay on the coast of NS)
1. Bangor class minesweeper, J168. 27 Sep 1941–21 Oct 1943, collided with the cable vessel *Lord Kelvin* and sank 30 miles off Rimouski, QC.

CHERRY LAKE
1. Lake class minesweeper, J485. cancelled 22 Oct 1945.

CHERRY PICKER
1. Auxiliary, circa 1942, at Esquimalt. Type & size not known.

CHICKADEE (CHICADEE, CHICADLE?) (N*)
1. Motor launch. Chartered 24 Apr–3 Nov 1915; 21 Nov 1915–Mar? 1917.

CHICOUTIMI (1 & 2. Geog, for the city in QC) 2. B
1. Flower class corvette, K156. 12 May 1941–16 Jun 1945.
2. Victoria class submarine, 879. To commission late in 2001. Ex HMS UPHOLDER.

CHIEF SEAGAY
1. Tender to GIVENCHY. (8 Nov?) 1939–(Apr 1940?) 1942? Type, pd. no. and source unknown.

CHIEF TAPEET
1. Tender to GIVENCHY. Circa 1939–1942? Type, pd. no. and source unknown.

CHIGNECTO (1, 2 & 3. Geog, for the bay between NB and NS) 3. B
1. Bangor class minesweeper, J160. 31 Oct 1941–3 Nov 1946.
2. Bay class minesweeper, 156. 1 Dec 1953–31 Mar 1954, transferred to French Navy as LA BAYONNAISE.
3. Bay class minesweeper, 160. 1 Aug 1957–29 Jan 1964; 31 Mar 1969–?; 1 May 1970–19 Dec 1998.

CHILLIWACK (Geog, for the town in BC)
1. Flower class corvette, K131. 8 Apr 1941–14 Jul 1945.

CHIMO
1. Naval radio station, Ungava Bay, QC. Sep 1948–late 1952.

CHIMON (N*)
1. RCSC training vessel, Midland, ON circa 1943–Apr 1946. Chartered.

CHIPPAWA (after HMS CHIPPAWA, one of the ships on Lake Erie, 1812-13) B
1. Naval reserve division, Winnipeg, MB. Originally located in Security Storage Bldg, 583 Ellice. Moved to the Winter Club Bldg, 51 Smith St Aug/Oct 1942. First block of Smith St renamed Navy Way 5 May 1985. Moved to Hangar 11, CFB Winnipeg 2 May 1988 while old quarters torn down and new facilities constructed. Moved back to 1 Navy Way 21 Nov 1999, officially reopening 28 Nov 1999.
   a. 1 Nov 1941–1 Sep 1942. Tender to NADEN.
   b. 1 Sep 1942–SIS.

CHRISTINE (N*)
1. Auxiliary. Chartered 21 Apr–Nov 1914. ex steamship *Christine*.

CHURCHILL (1 & 2. Geog, for the town in MB) 2. B
1. Flower class corvette. Circa 1940. Never com'd; became MOOSE JAW.
2. Naval radio station, Churchill, MB.
   a. established 1 Aug 1943.
   b. HMC NRS. 1 Dec 1950–1 Jul 1956.
   c. HMCS. 1 Jul 1956–11 Jul 1966. Became CFS Churchill.

CITADEL (CITADELLE?) (N*)
1. Examination vessel, Halifax. (21?) 23 Dec 1939–25 Jan 1940? ex DOT tug.

CLAIRE L
1. Harbour craft, HC39. 28 Dec 1940–15 Jan 1942. Became HC39.

CLAYOQUOT (Geog, for the Sound on Vancouver Island)
1. Bangor class minesweeper, J174. 22 Aug 1941–24 Dec 1944, torpedoed by U806 and sunk three miles off the Sambro Light Vessel. ex ESPERANZA.

CLEOPATRA (N*)
1. Patrol vessel, Fy 89/Z35. 27 Jul 1940–20 Sep 1945. ex motor launch.

CLIFTON
1. a. Norton class tug, W36. 21 Nov 1944–1946?
   b. CNAV/CFAV, Ton class tug, W36/529. 1946?–circa 1976.

CLIMAX (N*)
1. Tug? 24 Apr–18 May 1918, sunk in collision with HM submarine H-1.

COASTGUARD (N*)
1. Tug. Chartered late 1916–31 Jan 1919. ex Southern Salvage Co tug.

COATICOOK (Geog, for the town in QC)
1. River class frigate, K410. 25 Jul 1944–29 Nov 1949.

COBALT (Geog, for the town in ON)
1. Flower class corvette, K124. 25 Nov 1940–17 Jun 1945.

COBOURG (Geog, for the town in ON)
1. Revised Flower class corvette, K333. 11 May 1944–16 Jun 1945.

COLLINGWOOD (Geog, for the town in ON)
1. Flower class corvette, K180. 9 Nov 1940–23 Jul 1945.

COLUMBIA (1 & 2. Geog, for the river in BC) 2. B
1. Town class destroyer, I49. 24 Sep 1940–17 Mar 1944. ex USS HARADEN.
2. Restigouche class destroyer escort, 260. 7 Nov 1959–18 Feb 1974. Was a harbour training ship for Fleet School Esquimalt from Jun 1984 to spring 1994.

COLVILLE
1. Ville class tug, W?. 27 May 1944 to circa 1946.
2. CNAV, Ville class tug, 576. Circa 1946–31 Mar 1964.

COMBAT
1. Patrol vessel. 1940?–23 Aug 1941, transferred to RCAF.

COMBER (alternative name–water related)
1. Patrol vessel, Fy 37. 11 Mar 1942–16 Oct 1944. ex fishing vessel *C.S.C. II.*

COMOX (1 & 2. Geog, for the harbour, Vancouver Island, BC) 2. B
1. Basset/Fundy class minesweeper, N64/J64. 23 Nov 1938–27 Jul 1945.
2. Bay class minesweeper, 146. 2 Apr 1954–11 Sep 1957. Transferred to Turkish Navy 31 Mar 1958 as TIREBOLU.

CONESTOGA (a local name picked by the WRCNS community in BYTOWN II)
1. WRCNS training establishment, Galt, ON. 1 Jun 1943–31 Mar 1945. ex BYTOWN II. Former Grandview Correctional School for girls located west of Hespeler & Mulch St, NW of the present Police Station, Cambridge, ON. By Mar 1943, also included the Preston Springs Hotel, used as extension quarters. See note under BYTOWN.

CONSTANCE (N*)
1. Minesweeper/patrol craft/examination vessel, D76. Aug 1914–31 Jan 1919. ex Customs vessel *Constance.* In naval service but commissioning is in doubt.

CONTRECOEUR (N*)
1. Tug. Aug 1918–Oct 1919? ex Dept of Marine & Fisheries tug.

COPPER CLIFF (1 & 2. Geog, for the town in ON)
1. Name assigned to an Algerine class minesweeper but never promulgated. Ship turned over to RN o/c as HMS FELICITY, J369.
2. Castle class corvette, K495. 25 Feb 1944–21 Nov 1945. ex HMS HEVER CASTLE, K521.

COQUITLAM (for the District in BC)
1. Llewellyn class minesweeper, J364. 25 Jul 1944–30 Nov (?) 1945.

CORDOVA (Geog, for the bay on Vancouver Island, near Victoria) B
1. Minesweeper, 158. 9 Aug 1952–12 Apr 1957. ex USS YMS 420.

CORNER BROOK (for the city in NF) B
1. Victoria class submarine, 878. To commission mid 2001. Ex HMS URSULA.

CORMORANT (1 & 2 bird) 1. B
1. Bird class seaward defence patrol craft, 781. 16 Jul 1956–23 May 1963.
2. a. CFAV. 30 Jun 1975–3 Aug 1977. ex Italian stern trawler *ASPA Quarto*. Note: ASPA is a company, the Armatoriale Sarda Pesca Atlantica-Sassari.
   b. HMCS, Fleet diving support vessel, 20. 10 Nov 1978–2 Jul 1997.

CORNWALLIS (after Colonel the Honourable Edward Cornwallis, founder of Halifax and 1st Governor of NS) 2. B
1. a. Naval training establishment, Halifax, NS. 1 May 1942–14 Apr 1943. Located in Nelson Barracks and various bldgs scattered throughout the dockyard and barracks area.
   b. Naval training establishment, Deep Brook, NS. 14 Apr 1943–28 Feb 1945; 1 May 1949–1 Apr 1966(?) Became CFB Cornwallis.
Note: The sign over the main gate remained HMCS CORNWALLIS as late as 1968.

COUGAR (animal) 2. B
1. Armed yacht, P15/Z15. (P) 11 Sep 1940–23 Nov 1945. ex *Breezin' Thru*.
2. Fairmile B Type. 27 Apr 1953–1955; 4 May 1956–16 Oct 1956. ex PTC704, ex ML704, ex ML104.

COURTENAY (Geog, for the city in BC)
1. Bangor class minesweeper, J262. 21 Mar 1942–5 Nov 1945.

COVERDALE (Geog, for the community near Moncton, NB) B
1. Naval radio station, Coverdale, NB.
   a. Est'd as an H.F.D.F. station, circa 1941.
   b. HMC NRS. 1 Dec 1949–1 Jul 1956.
   c. HMCS. 1 Jul 1956–19 Jul 1966. Became CFS Coverdale.

COWICHAN (1, 3 & 4 Geog, for the bay on Vancouver Island, BC) 4. B
1. Bangor class minesweeper, J146. 4 Jul 1941–9 Oct 1945.
2. Water boat, Esquimalt, HC110. Second World War. Dates not known.
3. Bay class minesweeper, 147. 10 Dec 1953–31 Mar 1954, transferred to French navy as LA MALOUINE.
4. Bay class minesweeper, 162. 12 Dec 1957–28 Feb 1964; 1 May 1970–22 Aug 1997.

CRANBROOK (Geog, for the town in BC)
1. Llewellyn class minesweeper, J372. 12 May 1944–3 Nov 1945.

CREE (for one of the most prominent prairie First Nations tribes)
1. CFAV, Ville class tug, 584. 1972–1978. Tender to CHIPPAWA. ex LAWRENCEVILLE.

CRESCENT (N*, a type of moon; name dates from a coaster hired during the Armada) B
1. a. C/Crescent class destroyer, R16/D16/226. 10 Sep 1945–1 Dec 1949; 26 Sep 1950–25 Feb 1953. ex HMS CRESCENT.
   b. Algonquin class destroyer escort, 226. 31 Oct 1955–12 Aug 1966.

CREST (alternative name—water related)
1. Patrol vessel, Fy 38. 23 Feb 1942–16 Nov 1944. ex fishing vessel *May S*, 154437.

CROSSBOW (name taken from main device in the badge of HUNTER for which she was a tender)
  1. Patrol boat, 116. 1976–circa Jun 1995. ex YMU 116.

CRUSADER (1. N*. 2. N*, a participant in any of nine crusades, 1095-1272) 2. B
  1. Patrol vessel, Z13 (P). 27 Mar 1940–8 Aug 1944. ex yacht *Crusader*, ex MV *Invader*.
  2. C/Crescent/Algonquin class destroyer, R20/D120/228. 15 Nov 1945–21 Jan 1946; 2 Apr 1951–15 Jan 1960. ex HMS CRUSADER.

CULVER (N*)
  1. Auxiliary schooner. Circa Jul 1944–Oct 1947? Requisitioned 28 Apr 1944. ex Royal Society of London (?) yacht *Culver*, ex *Lady Nancy*.

CURLEW (N*)
  1. Minesweeper/patrol craft/examination vessel. Aug 1914–1921. ex Marine & Fisheries vessel *Curlew*. Commissioning in doubt.

CYRUS FIELD (N*)
  1. Cable layer. 7 Jun 1943–Dec 1943. ex British Union Telegraph Co Vessel *Cyrus Field*.

D

DAERWOOD (alternative name for the town of Selkirk, MB)
  1. Llewellyn class minesweeper, J357. 22 Apr 1944–28 Nov 1945.

DAISY (N*)
  1. Tug. Circa 1942. ex tug *Daisy*.

DALEHURST
  1. Patrol vessel, Fy 35. 1 May 1944–Jun 1945. ex GLENDALE V, 172338.

DALHOUSIE (Geog, for the town in NB)
  1. Flower class corvette, circa 1940. Before commissioning, became SACKVILLE.

DANIEL II (N*)
  1. Tug. 9 Jan–28 Jun 1943. ex Atlantic Towboat Lines tug *Daniel II*.

DAUPHIN (Geog, for the town in MB)
  1. Flower class corvette, K157. 17 May 1941–20 Jun 1945.

DAVY JONES (N*)
  1. Auxiliary. 31 Oct?–28 Dec 1914.

DAWSON (Geog, for the town in the Yukon)
  1. Flower class corvette, K104. 6 Oct 1941–19 Jun 1945.

DELBERT D (N*)
  1. Tug. 11 Mar 1917–Oct 1918? ex Southern Salvage Co tug.

DELIVERANCE (N*)
  1. Patrol vessel. Chartered 1 Dec 1914–15 Jun 1917. ex Southern Salvage Co Steam Trawler *Deliverance*.

DEPARTURE BAY (N*)
  1. Patrol vessel, Fy 48. 17 Jan 1942–16 Nov 1944. ex fishing vessel *Departure Bay*.

DESCHAILLONS (N*)
  1. Tug. May?–20 Nov 1918. ex Dept of Marine & Fisheries tug.

DETECTOR (N*)
  1. Detachment class patrol craft, 192. 17 Mar 1976–circa 1988. ex RCMP *Detector*.

D.G. WHALER (N*)

1. Harbour auxiliary. Circa 1941–?. Type and source not known.

DIANA (1. probably named after the daughter of Adm Kingsmill. 2 & 3 after 1?)

   1. a. Tender to RN College of Canada. 25 Aug 1911–1914? ex schooner *Advocate*. Never com'd.

      b. Depot ship, Halifax. 20 Aug 1914–7 Sep 1915, became Boom Gate Vessel No 2 and as such served until 1 Feb 1919.

   2. Shore barracks, Halifax. Nov 1914–6 Sep 1915.

   3. Tender to RN College of Canada. 7 Sep 1915–17 Mar 1919. ex schooner *Arthur W.*

D'IBERVILLE (1 & 2. Named for Pierre le Moyne, Sieur D'Iberville, one of the first French Naval Officers in North America, born Montréal 1661) 1. B

   1. New Entry Training Establishment, Québec City. Established Feb 1952 in MONTCALM. In commission 21 Oct 1952–31 Jul 1961. see also HOCHELAGA.

Note: In DHH files, these dates are listed under the second commissioning but there is no reference to a first commissioning.

   2. Naval reserve division, 446 Rue de l'Expansion, Rimouski, Québec. 14 Nov 1987–SIS.

DIGBY (Geog, for the town in NS) B

   1. Bangor class minesweeper J267/179. 26 Jul 1942–31 Jul 1945; 29 Apr 1953–14 Nov 1956.

DISCOVERY (named for one of the ships on Capt Cook's third voyage, Captain Vancouver's ship, and Henry Hudson's ship) B

   1. Naval reserve division, Vancouver, BC. Located in the Royal Vancouver Yacht Club bldg, Stanley Park; sick bay located on upper deck of Vancouver Rowing Club bldg, Coal Harbour. Moved to Deadman's Island 26 Jan 1944 (officially opened 21 Oct 1944).

      a. 1 Nov 1941–1 Sep 1942. Tender to GIVENCHY.

      b. 1 Sep 1942–SIS.

DISPATCH II (N*)

   1. Tug, W07. 23 Aug 1943–1945. ex Nemago (Neways?) Timber Co tug *Dispatch II*, 154966.

DIXIE (N*)

   1. RCSC training vessel, Port Arthur (now Thunder Bay), ON. 1 May–Oct 1944. ex DOT motor boat *Dixie*.

DOLPHIN II

   1. Auxiliary, HC158. Dates, source and type not known, Second World War.

DOMINION (probably from HMS DOMINION, battleship 1905-21) (B*)

   1. Manning Depot, Devonport, Eng. 1 Oct 1940–1 Mar 1941. Became NIOBE. Located in Stoke Dameral School; then in a private house at 6 Havelock Terrace; finally in the United Services Orphanage.

DONNACONA (probably for First Nations Chief who met Jacques Cartier in 1535) B

   1. Naval reserve division, Montréal. 26 Oct 1943–SIS. ex MONTREAL. Located at 1464 Mountain St. Moved to 1475 Drummond St, 9 Jun 1944. Moved to 2055 Drummond late 1958.

Note: Originally, a French-speaking division. Amalgamated with CARTIER, 9 Jun 1944. Both located at 1475 Mountain Street, and earlier, 1007 Mountain Street.

DONNACONA II

   1. Training vessel, Montréal. 26 Oct 1943–Jul 1946? ex MONTREAL II, ex *Stumble Inn 1*, ex Patrol Boat No. 4.

DORCAS II
    1. Former name of a work boat, HC147. 18 Dec 1942–1945?

DORET (N*)
    1. Auxiliary patrol vessel. Circa Jul 1919.

DORIS MARY
    1. Harbour craft, HC40. Circa Oct 1940–15 Jan 1942. Became HC40. Type and source not known.

DRUID (N*)
    1. Harbour craft. (14?) Oct 1939–1 Apr 1942. ex CGS *Druid*, on loan from DOT.

DRUMHELLER (Geog, for the town in AB)
    1. Flower class corvette, K167. 13 Sep 1941–11 Jul 1945.

DRUMMONDVILLE (Geog, for the town in QC)
    1. a. Bangor class minesweeper, J253. 30 Oct 1941–29 Oct 1945.

DUNDALK (Geog, for the town in ON)
    1. a. Dun class tanker, Z40. 13 Nov 1943–9 Apr 1946.
       b. CNAV/CFAV, 501. 9 Apr 1946?–17 Dec 1982.

DUNDAS (Geog, for the town in ON)
    1. Flower class corvette, K229. 1 Apr 1942–17 Jul 1945.

DUNDEE
    1. Auxiliary? Date, type and source not known, Second World War.

DUNDURN (Geog, for the town in SK?)
    1. a. Dun class tanker, Z41. 25 Nov 1943–2 Jan 1947.
       b. CNAV/CFAV, 502. 2 Jan 1947–circa 1993.

DUNVEGAN (Geog, for the town in NS)
    1. Flower class corvette, K177. 9 Sep 1941–3 Jul 1945.

DUNVER (alternative name for Verdun, QC)
    1. River class frigate, K03. 11 Sep 1943–23 Jan 1946..

D.W. MURRAY
    1. Tug, W17. 24 Aug 1942–46. Requisitioned by RN. ex Minas Basin vessel *D.W. Murray*.

The oiler DUNDURN, 14 Sep 1959. (RCN E-52095. KM Coll.)

E

EARL GREY (N*)
1. Icebreaker. ?–Jul 1912; 4–29 Oct 1914. ex Dept of Marine and Fisheries icebreaker *Earl Grey*. Com'd (?) in 1912 for Governor General's Tour. Com'd in 1914 for transfer to Russia.

EARLY FIELD (N*)
1. Patrol vessel, Fy 40. 2 Apr 1942–16 Nov 1944. ex fishing vessel.

EASTORE
1. a. Supply vessel, Z56. 7 Dec 1944–8 Apr 1946. ex US Army vessel.
   b. CNAV, 515. 8 Apr 1946–31 Mar 1964.

EASTVIEW (alternative name for Ottawa, ON)
1. River class frigate, K665. 3 Jun 1944–17 Jan 1946.

EASTWOOD
1. Wood class tug, Z49. 10 (26) Oct 1944–circa 1946.
2. CNAV/CFAV, Wood class tug, 550. Circa 1946–1979.

ECKVILLE
1. Ville class tug, W58. 22 Mar 1944–circa 1946.
2. CNAV, Ville class tug, 580. Circa 1946–31 Mar 1964.

EDITH I (N*)
1. Diving boat, HC41. 24 Jun 1940–15 Jan 1942. Became HC41.

EDMONTON (Geog, for the city in AB) B
1. Kingston class mine warfare vessel, 703. 21 Jun 1997–SIS.

EDMUNDSTON (Geog, for the town in NB)
1. Flower class corvette, K106. 21 Oct 1941–16 Jun 1945. ex MEDICINE HAT.

EDNORINA (N*)
1. Harbour craft, Z42/HC42. 19 Apr? 1941–15 Jan 1942. Former tug. Became HC42.

EGRET (EGRET PLUME?) (1&2 N*. 3. bird)
1. Tender, Z27. Nov 1914–Dec 1915. ex Dept of Marine & Fisheries vessel.
2. Crash boat, 925. 1 Apr 1965–1984. ex RCAF *Egret*.
3. Crash boat, 3. 15 Nov 1983–circa June 1994.

EHKOLI (Chinook word for whale)
1. a. "Nenamook" class patrol vessel, Fy 12. 1 Dec 1941–circa late 1949.
   b. CNAV, 532. Circa 1950–circa May 1991.

EILEEN (N*)
1. Patrol vessel. 6 Apr–27 Dec 1940. ex motor boat.

ELAINE U (N*)
1. Auxiliary, Second World War. Dates, type and source not known.

ELIZABETH (1. N*. 2. N*)
1. Auxiliary, 12 Jan–8 May 1916. ex Dept of Marine & Fisheries vessel.
2. RCSC vessel, RCSC Camp "William Swing," Choisy, QC. Circa 1945. ex MV *Elizabeth*.

ELK (1 & 2. animal) 2. B
1. Armed yacht, S05/Z27. 10 Sep 1940–4 Aug 1945. ex *Arcadia*.
2. Fairmile B Type, 724. 29 Dec 1953–23 Jul 1954. ex PTC724, ex ML724, ex ML124.

ELLEN BERNICE (N*)
1. Motor boat. Chartered 18 Apr 1917–?

ELLSWORTH (N*)
1. Harbour craft, HC43. 18 Sep 1939–15 Jan 1942. Became HC43. ex RCMP *Ellsworth*.

ELM LAKE
1. Lake class minesweeper, J486. Completed 18 Nov 1945 but never com'd.

EMOH
1. Harbour craft, Z44/HC44. Circa 1941–15 Jan 1942. Became HC44. Type and source not known.

E. NANCY LEE
1. Harbour craft, HC45. Circa 1941–15 Jan 1942. Became HC45. Type and source not known.

ENDEAVOUR (functional name; believed to be named after HMS ENDEAVOUR, Capt Cook's vessel.)
1. CNAV/CFAV, research vessel, 171. 9 Mar 1965–SIS.

ESPERANZA (for the inlet on west coast of Vancouver Island)
1. Gaspé class minesweeper. Launched 3 Oct 1940. Before commissioning, became CLAYOQUOT circa Dec 1940.

ESQUIMALT (Geog, for the municipality in BC)
1. Bangor class minesweeper, J272. 26 Oct 1942–16 Apr 1945, torpedoed by U190 and sank five miles off Chebucto Head, NS.

ETHEL (N*)
1. Motor boat. Chartered 7 Jul–Nov 1917.

ETTRICK (N*, for a stream in Selkirk, Scotland)
1. River class frigate, K254. 29 Jan 1944–30 May 1945. ex HMS ETTRICK.

CNAV ENDEAVOUR, just after her launch at Yarrows, Esquimalt. 4 Sep 1964. (PNL 4306-5. FDN Coll.)

EVA CLARE (N*)
1. Guard ship, Toronto. 14 Aug 1943–1 Jan 1944. ex MV *Eva Clare*, ex RCAF M298.

EYEBRIGHT (a flower)
1. Flower class corvette, K150. 15 May 1941–17 Jun 1945. In commission as RN vessel from 26 Nov 1940–15 May 1941.

EYOLFUR (N*)
1. RCSC training vessel, Toronto. 2 Feb 1944–1 Apr 1946 (?) ex motor boat.

F

FAHE
1. Former name for harbour craft, HC130. Jul 1942–1945. ex MB. Purchased.

FALCON (N*)
1. Auxiliary. Nov 1914–11 Jan 1915. ex Dept of Fisheries vessel.

FANTOME (N*)
1. Motor launch. Circa Jan 1918–Mar 1919.

FELICITY D (N*)
1. Tug. Chartered Apr–Nov 1917; 15 Apr–Nov 1918. ex Sincennes-McNaughton Co tug.

FENNEL (for the flower on the herb)
1. Flower class corvette, K194. 15 May 1941–12 Jun 1945. In commission as RN vessel from 15 Jan–15 May 1941.

FERNAND RINFRET (N*)
1. Patrol vessel, HC46. 3 Sep 1939–15 Jan 1942. Became HC46. ex RCMP motor boat *Fernand Rinfret*.

FERGUS (Geog, for the town in ON)
1. Revised Flower class corvette, K686. 18 Nov 1944–14 Jul 1945. ex FORT FRANCES.

FESTUBERT (after a First World War battle)
1. a. Battle class trawler. 13 Nov 1917–1918?
   b. Training ship, N46/J46. ?–? 1922; 1 May 1926–Nov 1932; 1934–1935; 6 Sep 1939–1 May 1942. Became Gate Vessel 17.

FIFER (N*)
1. Patrol vessel, Z30/Fy 00. 5 Dec 1941–11 Dec 1945. ex yacht *Fifer*.

FIR LAKE
1. Lake class minesweeper, J487. Completed 1947 as mission ship *Regina Polaris*. Never commissioned.

FIREBIRD
1. CFAV, fire/rescue vessel, 561. 1978–SIS.

FIREBRAND
1. CFAV, fire/rescue vessel, 562. 1978–SIS.

FISPA (N*)
1. Motor launch. 18 Oct 1916–30 Apr 1917. ex Dept of Fisheries vessel.

FLAMINGO (N*)
1. Crash boat, 847. 1 Apr 1965–circa 1984. ex RCAF *Flamingo*.

FLEUR DE LIS (N*)
1. Patrol craft, later examination vessel, Z31/J16. 16 Nov 1939–29 Nov 1945. ex RCMP *Fleur de Lis*.

FLORENCE (N*)
1. Patrol vessel. 19 Jul 1915–21 Sep 1916. ex steam yacht *Florence*, ex *Emeline*, ex *Czarina*. Presented to the RCN by John Eaton.

FLORES (N*)
1. Patrol vessel, Z25 (P). 1 Jan 1942–1944. ex American Can Co vessel *Cancolim II*.

FOAM (1. N* 2. alternative name–water related)
1. Motor launch. Jun 1917–?, 1 Jul–22 Jul 1918, sank in Sydney harbour. Raised and reused until Nov 1918(?). ex SPRAY.
2. Patrol vessel, Fy 22/Z25. 7 Apr 1942–1944. ex LOYAL II.

FOREST HILL (1 & 2. Geog, for the village in ON, now part of Toronto)
1. Name assigned to an Algerine class minesweeper which was renamed and turned over to the RN o/c in 1943 as HMS PROVIDENCE, J325.
2. Revised Flower class corvette, K486. 1 Dec 1943–9 Jul 1945. ex HMS CEANOTHUS, K360.

FORT ERIE (1 & 2. Geog, for the city in ON) 2. B
1. River class frigate, K645(?). Cancelled.
2. a. River class frigate, K670. 27 Oct 1944–22 Nov 1945. ex LA TUQUE.
   b. Prestonian class frigate, 312. 17 Apr 1956–17 Jan 1958; 3 Jul 1958–26 Mar 1965.

FORT FRANCES (Geog, for the town in ON) B
1. a. Algerine class minesweeper, J396/F396. 28 Oct 1944–3 Aug 1945; 23 Oct 1945–5 Apr 1946. ex FERGUS. Loaned to Dept of Mines and Technical Surveys 1948–1958.
   b. CNAV/CFAV Oceanographic research vessel, 170. 1958–1974.

FORT RAMSAY (from Fort Ramsey House, Gaspé, QC)
1. Naval officer-in-charge, Gaspé, QC. 1 May 1942–31 Jul 1945. ex GASPE?

FORT STEELE (N*) B
1. Fort class patrol craft, 140. 1973–26 Aug 1996. ex RCMP *Fort Steele*.

FORT WILLIAM (Geog, for the city in ON; now part of the city of Thunder Bay)
1. a. Bangor class minesweeper, J311. 25 Aug 1942–23 Oct 1945. ex LA MALBAIE ex FREDERICTON. In strategic reserve 1946–1951.
   b. Reacquired, modernized but never commissioned, 195. Jun 1951–29 Nov 1957, transferred to Turkish Navy as BODRUM.
Note: for another use of the name, see AVALON III, HMS

FORTUNA
1. Despatch boat, HC134. 15 Jul 1942–46. Became HC134.

FORTUNE (Geog, for the bay in NF) B
1. Bay class minesweeper, 151. 3 Nov 1954–28 Feb 1964.

FOSTER (alternative name for Waterloo, QC)
1. River class frigate. Cancelled Dec 1943.

FOUNDATION JUPITER (N*)
1. Tug. Circa 1941–circa Sep 1943.

FOUNDATION MARY (N*)
   1. Tug. Circa 1941–1945.

FOUNDATION MASSON (N*)
   1. Derrick scow. 16 Aug 1942–9 Oct 1943.

FOUNDATION MERSEY (N*)
   1. Tug? circa 1941–1945?

FRANCES MARTIN
   1. Auxiliary? Dates, type and source not known, Second World War.

FRANCOIS (N*)
   1. RCSC vessel. 1 Sep 1944–Oct 1946. ex MV *Francois*.

FRANK T. COOTE (N*)
   1. Motor boat. Chartered 1916?–?

FRANK DIXON (N*)
   1. Tug, tender to PROTECTOR II, W12. 8 Jun 1941–8 Jun 1945. ex Canadian Dredge Co tug.

FRASER (1 & 2. Geog, for the river in BC) 2. B
   1. C/River class destroyer, H48. 17 Feb 1937–25 Jun 1940, sunk in collision with HMS CALCUTTA in the Gironde River estuary, France. ex HMS CRESCENT.
   2. a. St Laurent class destroyer escort, 233. 28 Jun 1957–2 Jul 1965.
      b. Improved St Laurent class destroyer escort, helicopter carrier, 233. 22 Oct 1966–12 Apr 1973; Mar 1974–5 Oct 1994.

FREDERICK H PONTIN
   1. Auxiliary? Dates, type and source not known, Second World War.

FREDERICTON (1 & 2. Geog, for the city in NB)
   1. Revised Flower class corvette, K245. 8 Dec 1941–14 Jul 1945. ex FORT WILLIAM.
   2. Halifax class frigate, 337. 10 Sep 1994–SIS.

HMCS FRENCH at Halifax during the Second World War. (RCN H-605. KM Coll.)

FRENCH (N*)
1. Patrol vessel, later examination vessel, S01/Z23. 18 Sep 1939–2 Jan 1946. ex RCMP *French*.

FRIENDSHIP
1. Auxiliary? Dates, type and source not known, Second World War.

FROBISHER BAY (Geog, for the community in the NWT)
1. Naval radio station, Frobisher Bay, NWT.
   a. established Jul 1953(?)–30 Jun 1957(?).
   b. HMC NRS. 30 Jun 1957(?)–11 Jul 1966. Became CFS Frobisher Bay.

FRONTENAC (alternative name for Kingston, ON, taken from the county)
1. Revised Flower class corvette, K335. 26 Oct 1943–22 Jul 1945.

FUNDY (1, 2 & 3. Geog, for the bay between NB & NS) 3. B
1. Basset/Fundy class minesweeper, N88/J88. 2 Sep 1938–27 Jul 1945.
2. Bay class minesweeper, 145. 19 Mar 1954–31 Mar 1954, transferred to French Navy as LA DUNKERQUOISE.
3. Bay class minesweeper, 159. 27 Nov 1956–7 Feb 1964; 14 Apr 1967–?; 31 Mar 1969–?; 1 May 1970–19 Dec 1996. Bent a shaft in 1992 and lay alongside without a crew until paid off.

G

GALIANO (N*)
1. Patrol craft. 15 Dec 1917–30 Oct 1918, when she foundered in Barkley Sound, BC. ex Fishery patrol craft *Galiano*. In service from Jan 1916?

GALT (Geog, for the city in ON, now part of Cambridge)
1. Flower class corvette, K163. 15 May 1941–21 Jun 1945.

GANANOQUE (Geog, for the town in ON)
1. Bangor class minesweeper, J259. 8 Nov 1941–13 Oct 1945. In reserve until Feb 1959.

GANDER (Geog, for the town in NF)
1. Naval radio station, Gander, NF.
   a. Est'd 1938. Taken over from DOT in 1941. 1941–1957?
   b. HMC NRS. May 1957?–10 Jul 1966. Tender to GLOUCESTER.

GANNET (1. N/K 2. bird)
1. Depot ship for motor launches, Halifax. 6 May–12 May 1943. Became VENTURE (4th). ex VENTURE II. See note to third VENTURE II.
2. Crash boat, 873. 1 Apr 1965–SIS. ex RCAF *Gannet*.

GASPE (1 & 2. Geog, for the bay in QC) B
1. Basset/Fundy class minesweeper, N94/J94. 21 Oct 1938–23 Jul 1945.
2. Bay class minesweeper, 143. 26 Nov 1953–22 Aug 1957. Transferred to Turkish navy as TRABZON, 31 Mar 1958.

GATINEAU (1 & 2. Geog, for the river in QC) 2. B
1. E/River class destroyer, H61. 3 Jun 1943–10 Jan 1946. ex HMS EXPRESS.
2. a. Restigouche class destroyer escort, 236. 17 Feb 1959–29 Sep 1969.
   b. Improved Restigouche class destroyer escort, 236. 14 Apr 1971–1 Jul 1998.
Note: went into unmanned "extended readiness" in Jun 1996.

GEORGIAN (Geog, for the bay on Lake Huron)
1. Bangor class minesweeper, J144. 23 Sep 1941–23 Oct 1945.

GERALDINE
1. Auxiliary? Dates, type and source not known, Second World War.

GERTRUDE (N*)
1. Former name for a patrol craft, Corner Brook, NF. 1942-43. Became HC143 on 15 Jan 1942. ex Bowaters Ltd *Gertrude*.

GIFFARD (1, 2 & 3. Geog, for the town in QC)
1. Name assigned to Algerine class minesweeper which was renamed and turned over to the RN o/c, 1943.
2. River class frigate, Second World War. Became TORONTO.
3. Revised Flower class corvette, K402. 10 Nov 1943–5 Jul 1945. ex HMS BUDDLEIA, K275.

GILDA GRAY
1. Yacht. Dates, type and source not known, Second World War.

GIMLI (Geog, for the city in MB) B
1. Sea Cadet Training Centre, Hnausa, MB. 1985–1991. Commissioned each summer.

GIVENCHY (1. after a First World War land battle. 2 for 1.)
1. a. Battle class trawler. 22 Jun 1918–12 Aug 1919.
   b. Depot ship for auxiliary vessels, Esquimalt, P01/Z01. 25 Jun 1940–21 Oct 1940.
   c. known as GIVENCHY (hulk), 21 Oct 1940–18 Apr 1943. Became GIVENCHY II.
2. Shore establishment, (part of?) bldg 124 on the Dockyard Jetty, Esquimalt, BC. 21 Oct 1940–3 Mar 1947. Also occupied Bldg 77, the old RN College of Canada, circa late 1942.
Note: The buildings in the Dockyard, later to become known as VENTURE, were built to house GIVENCHY and were occupied from 9 Aug 1943–3 Mar 1947. From 1947–1954, they were used as a reserve training centre. The accommodation block (Bldg 29) was officially opened Jul 1943. Bldg 38 in the Dockyard was taken over by GIVENCHY in Dec 1943 and used until 19 Feb 1944 when it was returned to NADEN.

The tug CFAV GLENDYNE, 2nd of name, entering Esquimalt harbour in 1984 past Fisgard Light. (CF HC84-578. FDN Coll.)

The auxiliary GRYME in Burrard Inlet, Vancouver, c.1944. (CF U-322. KM Coll.)

GIVENCHY II
1. a. Trawler. Barracks for Fishermen's Reserve. 18 Apr 1943–7 Dec 1943.
    b. Floating barracks in Vancouver 7 Dec 1943–Jul 1944(?) as GIVENCHY (hulk)?; at Esquimalt as GIVENCHY II (hulk)? Jul 1944–17 Oct 1945(?); sold 19 Sep 1946.

GIVENCHY III
1. Seamanship training establishment, Comox spit, Comox, BC. 1 Oct 1943–1 Mar 1946. ex NADEN III. Became NADEN II, 1 Mar 1946 and later, QUADRA.

GIVENCHY PUP
1. Auxiliary, circa 1942 at Esquimalt. Type & size not known.

GLACE BAY (1, 2 & 3. Geog, for the town is NS) 3. B
1. River class frigate, Second World War. Before commissioning, became LAUZON.
2. River class frigate, K414. 2 Sep 1944–17 Nov 1945. ex LAUZON.
3. Kingston class mine warfare vessel, 701. 26 Oct 1996–SIS.

GLADIATOR (N*)
1. Auxiliary vessel. Aug 1914–mid Jan 1915. ex Halifax Tow Boat Co tug.

GLENADA
1. Glen class tug, W30. 23 Nov 1943–Dec 1945.

GLENBRAE
1. Glen class tug?, W28. Dates not known, Second World War.

GLENBROOK
1. a. Glen class tug, W64. 5 Oct 1944–1946?
    b. CNAV/CFAV, Glen class tug, 501. Circa 1946–1977.
2. CFAV, Glen class tug, 643. 16 Dec 1976–SIS.

GLENCAIRN (N*)
1. Auxiliary ketch. 28 Aug 1938–1 May 1944. Became CAIRN.
2. Glen class tug, no? circa 1944–?

GLENCLOVA (N*)
1. Tug, Montréal, W29. 11 Jun 1942–1 Apr 1945? ex Consolidated OKA Sand & Gravel Co tug *Glenclova*.

GLENCOVE
1. Glen class tug, W37. 7 Jul 1944–16 Oct 1945.

GLENDALE
1. CFAV, Glen class tug, 641. 1975–SIS.

GLENDALE V (N*)
1. Patrol vessel, Fy 35. 17 Feb 1942–1 May 1944. Became DALEHURST. ex fishing vessel *Glendale V*.

GLENDENNING
1. Despatch boat, NOIC Montréal, HC136. 27 Jul 1942–?

GLENDEVON
1. a. Glen class tug, W38. 19 Jun 1945–26 Mar 1946.
   b. CNAV, Glen class tug, 505. 26 Mar 1946–31 Mar 1964.

GLENDON
1. a. Glen class tug, W39. 25 May 1945–26 Mar 1946.
   b. CNAV, Glen class tug, 506. 26 Mar 1946–31 Mar 1964.

GLENDOWER
1. Glen class tug, W24. 18 Jun 1943–17 Dec 1945.

GLENDYNE
1. a. Glen class tug, W68. 28 Apr 1945–1946.
   b. CNAV, Glen class tug, 503. 1946–Mar 1957, capsized and sank attending MAGNIFICENT.
2. CFAV, Glen class tug, 640. 1975–SIS.

GLENEAGLE
1. Glen class tug, W40. 3 May 1945–Mar 1946.

GLENELLA
1. Glen class tug, W41. 17 Apr–Jun 1945.

GLENEVIS
1. a. Glen class tug, W65. 3 Nov 1944–1946?
   b. CNAV/CFAV, Glen class tug, 502. Circa 1946–1977.
2. CFAV, Glen class tug, 642. 1976–SIS.

GLENFIELD
1. Glen class tug, W42. 14 Nov 1944–Nov 1945.

GLENFRUIN (N*)
1. RCSC training vessel, Gananoque, ON. Circa 1944. ex MV *Glenfruin*.

GLENHOLME
1. Glen class tug. Built but never accepted into RCN service.

GLENKEEN
1. Glen class tug, W67. 30 Apr 1945–Mar 1946.

GLENLEA
1. Glen class tug, W25. 16 Aug 1943–29 Nov 1945.

GLENLIVET
1. Glen class tug, W43. 21 Jul 1944–1946. Same vessel as GLENLIVET II?

GLENLIVET II
1. a. Glen class tug, W43. 21 Jul 1944–1946?
   b. CNAV/CFAV, Glen class tug, 504. 1946?–1977. Loaned for a period to DPW.

GLENMONT
1. Glen class tug, W27. 2 Nov 1943–10 Dec 1945.

GLENORA
1. Glen class tug, W26. 1 Oct 1943–19 Oct(?) 1945.

GLENSIDE
1. a. Glen class tug, W63. 1 Sep 1944–1946?
   b. CNAV/CFAV Glen class tug, 500. 1946–1977.
2. CFAV Glen class tug, 644. 1977–SIS.

GLENVALLEY
1. Glen class tug, W44. 4 Dec 1944–Dec 1945.

GLENVILLE (alternative name for Inverness, NS)
1. River class frigate. Cancelled Dec 1943.

GLENWOOD
1. Glen class tug, W54. Contract cancelled when vessel 59% complete, 24 Aug 1945.

GLOUCESTER (Geog, for the township south of Ottawa) B
1. Naval radio station, Ottawa, ON.
   a. Est'd 1943 as HFDF station. School for Radioman Special Branch, 1948–?
   b. HMC NRS. 1 Dec 1950–1 Apr 1953.
   c. HMCS. 1 Apr 1953–11 Jul 1966. Became CFS Gloucester. Name is commemorated by bldg B69, E Sqn, CFSCE, CFB Kingston.

GODERICH (Geog, for the town in ON)
1. Bangor class minesweeper, J260. 23 Nov 1941–6 Nov 1945. In reserve until Feb 1959.

GOOSE BAY (Geog, alternative name for Happy Valley–Goose Bay, Labrador) B
1. Kingston class mine warfare vessel, 707. 26 Jul 1998–SIS.

GOPHER (N*)
1. Trawler sweeper. 12 May 1915–30 Apr 1918. ex Québec Salvage & Wrecking Co tug *Gopher*.

GRAEME STEWART (N*)
1. Tug. Circa 1943-44. ex Sincennes-McNaughton Co tug *Graeme Stewart*.

GRAHAM BELL
1. Auxiliary? Dates, type and source not known, Second World War.

GRANBY (1. Geog, for the city in QC. 2 for 1.) 1. B
1. a. Bangor class minesweeper, J264. 2 May 1942–31 Jul 1945.
   b. Deep diving tender, 180. 23 May 1953–20 Nov 1953; 19 Dec 1953–15 Dec 1966.
2. Prestonian class frigate, deep diving tender, 180. 21 Dec 1966–31 Dec 1973. ex VICTORIAVILLE.

GRANDMERE (Geog, for the city in QC)
1. Bangor class minesweeper, J258. 11 Dec 1941–23 Oct 1945.

GRAYLING (N*)
1. Motor boat. Chartered 1 Jun 1916–Nov 1916?

GREENWOOD
1. Wood class tug, Z50. 4 (8?) Dec 1944–circa 1946.
2. CNAV/CFAV, Wood class tug, 551. Circa 1946–1977?

GRENVILLE
1. Ville class tug, W18. Sep 1942–Aug 1945.

GRIB (N*)
1. Auxiliary patrol vessel/whaler. Circa May 1917–1919? ex whaler *Grib*.

GRIFFIN
1. G class destroyer, H31. 20 Mar 1943–10 Apr 1943. ex HMS GRIFFIN. Renamed OTTAWA, 10 Apr 1943. NSHQ made the name Ottawa retroactive to ship's first commissioning as GRIFFIN, 20 Mar 1943.

GRIFFON (after a French vessel built by La Salle on Niagara River in 1679 and used on the upper Great Lakes) B
1. Naval reserve division, Port Arthur (later Thunder Bay), ON. From 2 Apr 1940, located at 232 Cooke St; moved to 125 North Algoma St 14 Aug 1944.
    a. 1 Nov 1941–1 Sep 1942. Tender to NADEN.
    b. 1 Sep 1942–SIS.

GRILSE (1. & 2. N/K. 3. for the fish and for 1. and 2) 3. B
1. Torpedo boat/destroyer, QW1. 15 Jul 1915–Dec 1916; 10 May 1917–10 Dec 1918. ex US Yacht *Winchester*.
2. Yacht. Circa 1945–circa 1956. ex *Dontaff*. Became GOLDCREST?
3. Unconverted, snorkel fitted Balao class submarine, S71. 11 May 1961–2 Oct 1969. ex USS BURRFISH.

GRIZZLY (animal)
1. Armed yacht, P14/Z14 (P). 17 Jul 1941–17 Jun 1944. ex *Michigonne*.

GROU. (named for a French martyr of 1690. Alternative name for the town of Pointe-aux-Trembles, QC)
1. River class frigate, K158. 4 Dec 1943–25 Feb 1946.

GRYME (N*)
1. Deperming vessel, Vancouver, BC, Z60. 15 Dec 1942–14 Feb 1946. ex MV *Gryme*, 130855.

G. S. MAYES (N*)
1. Tug. Chartered 16 Jun 1917–19 Jun 1918. ex Beaver Dredging Co tug.

GUARDIAN (N*)
1. Harbour craft, HC47. 3 Sep 1939–15 Jan 1942. Became HC47. ex United Towing & Salvage Co tug *Guardian*? (ex RCMP *Guardian*?)

GUELPH (1 and 2 N/K. 3. Geog, for the city in ON)
1. a. Patrol boat. 1 May 1918–31 Jan 1919; 8 Mar 1919–31 May 1920. ex CD 20.
    b. Patrols depot, Halifax. 1 May 1918–31 Jan 1919. ex STADACONA I.
2. Depot ship, Halifax. 31 May 1920–1 Jul 1923. ex CD 23. Became STADACONA (3rd). Note: crew paid off 22 Sep 1922.
3. Revised Flower class corvette, K687. 9 May 1944–27 Jun 1945. ex SEA CLIFF.

GUILLEMOT (1. N*)

    1. Crash boat, 849. 1 Apr 1965–1984. ex RCAF *Guillemot.*

    2. Crash boat, 2. 15 Nov 1983–circa summer 1995.

GUINEA GOLD

    1. Auxiliary? Dates, type and source not known, Second World War.

GULF RANGER (N*)

    1. Harbour craft, HC48. 10 Jun 1941–15 Jan 1942. Became HC48.

GULL

    1. Auxiliary? Dates, type and source not known, Second World War.

GULNARE (N*)

    1. Contraband control/examination vessel, 1916(?)–1919 (1924?). ex Fishery Protection vessel *Gulnare.* (never commissioned?)

GUYSBOROUGH (Geog, for the county in NS)

    1. Bangor class minesweeper, J52. 1 Jul(?) 1942–17 Mar 1945, torpedoed by U878 and sunk in the English channel off Ushant. In commission as RN vessel 22 Apr–1 Jul(?) 1942.

GWENNITH (N*)

    1. Tug. Chartered 14 Jun 1917–17 Dec? 1918. ex Dominion Dredging tug.

H

HAIDA (for the West Coast First Nations Tribe) B

    1. a. Tribal class destroyer, G63/D63/215. 30 Aug 1943–22 Feb 1946; 1 Feb 1947–1 Dec 1949. Pd. No. changed Jan 1950.

        b. Tribal class destroyer escort, 215. 15 Mar 1952–11 Oct 1963. Became a non-commissioned floating museum at Ontario Place, Toronto, G63. Aug 1964 to present day.

HAIDEE (N*)

    1. Tender to HUNTER. Circa Nov 1939–Jul 1945? ex MV *Haidee.*

HALIFAX (1 & 2. Geog, for the city in NS) 2. B

    1. Revised Flower class corvette, K237. 26 Nov 1941–12 Jul 1945.

    2. Halifax class frigate, 330. 29 Jun 1991–SIS.

The first HOCHELAGA in the First World War. (RCN CN 3399. KM Coll.)

HALIGONIAN
1. Naval reserve division, Halifax, NS. 1 Oct 1943–31 Aug 1946. See SCOTIAN.
Note: Originally located within STADACONA; moved Dec 1943 to King Edward Hotel on corner of North & Barrington Streets; moved 4–6 Oct 1944 to St Joseph's Parish Hall, 482 Gottingen St.

HALLOWELL (1 & 2. alternative name for Picton, ON)
1. River class frigate? Became?
2. River class frigate, K666. 8 Aug 1944–7 Nov 1945.

HAMILTON (N*, for the towns in Lanark, England, and Ohio, USA)
1. Town class destroyer, I24. 6 Jul 1941–8 Jun 1945. ex HMS HAMILTON.

HARDROCK (alternative name for Geraldton, ON)
1. River class frigate. Cancelled Dec 1943.

HARO (N*)
1. Patrol vessel, P06/Z06(P). 18 Oct 1939–Feb 1945. ex Island Tug & Barge Co Tug *Haro*.

HARTVILLE
1. Ville class tug, No.? 24 Nov 1944–Dec 1945.

HATTA VII (N*)
1. Patrol vessel, Fy 33. 17 Feb?–circa 7 Apr 1942. Became SPRAY. ex fishing vessel *Hatta VII*.

HAWKESBURY (Geog, for the town in ON)
1. Revised Flower class corvette, K415. 14 Jun 1944–10 Jul 1945.
Note: HMAS HAWKESBURY K363 was a River class frigate 1944–1962.

HAYSVILLE
1. Ville class tug, W119. Circa Jul 1944–circa 1946.
2. CNAV, Ville class tug, 575? circa 1946–1964.

HEATHERTON
1. a. Norton class tug, W22. 5 Jun 1944–1946?
   b. CNAV/CFAV, Ton class tug, 527. 1946 ?–circa 1970.
   c. HMCS, Ton class tug, 527. Com'd summer 1973 for reserve training.

HELENA (N*)
1. Tug, W33. 28 Feb 1944–?; 21 Jan 1945–Nov 1945. ex DOT tug *Helena*. Under charter by Navy to Dominion Coal and Steel, 11 Dec 1940–21 Jan 1944.

HELEN H (N*)
1. Tug. 7 Aug 1943–Aug 1945. ex Canada Dredging Co tug *Helen H*, 107695.

HELEN S (N*)
1. Tug, W13. 24 Aug 1943 (?)–Jul 1945? ex Canada Dredge & Dock Co tug *Helen S*, 107695.

HENRYVILLE (alternative name for Iberville, QC)
1. River class frigate. Cancelled Dec 1943.

HEPATICA (a flower)
1. Flower class corvette, K159. 15 May 1941–27 Jun 1945. In commission as RN vessel 12 Nov 1940–15 May 1941.

HERBERT N. EDWARDS (N*)
1. Auxiliary. Purchased 1917 and became PV III.

HERON (N*)
1. Crash boat, 848. 1 Apr 1965–1984. ex RCAF *Heron*.

HERON WING (N*)
1. Tender. Nov 1914–Dec 1915? ex Dept of Marine & Fisheries vessel.

HERRING GULL (a bird)
1. Name allocated to a Bird class patrol vessel, cancelled in 1956.

HESPELER (1 & 2. Geog, for the town, now part of Cambridge, ON)
1. Name assigned to an Algerine class minesweeper but never promulgated. Ship turned over to the RN o/c as HMS LYSANDER, J379.
2. Castle class corvette, K489. 28 Feb 1944–15 Nov 1945. ex HMS GUILDFORD CASTLE, K378.

HICKORY LAKE
1. Lake class minesweeper, J488. Completed 14 Aug 1945 but never com'd.

HIGHLAND MARY (N*)
1. Tug/Lighter. 2 May 1917–Jan 1919.

HOCHELAGA (1. For the First Nations village in existence at the time of Jacques Cartier. Also, an area in Montréal to the north on the waterfront. 2 and 3 after 1. 4 for 1, 2 & 3.) 3. B
1. a. Patrol vessel. 13 (15?) Aug 1915–1919? 26 Jul 1919–31 Mar 1920. ex yacht *Waturus*.
2. a. NOIC, 224 Youville Square, Montréal. 28 Sep 1939–5 Mar 1942.
   b. Depot ship & NOIC Montréal. 20 Sep 1943?–30 Sep 1945.
3. Depot ship. 12 May 1941–Aug? 1945. ex cabin cruiser *Margo V*.
4. Naval training establishment and supply centre, 557 Dollard St, Lasalle, QC. 1 Oct 1955–1 Apr 1966(?) when it became part of CFB Montréal.
Note: During Aug 1961 HOCHELAGA assumed the English language training and basic recruit training functions from D'IBERVILLE.

HOCHELAGA II
1. NOIC, Montréal. 1940?–5 Mar 1942.
2. Manning depot, Montréal. 306 Old Customs Bldg, 400 Youville Square, 1939–20 Dec 1941. Ogilvie Bldg, 224 Youville Square, 20 Dec 1941–20 Sep 1943? NOIC joined Manning Depot 5 Mar 1942. Partly located at Jacques Cartier Barracks, Longueuil(?)
3. Harbour Craft, HC49. 1939–15 Jan 1942? Became HC49, 15 Jan 1942? Pd off Sep 1945?
4. Pay division, Montréal(?) 20 Sep 1943(?)–30 Sep 1945.

HODGEVILLE
1. Ville class tug, W53. 9 Mar 1944–Nov 1945.

HOLLY LEAF (N*)
1. Tender. 9 Oct? 1915–23 Dec 1914. Loaned.

HOOSIER II (N*)
1. RCSC training vessel, Minnicog, ON. 3 Jul 1943–Nov 1945. ex *Diana*, 156432.

HORNET (N*)
1. Patrol craft, Corner Brook, NF. 1942-43. ex Bowaters Ltd *Hornet*.

HOWE SOUND I (N*)
1. Patrol vessel, Fy 19. Circa Jan 1943–Nov 1945. ex fishing vessel *Howe Sound I*.

HUGH D (N*)
1. Scow. Circa 1943?–Oct 1945. ex tug *Hugh D.*

HUMBERSTONE (1 & 2. Geog, for the town in ON, now part of Port Colborne)
1. Name assigned to an Algerine class minesweeper but never promulgated. Ship turned over to RN o/c as HMS GOLDEN FLEECE, J376.
2. Castle class corvette, K497. 6 Sep 1944–17 Nov 1945. ex HMS NORHAM CASTLE, K447.

HUNTER (after a vessel at the Battle of Lake Erie) B
1. Naval reserve division, Windsor, ON. 1 Nov 1941–SIS. Originally located at 2462 Howard St but moved to 960 Ouelette St late 1947.
    a. Nov 1941–1 Sep 1942. Tender to STADACONA.
    b. 1 Sep 1942–SIS.

HUNTSVILLE (1 & 2. Geog, for the town in ON)
1. Name assigned to an Algerine class minesweeper, but never promulgated. Ship turned over to the RN o/c as HMS PROMPT, J378.
2. Castle class corvette, K499. 6 Jun 1944–15 Feb 1946; 12 Apr–31 May 1946. ex HMS WOLVESEY CASTLE, K461.

HURON (1. for the First Nations Tribe, ON. 2 for 1.) 1. B
1. a. Tribal class destroyer, G24/D224. 19 Jul 1943–9 Mar 1946; 28 Feb 1950–29 Sep 1951.
    b. Tribal class destroyer escort, 216. 18 Nov 1952–1 Aug 1957; 28 Mar 1958–30 Apr 1963.
2. Iroquois class destroyer, helicopter carrier, 281. 16 Dec 1972–SIS.

HUSKY (animal)
1. Patrol craft, S06/Z13/Z28/Z24. 23 Jul 1940–3 Aug 1945. ex yacht *Xama II*, ex *Wild Duck.*

The tug HMCS HEATHERTON, temporarily back in commission in 1973 to train reservists. (FDN Coll.)

The Bangor class minesweeper INGONISH in the Second World War. (KM Coll.)

I

ICTHUS (ICTHUS M?) (N*)
1. Motor boat. Chartered 23 Jul–Nov? 1917; May 1918–May 1920.

IMPERATOR (N*)
1. Patrol vessel, Z18(P). 18 Sep 1939?–15 Jan 1942. Became HDC18.

INCH ARRAN (alternative name for the town of Dalhousie, NB) B
1. a. River class frigate, K667. 18 Nov 1944–28 Nov 1945.
   b. Prestonian class frigate, 308. 25 Nov 1959–23 Jun 1965.

INGERSOLL (Geog, for the town in ON)
1. Revised Flower class corvette, K336. Cancelled Dec 1943.

INGLEWOOD
1. Wood class tug, Z51. 1 Sep 1944–Nov 1945.

INGONISH (Geog, for the district in NS)
1. Bangor class minesweeper, J69. 1 Jul(?) 1942–2 Jul 1945. In commission as RN vessel 8 May–1 Jul(?) 1942.

INNISVILLE
1. Ville class tug. 24 Nov 1944–Jun 1946.

INTERCEPTOR (N*)
1. Detachment class patrol vessel, Z15(A)/Q15. 3 Sep 1939–Aug 1945. ex RCMP *Interceptor*.

INUVIK (Geog, for the town in the NWT) B
1. Naval radio station, Inuvik, NWT. Moved from Aklavik.
   a. HMC NRS. 12 Mar 1961–10 Sep 1963. Commenced operations 20 Mar 1961.
   b. HMCS. 10 Sep 1963–19 Jul 1966. Became CFS Inuvik.

INVADER (N*)
1. Patrol vessel, P13/Z09/HC50. 18 Sep 1939–15 Jan 1942. Became HC40. ex RCMP *Acadian*.

IROQUOIS (1. for the Confederacy of First Nations people in the Great Lakes area. 2 for 1.) 1. B

   1. a. Tribal class destroyer, G89/D89. 30 Nov 1942–22 Feb 1946; 27 May–24 Nov 1946; 24 Jun 1949–30 Sep 1949. ex ATHABASKAN. While still on the builder's ways, IROQUOIS was damaged during an air attack. She was "lead" ship but this damage meant she would be completed after ATHABASKAN. So the two vessels exchanged names. This is supposed to be the destroyer on the $1.00 stamp issued in 1942.

      b. Tribal class destroyer escort, 217. 21 Oct 1951–19 Nov 1957; 17 Oct 1958–24 Oct 1962.

   2. Iroquois class destroyer, helicopter carrier, 280. 29 Jul 1972–SIS.

ISLANDER (N*)

   1. Harbour craft, HC51. 3 Sep 1939–15 Jan 1942. Became HC51. ex RCMP *Islander*.

ISLAND DEFENDER

   1. CFAV, tug. Circa Mar 1997. Became TILLICUM. Commissioning as *Island Defender* in doubt.

ITORORO

   1. Auxiliary? Dates, type and source not known, Second World War.

IVANHOE (N*)

   1. Auxiliary. Circa 1941–?

IVY LEAF (N*)

   1. Auxiliary. 30 Sep?–23 Dec 1914. Loaned to RCN.

J

J. A. CORNETT (N*)

   1. Tug, tender to PROTECTOR II, W16. 7 Jun 1941–Mar 1946?

JACK I. INGALLS

   1. Harbour craft, HC52. 2 Oct 1939–15 Jan 1942. Became HC52. ex Canada Dredge Co vessel.

JALOBERT (N*)

   1. Harbour craft, HC53. 1939 (12 Dec 1941?)–15 Jan 1942. Became HC53. ex Dept of Marine & Fisheries pilot vessel *Jalobert*; ex quarantine vessel, ex Dept of Agriculture vessel *Polona*. Listed as JALOBERT in *Navy Lists* as late as Nov 1944. Referred to as CGS *Jalobert* in messages.

JAMES BAY (Geog, for an extension of Hudson Bay) B

   1. Bay class minesweeper, 152. 3 May 1954–28 Feb 1964.

JAMESVILLE

   1. Ville class tug. 16 Feb?–Oct 1945.

JASPER (probably for the town in AB)

   1. Flower class corvette. Circa 1940. Before commissioning, became KAMLOOPS.

J. E. MCQUEEN (N*)

   1. Tug. 21 Aug 1942–19 Dec 1942. ex tug *J. E. McQueen*. Became *Stoic*. See STOIC.

JEFFYJAN (JEFFY JAN?)

   1. Harbour craft, HC54. Circa 1941–15 Jan 1942. Supposedly became HC54 but a final paying off date as JEFFY JAN is recorded for 10 Oct 1945.

JELLICOE (N*)
1. Yacht, Montréal. Circa 1941-2. ex yawl *Jellicoe*.

JESSIE (N*)
1. Motor boat, tender to SHEARWATER II. Aug–Nov 1914.

JESSIE ISLAND
1. Auxiliary? Dates, type and source not known, Second World War.

JESSIE MAY
1. Harbour craft, HC55. 2 Aug 1940–15 Jan 1942. Became HC55. Type and source not known.

JOAN W. II (N*)
1. Auxiliary minesweeper, Fy 34. 4 Mar 1940–27 Apr 1944. ex fishpacker.

JOHANNA (N*)
1. Patrol vessel, Fy 28. 13 Sep 1939?–Aug 1942? ex fishing vessel *Johanna*.

JOHN W. MACKAY
1. Auxiliary? Dates, type and source not known, Second World War.

JOHNVILLE
1. Ville class tug. 29 Nov 1944–Aug 1945.

JOLIETTE (Geog, for the city in QC)
1. River class frigate, K418. 14 Jun 1944–19 Nov 1945.

JOLLIET (for the explorer) B
1. Naval reserve division, 701 boul. Laure, Sept-Iles, Québec. 7 Oct 1989–SIS.

JONQUIERE (Geog, for the city in QC) B
1. a. River class frigate, K318. 10 May 1944–4 Dec 1945.
    b. Prestonian class frigate, 318. 20 Sep 1954–18 Dec 1957; 16 Jun 1958–23 Sep 1966.

JUANITA (N*)
1. Motor launch. Chartered 7 Jul–Nov? 1917.

HMCS JALOBERT. (KM Coll.)

KIPAWO at St John's during the Second World War. (RCN NF 2104. KM Coll.)

K

KALAMALKA (alternative name for Vernon, BC)
1. Llewellyn class minesweeper, J395. 2 Oct 1944–16 Nov 1945.

KAM (N*)
1. Tug, W15. 14 Sep 1943–30 May 1944. ex Abitibi Power & Paper Co tug *Kam*, 170259.

KAMLOOPS (Geog, for the city in BC)
1. Flower class corvette, K176. 17 Mar 1941–27 Jun 1945. ex JASPER.

KAMSACK (Geog, for the town in SK)
1. Flower class corvette, K171. 4 Oct 1941–22 Jul 1945. ex CARLTON.

KAPUSKASING (Geog, for the town in ON) B
1. a. Algerine class minesweeper, J326/F326. 17 Aug 1944–27 Mar 1946. Loaned to Dep't of Mines and Technical Surveys, 1948–58.
   b. CNAV/CFAV, Survey ship and research vessel, 171. 1958–1978.

KARLUK (N*, Aleutian First Nations for fish)
1. Auxiliary, wooden hulled whaler. Jun 1913–11 Jan 1914, sank in Arctic Ocean after being caught in, and later holed by ice. Main vessel of Stefansson's Arctic Expedition.

KAYVILLE
1. Ville class tug. 4 Dec 1944–Aug 1947.

KELOWNA (Geog, for the city in BC)
1. Bangor class minesweeper, J261. 5 Feb 1942–22 Oct 1945.

KENOGAMI (Geog, for the town in QC)
1. Flower class corvette, K125. 29 Jun 1941–9 Jul 1945.

KENORA (Geog, for the town in ON)
1. Bangor class minesweeper, J281/191. 6 Aug 1942–6 Oct 1945. In strategic reserve 1946–1952. Reacquired but never recommissioned. 1952–29 Nov 1957, transferred to Turkish Navy as BANDIRMA.

KENTVILLE (Geog, for the town in NS)
1. a. Bangor class minesweeper, J312. 10 Oct 1942–28 Oct 1945; 10 May–30 Sep 1954. In reserve 1945–1954, 1954–57.
    b. Bangor class minesweeper, 182. 10 May–30 Sep 1954. Transferred to Turkish Navy, 29 Nov 1957, as BARTIN.

KIA ORA (KIARA?) (N*)
1. RNCAS Seaplane tender. 2 Sep 1918–? Former motor boat used to tow experimental hydroplanes at Baddeck by Alexander Graham Bell. Sold 9 Oct 1920.

KINCARDINE (1 & 2. Geog, for the town in ON)
1. Name assigned to an Algerine class minesweeper but never promulgated. Ship turned over to RN o/c as HMS MARINER, J380.
2. Castle class corvette, K490. 19 Jun 1944–27 Feb 1946. ex HMS TAMWORTH CASTLE, K393.

KINGFISHER (a bird)
1. Name allocated to a Bird class patrol vessel cancelled in 1956.

KINGS (Special–for the university)
1. Officers' Training Establishment, University of Kings College, Halifax, NS. 1 Oct 1941–19 May 1945. Est'd 24 May 1941 on the move of the officers' training establishment from STADACONA.

KINGSTON (Geog, for the city in ON) B
1. Kingston class mine warfare vessel, 700. 21 Sep 1996–SIS.

KINGSVILLE
1. Ville class tug, W20. Aug 1942–Aug 1945.

KIPAWO (KIPAWA?)
1. Tender to AVALON. 28 Aug 1941–Jul 1945? Boom maintenance vessel.

KIRKLAND LAKE (1 & 2. Geog, for the town in ON)
1. Flower class corvette. Cancelled Dec 1943.
2. River class frigate, K337. 21 Aug 1944–14 Dec 1945. ex ST JEROME.

KIRKWOOD
1. Wood class tug, Z53. 24 Aug 1944–Nov 1945.

KITCHENER (Geog, for the city in ON)
1. Revised Flower class corvette, K225. 28 Jun 1942–11 Jul 1945. ex VANCOUVER.

KOKANEE (alternative name for Nelson, BC)
1. River class frigate, K419. 6 Jun 1944–21 Dec 1945.

KOOTENAY (1 & 2. for the river in BC) 2. B
1. D/River class destroyer, H75. 12 Apr 1943–26 Oct 1945. ex HMS DECOY.
2. a. Restigouche class destroyer escort, 258. 7 Mar 1959–7 May 1970.
    b. Improved Restigouche class destroyer escort, 258. 7 Jan 1972–18 Dec 1995.

KUITAN (Chinook word for horse)
1. a. "Nenamook" class patrol vessel, Fy 14. 2 Dec 1941–29 Mar 1946.
    b. CNAV. 29 Mar 1946–11 Dec 1946.

KWABEETA
1. Former name of harbour craft, HPC22. 23 Aug 1943–? SIS 1 Apr 1945.

L

LABRADOR (Geog, after the territory) B
    1. Ice breaker and Arctic patrol vessel, 50. 8 Jul 1954–22 Nov 1957.

LA CANADIENNE (N*)
    1. Hydrographic survey ship. Circa 1910–1914.

LACHINE (Geog, for the city in QC)
    1. Bangor class minesweeper, J266. 20 Jun 1942–31 Jul 1945.

LACHUTE (Geog, for the town in QC)
    1. Revised Flower class corvette, K440. 26 Oct 1944–10 Jul 1945.

LADY BALTIMORE (N*)
    1. RCSC training vessel, Minnicog, ON. Circa 1944–46. Chartered.

LADY BETH II (N*)
    1. Auxiliary, HC121. Became HC121 circa March 1943. 173747?

LADY B. I.
    1. Auxiliary? Dates, type and source not known, Second World War.

LADY EVELYN (N*)
    1. Auxiliary patrol vessel. 21 Jun 1917–Feb? 1919. ex Postmaster General department vessel *Lady Evelyn*, ex *Deerhound*.

LADY RODNEY (N*)
    1. Auxiliary, Fy 46/F40. Second World War.

LA HAVE (1. Alternative name for Bridgewater, NS. 2. For the town in NS?)
    1. River class frigate. Cancelled Dec 1943.
    2. CNAV, 531. Circa 1956–1964.

LA HULLOISE (alternative name for the city of Hull, QC) B
    1. a. River class frigate, K668/F668/305. 20 May 1944–6 Dec 1945; 24 Jun 1949–13 Jan 1950; 1 Jun 1950–23 Nov 1953.
       b. Prestonian class frigate, 305. 9 Oct 1957–16 Jul 1965.

The "pup" tug LOGANVILLE in 1946 wearing a white ensign. (KM Coll.)

LAKEVILLE
1. Ville class tug, W21. Jul 1942–45.

LAKEWOOD
1. a. Wood class tug, Z63. 25 Apr 1944–Aug 1945.
   b. CNAV/CFAV, Wood class tug, 552. Circa 1946–circa 1965.

LA MALBAIE (Geog, for the town in QC)
1. Revised Flower class corvette, K273. 28 Apr 1942–28 Jun 1945. ex MALBAIE, ex FORT WILLIAM.
Note: This is the ship featured in the 1942/43 20-cent stamp.

LANARK (alternative name for the town of Perth, ON) B
1. a. River class frigate, K669. 6 Jul 1944–24 Oct 1945.
   b. Prestonian class frigate, 321. 26 Apr 1956–11 Jul 1958; 10 Mar 1959–19 Mar 1965.

LANGARA
1. CNAV, 513. Supply vessel circa 1957–1976. ex *Blue Goose*?

LANGHOLM
1. Harbour craft, HC56. 10 Jan 1941–15 Jan 1942. Became HC56. Type not known.

LANSDOWNE (1. N* 2 for 1.)
1. Auxiliary patrol vessel/gate vessel/accommodation ship, Sydney, NS. 2 Apr 1917–3 Jan 1918(?); 9 Mar 1918(?)–10 Dec 1918. ex CGS *Lansdowne*.
2. a. Patrols depot, 145 Esplanade, Sydney, NS. 16 May–30 Nov 1917.
   b. Shore establishment, 145 Esplanade, Sydney, NS. 1 May–10 Dec 1918.
Note: The dates in 1. above are suspect. She apparently served with the Marine Dept for various periods during 1917/18. Whether she was com'd in the RCN at this time is not known.

LARCH LAKE
1. Lake class minesweeper, J489. Completed 2 Nov 1945 but never com'd.

LASALLE (Geog, for the town in QC)
1. River class frigate, K519. 29 Jun 1944–17 Dec 1945.

LA TUQUE (Geog, for the town in QC)
1. River class frigate. Became FORT ERIE.

LAUREL LEAF (N*)
1. Motor boat. 1 Oct?–23 Dec 1914. Loaned to RCN.

LAURENTIAN (N*)
1. Patrol vessel. May 1917–8 Jan 1919. ex Canada Steam Ship Lines *Laurentian*, ex *King Edward*.

LAURIER (N*)
1. Patrol craft, later examination vessel, S09/Z34. (Sep 1939?) 12 Apr 1940–25 Mar 1946. ex RCMP *Laurier*.
Note: There was an ex USN MTB in commission in the RCN at the same time and her pendant numbers were also S09. She was com'd as HMCS S09.

LAUZON (1 & 2. Geog, for the town of Lauzon, QC) B
1. River class frigate. Became GLACE BAY.
2. a. River class frigate, K671. 30 Aug 1944–7 Nov 1945. ex GLACE BAY.
   b. Prestonian class frigate, 322. 12 Dec 1953–3 Oct 1958; 5 Jun 1959–24 May 1963.

LAVAL
1. Auxiliary. Circa 1941–?

LAVALLEE (after the composer of "O Canada" born at Verchères, QC, 1842)
1. Llewellyn class minesweeper, J371. 21 Jun 1944–18 Dec 1945.

LAVALTRIE (N*)
1. Tug. Jun–Dec 1918; Apr–Jun 1919? ex Dept of Fisheries tug.

LAVIOLETTE (N*)
1. Tug. Jun–12 Aug 1918. Became SEAGULL. ex Dept of Fisheries tug.

LAWRENCEVILLE
1. a. Ville class tug, 584. 8 Jan 1944–circa 1945.
   b. CNAV/CFAV, Ville class tug. 584, circa 1946–circa 1964. Became CREE.
2. CFAV, Ville class tug, 590. 17 Jan 1974–SIS.

LAYMORE
1. a. Mine recovery & supply vessel, Z57. 12 Jun 1945–17 Apr 1946; 19 Jul–30 Aug 1946 (for passage to west coast).
   b. CNAV, 516. 30 Aug 1946–circa 1968.
   c. Oceanographic research vessel, 516. 1968–15 Feb 1976.

LEASIDE (1 & 2. Geog, for the town in ON)
1. Name assigned to Algerine class minesweeper but never promulgated. Ship turned over to RN o/c as HMS SERENE, J354.
2. Castle class corvette, K492. 21 Aug 1944–16 Nov 1945. ex HMS WALMER CASTLE, K460.

LEELO (Chinook word for wolf)
1. a. "Nenamook" class patrol vessel, Fy 15. 24 Nov 1941?–Oct 1944.
   b. CNAV? ?–Apr 1947.

LEGAL LIMIT (N*)
1. Tender to SHEARWATER II. Chartered 4 Sep 1914–Jan 1916.

LEOLA VIVIAN (N*)
1. Patrol vessel, P11/Z11 (P). 29 Jan 1940?–Aug 1945. ex fishing vessel. Chartered then purchased 30 Nov 1942. 171808

LETHBRIDGE (Geog, for the city in AB)
1. Flower class corvette, K160. 25 Jun 1941–23 Jul 1945.

LEVIS (1 & 2. Geog, for the city in QC)
1. Flower class corvette, K115. 16 May 1941–19 Sep 1941, torpedoed and sunk by U74, 120 miles east of Cape Farewell, Greenland.
2. River class frigate, K400. 21 Jul 1944–15 Feb 1946.

LIL II (N*)
1. Patrol vessel, Z37/HC57(?). 6 Nov 1940–15 Jan 1942. Supposedly became HC57 but still listed in *Navy List* Jul 1944 and Jul 1945 as LIL II. Messages in her file at D HIST refer to her commissioning on 1 May 1944 and 17 May 1945 with final paying off date 5 Jun 1945.

LILA G (N*)
1. Harbour craft, HC58. 4 Nov 1940–15 Jan 1942. Became HC58.

LILLIAN (N*)
1. Motor launch. 30 Aug 1917–Oct 1918?

LILLOOET (for the town in BC?)
1. Hydrographic survey ship. Circa 1910–1919.

LILY (N*)
1. Motor launch. Chartered 1 Jun–Nov? 1917; 20 Jul–Nov? 1918.

LINDSAY (Geog, for the town in ON)
1. Revised Flower class corvette, K338. 15 Nov 1943–18 Jul 1945.

LINGANBAR (alternative name for the town of Dominion, NS)
1. River class frigate. Cancelled Dec 1943.

LIPARI (N*)
1. Ammunition lighter, HC300. 10 Oct 1936–15 Jan 1942. Became HC300. ex Justice Dept vessel *Lipari*. SIS 1 Apr 1945.

LISGAR (N*)
1. Tug, W06/W33. 25 Apr 1940 (18 Jan 1941?)–Nov 1945. ex DPW tug *Lisgar*.

LISTERVILLE
1. a. Ville class tug, 578. 5 Oct 1944–?
    b. CFAV, Ville class tug. 578, circa 1946–circa 1974. Became CAVALIER.
2. CNAV/CFAV, Ville class tug, 592. 31 Jul 1974–SIS.

LISTOWEL (1. Geog, for the town in ON)
1. Revised Flower class corvette, K439. Cancelled Dec 1943.
2. Examination vessel Halifax. 12 Jul 1944–circa May 1946.

LLEWELLYN (Geog, for the glacier in BC?) B
1. a. Llewellyn class minesweeper, M278/J278. 24 Aug 1942–14 Jun 1946.
    b. tender, 141. 25 Jul 1949–31 Oct 1951.

LLOYD GEORGE (Geog, for the mountain in BC?) B
1. Llewellyn class minesweeper, M279/J279. 24 Aug 1942–16 Jul 1948. In reserve, 142. 1948–1959.

LOCH ACHANALT (N*, for a small lake in western Ross, Scotland)
1. Loch class frigate, K424. 31 Jul 1944–20 Jun 1945. ex HMS LOCH ACHANALT, K424.

LOCH ALVIE (N*, for a small lake near Avienmore, Scotland)
1. Loch class frigate, K428. 10 Aug 1944–11 Jul 1945. ex HMS LOCH ALVIE, K428.

LOCH MORLICH (N*, for a lake in Scotland near Avienmore)
1. Loch class frigate, K517. 17 Jul 1944–20 Jun 1945. ex HMS LOCH MORLICH, K517.

LOCKEPORT (Geog, for the town in NS)
1. Bangor class minesweeper, J100. 1 Jul(?) 1942–2 Jul 1945. In commission as RN vessel 27 May–1 Jul(?) 1942.

LOGANVILLE
1. a. Ville class tug, W66/589. 13 Dec 1944–?
    b. CNAV/CFAV, Ville class tug 589. Circa 1946–circa 1991.

LOIS (N*)
1. Scow. 10 Dec 1942–Aug 1945. Used as a landing stage.

LONG BRANCH (1 & 2. Geog, for the village in ON)
1. Name assigned to an Algerine class minesweeper that was renamed and turned over to the RN o/c as HMS REGULUS, J327.
2. Revised Flower class corvette, K487. 5 Jan 1944–17 Jun 1945. ex HMS CANDYTUFT, K382.

LONGUEUIL (Geog, for the town in QC)
1. River class frigate, K672. 18 May 1944–31 Dec 1945.

LOON (bird) B
1. Bird class seaward defence patrol craft, 780. 30 Nov 1955–23 May 1963; 31 Jul–30 Aug 1965; 1966?–1 Apr 1970.

LOOS (after a First World War land battle)
1. a. Battle class trawler. 1 Aug 1918–circa 1920.
   b. Patrol vessel. 1 Aug (12 Dec?) 1940 (1 Jul 1941?)–1 May 1942. Became Gate Vessel No. 14.

LORAINE (1. LORRAINE?) (1. and 2. N*)
1. Motor boat. 9 Jun 1917–1919. Purchased. *Ex Lorraine II*.
2. Harbour craft, HC59. 27 Jun 1940–15 Jan 1942. Became HC59.

LOTTIE RUSSEL (N*)
1. Auxiliary patrol vessel. Chartered Jul ?–7 Sep 1915. Became Gate Vessel No. 1. ex schooner.

LOUIS HEBERT (N*)
1. Auxiliary? Fy 92/J22. Second World War.

LOUISBURG (1. Geog, for the town in NS. 2 for 1.)
1. Flower class corvette, K143. 20 Oct 1941–6 Feb 1943, sunk by Italian aircraft east of Oran, North Africa, during "Operation Torch."
2. Revised Flower class corvette, K401. 13 Dec 1943–25 Jun 1945.

LOYAL I (N*)
1. Patrol vessel, Fy 43. 21 May 1942–Oct 1945. ex fishing vessel *Loyal I*, 154648.

LOYAL II (N*)
1. Patrol vessel, Fy 22. 22 Jan–7 Apr 1942. Became FOAM. ex fishing vessel *Loyal II*, 156618.

LUCEVILLE
1. Ville class tug. 27 May 1944–Nov 1945.

LUCINDA II
1. Former name for patrol vessel HPC21. 17 Sep 1943–45. ex *Lucinda II*. Became HDC21.

LUNENBURG (Geog, for the town in NS)
1. Flower class corvette, K151. 4 Dec 1941–23 Jul 1945.

LYNN B. (N*)
1. Tug, W14. 21 Jul–7 Dec 1943. ex CS Boone Dredging Co tug, 154628.

LYNX (animal)
1. Patrol craft, S07/Z07. 25(?) May–6(?) Jun 1940; (21?) 26 Aug 1940–23 Apr 1942, condemned due to a lack of spare parts for her engines. ex MV *Ramona*.
2. Harbour craft, HC75 (ML13). 16 May 1941–15 Jan 1942?

M

MACKENZIE (Geog, for the river in the NWT) B
1. Mackenzie class destroyer escort, 261. 6 Oct 1962–(3 Aug?)31 Dec 1993.

MACDONALD (N*)
1. Patrol craft, P07/Z07. 11 Oct 1939–28 Jan 1945. ex RCMP *Macdonald*.

MACSIN (N*)
1. Examination vessel, W07/Z38. 10 Apr 1940–Nov 1941? 23 Apr 1942–? 2 Apr–20 Dec 1943; 4 Apr–22 Dec 1944; 5 Apr 1945–? ex Marine Industries Ltd vessel *Macsin*. ex *Gedeon L*, ex TR class naval trawler.

MADAWASKA (N*)
1. Patrol vessel, Z21 (A)/J21. 3 Sep 1939–c. Mar 1945. ex RCMP motor boat *Madawaska*.

MAGEDOMA (N*)
1. Tender to CATARAQUI. 14 Jul 1941–Dec 1945? ex yacht *Magedoma*.

MAGNIFICENT (N*, means "splendid in appearance") B (B*)
1. Majestic class Light Fleet aircraft carrier, 21. 7 Apr 1948–14 Jun 1957. ex HMS MAGNIFICENT.

MAGOG (Geog, for the town in QC)
1. River class frigate, K673. 7 May 1944–20 Dec 1944. Torpedoed by U1223 and damaged in St Lawrence River off Pointe des Monts, 14 Oct 1944.

MAHITA (N*)
1. RCSC training vessel, Lachine, QC. 30 Jun–1 Jul 1944. Burned.

MAHONE (Geog, for the bay on the coast of NS; name later associated with the town in NS.)
1. Bangor class minesweeper, J159. 29 Sep 1941–6 Nov 1945. In strategic reserve 1946–1951. In reserve 1951–29 Mar 1958 when transferred to Turkish Navy as BEYLERBEYI.

MALASPINA at Esquimalt, date unknown. (RCN E-75597. KM Coll.)

MALAHAT (1. probably for a now extinct Coast Salish tribe on Saanich Inlet.
2. Probably after 1) B

1. Naval reserve division, Victoria, BC. 15 Jan 1944–15 Jan 1946. Located at 1238 Government St and later in Bldg 188, HMC Dockyard.
2. Naval reserve division, Victoria, BC. 23 Apr 1947–SIS. From 1947–8 Oct 1951, located in the dockyard. 8 Oct 1951–14 May 1953 located in Moresby House (Bldg 91), 1350 Esquimalt Rd, until bldg turned into a Wrens barracks. Division moved on board SAULT STE MARIE until Jan 1955 when it moved into the basement of Moresby House. From the summer of 1955–31 Mar 1964, located in the Old Customs Bldg, 1002 Wharf Street in downtown Victoria. From the fall of 1964 to 14 Mar 1992, in Bldg 61 (Old Seamanship School) in NADEN. From 14 Mar 1992, at end of Huron St, Shoal Point, Victoria, BC.

MALASPINA (N*)

1. a. Patrol vessel, P00/Z00. 1 Dec 1917–31 Mar 1920. ex Fishery patrol vessel *Malaspina*. Note: from 1914–1917 she carried out various part-time duties under the control of the naval service but carried a civilian crew. Between the wars, she worked for the Dept of Fisheries.
   b. Patrol vessel, later training vessel for ROYAL ROADS, Z00. 6 Sep 1939–24 Jan (31 Mar?) 1945.

MALLARD (bird) B

1. Bird class seaward defence patrol craft, 783. 16 Jul 1956–30 Jun 1960(?); 1 Jan 1962–23 May 1963; May?–2 Sep 1965; May?–Sep 1966; ?–1 Apr 1970.

MALPEQUE (Geog, for the bay on the coast of PE)

1. Bangor class minesweeper, J148. 4 Aug 1941–9 Oct 1945. In reserve until Feb 1959. Note: name later associated with the town.

MANNVILLE

1. a. Ville class tug, W57. 6 Apr–Sep 1945.
   b. CNAV/CFAV, Ville class tug, 577. Circa 1946–1976.

MANX (N*)

1. Crash boat, 851. 1 Apr 1965–1981. ex RCAF *Manx*.

MAPLE LAKE

1. Lake class minesweeper, J490. Cancelled 18 Sep 1944.

MARAUDOR (MARAUDER?) (N*)

1. Patrol vessel, Fy 03. 7 Sep 1939–21 Dec 1944. ex Pachena Fishing & Navigation Co vessel *Maraudor*, 156633.

MARGAREE (1 & 2. Geog, for the river in NS) 2. B

1. D/River class destroyer, H49. 6 Sep 1940–22 Oct 1940, lost in collision with freighter *Port Fairy* off Ireland. ex HMS DIANA.
2. a. St Laurent class destroyer escort, 230. 5 Oct 1957–25 Sep 1964.
   b. Improved St Laurent class destroyer escort, helicopter carrier, 230. 15 Oct 1965–2 May 1992.

MARGARET (N*)

1. Patrol vessel. 3 Feb 1915–30 Oct? 1915; 30 Oct? 1915–3 Apr 1919. ex customs vessel *Margaret*.

MARGARET A. HACKETT (N*)

1. Tug. Chartered 24 Apr–25 Nov? 1916. ex Canada Shipping Co tug.

The auxiliary tanker MASTODON, 25 Feb 1943. (KM Coll.)

MARGARET I (N*)
1. Patrol vessel, Fy 29. 16 Sep 1939–circa Feb 1944. ex fishing vessel *Margaret I*, 150859.

MARIE THERESE (N*)
1. Patrol vessel, Q10/HC67. 22 Nov 1939–21 Jul 1944. ex diesel powered motor vessel *M. F. Thérèse.*

MARION B (N*)
1. Tug, W14. 14 May–22 Nov 1943; 30 Apr 1944–?; ?–8 Oct 1945. ex Price Navigation Co vessel.

MARLIS (N*)
1. Harbour craft, HC60. 31 Jul 1940–15 Jan 1942. Became HC60.

MARMAT (N*)
1. Harbour craft, HC61. 6 Jul 1940–15 Jan 1942. Became HC61.

MARTIN J. MARRAM (N*)
1. Purchased 1917 and became PV IV.

MARTINVILLE
1. Ville class tug, W61. 2 Nov 1944–Jan 1946.

MARVITA (N*)
1. Examination vessel, Z44. 7 Aug 1941–Jun 1945? ex Newfoundland government vessel *Marvita.*
Note: Apparently taken over 1 May 1941, returned 21 Jun 1945.

MARY GOREHAM
1. Former name of harbour craft, HC160. 8 Feb 1943–46.

MARYSVILLE
1. a. Ville class tug, Z62. 20 Jan 1944–? Sank 3 May 1944 after striking a rock but raised the next day and repaired.
   b. CNAV/CFAV, 585. Circa 1946–1976.
2. CFAV, Ville class tug, 594. 11 Sep 1974–SIS.

MASSET (Geog, for the town in BC)
1. Naval radio station, Masset, Queen Charlotte Islands, BC.
   a. NRS. 1943–late 1945. ex RCAF station.
   b. HFDF station. 1949–1957?
   c. HMC NRS. 1957 ?–11 Jul 1966. Tender to GLOUCESTER. Became CFS Masset.

MASTODON
1. Auxiliary Tanker. 9 Dec 1942–12 Mar 1946. ex DPW Dredge 306.

MATANE (Geog, for La Ville de Matane, QC)
1. River class frigate, K444. 22 Oct 1943–11 Feb 1946. ex STORMONT.

MATAPAN (MARAPAN?)
1. Harbour craft, HC62. Became HC62, 15 Jan 1942. SIS 1 Apr 1945.

MATAPEDIA (Geog, for the town in QC)
1. Flower class corvette, K112. 9 May 1941–16 Jun 1945.

MATSQUI (Geog, for the town in BC)
1. Naval transmitter site, Sumas, BC. ex SUMAS. Came under ALDERGROVE Dec 1942–Dec 1945 after which it became a separate establishment with own OIC. Became part of ALDERGROVE again 1 Jun 1955.

MAUDE MOSHER (N*)
1. Motor launch. Chartered 1 Jun–Nov? 1916; Jun–Nov 1917?

MAXWELLTON
1. Norton class tug, W46. 20 Oct 1944–10 Dec 1945.

MAYFLOWER (a flower)
1. Flower class corvette, K191. 15 May 1941–15 May 1945. In commission as RN vessel from 9 Nov 1940–15 May 1941. Not named for but later sponsored by, town in Nova Scotia.

MEAFORD (Geog, for the town in ON)
1. Revised Flower class corvette. Cancelled Dec 1943.

MEANDER (N*)
1. Patrol vessel. P04/Z04(P). 4 Nov 1939–May (19 Jul?) 1945. ex yacht *Meander*.

MEDICINE HAT (1 & 2. Geog, for the city in AB)
1. Flower class corvette. Before commissioning, became EDMUNDSTON.
2. Bangor class minesweeper, J256. 4 Dec 1941–6 Nov 1945. In reserve until 29 Nov 1957 when transferred to Turkish navy as BIGA.

MEGANTIC (Geog, for the town in QC)
1. River class frigate. Became SEA CLIFF.

MELVILLE (Geog, for the town in SK)
1. Bangor class minesweeper, J263. 4 Dec 1941–18 Aug 1945.

MELVIN SWARTOUT (N*)
1. Harbour craft, HC166. Second World War.

MEON (N*, for a river in Hampshire, England)
1. River class frigate, K269. 7 Feb 1944–23 Apr 1945. ex HMS MEON.

MEPSYA (see NEPSYA)

MEREDITH (N*)
1. Motor launch. Circa Jul 1917–Jul 1919. Purchased.

MERRICKVILLE
1. a. Ville class tug, 581. 7 Nov 1944–?
   b. CNAV/CFAV, 581. Circa 1946–1976.
2. CFAV, Ville class tug, 593. 11 Sep 1974–SIS.

MERRITTONIA (1 & 2. alternative name for Merritton, ON)
1. River class frigate. Cancelled Dec 1943.
2. Revised Flower class corvette, K688. 10 Nov 1944–11 Jul 1945. ex POINTE CLAIRE.

MERRY CHASE (N*)
1. a. patrol vessel, Fy 46. Mar 1942–28 Mar 1946. ex fishing seiner *Merry Chase*, 155235. Still a working seiner as late as Aug 1985.
   b. CNAV?

MESSINES (after a First World War battle)
1. Battle class trawler. 13 Nov 1917–1920.

M. E. WHERRY (N*)
1. Motor boat? Chartered 5 Jul 1918 and later purchased. Sold 1919?

M. F. THERESE
1. Harbour craft, HC67. 21 Nov 1939–15 Jan 1942. Became HC67, in service until Jun 1944. 165482?.

MICMAC (1. for the First Nations Tribe in NS. 2 for 1.) 1. B
1. a. Tribal class destroyer, R10/D100/214. 12 Sep 1945–5 Sep 1947; 16 Nov 1949–30 Nov 1951. Pd. No. changed 1 Oct 1949. ex NOOTKA.
   b. Tribal class destroyer escort, 214. 14 Aug 1953–13 Jun 1958; 10 Mar 1959–31 Mar 1964.
2. Royal Canadian Sea Cadet camp, Halifax, NS. 1979–c. 1982. Commissioned each summer.

MIDDLESEX (alternative name for London, ON)
1. Algerine class minesweeper, J328. 8 Jun 1944–31 Dec 1946. On 2 Dec 1946, ran ashore on Half Island Point, near Halifax. Ensign struck 12 Dec 1946.

MIDLAND (Geog, for the town in ON)
1. Flower class corvette, K220. 7 Nov 1941–15 Jul 1945. ex BRANTFORD.

MILDRED (N*)
1. Motor launch. 7 Sep 1915–? ex *Mildred McColl*.

MILICETTE (N*)
1. Training vessel. 8 May 1941–Nov 1945. ex yacht, 122201.

MILL COVE, CFS (Geog, for the community in NS)
1. CFS, Mill Cove, NS. Became CFS Mill Cove vice NRS BLANDFORD 11 Jul 1966. Operational mid Sep 1967, officially opened 19 Dec 1967. Never com'd as HMCS or HMC NRS.

MILLTOWN (Geog, for the town in NB)
1. Bangor class minesweeper, J317. 18 Sep 1942–16 Oct 1945. In reserve 1946–Feb 1959.

MIMICO (1 & 2. Geog, for the town in ON)
1. Name assigned to an Algerine class minesweeper which was turned over to RN o/c and renamed HMS MOON, J329.
2. Revised Flower class corvette, K485. 8 Feb 1944–18 Jul 1945. ex HMS BULRUSH, K307.

MINAS (Geog, for the basin in the Bay of Fundy. Name later associated with the town of Minasville in NS.) B
1. Bangor class minesweeper, J165. 2 Aug 1941–6 Oct 1945; in reserve to 1955; com'd 15 Mar 1955–7 Nov 1955.

MINNICOG (N*)
   1. RCSC training vessel, Minnicog, ON. Jun 1944–46. Chartered.

MINORU (N*)
   1. Motor launch. Circa Jul 1919.

MIRAMICHI (1, 2 & 3. Geog, for the bay on the coast of NB) 2. B
   1. Bangor class minesweeper, J169. 26 Nov 1941–24 Nov 1945.
   Note: Name was later associated with the town in NB.
   2. Bay class minesweeper, 150. 30 Jul 1954–1 Oct 1954. 9 Oct 1954 transferred to French Navy as LA LORIENTAISE.
   3. Bay class minesweeper, 163. 29 Oct 1957–28 Feb 1964; 16 May 1968–?; 5 Jan 1970 (?)–16 Sep 1998.

MISS GRAY
   1. Harbour craft, HC78. ?–15 Jan 1942. Became HC78 and SIS 1 Apr 1945.

MISS KELVIN
   1. Harbour craft, HC79. 25 May 1941–15 Jan 1942. Became HC79. SIS 1 Apr 1945.

MITCHELL BAY (N*)
   1. Auxiliary minesweeper, Fy 05. 10 Sep 1939?–Mar 1944. ex fishpacker *Mitchell Bay*, 170409.

MOBY DICK
   1. Harbour craft, HC80/Z04. 5 Oct 1939–15 Jan 1942. Became HC80 but still listed under her name in *Navy List*, Jul 1945.

MOHAWK (MOWHAWK?) (N*)
   1. Motor launch. 11 Jun 1917–c. Mar 1918?

MONCTON (1 & 2. Geog, for the city in NB) 2. B
   1. Flower class corvette, K139. 24 Apr 1942–12 Dec 1945. ex CAMPBELLTOWN.
   2. Kingston class mine warfare vessel, 708. 12 Jul 1998–SIS

MONNOW (N*, for the river in the counties of Hereford, Eng. and Gwent, Wales)
   1. River class frigate, K441. 8 Mar 1944–11 Jan 1945. ex HMS MONNOW.

MONTCALM (1. after the brig built at Fort Frontenac, 1755) 1. B
   1. Naval reserve division, Québec City. From 1 Nov 1941, located at 322 Saint John St. From 4 Dec 1941, located at the Québec Winter Club, 30 Laurier. Moved to the Inspection Bldg, 39 Laurier, 22 Jun 1947. Moved to Pointe-à-Carcy, 27 Jun 1995.
      a. 1 Nov 1941–1 Sep 1942. Tender to CHALEUR II.
      b. 1 Sep 1942–SIS.
   2. Harbour craft, HC133. Circa 1942–45. ex MB.

MONT JOLI (N*)
   1. a. Examination vessel, Fy 93/Z02/Z24. 5 Jul 1940–29 Mar 1946. Chartered until 29 Jun 1943, then purchased. ex *Mont Joli*.
      b. CNAV, 1946 until sold Mar 1947.

MONTOUR
   1. Harbour craft, HC81. 9 Jul 1941–15 Jan 1942. Became HC81. Became SAMBRO (II) in 1943.

MONTREAL (1. after a ship on Lake Ontario during the War of 1812; 2 & 3 for the city in QC) 3. B
1. Naval reserve division, 1464 Mountain St, Montréal, QC.
    a. 21 Nov 1941–1 Sep 1942. Tender to HOCHELAGA II.
    b. 1 Sep 1942–26 Oct 1943. Became DONNACONA.
2. River class frigate, K319. 12 Nov 1943–15 Oct 1945. ex STORMONT 2nd.
3. Halifax class frigate, 336. 21 Jul 1994–SIS.

MONTREAL II
1. Harbour craft, Montréal. 20 Jul 1942–26 Oct 1943. Became DONNACONA II. Donated by Marine Industries Ltd.

MONTREAL CIRCLE (for the street that circles the water reservoir, Prince Rupert, BC.)
1. NRS, Prince Rupert, BC. Circa Jul 1953–Jul 1960. Located in ex RCN Second World War bldg, now called Applewhaite Hall, on Montréal Circle.

MOOLOCK (Chinook word for elk)
1. "Nenamook" class patrol vessel, Fy 16. 2 Dec 1941–13 Mar 1946.

MOONBEAM
1. Fuel oil carrier, Z43/J43. 4 Dec 1940–13 Nov 1945. ex Dept of Transport "Hopper Barge No 1."

MOOSE (animal) B
1. Armed yacht, Z14/S03. 8 Sep 1940–20 Jul 1945. ex *Cleopatra*, ex *Centaur*, ex *Naroma*, ex *Shogun*.
2. Harbour craft, HC74 (ML11). 19 Oct 1940–15 Jan 1942?
3. Fairmile B type, 711. 17 May(?) 1954–11 Oct 1956? ex PTC711, ex ML711, ex ML111.

MOOSE JAW (1 & 2. Geog, for the city in SK)
1. Flower class corvette. Became SOREL.
2. Flower class corvette, K164. 19 Jun 1941–8 Jul 1945. Ex CHURCHILL.

MORDEN (1 & 2. Geog, for the town in MB)
1. Bangor class minesweeper. Became TRANSCONA circa Apr 1941.
2. Flower class corvette, K170. 6 Sep 1941–29 Jun 1945.

MORESBY (for the island in BC) B
1. Anticosti class minesweeping auxiliary vessel, 110. 7 May 1989–10 Mar 2000. ex *Joyce Tide*, ex *Lady Joyce*.

MORESBY III (N*)
1. Patrol vessel, Fy 42. 27 Apr 1942–16 Nov 1944. ex fishing vessel.

MOTO (N*)
1. Motor launch. 1 Oct 1918–? Sold 1921.

MUDATHALAPADU
1. Former name for harbour craft, HC202. 19 Jul 1943–46. Used as ferry boat in Halifax.

MULGRAVE (1 & 2. Geog, for the town in NS)
1. Chief examination officer, Mulgrave, NS. 1941–?
2. Bangor class minesweeper, N313/J313. 4 Nov 1942–7 Jun 1945.

MURRAY STEWART (N*)
1. Examination vessel, Z19/J19. 3 Oct 1940–?; Jan? 1942–22 Aug 1945. ex Dept of Transport vessel *Murray Stewart*.

MUSH

1. Former name for harbour craft, HC159. 5 Feb 1943–46.

MUSQUASH (N*)

1. Trawler sweeper. 12 May 1915–30 Apr 1918; ?–4 Jul 1918. ex Québec Salvage & Wrecking Co tug *Musquash*. This vessel was damaged at the explosion in Halifax, 1917.

MYSTIC

1. Auxiliary? Dates, type and source not known, Second World War.

M. W. WEATHERSPOON (N*)

1. Tug. 2 Mar–16 Jun 1917. ex Hendry's Ltd tug.

N

NABOB, HMS (for a native district ruler in the Mogul Empire of India)

1. Ruler class escort aircraft, D77. Com'd 7 Sep 1943 as HMS NABOB but had RCN ship's company from 15 Oct 1943–30 Sep 1944. Torpedoed by U354 in the Barents Sea 22 Aug 1944. Pd off 10 Oct 1944. Never com'd in RCN. ex MV *Edisto*.

Note: Some authorities list her as a Smiter class carrier.

NADEN (N* 1. CGS *Naden* was named for the river in the Queen Charlotte Islands. The name is a corruption of the term "ne dan xada i," meaning the Nedan River People, part of the Koetas family of the Raven clan of the Haida tribe on Graham Island, Queen Charlotte Islands, BC. 2 & 3 for 1.) 2. B

1. a. Tender to RN College of Canada. Jun 1918–1 Jun 1920. ex hydrographic survey sailing schooner, CGS *Naden*.

   b. Depot ship for barracks, Esquimalt, BC. 1 Jun 1920–31 Jul 1922; 1 Nov 1922–Jul 1925.

2. Shore barracks and naval training establishment, Esquimalt, BC. 1 Jun 1920–31 Jul 1922; 1 Nov (3 Sep?) 1922–1 Apr 1966. Became part of CFB Esquimalt.

Note: In 1999, "Naden" consists of that part of CFB Esquimalt bounded by Constance Cove, the government dry dock, Admiral's Road and Constance St, Esquimalt Road and the former Yarrows Ltd. Certain places are outside these general boundaries, e.g. the Wardroom, the former hospital, and some playing fields along Colville Rd.

3. Motor boat. Circa 1925–1935? (1941?) ex *Blue Boat*, ex motor boat for the Royal Naval College of Canada.

NADEN II

1. Mechanical training establishment barracks, Bldg 38, HMC Dockyard, Esquimalt, BC. Circa Dec 1941–Dec 1943. Became part of GIVENCHY.

2. Seamanship training establishment, Comox Spit, Comox, BC. 1 Mar 1946–1947? ex GIVENCHY III. Eventually became QUADRA.

NADEN III

1. Training establishment, Comox Spit, Comox, BC. Circa Dec 1941–1 Oct 1943. Became GIVENCHY III.

NADUR (name seems to be a spelling error for Adur, a river in Sussex, England)

1. River class frigate, turned over to USN prior to commissioning, Aug 1942? ex HMS ADUR, K296. Became USS ASHEVILLE.

NANAIMO (1 & 2. Geog, for the city in BC) 2. B

1. Flower class corvette, K101. 26 Apr 1941–28 Sep 1945.

2. Kingston class mine warfare vessel, 702. 10 May 1997–SIS

The tug NORTH LAKE circa 1945. (KM Coll.)

NANCY C
1. Harbour craft, HC85. Jul 1940–15 Jan 1942. Became HC85.

NANCY LEE
1. Harbour craft, HC45. 29 Jul 1941–15 Jan 1942. Became HC45.

NANOOSE (Geog, for the bay on the east coast of Vancouver Island, BC)
1. Basset class minesweeper, J35. 1 Apr 1943–(23?) 29 Jul 1945. ex NOOTKA.

NAPANEE (Geog, for the town in ON)
1. Flower class corvette, K118. 12 May 1941–12 Jul 1945.

NARADA (N*)
1. Tender. Chartered 12 Nov 1914–31 Aug 1916; 25 Sep 1916–? ex MV *Narada*.

NARASPUR (N*)
1. ex penitentiary vessel. 1 Nov 1935–?

NASHWAAK (N*)
1. a. Tug, W03. 4 Jun 1942–?
   b. Fire tug. 7 Mar 1945–circa late 1946.

NENAMOOK (Chinook word for otter)
1. "Nenamook class" patrol vessel, Fy 13. 7 Jan 1941–12 Mar 1946. Requisitioned 7 Jan, purchased 12 Mar 1941.

NENE (N*, for a river in the counties of Cambridge and Lincoln, England)
1. River class frigate, K270. 6 Apr 1944–11 Jun 1945. ex HMS NENE.

NEPSYA
1. Harbour craft, HC86. 17 Jun 1941–15 Jan 1942. Became HC86.

NEREID (N*)
1. Tug. Chartered 23 Jul 1917–28 Feb 1918; Jan?–Jun? 1919.

NEVILLE
1. Ville class tug. 7 Nov 1944–Sep 1945.

NEW AMERICA (N*)
1. Harbour craft, HC87. Circa 1941–15 Jan 1942. Became HC87. Type and source not known.

NEW BRUNSWICKER
1. Harbour craft, HC88. 3 Sep 1939–15 Jan 1942. Became HC88. ex RCMP motor launch.

NEW GLASGOW (Geog, for the town in NS) B
1. a. River class frigate, K320. 23 Dec 1943–5 Nov 1945.
   b. Prestonian class frigate, 315. 30 Jan 1954–15 Nov 1957; 5 May 1958–30 Jan 1967.

NEW LISKEARD (Geog, for the town in N. ON) B
1. a. Algerine class minesweeper, J397/F37. 21 Nov 1944–23 Oct 1945.
   Cadet training ship, 169. 9 Apr 1946–28 Oct 1949; 22 Mar 1950–22 Apr 1958.
   b. CNAV, Oceanographic survey ship, 160. ?–1 (May?) Dec 1969.

NEW WATERFORD (Geog, for the town in NS) B
1. a. River class frigate, K321/F321. 21 Jan 1944–7 Mar 1946; 9 Jan–28 Aug 1953;
   b. Prestonian class frigate, 304. 31 Jan 1958–27 Sep 1965?; 7 Jul 1966–22 Dec 1966.

NEW WESTMINSTER (Geog, for the city in BC)
1. Flower class corvette, K228. 31 Jan 1942–21 Jun 1945.

NEWINGTON (N*)
1. Minelayer and patrol vessel, 1914–1918 (?). ex lighthouse tender *Newington*, ex fishing trawler.

NEWPORT CORNER (Geog, for the community in NS)
1. Naval radio station, Newport Corner, NS (near Brooklyn).
   a. est'd as a transmitter site 1940 but not operational until May 1943.
   b. HMC NRS. 1957?–11 Jul(?) 1966. Tender to STADACONA.

NIAGARA (1. Geog, for the river flowing between ON and New York State. 2. after HMS NIAGARA, 20-gun vessel on Great Lakes circa 1832–1842) 2. B
1. Town class destroyer, I57. 24 Sep 1940–15 Sep 1945. ex USS THATCHER.
2. Canadian Naval Attaché and Naval Member, Canadian Joint Staff, Washington, DC. 7 Sep 1951–1 Apr 1966 (but made retroactive to 1 Sep 1965). Located at 1700 and after mid 1953, at 2450 Massachusetts Ave NW.

NICHOLSON (N*)
1. Detachment class patrol craft, 196. 28 Sep 1976–5 May 1992. ex RCMP *Nicholson*.

NIMPKISH (N*)
1. CNAV/CFAV, torpedo recovery vessel, YMR 120. 1953? (1944?)–circa May 1991. ex RCAF *Nimpkish*.

NIMPKISH II
1. Harbour craft, circa 1965. Became YAG 314. ex YFP 314.

NIOBE (1. N*, mythology, for the wife of King Amphion. 2 & 3 for 1.) 3. B
1. a. Diadem class: first class protected cruiser/cruiser. 21 Oct 1910–6 Sep 1915. ex HMS NIOBE. Com'd as RN ship 16 Sep 1910 and legally did not become RCN vessel until arrival in Halifax 21 Oct 1910. Apparently com'd and pd off on several occasions between 1910 and 1915.
   b. Depot ship, Halifax, NS. 6 Sep 1915–31 May 1920.
   Note: Paying off date sometimes listed as 1 Jun 1920.
2. a. Manning depot, Plymouth, England. 1 Mar–30 Jun 1941. ex DOMINION.
   b. Manning depot, Canada House, London, Eng. 30 Jun–15 Dec 1941.
   c. Manning depot, Greenock, Scot. 15 Dec 1941–9 Feb 1946. Located in the Smithson Institute on Inverkip Rd. After NIOBE paid off, the bldg became Ravenscraig Hospital.
3. Senior Canadian naval officer, London, England. 9 Feb 1946–1 Apr 1966. Located at 10 Haymarket, then 11 Hill St, then 66 Ennismore Gardens and later 1 Grosvenor Square. Dates not known. Became Canadian Defence Liaison Staff (CDLS) London, 1 Apr 1966, but date made retroactive to 1 Sep 1965.

NIOBE II
1. Depot, Belfast, N. Ireland. 9 Apr 1956–17 Jan 1957. Est'd to carry on her books the personnel standing by BONAVENTURE when she was fitting out.

NIPIGON (Geog, 1. bay in N. ON. 2. river in N. ON) 2. B
1. Bangor class minesweeper, J154. 11 Aug 1941–13 Oct 1945. In reserve until transferred to Turkish Navy as BAFRA, 29 Nov 1957.
2. Annapolis class destroyer, helicopter carrier, 266. 30 May 1964–1 Jul 1998.

NITINAT (N*)
1. Patrol craft, P03/Z03. 18 Sep 1939?–Jun 1945. ex Dept of Fisheries *Nitinat*.

NONSUCH (1. for Hudson's Bay Co vessel which arrived in Canada 1668. 2 for 1.) 1. B
1. Naval reserve division, Edmonton, AB. Located at 9722 102nd St.
   a. 1 Nov 1941–1 Sep 1942. Tender to NADEN.
   b. 1 Sep 1942–30 Nov 1964.
2. Naval reserve division, Edmonton, AB. 27 Sep 1975–SIS. Located at 11440 117th St.

NOOTKA (1. Geog, sound on Vancouver Island, BC. 2. First Nations Tribe in BC) 2. B
1. Basset/Fundy class minesweeper, N35/J35. 6 Dec 1938–1 Apr 1943. Became NANOOSE to release name for the destroyer in 2. below.
2. a. Tribal class destroyer, R96/D196/213. 7 Aug 1946–15 Aug 1949; 29 Aug 1950–16 Jan 1953. Pt. no. changed 1 Dec 1949. ex MICMAC.
   b. Tribal class destroyer escort, 213. 15 Dec 1954–6 Feb 1964.

NOOTKA SOUND
1. Auxiliary? Dates, type and source not known, Second World War.

NORANDA (Geog, for the city in QC)
1. Bangor class minesweeper, J265. 15 May 1942–28 Aug 1945.

NORSAL (N*)
1. Patrol craft, P12/Z12(P). 1940–Jan 1945. ex Powell River Co yacht *Norsal*, 150654.

NORSYD (alternative name for the town of North Sydney, NS)
1. Revised Flower class corvette, K520. 22 Dec 1943–25 Jun 1945.

NORTH BAY (Geog, for the city in ON)
1. Revised Flower class corvette, K339. 25 Oct 1943–1 Jul 1945.

NORTH LAKE
1. Tug, W08. 7 Sep 1943–Nov 1945. Former USN tug.

NORTH SHORE
1. Tug, W09. 21(?) Sep 1942–Nov 1945(14 Jan 1946?). Former USN tug.

The cruiser NIOBE as a depot ship at Halifax after the 1917 explosion. Note only two funnels—a third one appears to be under construction—and a wooden structure enclosing her quarterdeck. (RCN CN 3310.)

NORTH STAR
1. Tug, W10. 5 Dec 1941–17 Dec 1945. Former USN tug.

NORTHUMBERLAND (alternative name for Chatham, NB)
1. River class frigate. Cancelled Dec 1943.

NORTH WIND (NORTHWIND?)
1. Tug, W11. 9(?) Dec 1941–5 Dec 1945. Former USN tug. Tender to AVALON.

NORTON
1. Norton class tug, W31. 20 Dec 1943–Nov 1945.

O

OAK LAKE
1. Lake class minesweeper, J491. Cancelled 18 Sep 1944.

OAKVILLE (Geog, for the town in ON)
1. Flower class corvette, K178. 18 Nov 1941–20 Jul 1945. ex SELKIRK.

OAKWOOD
1. a. Wood class tug, Z64/554. 30 Mar 1944–Jan 1947.
   b. CNAV Wood class tug. Circa 1947?–1977? Loaned to DOT circa 1957.

OCEAN EAGLE (N*)
1. Tug, Fy 71/J07. Circa 1941–Jun 1944. Ex First World War rescue tug, 143330.

OJIBWA (For one of the most numerous of all First Nations tribes) B
1. Standard Admiralty O class submarine, S72. 23 Sep 1965–21 May 1998. ex HMS ONYX. Another form of this name is Chippawa.

OKANAGAN (For one of the five tribes of the Interior Salish Nation in BC) B
1. S22 super O class submarine, S74. 22 Jun 1968–14 Sep 1998. Paying off and 30th anniversary celebrations were held 28 Sep 1998.

OLYMPIA II
1. Auxiliary? Dates, type and source not known, Second World War.

ONONDAGA (For one of the Six Nations Iroquois tribes in the Lake Ontario region) B
1. S22 super O class submarine, S73. 22 Jun 1967–SIS.

ONTARIO (1. Geog, for the province. 2 for 1.) B
1. Minotaur class cruiser, 53/32. 26 Apr 1945–15 Oct 1958. ex HMS MINOTAUR (RN class name changed to Swiftsure after HMS MINOTAUR transferred).
2. Sea Cadet training centre, RMC, Kingston, ON. From 1982–SIS. ex Sea Cadet Camp Frontenac.

ORACLE (N*)
1. Training vessel/harbour craft, HC128? circa Sep 1941–9 Oct 1941? Became BYTOWN, and later HC128. ex HC128, ex *Oracle*. ORACLE sailed from Gaspé, QC, to Ottawa in Sep 1941.

ORANGEVILLE (1 & 2. Geog, for the town in ON)
1. Name assigned to an Algerine class minesweeper but never promulgated. Ship turned over to RN o/c as HMS MARMION, J381.
2. Castle class corvette, K491. 24 Apr 1944–12 Apr 1946. ex HMS HEDINGHAM CASTLE, K396.

ORILLIA (Geog, for the town in ON)
1. Flower class corvette, K119. 25 Nov 1940–2 Jul 1945.

ORIOLE (bird) B
1. Bermuda-rigged sail training ketch, 3/408. 19 Jul 1954–SIS. ex ORIOLE IV.
Note: On charter from Navy League until purchased by the RCN May 1957.

ORIOLE IV (N*)
1. a. RCSC training vessel (sail) tender to HMCS YORK. 16 Sep 1943–26 Sep 1946 (commissioning in doubt). ex yacht *Oriole IV*.
   b. Tender to CORNWALLIS. 16 Jan 1950–3 Nov 1950; 13 Jun 1952–19 Jul 1954. Became ORIOLE.
Note: For duration of her service, she was on charter from the Navy League.

ORKNEY (alternative name for Yorkton, SK)
1. River class frigate, K448. 18 Apr 1944–22 Jan 1946.

OSHAWA (Geog, for the city in ON) B
1. a. Algerine class minesweeper, J330/F330. 6 Jul 1944–28 Jul 1945; 24 Oct 1945–26 Feb 1946. In reserve 1946–1956. 11 Apr 1956–7 Nov 1958.
   b. CNAV, oceanographic research vessel, 174. 1958–1966.

OTTAWA (1, 2 & 3. Geog, for the river between ON & QC. 4. for the city.) 3. B
1. C/River class destroyer, H60. 15 Jun 1938–13 Sep 1942, torpedoed by U91 and sunk in the North Atlantic. ex HMS CRUSADER.
2. G/River class destroyer, H31. 20 Mar 1943–31 Oct 1945. ex GRIFFIN, ex HMS GRIFFIN.
Note: The actual date of commission was 10 Apr 1943. The name Ottawa was made retroactive to the date of her commissioning as HMCS GRIFFIN. See GRIFFIN.
3. a. St Laurent class destroyer escort, 229. 10 Nov 1956–24 May 1963.
   b. Improved St Laurent class destroyer escort, helicopter carrier, 229. 28 Oct 1964–31 Jul 1992.
4. Halifax class frigate, 341. 28 Sep 1996–SIS.

OTTER (animal)
1. Armed yacht, S04. 4 Oct 1940–26 Mar 1941, destroyed by accidental explosion and fire off Halifax Light Ship. ex yacht *Conseco*.

OTTERVILLE
1. a. Ville class tug, W51/W32. 29 Jan 1944–Jan 1946.
   b. CNAV/CFAV, Ville class tug, 590. Circa 1946?–circa 1975/76.

OUGANDA III (N*)
1. Auxiliary. Requisitioned 27 Aug 1941. Caught fire and sank in St. John's harbour, 30 Nov 1941. ex Shaw Steamship Ltd vessel.

OUTARDE (Geog, for the bay on the St Lawrence R.)
1. Bangor class minesweeper, J161. 4 Dec 1941–24 Nov 1945.
Note: Name later associated with the town.

OUTREMONT (Geog, for the city in QC) B
1. a. River class frigate, K322. 27 Nov 1943–5 Nov 1945. ex VALLEYFIELD.
   b. Prestonian class frigate, 310. 2 Sep 1955–7 Jun 1965.

OWEN SOUND (Geog, for the city in ON)
1. Revised Flower class corvette, K340. 17 Nov 1943–19 Jul 1945.

The first OTTAWA (at Iceland?) circa 1942. (FDN Coll.)

P

PACIFIC CROWN
1. Auxiliary? Dates, type and source not known, Second World War.

PADLOPING ISLAND (Geog, for the island off east coast of Baffin Island)
1. Naval radio station, Padloping Island, NWT. 10 Sep 1953–Aug? 1955. Taken over by DOT.

PAL-O-MINE
1. Former name for harbour craft, HC165. 11 Feb 1943–46. 43 ft MB.

PAMELA
1. Harbour craft, HC89. ?–15 Jan 1942. Became HC89. ex Seminaire de Québec MB. ex *Laval* (Luval?).

PANSY
1. Auxiliary? Dates, type and source not known, Second World War.

PAPOOSE
1. Harbour craft, W49/Z90/HC90. Circa Nov 1940–? ex motor launch.

PARAGON (N*)
1. Motor launch. 31 May 1917–Jul 1919. Purchased. ex Phoenix Foundry & Locomotive Works vessel. Sold Jan 1921.

PARAGON II
1. Former name of HC207. 21 Aug 1943–2 Jan 1945. ex MB.

PARKSVILLE
1. a. Ville class tug, W49. 27 Jan 1944–1946?
   b. CNAV/CFAV, Ville class tug,, 579. 1946–1974.
2. CFAV, Ville class tug, 591. 17 Jan1974–SIS.

PARRY SOUND (Geog, for the town in ON)
1. Revised Flower class corvette, K341. 30 Aug 1944–10 Jul 1945.

PATHFINDER (N*)
1. a. Patrol vessel, Atlantic coast. 1915–1918. ex yacht *Pathfinder*.
   b. Tender to naval reserve division, Toronto. 26 May 1941–Nov 1945. (Tender to STAR from 27 Nov 1941). ex yacht *Pathfinder*, ex *Conestoga*, ex *Pathfinder*, 138220.

PATRICIA DON (N*)
1. RCSC launch, Shepley Island, SK. Circa 1944–1946. Chartered.

PATRICIA MCQUEEN (N*)
1. Tug, W12/W02. 9 Jun 1941–30 Aug 1945. ex tug *Patricia McQueen*.

PATRICIAN (N*, a member of the ancient Roman aristocracy)
1. M class destroyer, G57/H57/H87. 1 Nov 1920–1 Jan 1928. ex HMS PATRICIAN.
Note: as HMS PATRICIAN, wore pt. nos G48 (Sep 1915), F23 (Jan 1917), F15 (Jan 1918), GA1 (Sep 1918).

PATRIOT (1. N*, one who loves and loyally supports his country. 2 for 1.) 2. B
1. M class destroyer, G56/H56/H86. 1 Nov 1920–Dec 1927. ex HMS PATRIOT.
Note: As HMS PATRIOT, wore pt. nos G56 (Sep 1915) and G63 (Jan 1917).
2. Commanding Officer Naval Divisions, Hamilton, ON. Began operation 28 Mar 1953 when located in STAR. Moved to new bldg at Catharine St N May 1955. In commission 1 Feb 1956–circa 1966.

PATROL BOAT III
1. Former name for harbour craft, HC91. 1942–1945? ex Dept of Fisheries MB.

PELICAN (bird)
1. Crash boat, 4. July 1985–SIS.

PENETANG (1 & 2. alternative name for Penetanguishene, ON) 2. B
1. Flower class corvette. Cancelled Dec 1943. ex RIVERSIDE.
2. a. River class frigate, K676. 19 Oct 1944–10 Nov 1945. ex ROUYN.
   b. Prestonian class frigate, 316. 1 Jun 1954–2 Sep 1955; 9–25 Jan 1956. Loaned to Norwegian Navy as DRAUG.

PEREGRINE (bird. 2. Named for 1?)
1. Vessel, WWI?
2. Drafting depot and manning pool, Halifax, NS. 1 Oct 1944–29 Mar 1946. ex STADACONA II.
Note: Took over the exhibition grounds and the former RCAF depot at Windsor Park.

PESAQUID (alternative name for Windsor, NS)
1. River class frigate. Cancelled Dec 1943.

PETERBOROUGH (Geog, for the city in ON)
1. Revised Flower class corvette, K342. 1 Jun 1944–19 Jul 1945.

PETREL (N*)
1. Patrol vessel. 1 Apr 1915–31 Mar 1917? 17 Sep 1917–? 1 May–6 Jun 1918; 24 Oct 1918–31 Dec 1918. ex Fisheries patrol vessel *Petrel*.
Note: This vessel alternated periods in naval service with Fisheries duties.

PETROLIA (1 & 2. Geog, for the town in ON)
1. Name assigned to an Algerine class minesweeper but never promulgated. Ship turned over to RN o/c as HMS LIONESS, J377.
2. Castle class corvette, K498. 29 Jun 1944–8 Mar 1946. ex HMS SHERBORNE CASTLE, K453.

PICKLE
1. Sailing yawl, QW7. Circa 1955–1975. ex British, ex German vessel.

PICTOU (Geog, for the town in NS)
1. Flower class corvette, K146. 29 Apr 1941–12 Jul 1945.

PIERREVILLE
1. Ville class tug. 13 Dec 1944–Jul 1945.

PILOT (N*)
1. Auxiliary. Aug–Nov 1914? ex steamship *Pilot.*

PILOT BOAT (N*)
1. RCSC training vessel, Minnicog, ON. Circa 1944/5.

PINE BRANCH
1. Auxiliary? Dates, type and source not known, Second World War.

PINE LAKE
1. Lake class minesweeper, J492. Completed 22 Sep 1945 but never com'd. ex BEECH LAKE.

PINE LEAF (N*)
1. Auxiliary. 23 Sep–11 Nov 1939.

PLAINSVILLE
1. a. Ville class tug, W01. 24 Nov 1944–Jan 1946.
   b. CNAV/CFAV, Ville class tug, 587. Circa 1946–circa 1991.

PLESSISVILLE (Geog, for the town in QC)
1. River class frigate. Cancelled Dec 1943.

The first PROVIDER 17 Jan 1943. (RCN H-5857. KM Coll.)

POGO (after the Walt Kelly cartoon character)
1. Patrol boat, 104. Circa 1980–circa 1996. Tender to CARLETON. ex launch *Pogo*, originally carried onboard LABRADOR.

POINTE CLAIRE (Geog, for the town in QC)
1. Flower class corvette. Became MERRITONIA.

POPLAR LAKE
1. Lake class minesweeper, J493. Completed 9 Sep 1946 but never com'd.

PORTAGE (alternative name for Portage la Prairie, MB) B
1. Algerine class minesweeper, J331/F31/164. 22 Oct 1943–31 Jul 1946; 12 Apr–30 Sep 1947; 24 Mar–18 Aug 1948; 12 Apr 1949–25 Nov 1954; 23 Apr 1955–24 Sep 1957; 1 Apr–26 Sep 1958.

PORT ARTHUR (Geog, for the city in ON, now part of Thunder Bay)
1. Revised Flower class corvette, K233. 26 May 1942–11 Jul 1945.

PORT COLBORNE (Geog, for the town in ON)
1. River class frigate, K326. 15 Nov 1943–7 Nov 1945.

PORT EDWARD (Geog, for the community 16 kms south of Prince Rupert, BC)
1. NRS, Port Edward, BC. Circa Jul 1953–Jul 1960.

PORT HOPE (Geog, for the town in ON)
1. a. Bangor class minesweeper, J280. 30 Jul 1942–13 Oct 1945. In strategic reserve 1945–52.
   b. re-acquired but not recommissioned, 183. 1952–1959.

PORTE DAUPHINE (for a gate in the fortress of Louisbourg, NS) B
1. a. Porte class gate vessel, 186. 10–23 Dec 1952; 17 Mar–18 Dec 1953; 16 May–21 Oct 1955. Loaned to MOT 1955–1974.
   b. circa Oct 1974–circa Dec 1995.

PORTE DE LA REINE (for a gate in the fortress of Louisburg, NS) B
1. Porte class gate vessel, 184. 7–14 Oct 1952; 1 Jun 1966–19 Dec 1996.

PORTE QUEBEC (for a gate in the city of Montréal) B
1. Porte class gate vessel, 185. 19 Sep 1952–1 Nov 1957. 1966?–19 Dec 1996.

PORTE SAINT JEAN (for a gate in Québec city) B
1. Porte class gate vessel, 180. 5 Dec 1951–25 Jul 1952; 9 May–18 Sep 1953; 16 May–22 Sep 1955; 2 Jun 1958–31 Mar 1996.

PORTE SAINT LOUIS (for a gate in Québec city) B
1. Porte class gate vessel, 183. 29 Aug 1952–30 Oct 1952; 9 May–18 Sep 1953; 16 May–22 Sep 1955; 7 Jun 1962–31 Mar 1996.

POUNDMAKER (alternative name for the town of North Battleford, SK. Poundmaker was a First Nations chief from the area of North Battleford.)
1. River class frigate, K675. 17 Sep 1944–25 Nov 1945.

PREMIER (N*)
1. Patrol vessel. 21 Aug 1915–2 Jun 1917, wrecked on Pollock Rock off Halifax. ex oceangoing tug *Premier*.
Note: This vessel was chartered 1 Dec 1914 from the Canadian Dredging, Co., Midland, ON, and apparently purchased in 1915.

PRESCOTT (Geog, for the town in ON)
1. Flower class corvette, K161. 26 Jun 1941–20 Jul 1945.

PRESERVER (1. N/K. 2. for 1.) 2. B
1. Fairmile depot ship, F94. 11 Jul 1942–6 Nov 1945.
2. Protecteur class operational support ship, 510. 30 Jul 1970–SIS.

PRESTONIAN (1 & 2. alternative name for Preston, ON) 2. B
1. Flower class corvette. Cancelled Dec 1943.
2. a. River class frigate, K662. 13 Sep 1944–9 Nov 1945. ex BEAUHARNOIS, ex BUCKINGHAM.
   b. Prestonian class frigate 307. 22 Aug 1953–24 Apr 1956. Became R Nor N TROLL.

PREVOST (1. after the LADY PREVOST, a ship in the Battle of Lake Erie in 1813. 2 for 1.) 1. B
1. Naval reserve division, London, ON. Originally located in Carling Block, Richmond St. Moved to 19 Becher St Sep 1957.
   a. 1 Nov 1941–1 Sep 1942. Tender to STADACONA.
   b. 1 Sep 1942–30 Nov 1964.
2. Naval reserve division, London, ON. 19 Becher St, London. 29 Sep 1991–SIS.

PRINCE ARTHUR (N*)
1. ex CPR passenger vessel. Chartered Aug–Sep 1914. Then to RN?

PRINCE DAVID (N*, named for a vice-president of the CNR)
1. a. Prince class armed merchant cruiser, F89. 28 Dec 1940–1 May 1943. ex CNR passenger vessel *Prince David*.
   b. Infantry landing ship, F89. 20 Dec 1943–11 Jun 1945.

PRINCE GEORGE (N*)
1. ex CPR passenger vessel. Chartered 8 Aug–23 Sep 1914. Then to RN?

PRINCE HENRY (N*, named for the first president of the CNR)
1. a. Prince class armed merchant cruiser, F70. 4 Dec 1940–30 Apr 1943. ex *North Star*, ex CNR passenger vessel *Prince Henry*.
   b. Infantry landing ship, F70. 4 Jan 1944–15 Apr 1945. Became HMS PRINCE HENRY Jul 1945–Jul 1946.

PRINCE ROBERT (N*, named for a vice-president of the CNR)
1. a. Prince class armed merchant cruiser, F56. 31 Jul 1940–2 Jan 1943. ex CNR passenger vessel *Prince Robert*.
   b. Auxiliary anti-aircraft ship, F56. 7 Jun 1943–18 (20?) Dec 1943; 4 Jun–10 Dec 1945.

PRINCE RUPERT (Geog, for the city in BC)
1. River class frigate, K324. 30 Aug 1943–15 Jan 1946.

PROTECTOR (1. N* 2. from 1)
1. a. Vessel for NOIC, Sydney, NS, T98, later HC63. 3 Sep 1939–? ex RCMP motor boat *Protector*.
Note: Vessel obtained 28 Aug 1939. NOIC established Sep 1939 and took name from vessel.
2. Naval base, Post Record (newspaper) Building(?), Sydney, NS. 22 Jul 1940–27 Mar 1946.

PROTECTOR II
1. Naval base, Point Edward, NS. 15 Mar 1943–Oct 1943. Became part of PROTECTOR, Oct 1943.
Notes: a. Listed in the 15 Nov 1940 *Navy List*.
   b. The use of this site as a naval base dates from 5 Sep 1915. Although not given a separate name, it came under the command and control of various SNO's in MARGARET (1 Jul–Nov 1915), NIOBE (1 Nov 1915–Nov 1917), and

STADACONA (Nov 1917–3 Apr 1918). During the Second World War, came under STADACONA, VENTURE, and PROTECTOR. After the war, under SCOTIAN and STADACONA. Property retained and became RCSC TE PROTECTOR circa 1953. Became ACADIA 15 May 1956. Became the Coast Guard College.

PROTECTEUR (French version of PROTECTOR) B
1. Protecteur class operational support ship, 509. 30 Aug 1969–SIS.

PROVIDER (1. N/K. 2 for 1.) 2. B
1. Fairmile depot ship, F100. 1 Dec 1942–22 March 1946.
2. Provider class operational support ship, 508. 28 Sep 1963–24 Jun 1998. Note: retained in the service as a replacement AOR during long refits of Protecteur class vessels.

PUGWASH (N*)
1. Tug, W01. Dec 1943–15 May 1945. ex DPW tug *Pugwash*.

PUNCHER, HMS (descriptive name for one who strikes with the fist)
1. Smiter class escort aircraft carrier, D79. Com'd 5 Feb 1944 as HMS PUNCHER but had RCN ship's company. Pd off 16 Jan 1946. Never com'd in RCN. ex MV *Willapa*.
Note: Some authorities list her as a Ruler class carrier.

Q

QUADRA (for the Spanish naval captain and navigator, Juan Francisco de la Bodega y Quadra, who explored the NW coast of North America circa 1775–1790.) B
1. Sea Cadet training establishment on Comox Spit, Comox, BC. 1 Jul–15 Sep 1956; 1 Jun–15 Sep 1957; 2 Jun–14 Sep 1958; 1 Jun–15 Sep 1959; 1 Jun–15 Sep 1960; 5 Jun–15 Sep 1961; 4 Jun–14 Sep 1962; 3 Jun–13 Sep 1963; 7 Jun–12 Sep 1964; 8 Jun–10 Sep 1965. Commissions each summer.
Note: Started life as a rifle range as early as 1895. ex NADEN III, GIVENCHY III, NADEN II. Became a RCSC Camp in the summer of 1952.

QUEBEC during full power trials in the Strait of Juan de Fuca, 20 Mar 1953. (RCN E-18307. FDN Coll.)

QU'APPELLE (1 & 2. Geog, a river in SK. 3 for 1 & 2.) 2. B
1. F/River class destroyer, H69. 8 Feb 1944–27 May 1946. ex HMS FOXHOUND. Became a stationary training ship, 12 Oct 1945–Jan 1946.
2. Mackenzie class destroyer escort, 264. 14 Sep 1963–(13 Mar?) 4 Apr 1992.
3. Sea Cadet training centre, Fort San, SK. 1992–SIS. Commissions each summer.

QUATSINO (Geog, for the sound on Vancouver Island, BC)
1. Bay class minesweeper, J152. 3 Nov 1941–26 Nov 1945.
Note: Name later came to be associated with the town.

QUEBEC (1. Geog, for the city. 2. Geog, for the province. 3 for 2.) 2. B
1. Revised Flower class corvette. Became VILLE DE QUEBEC circa Apr 1942.
2. Uganda/Ceylon class cruiser, 66/31. 14 Jan 1952–13 Jun 1956. ex UGANDA, ex HMS UGANDA. See also VILLE DE QUEBEC.
3. Sea Cadet Training Centre:
   a. Farnham, Québec. Summer 1982.
   b. Ste-Angele-de-Laval, Québec. Summer 1983–SIS. Commissions each summer.

QUEEN (probably for the English meaning of the Latin word Regina) B
1. Naval reserve division, Regina. Originally located in the New Armouries, Elphinstone St., Wascana Winter Club acquired 1939 but move here delayed until circa 1943. Moved to ex CWAC Barracks Aug 1945. Apparently moved to Elphinstone & 10th Ave in 1947. Moved to the Queen Bldg, 2833 Broad St in Jun 1955.
   a. 1 Nov 1941–1 Sep 1942. Tender to NADEN.
   b. 1 Sep 1942–30 Nov 1964.
2. Naval reserve division, Regina. 28 Sept 1975–SIS. 2833 Broad St.

QUEEN BEE
1. Harbour craft, HC110, Prince Rupert, BC, second World War.
2. a. Harbour launch, YFL 100, Esquimalt. Circa 1972–Aug 1984. Became ADMIRAL'S LADY.
   b. Harbour launch, YFL 100, Esquimalt. Circa 1991–SIS. Ex ADMIRAL'S LADY.

QUEEN CHARLOTTE (1. after a Provincial Marine corvette built in 1809 at Amherstburg for service on Lake Erie and named in honour of the consort of the reigning monarch, King George III. 2 for 1.) 1. B
1. Naval reserve division, Simms Bldg, Charlottetown, PE.
   a. 1 Nov 1941–1 Sep 1942. Tender to STADACONA.
   b. 1 Sep 1942–15 Dec 1964.
2. Naval reserve division, Charlottetown, PE. 17 Sep 1994–SIS. First located at 22 1st Ave, West Royalty Industrial Park. Moved to Water Street, Charlottetown, 27 Sep 1997–SIS.

QUEENSVILLE
1. a. Ville class tug, W?. 5 Dec 1944–?
   b. CNAV/CFAV, Ville class tug, 586. Circa 1946–circa 1991.

QUEST (functional name)
1. CNAV/CFAV, Research vessel, 172. 21 Aug 1969–SIS.

QUESNEL (Geog, for the town in BC)
1. Flower class corvette, K133. 23 May 1941–3 Jul 1945.

QUINTE (1 & 2. Geog, for the bay on Lake Ontario) 1. B
1. Bangor class minesweeper, J166. 30 Aug 1941–25 Oct 1946.
2. Bay class minesweeper, 149. 15 Oct 1954–26 Feb 1964.

HMCS RAINBOW (2nd) in 1971. (FDN Coll.)

R

RACOON (N*)
1. Harbour craft, HC72. 19 Jun 1940–? ex yacht.

RACCOON (animal) 2. B
1. Armed yacht, pt. no? 17 May 1940–7 Sep 1942, torpedoed by U165 and sunk in the St Lawrence River. ex *Halonia*.
2. Fairmile B type, 779. 11 May 1956–22 Oct 1956. ex PTC779, ex ML779, ex ML079.

RADISSON (for the explorer) B
1. Naval reserve division, Cap-de-la-Madeleine, Québec. 3 Oct 1987–SIS. First located at 175 Rue Alphonse; moved 3 May 1992 to a new facility, Ile St Christophe.

RADVILLE
1. Ville class tug, W52. 3 Feb 1944–Sep 1945.

RAFFICER
1. Harbour craft, HC64. 6 Dec 1940–15 Jan 1942. Became HC64. ex M.B. 248?

RAINBOW (1. N*, weather phenomenon. 2. species of trout) 2. B
1. a. Apollo class: 2nd class protected cruiser/light cruiser. 7 Nov 1910–8 May 1917. ex HMS RAINBOW. Com'd as RN ship 4 Aug 1910 but legally did not become RCN vessel until arrival in Esquimalt 7 Nov 1910.
   b. Depot ship, Esquimalt, BC. 5 Jul 1917–1 Jun 1920. Duties taken over by NADEN.
2. Modernized (Guppy II) Tench class submarine, 75. 2 Dec 1968–31 Dec 1974. ex USS ARGONAUT.

RAINBOW II
1. Former name for despatch boat, Cornwallis, HC139. 16 Oct 1942–1945?

RALLY (N*)
1. R class patrol boat, 141. 22 Jul 1982–24 Oct 1992. ex DOT Vessel *Rally*.

RAMBLER (N*)
1. Motor launch. Chartered 30 May–? 1916; 1 Jun–? 1917; 1918?

RANNEY FALLS (alternative name for Campbellford, ON)
1. River class frigate. Cancelled Dec 1943.

RAPID (N*)
1. R class patrol boat, 142. 22 Jul 1982–24 Oct 1992. ex DOT vessel *Rapid*.

RAYON D'OR (N*)
1. Auxiliary minesweeper, J13/J11/Z11. 11(15?) Sep 1939–Apr 1945. ex Maritime Fish Corporation steam fishing trawler *Rayon d'Or*.

RED DEER (Geog, for the city in AB)
1. Bangor class minesweeper, J255. 24 Nov 1941–30 Oct 1945. In reserve until Feb 1959.

RED WING
1. Auxiliary? Dates, type and source not known, Second World War.

REGAL
1. Auxiliary? Dates, type and source not known, Second World War.

REGINA (1 & 2. Geog, for the city in SK) 2. B
1. Revised Flower class corvette, K234. 22 Jan 1942–8 Sep 1944, torpedoed and sunk by U667 off Trevose Head, Cornwall, England.
Note: Various sources incorrectly state date of loss as 11 instead of 8 Sep. Further, REGINA is not listed in Appendix III of *The Far Distant Ships* with other Principal Ships of the RCN.
2. Halifax class frigate, 334. 30 Sep 1994–SIS.

REINDEER (animal)
1. Armed yacht, S08/Z08. 25 Jul 1940–20 Jul 1945. ex *Mascotte*, ex *Josephine*.
2. Harbour craft, HC71 (ML8). 24 Jun 1940–?
3. Fairmile B Type, 716. 30 Apr 1954–circa 1957. ex PTC716, ex ML716, ex ML116.

RENARD (animal; Fr. for fox)
1. Armed yacht, S13/Z13. 27 May 1940–1 Aug 1944, condemned. ex *Winchester*.

RENFREW (Geog, for the town in ON)
1. Revised Flower class corvette, K452. Cancelled Dec 1943.

REO II (N*)
1. Auxiliary minesweeper, Z33/J08. 23 Jan 1941–19 Oct 1945. ex Dover Shipping Co coaster *Reo II*.

RESOLUTE (Geog, for the bay on Cornwallis Island, Nunavut) B
1. Bay class minesweeper, 154. 16 Sep 1954–14 Feb 1964.

RESTIGOUCHE (1 & 2. Geog, for the river in NB) 2. B
1. C/River class destroyer, H00. 15 Jun 1938–6 Oct 1945. ex HMS COMET.
2. a. Restigouche class destroyer escort, 257. 7 Jun 1958–3 Aug 1970.
   b. Improved Restigouche class destroyer escort, 257. 12 May 1972–31 Aug 1994.

RESTLESS (N*)
1. Examination vessel and later training vessel for RN College of Canada. Circa Jan 1918–1920. ex Fishery patrol vessel *Restless*, ex examination vessel *Restless*.

RETLAS
1. Former name of harbour craft, HC218. 18 Oct 1943–4 Jan 1945.

REVELSTOKE (Geog, for the town in BC) B
1. Llewellyn class minesweeper, J373/140? 4 Jul 1944–12 Nov 1945; 17 Jun–20 Nov 1952; 11 Jun–23 Oct 1953.
2. CNAV, 140? Circa 1956.

RIBBLE (N*, for a river in Lancashire, England)
1. River class frigate, K525. 24 Jul 1944–11 Jun 1945. ex HMS RIBBLE.

RIMOUSKI (Geog, for the town in QC)
1. Flower class corvette, K121. 26 Apr 1941–24 Jul 1945.

RIO CASMA (N*)
1. Harbour craft, HC92. 17 Sep 1941–15 Jan 1942. Became HC42. ex MB.

The auxiliary ROSS NORMAN in the Second World War. (RCN 2685. KM Coll.)

RIO SAMA (N*)
1. Tug. 3 Jul 1943–31 Jan 1944. ex Victory Transport & Salvage Co tug. Chartered.

RIPPLE (alternative name–water related)
1. Patrol vessel, Z08(P). 19 May 1942–12 Jun 1945. ex BCPP vessel PML 14. Com'd as PML 14 from 12-19 May 1942.

RIVERSIDE (Geog, for the town in ON)
1. Flower class corvette. Cancelled Dec 1943. ex PENETANG.

RIVERTON
1. a. Norton class tug, W47. 3 Aug 1944–1946?
   b. CNAV/CFAV, Ton class tug, 528. 1946?–circa 1979.
2. CFAV, Support vessel, 121. 3 Mar 1989(?)–SIS. ex *Smit-Lloyd 112*.

RIVIERE DU LOUP (Geog, for the town in QC)
1. Revised Flower class corvette, K537. 21 Nov 1943–2 Jul 1945.

R.J. FOOTE
1. Tug, HC93. 1 Jun 1941–15 Jan 1942. Became HC93. ex Canada Dredging Co tug.

ROAMER (N*)
1. Motor launch. Chartered 30 May–Nov 1916; 3 Mar–Nov? 1917; 1 Jun–Nov? 1918.

ROANOKE (N*)
1. Motor launch. Chartered 30 May–Nov? 1917.

ROCKCLIFFE (Geog, for the village of Rockcliffe, ON, now part of Ottawa) B
1. a. Algerine class minesweeper, J355. 30 Sep 1944–28 Jul 1945; 24 Oct 1945–14 Jan 1946.
   b. Training ship, 173. 3 Mar 1947–15 Aug 1950.

ROLLIN E. MASON (N*)
1. Auxiliary. Purchased 1917 and became PV V.

ROSE (N*)
1. Motor launch. Circa Jan 1918–Mar 1919.

ROSEMARY (N*)
1. Harbour craft, HC94. Circa 1941–15 Jan 1942. Became HC94 and as such SIS 1 Apr 1945. ex MB.

ROSEVILLE
1. Ville class tug. Mar 1944–Nov 1945.

ROSSLAND (Geog, for the town in BC)
1. Llewellyn class minesweeper, J358. 15 Jul 1944–1 Nov 1945.

ROSS NORMAN (N*)
1. Auxiliary minesweeper, and later mobile deperming vessel, Z09/J01/J09. Chartered 19 Jun 1940–26 Aug 1943, when purchased. 26 Aug 1943–8 Apr 1946. ex Ross Norman Shipping Company coaster *Ross Norman.*

ROSTHERN (Geog, for the town in SK)
1. Flower class corvette, K169. 17 Jun 1941–19 Jul 1945.

ROVER (N*)
1. Motor launch. Circa Jan 1918–Mar 1919.

ROUYN (1 & 2. Geog, for the town in QC)
1. River class frigate. Became PENETANG.
2. River class frigate. Cancelled Dec 1943.

ROYALMOUNT (1 & 2. alternative name for Mount Royal, QC)
1. River class frigate. Became BUCKINGHAM, 5 Apr 1944.
2. River class frigate, K677. 25 Aug 1944–17 Nov 1945. ex ALWINGTON.

ROYAL ROADS (for the roadstead outside Esquimalt harbour and off the college grounds)
1. a. RCNVR Officer's training establishment, Colwood, BC. 13 Dec 1940–Feb 1942.
   b. Royal Canadian Naval College, Colwood, BC. 21 Oct 1942–29 Jul 1948.
   c. became HMCS ROYAL ROADS, the RCN–RCAF College circa 1947/8.
   d. became Royal Roads Military College, circa 1948–1996.
Note: Originally a mansion called Hatley Park. Still referred to as a fleet establishment and HMCS as late as 1956.

RPS (N*)
1. Auxiliary. Jun 1918–Sep 1919. ex schooner *RPS.*

RUNNYMEDE (alternative name for township of York, ON)
1. River class frigate, K678. 14 Jun 1944–19 Jan 1946.

RUTH (N*)
1. Motor launch. Chartered 31 May–Nov? 1916.

S

SABLE I (SABLE 1; SABLE ISLAND) (N*)
1. Auxiliary. Chartered 3 Dec 1914–?; 12 Aug 1915–Apr(?) 1916. Tender to MARGARET. ex Farquhar & Co vessel.

SACKVILLE (Geog, for the town in NB) Note: her badge is unofficial.
1. a. Flower class corvette, K181. 30 Dec 1941–Nov 1944. ex DALHOUSIE.
   b. Loop layer, Z62. 21 May 1945–8 Apr 1946.
   c. Loop layer, depot ship, reserve fleet, 532. 4 Aug 1950–Dec 1953.
   d. CNAV, loop layer, 532. Dec 1953–circa Aug 1954
   e. CNAV, Survey vessel, 113. Circa Aug 1954–Jan 1964.
   f. CNAV/CFAV, research vessel, 113. May 1964–16 Dec 1982.
   g. Non commissioned floating museum, Halifax. Restored. Flower class corvette, K181. 4 May 1985 to present.

SAGUENAY (1 & 2. Geog, for the river in QC) 2. B
1. Acasta/River class destroyer, H01/D79/I79/I89. 22 May 1931–30 Jul 1945.
2. a. St Laurent class destroyer escort, 206. 15 Dec 1956–22 Aug 1963.
   b. Improved St Laurent class destroyer escort, helicopter carrier, 206.
      14 May 1965–31 Aug 1990. Became a harbour training ship in Halifax.

SAINTE AGATHE (alternative name for Sainte Agathe des Monts, QC)
1. River class frigate. Cancelled Dec 1943.

STE ANN (ST ANNE) (probably for the Bay in QC or NB)
1. Bangor class minesweeper. Circa 1940. Became BURLINGTON.

ST ANNE (N*)
1. Tug, W02. Oct 1939–May 1940; 27 Oct 1940–26 Apr 1941; 18 Nov 1941–14 May 1942;
   10 (12?) Oct 1942–7 Jun 1943. ex Bathurst Power & Paper Co tug *St Ann*. Became
   CASCAPEDIA.

ST ANTHONY (in honour of Father Anthony Daniel, one of the early Jesuit Missionaries. He was killed by
the Iroquois while defending his mission near present day Hillsdale, ON, 4 Jul 1648) B
1. CNAV/CFAV, Saint class tug, 531. 22 Feb 1957–1958; ?–30 Jun 1995?

ST BONIFACE (Geog, for the city in MB)
1. Algerine class minesweeper, J332. 10 Sep 1943–25 Sep 1946.

ST CATHARINES (Geog, for the city in ON)
1. River class frigate, K325. 31 Jul 1943–18 Nov 1945. Later employed by DOT as a weather
   ship with naval pt. no. 324.

ST CHARLES (for Charles Garnier, a Jesuit Missionary killed by the Iroquois in 1649) B
1. CNAV/CFAV, Saint class tug, 533. 7 Jun 1957–31 Mar 1964; ?–circa 1993.

ST CLAIR (Geog, for the river flowing between Ontario and Michigan)
1. Town class destroyer, I65. 24 Sep 1940–23 Aug 1944. ex USS WILLIAMS. Attached to the
   Damage Control and Fire Fighting school, 1944–45.

The armed yacht SANS PEUR in the Second World War. (KM Coll.)

ST CROIX (1 & 2. Geog, for the river flowing between NB & the state of Maine) 2. B
  1. Town class destroyer, I81. 24 Sep 1940–20 Sep 1943, torpedoed by U305 and sunk south of Iceland. ex USS McCOOK.
  2. Restigouche class destroyer escort, 256. 4 Oct 1958–15 Nov 1974. Became a harbour training ship, circa 1984–1989.

ST EDOUARD (alternative name for Port Alfred, QC)
  1. River class frigate. Cancelled Dec 1943.

ST ELOI (after a First World War land battle)
  1. a. Battle class trawler, 13 Nov 1917–1920.
    b. Became Gate Vessel 12, 15 Jun 1940–Jun 1945. ex DOT
Note: Apparently had pt. no. Fy 37 assigned to her.

ST FRANCIS (Geog, for the river flowing between QC/NB and the State of Maine)
  1. Town class destroyer, I93. 24 Sep 1940–11 Jun 1945.

ST HYACINTHE (Geog, for the city in QC)
  1. Signal training school, St Hyacinthe, QC. 1 Oct 1941–20 Feb 1946.
Notes: a. This school was formerly located in the Exhibition grounds, Halifax. See STADACONA II.
    b. School established at St. Hyacinthe some time prior to actual commissioning date. In St. Hyacinthe, the school was located in the former Militia Training Centre in an area bounded by the CNR tracks, Sicotte and Larocque Streets. An unofficial badge was designed and used.

ST JEROME (Geog, for the city in QC)
  1. River class frigate. Became KIRKLAND LAKE.

SAINT JOHN (Geog, for the city in NB)
  1. River class frigate, K456. 13 Dec 1943–27 Nov 1945.

ST JOHN (In honour of Father Jean deBrebeuf, a Jesuit missionary who died at the hands of the Iroquois, 16 Mar 1649) B
  1. CNAV/CFAV, Saint class tug, 532. 23 Nov 1956–circa 1971.

ST. JOHN'S (for the city in NF) B
  1. Halifax class frigate, 340. 18 Jul 1996–SIS

ST JOSEPH (alternative name for St Joseph de Grantham, QC)
  1. Llewellyn class minesweeper, J359. 24 May 1944–8 Nov 1945.

ST JULIEN (after a First World War land battle)
  1. Battle class trawler. 13 Nov 1917–1920.

ST LAMBERT (Geog, for the town in QC)
  1. Revised Flower class corvette, K343. 27 May 1944–20 Jul 1945.

ST LAURENT (1 & 2. Geog, the Fr. name for the St Lawrence River) 2. B
  1. C/River class destroyer, H83. 17 Feb 1937–10 Oct 1945. ex HMS CYGNET.
  2. a. St Laurent class destroyer escort, 205. 29 Oct 1955–26 Oct 1962.
    b. Improved St Laurent class destroyer escort, helicopter carrier, 205. 4 Oct 1963–14 Jun 1974.

ST PIERRE (Geog, for the town in QC)
  1. River class frigate, K680. 22 Aug 1944–22 Nov 1945.

ST ROMAULD (alternative name for Farnham, QC)
  1. River class frigate. Cancelled Dec 1943.

ST STEPHEN (Geog, for the town in NB) B
  1. River class frigate, K454/F454/323. 28 Jul 1944–30 Jan 1946; 27 Sep 1947–31 Aug 1950.

STE THERESE (alternative name for Ste Thérèse-de-Blainville, QC) B
  1. a. River class frigate, K366. 28 May 1944–22 Nov 1945.
     b. Prestonian class frigate, 309. 22 Jan 1955–25 Apr 1958; 24 Jan 1959–30 Jan 1967.

ST THOMAS (1 & 2. Geog, for the town in ON)
  1. Name assigned to Algerine class minesweeper which was renamed and turned over to RN o/c, 1943 as HMS SEABEAR, J333.
  2. Castle class corvette, K488. 4 May 1944–22 Nov 1945. ex HMS SANDGATE CASTLE, K373.

SAKER II (SAKAR II?)
  1. Harbour craft, HC65. 27 Nov 1940–26 Mar 1943. Became HC65. ex M.B. 626? Depot ship for HMS SAKER? Depot ship for RN FAA 12 Feb 1942–26 Mar 1943.

SALABERRY
  1. Name assigned to naval reserve division, Salaberry-de-Valleyfield, Québec, in 1993. Never com'd. Cancelled 1994.

SALTPETRE (N*?)
  1. Harbour craft, P09/Z95/HC95. Circa 1941–15 Jan 1942. Became HC95.

SAMBRO (1 & 2. Geog, for the cape south of Halifax, NS)
  1. Shore establishment, depot ship for destroyers and corvettes, Halifax, NS, 510/25. 28 Jul 1941–1 May 1942.
  2. Depot ship for destroyers and auxiliaries, Halifax, NS. 1 Oct 1941–30 Apr 1942. ex HMS SEABORN, ex *Charles A. Dunning*, ex *Seaborn*. Became VENTURE II, 6 Mar 1942. "Particulars of Canadian War Vessels 1944" lists an HC81 as HMCS SAMBRO, ex *Montour*. See notes under third VENTURE II.

SAMBRO II (I?)
  1. Former name for harbour craft, HC157. 31 Jan 1943–46. ex HC81, ex MONTOUR.

SANDPIPER (bird) B
  1. Name allocated to a Bird class patrol vessel that was cancelled in 1956.

SANDY
  1. Barge, Prince Rupert, BC. ?–28 Jul 1943.

SANKATY (N*)
  1. Minelayer, looplayer and maintenance vessel, Fy 61/Z29/M01. 24 Sep 1940–18 Aug 1945. ex ferry *Sankaty*.

SANS PEUR (N*)
  1. Armed yacht, P02/Z02/Z52/Z53. (3?) 5 May 1940–Jan 1946; 25 Oct 1946–31 Jan 1947. ex yacht *Sans Peur*. On charter from 12 Oct 1939.

SANTA MARIA (N*)
  1. Patrol vessel, Fy 08. 4 Apr 1940–Jul 1944. ex fishing vessel *Santa Maria*, 158915. Chartered.

SAN TOMAS (SAN THOMAS?) (N*)
  1. Patrol vessel, Fy 02. 15 Jan 1940–Apr 1944. ex fishing vessel *San Tomas*, 170951.

SARAVAN
  1. Boom defence tug, HC96. Circa 1941–15 Jan 1942. Became HC96.

SARNIA (Geog, for the town in ON)
1. a. Bangor class minesweeper, J309. 13 Aug 1942–28 Oct 1945.
   In strategic reserve, 1946–1951.
   b. reacquired but not recommissioned, 190. 1951–29 Mar 1958. Transferred to
   Turkish Navy as BUYUKDERE.

SASKATCHEWAN (1 & 2. Geog, for the river in the prairies) 2. B
1. F/River class destroyer, H70. 31 May 1943–28 Jan 1946. ex HMS FORTUNE.
2. Mackenzie class destroyer escort, 262. 16 Feb 1963–28 Mar 1994.

SASKATOON (1 & 2. Geog, for the city in SK) B
1. Flower class corvette, K158. 9 Jun 1941–25 Jun 1945.
2. Kingston class mine warfare vessel, 709. 5 Dec 1998–SIS.

SAULT STE MARIE (Geog, for the city in ON) B
1. a. Algerine class minesweeper, J334/F3. 24 Jun 1943–12 Jun 1946. ex THE SOO.
   b. Reserve training ship, 176. 7 May 1949–10 Jan 1955; 8 Nov 1955–24 Sep 1957;
   1 Apr–1 Oct 1958.

SAXON
1. Auxiliary? Dates, type and source not known, Second World War.

SCATARIE (N*, for the island off the east coast of Cape Breton)
1. Patrol vessel, Z22. 7 Nov 1939–1945. ex RCAF *Scatarie*, 151156; ex civilian craft.

SCATARI (for the island off the east coast of Cape Breton)
1. Stores carrier and general harbour craft, 604/514. Circa 1952–1968. ex RCAF tug *Malahat*.
Note: SCATARI and SCATARIE were named for the same island.

SCOTIAN (source of name unknown) 2. B
1. Commodore Superintendent, Halifax. 1 Jun 1944–28 Feb 1947.
2. Naval reserve division, Halifax, NS. 23 Apr 1947–SIS. see HALIGONIAN. Originally
   located in H Block & Dockyard Gym. Apr 1951 located in Bldg D-14, HMC Dockyard.
   Aug 1951–Aug 1953 in St Mary's College, Windsor St. Moved late 1958 from FOAC Bldg
   to F Block, STADACONA. Early 1961(?)–3 Nov 1961 in G Block. Then located at
   Seaward Defence Base (later Dockyard South Annex and now a container pier). Officially
   moved to ex RCAF Stn Gorsebrook, South St, 17 Sep 1969. Moved to Bldg D-167, HMC
   Dockyard 2 Jan 1985 and officially opened there 16 Mar 1985.

SCOTSMAN (N*)
1. Tug. 7 Aug 1914–mid Jan 1915. ex Halifax Tow Boat Co tug.

SCRETA
1. H/F D/F vessel. Circa 1944.

SEABIRD
1. Despatch boat, HC223. 15 Oct 1943–46. ex motor boat from ST CLAIR.

SEABORN, HMS
1. RN Headquarters ship, Rear Admiral Third Battle Squadron, Halifax, NS. In non com'd
   service 1 Sep 1940–Jan 1940(?). Com'd Jan 1940 (7 Dec 1939?)–30 Sep (1 Oct?) 1941. ex
   VENTURE II (1st). Became SAMBRO.
2. RN Air Station, Eastern Passage, Dartmouth, NS. In non com'd service 14 Sep 1939–Dec
   1943. Com'd Dec 1943–28 Jan 1946.
Note: Co-located with RCAF Station Dartmouth, which was eventually to become SHEAR-
WATER.

SEABORN II, HMS
   1. RN establishment, Halifax, NS. Sep 1940–31 Dec 1940.
   Note: Formed to assist in the take-over of the Town class destroyers from the USN.

SEA CLIFF (1 & 2. alternative name for Leamington, ON)
   1. Flower class corvette. Cancelled Dec 1943. ex GUELPH.
   2. River class frigate, K344. 26 Sep 1944–28 Nov 1945. ex MEGANTIC.

SEA FLASH (N*)
   1. Patrol vessel, Fy 45. 21 May 1942–11 Aug 1944? Became HC339. ex fishing vessel *Sea Flash*.

SEAGULL (1. N/K. 2 for 1.)
   1. Tug, CD 74. 12 Aug 1918–31 Jan 1919. ex LAVIOLETTE.
   2. Patrols depot, 145 Esplanade, Sydney, NS. 1 May 1918–10 Dec 1918. ex STADACONA II.

SEA LARK (N*)
   1. Motor launch. Circa 1919. Sold 1921.

SEAMAN (N*)
   1. RCSC training vessel, Wabamum, AB. 5 Jun 1943–Sep 1945.

SEA PRIDE II (N*)
   1. Patrol vessel, Z126. Mar 1943–Aug 1944. ex fishing vessel *Sea Pride II*, 172296.

SEA RANGER
   1. Auxiliary? Dates, type and source not known, Second World War.

SEA WAVE (alternative name–water related)
   1. Patrol vessel, Fy 47. 13 Jun 1942–1 Oct 1945. Became HC322. ex CHATHAM S, ex fishing vessel *Chatham S*, 138606.

SECHELT (Geog, for the small town in BC)
   1. a. CFAV, S class torpedo recovery vessel, YPT 610. 8 Feb 1991–Oct 1996
      b. CFAV, S class yard diving tender, YDT 610. Feb 1997–SIS.

SEINER (N*)
   1. Patrol vessel, Fy 32. 13 Feb 1942–16 Nov 1944. ex fishing vessel *Seiner*, 152892.

SELKIRK (probably for the town in MB)
   1. Flower class corvette. Circa 1940. Became OAKVILLE.

SERETHA II (N*)
   1. Patrol vessel, Fy 45/Z45. 26 Oct 1943–22 Mar 1945.

SERVICE (from the motto of CHIPPAWA)
   1. Patrol boat, tender to CHIPPAWA, 198. Jul 1978–27 Sep 1995. ex cabin cruiser *Latinozza*?

SHAMROCK (N*)
   1. Motor launch. Circa Jan 1918–Jul 1919.

SHANNON (N*)
   1. Tug. 8 Aug 1914–21 Sep 1914. ex Halifax Dredging Co tug.

SHARK
   1. Motor launch. 7 Sep 1917–c. 1918. ex motor boat *Nereid* (Note: she is not the tug).

SHAWINIGAN (1. alternative name for the town of Shawinigan Falls, QC. 2. Geog. for city in QC) 2. B
   1. Flower class corvette, K136. 19 Sep 1941–24 Nov 1944, torpedoed by U1228 and sank in the Cabot Strait.
   2. Kingston class mine warfare vessel, 704. 14 Jun 1997–SIS.

SHAWVILLE
1. Ville class tug, WPT34. 24 Apr 1944–?; 24 Apr 1945–?

SHEARWATER (1. N*, for the sea bird. 2 for 1.) 2. B
1. Condor class sloop, K02. 8 Sep 1914–13 Jun 1919. ex HMS SHEARWATER. From 8 Sep 1914, stripped of guns and employed as a depot ship and submarine depot ship at Esquimalt and known as SHEARWATER I. Transferred to east coast with CC1 and CC2 on 21 Jun 1917. Re-armed in 1918 for use as a patrol vessel.
Note: Only HMC ship to have a figurehead.
2. Naval air station, Eastern Passage, NS. 1 Dec 1948–1 Apr 1966. Became CFB Shearwater. ex RCAF station *Dartmouth*. see also SEABORN, HMS.

SHEARWATER II
1. Shore establishment, Esquimalt, BC. 5 Aug 1914(?)–circa Sep 1916.

SHEDIAC (Geog, for the town in NB)
1. Flower class corvette, K110. 8 Jul 1941–?; 23 Aug 1944–28 Aug 1945. ex AMHERST.

SHELBURNE (1 & 2. Geog, for the town in NS) 2. B
1. NOIC and naval establishment, Shelburne, NS. 1 May 1942–31 Jan 1946.
Note: NOIC established earlier than May 1942.
2. Joint RCN–USN oceanographic station. 1 Apr 1955–10 Aug 1967. Became CFS Shelburne.

SHERBROOKE (Geog, for the city in QC)
1. Flower class corvette, K152. 5 Jun 1941–28 Jun 1945.

SHIPTON (alternative name for Richmond, QC)
1. River class frigate. Cancelled Dec 1943.

SHIRL (N*)
1. Training vessel, tender to PREVOST. 13 Aug 1943–Jan 1946. ex MV *Shirl*, 153122.

SHIRLEY MAE
1. Harbour craft, HC97. Circa 1941–15 Jan 1942. Became HC97.

SHOVELER
1. CNAV, tug, 591. Circa 1940 ?–1966.

SHULAMITE (N*)
1. Examination vessel, Z39. 7 Aug 1941–3 Aug 1945. ex Newfoundland government customs vessel *Shulamite*, 156692.

SIDNEY (N*)
1. Detachment class patrol boat, 195. 17 Mar 1976–circa 1996. ex RCMP *Sidney*.

SIGNAL (N*)
1. Auxiliary minesweeper, Fy 30. 4 Apr 1940–31 May 1944. ex fishpacker *Signal*, 153310.

SIKANNI (Geog, for the small town in BC)
1. CFAV, S class torpedo recovery vessel, YPT 611. 26 Apr 1991–SIS.

SIMCOE (Geog, for the town in ON)
1. Flower class corvette. Cancelled Dec 1943.

SINMAC (N*)
1. Patrol vessel. Chartered 9 Jul 1915–30 Oct 1915. Tender to MARGARET. ex Sincennes-McNaughton line tug *Sinmac*.

SIOUX (for the prairie First Nations tribe) B
1. V/Algonquin class destroyer, R64/D164/225. 21 Feb 1944–27 Feb 1946; 18 Jan 1950–30 Oct 1963. ex HMS VIXEN.

SIYO II (N*)
1. RCSC training vessel, Gananoque, ON. Sep 1943–Jan 1946.

SKEENA (1 & 2. Geog, for the river in BC) 2. B
1. Acasta/River class destroyer, H03/H43/D59/I59. 10 Jun 1931–25 Oct 1944, wrecked on a rocky islet near Reykjavik, Iceland, after dragging her anchors in a storm. pt. no. changed to I79 after 1940.
2. a. St Laurent class destroyer escort, 207. 30 Mar 1957–26 Jul 1964.
   b. Improved St Laurent class destroyer escort, helicopter carrier, 207.
      14 Aug 1965–1 Nov 1993.

SKIDEGATE (Geog, for the town on Graham Island, BC)
1. Training vessel, Z20. 25 Jul 1938–18 Feb 1942. Ex yacht *Ochecac*, former seiner. Served until 1946 as non com'd vessel.

SKIFF (N*)
1. RCSC fourteen-foot skiff. 1943–1945.

SKIMMER I, II, III, IV & V
1. Harbour craft, HC53, 127, 171, 172, and 173 respectively. Dates and source not known. Second World War. Sixteen-foot stores boats.

SMITHS FALLS (Geog, for the town in ON)
1. Revised Flower class corvette, K345. 28 Nov 1944–8 Jul 1945.

SMITH SOUND (N*)
1. Patrol vessel, Fy 18. 5 Jan 1942–Jun 1945. ex fishing vessel *Smith Sound*. Acquired 15 Dec 1941.

SNOWBERRY (a flower)
1. Flower class corvette, K166. 15 May 1941–8 Jun 1945. In commission as RN vessel from 30 Nov 1940–15 May 1941.

SNOW PRINCE (N*)
1. Fishermen's Reserve vessel, tender to GIVENCHY. 29 Jun 1940–16 Sep 1941, transferred to RCAF. ex Nootka Packing Co vessel. Chartered.

SOMA
1. Harbour craft, HC98. 24 Jun 1941–15 Jan 1942. Became HC98. ex MB.

SOMERS ISLES (Geog, for one of the islands comprising Bermuda)
1. RCN training base, St George's, Bermuda. 1 Aug 1944–16 Oct 1945.
Note: Base was located at the site of an ex army barracks near the water, opposite Five Fathom Hole, near the town of St George's. There had been a RN base of this name but it was amalgamated with HMS MALABAR in May 1943.

SONGHEE (for the First Nations band in BC?)
1. CNAV/CFAV, S class torpedo recovery vessel, YPT 1. 1944–SIS. Acquired 1944 but not named until circa 1960.

SOOKE (Geog, for the small town in BC)
1. a. CFAV, S class torpedo recovery vessel, YPT 612. 21 Jun 1991–Nov 1996.
   b. CFAV, S class yard diving tender, YDT 612. Feb 1997–SIS.

SOREL (Geog, for the city in QC)
1. Flower class corvette, K153. 19 Aug 1941–22 Jun 1945. ex MOOSE JAW.

SPARROW
1. Auxiliary, F17. Dates, type and source not known.

SPARTAN III (SPARTON III?)
1. Harbour craft, P08/Z99/HC99. Circa 1941–15 Jan 1942. Became HC99.

SPEEDY (N*)
1. Examination vessel. 25(?) Nov 1914–?; 1 May–9(?) Dec 1918. ex DPW tug *Speedy* or *Speedy II.*

SPIKENARD (a flower)
1. Flower class corvette, K198. 15 May 1941–10 Feb 1942, torpedoed by U136 and sunk south of Iceland. In commission as RN vessel from 6 Dec 1940–15 May 1941.

SPRAY (1. N/K. 2. alternative name–water related)
1. Motor launch. Circa Jul 1917. Became FOAM.
2. Patrol vessel, Z09(P) (Fy 33?). Circa 7 Apr 1942–16 Nov 1944. ex HATTA VII, 171798.

SPRINGHILL (Geog, for the town in NS)
1. River class frigate, K323. 21 Mar 1944–1 Dec 1945.

SPRINGTIME V (N*)
1. Patrol vessel, Fy 09. 21 Feb 1942–(16 Nov 1944?) Jun 1945. ex fishing vessel *Springtime V.*

SPRUCE LAKE
1. Lake class minesweeper, J494. Completed 19 Mar 1946 but never com'd.

STADACONA (1. Origin of the name of the first vessel is not clear. Apparently named after the First Nations village near the present site of Québec City. 3 & 4 named after 1 & 2) 4. B
1. Patrol vessel. 13 Aug–Dec 1915? Mar 1916–31 Mar 1920. ex American yacht *Columbia* (this vessel was not the former USS WASP).
2. As STADACONA I, Patrols depot, Halifax: consisted of ship in 1. above plus shore establishment. 21 Mar–1 May 1918. Base became GUELPH (1st).
3. Depot ship (motor boat), Halifax, NS, HC131. 1 Jul 1923–Feb 1943. ex GUELPH (3rd), ex CD23.
4. Naval training establishment, Halifax, NS. 1 Jul 1923–1 Apr 1966. Originally located in the Dockyard, moved into Army's Wellington (later Nelson) Barracks alongside Admiralty House early 1941. Became that part of CFB Halifax bounded by Barrington, North, Gottingen and Russell Sts.

STADACONA II
1. Patrol depot, Sydney, NS. 21 Mar–1 May 1918. Became SEAGULL (2nd).
2. Naval Barracks and Signal School, Exhibition Grounds, Halifax, NS. 1 Aug 1940–30 Sep 1941. Moved and became ST HYACINTHE.
3. Training establishment, Halifax, NS. Circa Jan 1944–1 Oct 1944. Became PEREGRINE.

STANDARD COASTER (N*)
1. Auxiliary minesweeper and coil skid towing vessel, Z17/J10. 11 Feb 1942–25 Mar 1946. ex coaster *Standard Coaster*, 151159.

STANDOFF (N*)
1. Detachment class patrol boat, 199. 11 Mar 1980–14 May 1997. ex RCMP *Standoff.*

STANPOINT (N*)
1. Tug, P05/Z05(P). 28 May 1940–Feb 1946. Acquired 17 Oct 1939.

STAR (after one of the ships on Lake Ontario during the War of 1812) B
1. Naval reserve division, Hamilton, ON. First located in ex Dominion Vinegar Works bldg, Stuart and McNab Sts. Moved to Catherine St North into Bldg 2, 18 Oct 1943. On same site, moved into Bldg 1, the former PATRIOT quarters circa 1980. On same site, moved into new Bldg 40, 27 Sep 1997.
    a. 1 Nov 1941–1 Sep 1942. Tender to STADACONA.
    b. 1 Sep 1942–SIS.

STAR XVI (N*)
1. Auxiliary minesweeper, Z16/J00. Aug 1941–31 Aug 1945. ex Norwegian whale catcher *Star XVI*.

STARLING (1. N* 2. N/K)
1. Auxiliary. Jan 1916–23 Jan 1917. ex Lockeport Cold Storage vessel.
2. Patrol vessel, pt. no? Dates, type and source not known, Second World War.

STELLA (N*)
1. Motor launch. Chartered 10 Aug 1918–?

STELLA MARIS (N*)
1. Auxiliary. Chartered Sep 1916–6 Dec 1917, sunk by Halifax explosion. ex Southern Salvage Co vessel *Stella Maris*, ex HMS STARLING.

STELLARTON (Geog, for the town in NS)
1. Revised Flower class corvette, K457. 29 Sep 1944–1 Jul 1945.

STETTLER (Geog, for the town in AB and alternative name for Edmonton) B
1. a. River class frigate, K681. 7 May 1944–(8?) 9 Nov 1945.
    b. Prestonian class frigate, 311. 27 Feb 1954–31 Aug 1966.

STIKINE (Geog, for the small town in BC)
1. CFAV torpedo recovery vessel, YPT 613. 25 Jul 1991–SIS.

STOIC (N*)
1. Tug. Chartered for short period 1944. ex *Stoic*. ex *J.E. McQueen*. See J.E. MCQUEEN

STONECHAT
1. Tanker ? 28 Aug 1944–circa 1945.

STONE FRIGATE (after a dormitory at RMC, originally a stone warehouse built in the early 1800's for the RN)
1. RCNVR Officer's training establishment, Royal Military College, Kingston, ON. 8 Jan–27 Jun 1940.
Note: Bldg 38 in the Esquimalt Dockyard is also known as Stone Frigate but was never com'd. It was used as a barracks for NADEN circa 1922–24 until the latter's buildings were completed.

STONE TOWN (alternative name for St Marys, ON)
1. River class frigate, K531/302. 21 Jul 1944–13 Nov 1945.

STORM KING (N*)
1. Tug. Sep–17 Dec 1918. ex DW tug.

STORMONT (1 & 2. alternative name for Cornwall, ON)
1. River class frigate. Became MATANE.
2. River class frigate, K327. 27 Nov 1943–9 Nov 1945. ex MONTREAL.

STRATFORD (Geog, for the city in ON)
1. Bangor class minesweeper, J310. 29 Aug 1942–4 Jan 1946.

STRATHADAM (alternative name for Newcastle, NB)
1. River class frigate, K682. 29 Sep 1944–7 Nov 1945.

STRATHROY (Geog, for the town in ON)
1. Revised Flower class corvette, K455. 19 Nov 1944–12 Jul 1945.

STREETSVILLE
1. Ville class tug, W55. 10 Mar 1944–Jan 1946.

STUYWUT (Musquem word for "south wind")
1. CFAV, sonabuoy recovery vessel, YAG 680. 22 Jun 1995–SIS.
Note: name received MND approval 16 Aug 1995 but vessel not informed until mid Sep 95.

SUDBURY (Geog, for the town in Northern Ontario)
1. Flower class corvette, K162. 15 Oct 1941–28 Aug 1945.

SUDEROY I (N*)
1. Auxiliary minesweeper, Z01/J01. 17 Oct 1940–10 Jan 1941? ex Norwegian whale catcher *Suderoy I.*

SUDEROY II (N*)
1. Auxiliary minesweeper, Z02/J02. 17 Oct 1940–10 Jan 1941? ex Norwegian whale catcher *Suderoy II.*

SUDEROY IV (N*)
1. Auxiliary minesweeper, Z04/J03. Jun 1941–31 Aug 1945. ex Norwegian whale catcher *Suderoy IV.*

SUDEROY V (N*)
1. Auxiliary minesweeper, Z05/J05. 2 Jun 1941–7 Aug 1945. ex Norwegian whale catcher *Suderoy V.*

SUDEROY VI (N*)
1. Auxiliary minesweeper, Z06/J06. 19 Mar 1941–31 Aug 1945. ex Norwegian whale catcher *Suderoy VI*, ex British *Southern Gem.*

SUMAS (Geog, for the town in BC)
1. Transmitter station, Sumas, BC. Dec 1942–circa 1959? Became MATSQUI.

SUMMERSIDE (1 & 2. Geog, for the town in PE) 2. B
1. Flower class corvette, K141. 11 Sep 1941–6 Jul 1945.
2. Kingston class mine warfare vessel, 711. 18 Jul 1999–SIS

SUNBEAM
1. Fuel oil carrier, Z42. 11 Nov 1940 (8 May 1941?)–13 Dec 1945. ex Dept of Transport "Hopper Barge No. 4," 132590.

SURF (alternative name–water related)
1. Patrol vessel, Fy 24. 4 Feb 1942–10 Jan 1943, when she went aground on west coast of Vancouver Island. She was freed but hull had to be scrapped. ex ARAISHO; ex fishpacker *Araisho*, 171791.

SUSAN S
1. Former name for harbour craft, HC219. 16 Oct 1943–SIS 1 Apr 1945.

SUSSEXVALE (1 & 2. alternative name for Sussex, NB) 2. B
1. River class frigate. Cancelled Dec 1943.
2. a. River class frigate, K683. 29 Nov 1944–16 Nov 1945. ex VALDORIAN.
   b. Prestonian class frigate, 313. 18 Mar 1955–23 Jun 1958; 28 Nov 1958–6 Dec 1966.

SWAN (N*)
1. Motor launch. Chartered 1 Jun–Nov? 1917.

SWANSEA (Geog, for the village in ON, now part of Toronto) B
1. a. River class frigate, K328/F328. 4 Oct 1943–2 Nov 1945; 12 Apr 1948–15 Aug 1952; 14 Apr–10 Nov 1953.
   b. Prestonian class frigate, 306. 14 Nov 1957–14 Oct 1966.

SWIFT CURRENT (Geog, for the city in SK)
1. a. Bangor class minesweeper, J254. 11 Nov 1941–31 Oct 1945. In reserve until 29 Mar 1958 when transferred to the Turkish Navy as BOZCAADA.

SYDNEY RIVER
1. Harbour craft, HC100. 4 Nov 1941–15 Jan 1942. Became HC100. ex MB.

T

TAKLA (N*)
1. Auxiliary minesweeper, Fy 27. 13 Sep 1939?–May 1944? ex fish packer *Takla*.

TALAPUS (Chinook word for coyote)
1. "Nenamook" class patrol vessel, Fy 11. 15 Nov 1941–1946. From 1946–1969 on loan to Dept of Mines and Technical Surveys as *Parry*(?). Spelt TELAPUS in *Naval Service of Canada*.

TAUTOG
1. Auxiliary, circa 1942 at Vancouver. Type & size not known.

TANNIS (N*)
1. Auxiliary. Aug 1914–circa Apr 1915. Loaned. Motor boat?

TANTRAMAR
1. Harbour craft, HC101. 5 Aug 1941–15 Jan 1942. Became HC101.

TASEKO (N*)
1. Motor launch. Chartered 26 Aug 1940–30 Nov 1941.

TAYUT
1. Tender to Royal Roads, YAG 1. Feb 1978–SIS. Purchased without authority Dec 1976. Officially acquired Feb 1978.

TECO III (N*)
1. Motor launch. Sep–24 Nov 1939. ex MV *Teco III*.

TECUMSEH (after a vessel built on the Niagara River, 1814–15) B
1. Naval reserve division, Calgary, AB. 1 Nov 1941–SIS. Located at 337 7th Ave W. Moved to 1820 24th St SW late 1947.

TEME (N*, for a river in South Wales and Worcestershire, Eng.)
1. River class frigate, K458. 28 Feb 1944–4 May 1945. Rammed by escort carrier HMS TRACKER, 10 Jun 1944; torpedoed by U246 but not sunk, 29 Mar 1945. ex HMS TEME.

TERRA NOVA (Geog, for the river in NF) B
1. a. Restigouche class destroyer escort, 259. 6 Jun 1959–circa Aug 1967.
    b. Improved Restigouche class destroyer escort, 259. Circa Aug 1967–1 Jul 1998.
    From 11 Jul 1997 placed in "extended readiness" with no crew, fuel, or ammunition.
    Note: Since she did not pay off for the conversion, there is no exact date for her change of
    class. Aug 1967 is the month her class changed in the ship's log.

THE PAS (Geog, for the town in MB)
1. Flower class corvette, K168. 21 Oct 1941–24 Jul 1945.

THE SOO (alternative name for Sault Ste Marie, ON)
1. Algerine class minesweeper. Circa 1943. Became SAULT STE MARIE before being com'd.

THETFORD MINES (Geog, for the town in QC)
1. River class frigate, K459. 24 May 1944–18 Nov 1945.

THIEPVAL (after a First World War land battle)
1. Battle class trawler. 24 Jul 1918–19 Mar 1920; 1 Apr 1923–27 Feb 1930, wrecked on an
    uncharted rock in Barkley Sound, BC.

THISTLE (N*)
1. Motor launch. Circa Jan 1918–Jul 1919.

THORLOCK (alternative name for Thorold, ON)
1. Revised Flower class corvette, K394. 13 Nov 1944–15 Jul 1945.

THREE COUSINS (N*)
1. Auxiliary. Chartered 1 Jun–Nov? 1916.

THREE RIVERS (1 & 2. English name for Trois-Riviéres, QC)
1. Bangor class minesweeper. Became TROIS RIVIERES 17 Oct 1941.
2. Tender to HOCHELAGA II? Second World War.

HMCS TALAPUS, a Nenamook class patrol vessel, 20 Nov 1944. (RCN E-1570. KM Coll.)

THUNDER (1, 2 & 3. Geog, for the bay on Lake Superior) 3. B
1. Bangor class minesweeper, J156. 14 Oct 1941–4 Oct 1945.
2. Bay class minesweeper, 153. 15 Dec 1953–31 Mar 1954, transferred to French Navy as LA PAIMPOLAISE.
3. Bay class minesweeper, 161. 3 Oct 1957–6 Mar 1964; 31 Mar 1969–22 Aug 1997.

TILLICUM
1. RCSC training centre, North Bay, ON, c. 1980. Commissioned each summer.
2. Tug, 555. 19 Mar 1997–SIS. Former *Island Defender*.

TILLSONBURG (1 & 2. Geog, for the town in ON)
1. Name assigned to an Algerine class minesweeper but never promulgated. Ship turned over to RN o/c as HMS FLYING FISH, J370.
2. Castle class corvette, K496. 29 Jun 1944–15 Feb 1946. ex HMS PEMBROKE CASTLE, K450.

TIMMINS (Geog, for the town in ON)
1. Flower class corvette, K223. 10 Feb 1942–15 Jul 1945.

TISDALE (alternative name for South Porcupine, ON)
1. River class frigate. Cancelled Dec 1943.

TOPSY (N*)
1. RCSC training vessel, Minnicog, ON. 1943–1945.

TORDO (N*)
1. Patrol vessel, Fy 20. 1939? (Dec 1941?)–16 Nov 1944. ex fishing vessel *Tordo*, 172556.

TORONTO (1, 2 & 3. Geog, for the city in ON) 2. B
1. Name assigned to an Algerine class minesweeper but never promulgated. Ship was turned over to the RN o/c as HMS MARY ROSE, J360.
2. a. River class frigate, K538. 6 May 1944–27 Nov 1945. ex GIFFARD.
   b. Prestonian class frigate, 319. 25 Nov 1953–14 Apr 1956. Loaned to Norwegian Navy as GARM.
3. Halifax class frigate, 333. 29 Jul 1993–SIS.

TRAIL (Geog, for the city in BC)
1. Flower class corvette, K174. 30 Apr 1941–17 Jul 1945.

The former torpedo boat TUNA just prior to being sold, circa June 1918. (RCN O-10330. KM Coll.)

TRANSCONA (Geog, for the town in MB)

1. Bangor class minesweeper, J271. 25 Nov 1942–31 Jul 1945. ex MORDEN.

TRANSRIVER (N*)

1. Tanker. 5 Dec (5 Jan?) 1942–22 May 1943. ex Transit Tankers & Terminals vessel.

TRENTONIAN (alternative name for the town of Trenton, ON)

1. Revised Flower class corvette, K368. 1 Dec 1943–22 Feb 1945, torpedoed by U1004 and sunk off Falmouth, England.

TRILLIUM (a flower)

1. Flower class corvette, K172. 15 May 1941–27 Jun 1945. In commission as RN vessel from 22 (31?) Oct 1940–15 May 1941.

TRINITY (Geog, for the bay on the Avalon Peninsula of NF) B

1. Bay class minesweeper, 157. 16 Jun 1954–21 Aug 1957. Transferred to Turkish Navy 31 Mar 1958 as TERME.

TROIS RIVIERES (Geog, for the city in QC)

1. Bangor class minesweeper, J269. 12 Aug 1942–31 Jul 1945. ex THREE RIVERS.

TROUT (N*)

1. Motor launch. Circa Jul 1919.

TRURO (Geog, for the town in NS)

1. Bangor class minesweeper, J268. 27 Aug 1942–31 Jul 1945.

TRUSTY (N*)

1. Tug. 16 May 1917–Oct? 1918. ex Hendry Ltd. tug.

TUNA

1. Torpedo boat, tender to DIANA, QW2. 5 Dec 1914–10 May 1917. ex yacht *Tarantula*. Name changed to TUNA on 25 Sep 1914 but vessel was not officially purchased until 1 Oct 1914.
2. Harbour craft, HC102. 9 Dec 1940–15 Jan 1942. Became HC102. ex MB.
3. Yacht. Circa 1945–circa 1977. ex *Seerauber*.

TWO BROTHERS

1. Motor launch. Dates, type and source not known, Second World War.

U

U190 (N*)

1. Type IXC/40 submarine, 19 May 1945–24 Jul 1947. ex German U190.

Note: Surrendered to VICTORIAVILLE and THORLOCK, 12 May 1945. Com'd in June but date made retroactive to 19 May so mixed RN/RCN crew could receive submarine & hard lying pay from date they commenced their duties. Sunk by RCN ships and aircraft 21 Oct 1947 near the site where she sank ESQUIMALT in April 1945.

U889 (N*)

1. Type IXC/40 submarine. 14 May 1945–12 Jan 1946? ex German U889.

Note: Surrendered to RCAF Liberator at sea. Escorted into Shelburne by DUNVEGAN and ROCKCLIFFE. Com'd in June but date made retroactive to 19 May so mixed RN/RCN crew could receive submarine and hard lying pay from date they commenced their duties. Turned over to USN 12 Jan 1946.

UGANDA (N*, for the country in Africa) (B*)
1. Uganda class cruiser, 66/53. 21 Oct 1944–1 Aug 1947. Became QUEBEC. ex HMS UGANDA. Note: RN class name changed to Ceylon after UGANDA was transferred.

ULALLA (ULULA?) (N*)
1. Motor launch. 7 Jun 1917–Oct? 1918. Sold Apr 1919.

ULNA (1. N*. 2. N*)
1. Auxiliary vessel? circa 1918. ex schooner?
Note: Only reference is Tucker, 124518. Sometimes listed incorrectly as UNA.
2. Examination vessel, Halifax. (11?) 25 Sep 1939–25 May 1940. ex Canso Steamship Co vessel, ex RCMP vessel, 124518.

UNA (N*)
1. Gate vessel. Circa Jul 1917–1918. ex schooner. Purchased.

UNGAVA (1 & 2. Geog, for the bay on the NE coast of QC) 2.B
1. Bay class minesweeper, J149. 5 Sep 1941–3 Apr 1946.
2. Bay class minesweeper, 148. 4 Jun 1954–23 Aug 1957. Transferred to Turkish Navy 31 Mar 1958 as TEKIRDAG.

UNICORN (after a ship of Jens Munck, Danish Navy, one of the earliest explorers in Hudson Bay, who visited the site of Ft. Churchill in the *Unicorn*, 1619.) B
1. Naval reserve division, Saskatoon, SK. Originally located in an ex automobile showroom at 1st Ave & 25th St. Moved to 405 24th St East 4-6 Mar 1944 and officially opened 25 May 1944.
   a. 1 Nov 1941–1 Sep 1942. Tender to NADEN.
   b. 1 Sep 1942–SIS.

UNIVERSE
1. a. Harbour craft, Z125/HC125, Esquimalt, BC. Circa May 1943–19 Mar 1946.
   b. CNAV. 19 May 1946–?

UNO
1. Harbour craft, HC145. Circa late 1942. Type and source not known.

The second UNGAVA circa 1955 on the east coast. Her funnel marking denotes her as a member of the 1st Minesweeping Squadron. (RCN H-535849. KM Coll.)

HMCS U889 at sea about 1946. (RCN CN-6292. KM Coll.)

V

VALDES
1. Patrol vessel, Fy 21. 17 Jan 1942–Sep 1944? ex *Departure Bay II*.

VALDORIAN (alternative name for Val d'Or, QC)
1. River class frigate. Became SUSSEXVALE.

VALIANT
1. Motor launch, 375. Circa Nov 1914–Jul 1919. One time tender to SHEARWATER II.
2. a. Tug, Esquimalt, BC. HC109. Second World War.
   b. CNAV, tug, 575. Circa 1946–1966.

VALINDA (VELINDA?)
1. Harbour craft, HC103. 29 Aug 1941–15 Jan 1942. Became HC103 but still listed by name as late as *Navy List* for Jul 1945.

VALLEYFIELD (alternative name for city of Salaberry-de-Valleyfield, QC)
1. River class frigate, K329. 7 Dec 1943–7 May 1944, torpedoed by U548 and sunk 50 miles SE of Cape Race. ex OUTREMONT.

VANCOUVER (1. for the explorer Capt George Vancouver, RN. 2 & 3. Geog, for the city in BC) 3. B
1. S class destroyer, D05/F6A/H55. 1 Mar 1928–25 Nov 1936. ex HMS TOREADOR.
2. Flower class corvette, K240. 20 Mar 1942–26 Jun 1945. ex KITCHENER.
3. Halifax class frigate, 331. 23 Aug 1993–SIS.

VANISLE (N*)
1. Patrol vessel, Fy 01. 4 Apr 1940–29 Jul 1944. ex fishing vessel *Vanisle*. Note: Some authorities list this name as VAN ISLE, others as VAN ISLES.

VEGREVILLE (Geog, for the town in AB)
1. Bangor class minesweeper, J257. 10 Dec 1941–6 Jun 1945.

VENCEDOR (N*)
1. Auxiliary vessel, Z21 (P). 18(?) Aug 1941–Aug 1945. ex yacht *Vencedor*, ex three-masted topsail schooner *Exmouth II*, 135254.

VENETIA (N*)
1. Tender to YORK. (3?) 25 Nov 1941–8 Sep 1945. ex steam yacht *Venetia*, 115669; ex USS VENETIA. This vessel was not HMS VENETIA of the First World War.

VENNING
1. Harbour craft, HC137. 27 Jul 1941–?. ex Dept of Fisheries vessel *Venning*? Became HC137 circa 1943. SIS 1 Apr 1945.

VENOSTA (N*)
1. Gate vessel & auxiliary schooner, Cy 509/J11. 17 Nov 1939–22 Jan (23 May?) 1942. ex Venosta Ltd trawler *Venosta*, 139959; ex RN m/s of First World War.

VENTURE (1. N* 2. for 1. 3. from 2. 4. N/K. 5. for 1 & 2?) 5. B

1. Training sloop (sail), tender to RN College of Canada. 26 May 1911–circa Sep 1920. ex sloop *Venture*, built 1908/9.

2. a. Training schooner (sail), D16/I16. 25 Oct 1937–1 Sep 1939. Became a non-com'd RN accommodation vessel at Halifax and sometime flagship for the RN until about Sep 1941. Name suggested by Commodore Nelles, CNS, in memory of first vessel.

Note: Some sources state she became HMS SEABORN II but in a report dated 20 May 1940, the RN refer to her as HMCS VENTURE.

   b. Tender to STADACONA and guard ship, HC190. 1 Nov 1941–5 Mar 1943. Became HC190 (and as such, SIS 1 Apr 1945) to avoid confusion with establishment at 3 below.

Note: Some sources state 13 May vice 5 Mar 1943 as the renaming date.

3. Shore establishment, Halifax, NS. 1 Feb 1940–30 Apr 1942. Employed as a depot ship for auxiliary vessels and an accounting base for destroyers. Duties taken over by STADACONA.

Note: Before the end of 1940, this establishment was split into two accounting sections, VENTURE and VENTURE II. One source also states that the name was temporarily used for the Signal School but research indicates this to refer only to classes in signalling and not a formal school.

4. a. Depot ship for Fairmile motor launches, Halifax, NS. 6 May 1943–30 Jun 1945. ex GANNET, ex VENTURE II, ex SAMBRO, ex HMS SEABORN, ex VENTURE II (?), ex *Charles A Dunning*, ex *Seaborn*. see GANNET.

Note: Actually com'd 6 May 1943 as GANNET but name changed 12 May and made retroactive to 6 May. Often referred to as VENTURE II but she was the only ship of this name then in service and she com'd as VENTURE.

   b. Tender to SCOTIAN, Halifax. 1 Jul 1945–14 Jan 1946.

5. Junior officer training establishment, Esquimalt, BC. 11 Aug 1954–1 Sep 1966.

Note: Although pd off in 1966, this establishment continued to train junior officers for both the RCN and the RCAF and later, the Army. The name Venture was still used up to sometime in 1968 when the CF officer training establishment was formed. This unit became CF Officer Candidate School (CFOCS) for a short time, eventually moving to CFB Chilliwack to merge with the other half of CFOCS in 1970. The "Venture" buildings then became the CF Warrant Officers' School, which later changed its name to the CF Leadership Academy before moving to CFB Borden in 1976. In Sep 1976, the Officer Training Division, Fleet School Esquimalt, was formed. This unit moved to the former VENTURE complex in 1977 and changed its name to the Naval Officers' Training Centre (NOTC). From 1984, referred to as NOTC Venture. This unit moved to Work Point Barracks in the fall of 1994. See also the second GIVENCHY.

VENTURE II

1. The Northumberland Ferries Ltd vessel *Charles A. Dunning* was taken over early in Sep 1939. Apparently named VENTURE II, she was almost immediately given to the RN and renamed SEABORN. ex *Charles A. Dunning*, 158808; ex US steam yacht *Seaborn*.

2. Accounting base, Halifax, NS. Late 1940–31 Jul 1941. Duties taken over by SAMBRO. See note to third VENTURE above.

3. Depot ship for Fairmile motor launches, Halifax, NS. 6 Mar 1942–April 1942. ex SAMBRO, ex HMS SEABORN, ex VENTURE II (1st).

Note: Apparently pd off at end of Apr 1942 but continued to serve as non com'd vessel VENTURE II until 12 May 1943 when she re com'd as VENTURE (4th).

Note: Still listed as depot ship VENTURE II in *Navy List* of Jul 1945; on a list of auxiliary vessels dated 1 Apr 1945.

The second HMS SAMBRO, circa late 1940 at Halifax, soon to become the third HMCS VENTURE. The bow of the second VENTURE can be seen behind HMS SAMBRO. (KM Coll.)

VERAINE

1. Admiral's barge, Halifax, 101. Circa 1952–1957? ex HC135? Became QMB101 circa 1957.

VERAINE I

1. Former name for despatch boat, HC135. 12 Aug 1942–1945. Became VERAINE?

VERCHERES (N*)

1. Auxiliary minesweeper, no? 1939–May 1943, lost? ex CGS(?) *Vercheres*.

VICTORIA (for the city in BC) B

1. Victoria class submarine, 876. To commission mid 2000. ex HMS UNSEEN.

VICTORIAVILLE (Geog. for the town in Québec) B

1. a. River class frigate, K684. 11 Nov 1944–17 Nov 1945.
   b. Prestonian class frigate, 320. 25 Sep 1959–16 Dec 1966. Became GRANBY
      21 Dec 1966.

VIERNOE (N*)

1. Boom defence vessel, J12. 11 (31?) Oct 1939–22 Jan (18 May?) 1942. ex trawler *Viernoe*,
   137002.

VIGIL II (N*)

1. Harbour craft, HC104. 3 Sep 1939–15 Jan 1942. ex RCMP *Vigil II*, 158836. Became
   HC104. SIS 1 Apr 1945.

VIGILANT (N*)

1. Patrol vessel. 1910(?)–Dec 1919. ex Dept of Marine & Fisheries vessel *Vigilant*.

VIKING (N*)

1. Motor launch. Chartered 9 Sep 1914–Dec 1919. One-time tender to SHEARWATER II. ex
   Dept of Marine & Fisheries vessel *Viking*.
2. Harbour craft, HC138. 21 May 1943–46. ex MB. SIS as HC138, 1 Apr 1945.

VILLE DE QUEBEC (1. alternative name for Québec City. 2 for 1.) 2. B
1. Revised Flower class corvette, K242. 24 May 1942–6 Jul 1945. ex QUEBEC.
2. Halifax class frigate, 332.14 Jul 1994–SIS.

VIMY (after a First World War land battle)
1. Battle class trawler, 13 Nov 1917–30 Nov 1918.

VINER (N*)
1. Auxiliary. 27 Oct 1914–1915.

VIRGINIA (N*)
1. Motor launch. Circa Oct 1918–Mar 1919.

VISON (animal–Fr. for mink)
1. Armed yacht, S11/Z30. 5 Oct 1940–4 Aug 1945. ex *Avalon*.

W

WALKERVILLE
1. Ville class tug, W36. Second World War.

WALLACEBURG (Geog, for the town in ON) B
1. a. Algerine class minesweeper, J336. 18 Nov 1943–7 Oct 1946.
   b. Cadet training vessel, 172. 1 Nov 1950–25 Nov 1954; 14 Apr 1955–24 Sep 1957.
      Transferred to Belgian Navy as GEORGES LECOINTE, 1 Aug 1959.

WANDERER
1. Auxiliary? Dates, type and source not known, Second World War.

WARRIOR (N*, a fighting man) B
1. Improved Colossus class light fleet aircraft carrier, 31. 24 Jan 1946–23 May 1948. ex HMS WARRIOR.

WASAGA (for the beach on Nottawasaga Bay, ON)
1. Bangor class minesweeper, J162. 1 Jul 1941–6 Oct 1945.
Note: Name came to be associated with the community of Wasaga Beach, ON.

WASKESIU (alternative name for Prince Albert, SK)
1. River class frigate, K330. 16 Jun 1943–29 Jan 1946.

CNAV WHITETHROAT. (RCN E 71548. KM Coll.)

WATAMBA (N*)
1. Motor launch. 6 Jul? 1916–? Given to RCN by Col T. Cantley. Collided with PV IV, 1 Aug 1917 and broken up Oct 1917.

WAUSAU II (N*)
1. RCSC vessel, Kingston, ON. 28 Jun 1944–Jan 1946. Chartered.

WAWBEC IV (N*)
1. RCSC vessel, Minnicog, ON. 5 Jul 1943–Nov 1945. Chartered.

WEATHERSPOON see M. W. WEATHERSPOON

WEETIEBUD
1. Former name of harbour craft at Cornwallis, HC298. 24 May 1944–SIS 1 Apr 1945.

WENTWORTH (alternative name for Dartmouth, NS)
1. River class frigate, K331. 7 Dec 1943–10 Oct 1945.
Note: A letter dated 12 Jan 1961 from EC Russell the naval historian, to Adm Pullen, explained that WENTWORTH was named after Sir John Wentworth, a Lt Gov of NS, and was to honour Dartmouth, NS. Some authorities have stated incorrectly that this name is to honour the city of Hamilton, located in Wentworth County, ON.

WESTBURY (alternative name for East Angus, QC)
1. River class frigate. Cancelled Dec 1943.

WEST COAST (N*)
1. Patrol vessel, Fy 04. 4 Apr 1940–3 May 1944. ex fishing vessel *West Coast,* 156591.

WESTERN CHIEF
1. Auxiliary? Dates, type and source not known, Second World War.

WESTERN MAID (N*)
1. Patrol vessel, Fy 36. 11 Mar 1942–16 Mar 1944. ex fishing vessel *Western Maid,* 158916.

WESTMOUNT (Geog, for the city in QC)
1. Bangor class minesweeper, J318. 15 Sep 1945–13 Oct 1945. Placed in strategic reserve 1946. Reacquired but never recommissioned, 187. 1951–29 Mar 1958, when transferred to Turkish Navy as BORNOVA.

WESTORE
1. Name allocated to a small supply ship (a sister to EASTORE and LAYMORE), Z58. Never acquired. Name also spelt WESTMORE.

WESTVILLE (Geog, for the town in NS)
1. River class frigate. Cancelled 1944.

WEST YORK (alternative name for Weston, ON)
1. Revised Flower class corvette, K369. 6 Oct 1944–9 Jul 1945.

WETASKIWIN (Geog, for the town in AB)
1. Flower class corvette, K175. 17 Dec 1940–19 Jun 1945. ex BANFF.

WEYBURN (Geog, for the town in SK)
1. Flower class corvette, K173. 26 Nov 1941–22 Feb 1943, mined and sunk off Gibraltar.

W.H. LEA (W.H. LEE?) (N*)
1. Tug. 1915–7 Sep 1915. Became G.V. No 3. ex derrick tug.

WHISPER (N*)
1. RCSC motor launch, Hamilton, ON. Jul 1944–Aug 1945. ex *Whisper,* ex *Nancy,* 156438.

WHITBY (Geog, for the town in ON)
1. Revised Flower class corvette, K346. 6 Jun 1944–16 Jul 1945.

WHITETHROAT (a bird. Named to correspond with the Bird class minelayers in the RN) B
1. a. Minelayer, M03/M53. 7 Dec 1944–6 May 1946. ex Isles class trawler.
   b. CNAV, 113. 6 May 1946–17 Apr 1951.
   c. Loop layer, 113. 17 Apr 1951–30 Sep 1954.
   d. CNAV, oceanographic vessel, 113. 30 Sep 1954–Nov 1967.

WHITEHORSE (Geog, for the city in the Yukon) B
1. Kingston class mine warfare vessel, 705. 17 Apr 1998–SIS.

WILD DUCK
1. Harbour craft, HC69 (ML5). 22 Jun 1940–15 Apr 1942? Became HC69. ex MB.
2. Harbour craft, HC105. Circa 1941–15 Apr 1942. Became HC105. ex yacht.

WILDWOOD
1. a. Wood class tug, Z65. 22 May 1944–?
   b. CNAV/CFAV, Wood class tug, 553/YMR2. Circa 1946–circa 1991.

WILFRED C (N*)
1. Tug. Jul 1917–c. 1918? Name changed to WILFRED 15 Aug 1917. Sold Nov 1919. ex Shepody Navigation tug. Purchased.

WILLEENA F.
1. Auxiliary? Dates, type and source not known, Second World War.

WILLIAM B. MURRAY (N*)
1. Auxiliary. Purchased 1917 and became PV I.

WILLIAM J. STEWART
1. Auxiliary? Dates, type and source not known, Second World War.

WILLOW LAKE
1. Lake class minesweeper, J495. Completed 11 Mar 1946 but never commissioned.

WINCHESTER see A.B. WINCHESTER

WINDFLOWER (a flower)
1. Flower class corvette, K155. 15 May 1941–7 Dec 1941, when rammed and sunk in dense fog on Grand Banks of Newfoundland by Dutch freighter *Zypenberg*, while escorting convoy SC58. In commission as RN vessel from 26 Oct 1940–15 May 1941.

WINDSOR (for the city in ON) B
1. Victoria class submarine, 877. To commission late in 2000. Ex HMS UNICORN.

WINGS
1. Harbour craft, HC106. 19 Jul 1940–15 Jan 1942. Became HC106.

WINNIPEG (1 & 2. Geog, for the city in MB) 1. B
1. Algerine class minesweeper, J337. 29 Jul 1943–11 Jan 1946. In reserve fleet, 177. 12 Jan 1946–7 Aug 1959 when transferred to Belgian Navy as A.F. DUFOUR.
2. Halifax class frigate, 338. 23 Jun 1995–SIS.

W. M. WEATHERSPOON see M.W. WEATHERSPOON

WOLF (1 & 2. an animal) 2. B
1. Armed yacht, P16/Z16. 2 Oct 1940–16 May 1945. ex *Blue Water*.
2. Fairmile B Type, 762. May 1954–? 17 May–Oct 1955; 8 May–Oct 1956. ex PTC762, ex ML762, ex ML062.

WOODCOCK (N*)

1. Crash boat, 809. 1 Apr 1965–circa 1982. ex RCAF *Woodcock*.

WOODSTOCK (Geog, for the city in ON)

1. Revised Flower class corvette, K238. 1 May 1942–27 Jan 1945; 17 May 1945–18 Mar 1946.

WORKBOY

1. Harbour craft, W00/HC107. Circa 1941–15 Jan 1942. Became HC107 and as such SIS 1 Apr 1945.

WREN (N*)

1. Patrol vessel. Chartered 22 Apr–22 May 1915. ex Atlantic Fish and Transportation Co steam trawler *Wren*.

WULASTOCK (alternative name for Woodstock, NB)

1. River class frigate. Cancelled Dec 1943.

WYE

1. Unknown vessel. Circa Jul 1944.

Y

YELLOWKNIFE (Geog, for the city in NWT) B

1. Kingston class mine warfare vessel, 706. 18 Apr 1998–SIS.

YENDYS (YENLYS?)

1. Former name for harbour craft, HC201. 28 Jul 1943–1945.

HMCS YELLOWKNIFE in 1998. (CF ETC98-0226-1. NPA)

YORK (after the name of the first commercial craft on Lake Ontario, a 66-ton schooner) B
1. Naval reserve division, Toronto, ON. Originally located at 165 Lakeshore Blvd. Moved
    to the Automotive Bldg, Exhibition Park circa 1941 returning to 57 Lakeshore Blvd circa
    Jul 1946. Moved to 659 Lakeshore Blvd circa late 1959.
    a. 1 Nov 1941–1 Sep 1942. Tender to STADACONA.
    b. 1 Sep 1942–SIS.

YORKHOLM
1. Auxiliary, circa 1942 at Esquimalt. Type & size not known.

YOUVILLE
1. a. Ville class tug, W? 14 Dec 1944–Mar 1946.
    b. CNAV/CFAV, Ville class tug, 558. Circa 1946–circa 1991.

YPRES (after a First World War land battle)
1. a. Battle class trawler. 13 Nov 1917–1920.
    b. Training ship, N70/J70. 1 May 1923–Nov 1932. In reserve 1932–1938. Became Gate
        Vessel 1, 1938–12 May 1940, when she sank after being run down by the battleship
        HMS REVENGE in Halifax harbour.

YUKON (Geog, for the river in the Yukon Territory) B
1. Mackenzie class destroyer escort, 263. 25 May 1963–(3 Dec 1993?) 1 Jan 1994. Became a
    non-commissioned harbour training ship in Esquimalt.

Z

ZIG ZAG
1. Auxiliary vessel, Second World War. Became HMS AVALON III circa Jan 1941.

ZOARCES (N*)
1. Examination vessel at Saint John, Fy 62/Z36. 27 Jun 1940–14 Aug 1945. ex Dept of
    Fisheries vessel *Zoarces*.

The auxiliary ZOARCES during the Second World War. (KM Coll.)

Appendices

APPENDIX A

Alternative Names for HMC Ships

During the Second World War, the names of cities and towns with a population over 2,800 were used to name most frigates, corvettes and minesweepers. This list contains those cities and towns whose name in its original form could not be used and for which an alternative had to be devised.

The "Reason" for that alternative name is taken from NSHQ lists and was often simple: another Allied ship with the same or similar name. Such reasons, however, were often incorrectly stated and where known, accurate reasons are listed. "Alternatives" are names generally suggested by someone in the community. "Objections", if any, are NSHQ beliefs as to why an alternative suggestion should not be used. "Notes" are listed following the table.

ALGONQUIN, PROTECTEUR and WINNIPEG conducting a replenishment at sea c. 1996.

Alternative names listed by city

City/Town(name chosen)	Reason	Alternatives	Objections	Notes
Algoma Mills, ON (ALGOMA)	too long?			
Aylmer, ON	USS AYLWIN			
Aylmer, QC	USS AYLWIN	Aylmer East		25
Amherstburg, NS (MALDEN)	AMHERST			
Aurora, ON	HMS/USS AURORA			3
Baie-St Paul, QC	USS BAYSPRING			3
Bagotville, QC	HMS BAGSHOT	Ha Ha Baie Rivière á Mars Anse á Philippe Cape Eternity Cap Trinité Darling's Creek (Anse á Benjamin)		
Banff, AB	HMS BANFF			
Bathurst, NB (BUCTOUCHE)	HMAS BATHURST			21
Beauport, QC	HMS BEAUFORT			3
Bridgebury, ON	HMS BRIDGEWATER			12
Bridgewater, NS (LA HAVE)	HMS BRIDGEWATER	La Have	Fr vessel LA HAVRAISE	
Brampton, ON	BRANDON			
Brownsburg, ON	USS BROWNSON			6
Campbellford, ON (RANNEY FALLS)	HM Ships CAMPBELL & CAMPBELTOWN	Ranney Falls Crow Bay Alert Seymour		1
Campbellton, NB (ATHOLL)	as above	Sugar Loaf Atholl		
Carleton Place, ON (CARLPLACE)	CARLETON	Carlplace Carlbeck Carace		
Chatham, NB (NORTHUMBERLAND)	CHATHAM	Northumberland Escuminac Beaver Brook	HMS NORTHLAND BEAVER	1
Chatham, ON (CHATKENADA)	CHATHAM	Maple City William Pitt Tecumseh Baldwin William Iredell Chatamaple Chatkenada Chatapitt Chathamont	man's name TECUMSEH man's name man's name	22, 25

City/Town(name chosen)	Reason	Alternatives	Objections	Notes
Cochrane, ON (ABITIBI)	HMS COCHRANE			25
Cornwall, ON (STORMONT)	HMS CORNWALL	Peel		14
Cowansville, QC	COWICHAN			3
Dalhousie, NB (INCH ARRAN)	HMIS DALHOUSIE	Bon Ami Inch Arran Allain Colborne	HMS ALLAN PORT COLBORNE	
Dartmouth, NS (WENTWORTH)	HMS DARTMOUTH	Wentworth		
D'Iberville, QC	Fr vessel			
Dominion, NS (LINGANBAR)	DOMINION	Old Bridgeport Lingan Bar	USS BRIDGEPORT	1 6
Donnacona, QC	DONNACONA			
Dunnville, ON (LIVE OAK)	DUNVEGAN			25
East Angus, QC (WESTBURY)		Linda St Francis Westbury	HMS LINDI ST FRANCIS	1
Edmonton (STETTLER)	EDMUNSTON	City of Edmonton City of Edmonton Stettler	too long merchant ship	16
Farnham, QC (ST ROMAULD)	HMS FAREHAM	Missiquoi St Romauld Yamaska Hamfarn	USS MISSISSIPPI	
Fort Macleod, AB (MACLEOD)	Merchant ship			25
Geraldton, ON (HARDROCK)	HMS GERALDTON	Little Longlac MacLeod Hardrock		1, 26
Hanover, ON				15
Hull, QC (LA HULLOISE)	HMS HULL	La Hulloise Hull-Volent		
Iberville, QC (HENRYVILLE)	Fr sloop D'Iberville	Bleury d'Iberville Sabrevois Henryville		1
Inverness, NS (GLENVILLE)	HMAS INVERELL	Glenville Lake Loon Belle Cote		25
Jasper	HMS JASPER			

City/Town(name chosen)	Reason	Alternatives	Objections	Notes
Kingston (FRONTENAC)	HMS KINGSTON	Frontenac Cataraqui Rideau		14
Laprairie, QC	USS PRAIRIE			3
La Ville De Matane, QC (MATANE)	too long	Matane		
Laval des Rapides, QC	too long			
Leamington, ON (SEA CLIFF)	HMS LEAMINGTON	Talbot Sea Cliff	HMS TALBOT	
Liverpool, NS	HMS LIVERPOOL			4
London, ON (MIDDLESEX)	HMS LONDON	Middlesex		14
Louiseville, ON	LOUISBOURG USS LOUISVILLE			
Merritton, ON (MERRITTONIA)		Merrittonia Nottirem Merrittwell		
Montmorency, QC	USS(?)	Beauport	HMS BEAUFORT	5, 17
Montréal North (VIEL)	MONTREAL			25
Montréal West	MONTREAL	Ballantine	man's name	3
Mount Royal, QC (ROYALMOUNT)	MONTREAL	Mountroyaltown Royalmount Roymount	ROYAL ROADS HM Ships ROYAL SCOTSMAN, etc. USS ROYAL	
Nelson, BC (KOKANEE)	HMS NELSON	Kokanee Bonnington Silver King		10
Newcastle, NB (STRATHADAM)	HMS NEWCASTLE	Miramichi Douglastown Strathadam Maple Glen	MIRAMICHI HMS DOUGLAS HMS MAPLE	
Newmarket, ON	HMS NEWMARKET	Sentinel Simcoe Cane North York Loyal Combat		3, 9
New Toronto, ON (NEWTORO)	TORONTO	Newtoro Churchill Post #3		25
Nicolet, QC	USS NICHOLAS	Provencher Bécanour Dollard des Ormeaux		3

City/Town(name chosen)	Reason	Alternatives	Objections	Notes
North Battleford, SK (POUNDMAKER)	too long?	Poundmaker Northern City Thunderchild		
North Sydney, NS (NORSYD)	lengthy	Norsyd		
North Vancouver (CAPILANO)	VANCOUVER	Norvan Capilano Seaman Lynn Lions	tug Seaman USS LYNN HMS LION	11
Ottawa, ON (EASTVIEW)	OTTAWA			
Paris, ON	French ship under British operational control		4	
Pembroke, ON	HMS PEMBROKE			3
Penetanguishene, ON (PENETANG)	too long	Penetang		
Perth, ON (LANARK)	HMAS PERTH	Perth-on-the-Tay Tayville The Tay Lanark		20
Peterborough, ON	HMS PETERBOROUGH	Kawartha Ontonabee Chemong		
Picton, ON (HALLOWELL)	PICTOU	Glenora Athol Hallowell	HM Ships Glenevin, Glenroy & Glenarm ATHOLL USS HALAWA	
Pointe Aux Trembles, QC (GROU)	too long	Tremble Chevalier Colombet Grou Laval Fortin	unfortunate name USS CHEVALIER USS COLUMBIA & COLUMBUS	10 18
Porcupine, ON	HMS PORCUPINE			
Port Alfred, QC (ST EDOUARD)				
Portsmouth, ON (ALWINGTON)	HMS PORTSMOUTH	Oliver Mowat Alwington Hatter's Bay		19
Portage la Prairie, MB (PORTAGE)	too long	Portage		
Preston, ON (PRESTONIAN)	PRESCOTT, USS PRESTON	The Hub Cambridge Prestonian		

City/Town(name chosen)	Reason	Alternatives	Objections	Notes
Prince Albert, SK (WASKESIU)	Prins Albert	Waskesiu Kingsmere Mistawasis		24
Québec City, QC (VILLE DE QUEBEC)	HMS QUEBEC			
Richmond, QC (SHIPTON)	HMS/USS RICHMOND	Melbourne (note 8) Cleveland Shipton	MELVILLE HMS/USS CLEVELAND HMS SHIPPIGAN	
Sainte-Agathe-des-Monts, QC (SAINTE AGATHE)	too long			
Ste Anne de Bellevue, QC (STE ANNE)	too long	Ste Anne Bellevue	civilian tug BELLEVILLE	7 25
St Jean, QC	SAINT JOHN			4
St John's, QC	SAINT JOHN	L'Aigle Saint Jean	too long	
St Joseph D'Alma, QC (ALMA)	too long	Alma		
St Joseph de Grantham, QC (ST JOSEPH)	too long	St Joseph Ville de St Joseph		
St Marys, ON (STONE TOWN)	HMS ST MARYS	Stone Town Blanshard Little Falls		

Named for Sussex, NB, the Prestonian class frigate SUSSEXVALE as a cadet training ship, 4th Escort Squadron, 1963. The broad black band at the top of her funnel indicates she is senior ship. (RCN E 52093. FDN Coll.)

City/Town(name chosen)	Reason	Alternatives	Objections	Notes
St Michel de Laval, QC	too long			
Salaberry-de-Valleyfield, QC (VALLEYFIELD)	too long	Valleyfield		9
Selkirk, MB (DAERWOOD)	HMS SELKIRK	Rod Fidler Daerwood Wolverine	man's name reserved for a/s yacht	
Shawinigan Falls, QC (SHAWINIGAN)	too long			
South Porcupine, ON (TISDALE)	HMS PORCUPINE	Porcupine Tisdale Schumacher		
Sturgeon Falls, ON	HMS STURGEON			
Sussex, NB (SUSSEXVALE)	HMS SUSSEX	Sussex Vale Kennebecassis Sussexvale	USS Kennebec	
Sydney, NS (CAPE BRETON)	HMAS SYDNEY (note 8)	Cape Breton		2
Sydney Mines, NS	see above			10
Thorton	USS THORTON			
Thorold, ON (THORLOCK)	THORODD, vessel under British control	Flightlocks Old Thor Thorlock		
Trenton, ON (TRENTONIAN)	HMS TRENT USS TRENTON	Trentonia The Trent Mount Pelion Quinte	USS TRENTON HMS TRENT QUINTE	
Val d'Or, QC (VALDORIAN)	HMS VALOROUS USS VALOR	La Valdorien La Valdorienne La Ville de Val d'Or		
Verdun, QC (DUNVER)	HMS VERDUN	Beurling Crawford Dunver Verdun of Canada Verdun-Canada Verdun-Québec Verdun-Lasalle Ville de Verdun Argoulets	man's name USS CRAWFORD USS DENVER	
Vernon, BC (KALAMALKA)	HMS VERDUN	Kalamalka Silver Star		

City/Town(name chosen)	Reason	Alternatives	Objections	Notes
Victoria, BC (BEACON HILL)	HMS VICTORIA	Beacon Hill Race Rocks Clover Point	HMS RACER HMS CLOVER	
Waterloo, ON (FOSTER)		Shefford Foster Warden	HMS SHEFFIELD HM Rescue Tug	23
Welland, ON	HMS WELLARD			
Weston, ON (WEST YORK)	HMS WESTON	Westonia Westonian Westonite West York Alliance Sunset		
Windsor, NS (PESAQUID)	USS WINDSOR	Pesaquid Edward Avon	USS EDWARD HMS AVON	
Windsor, ON (BORDER CITIES)	USS WINDSOR	Walkerville Essex Border Cities	USS ESSEX	
Windsor, QC	USS WINDSOR			
Woodstock, NB (WULASTOOK)	WOODSTOCK	Wulastook Meduxnebeac	HMS WOOLSTON "inappropriate"	
Yarmouth, NS (CHEBOGUE)	HMS YARMOUTH	Chebogue Forchu Markland		6
York Township, ON (RUNNEYMEDE)	YORK	Runneymeade [sic] Mt Dennis Fairbank Roselands		13
Yorkton, SK (ORKNEY)	USS YORTOWN			

NOTES:

1. Name assigned but ship cancelled.
2. Names suggested by NSHQ (MNS?).
3. NSHQ wrote to the mayor or town council on several occasions.
4. Mayor/town council had no alternative name to suggest.
5. No agreement could be reached on an alternative name.
6. The reason listed was HMS YARMOUTH. In this period, no trace of such a vessel or establishment could be found in any of the Commonwealth navies.
7. NSHQ wrote and asked the Bathurst Power & Paper Co to change the name of their tug *Ste Anne*, to avoid any possible confusion.
8. Name reserved for use by RAN.
9. Alternative name(s) suggested by mayor.
10. Alternative name(s) suggested by town council.
11. Alternative names suggested by Victory Loan committee.
12. The mayor of Fort Erie replied to say that this town had amalgamated his city.
13. The reason listed was HMS YORK but she was sunk in the spring of 1941. HMCS YORK com'd Nov 1941 and she would be the correct reason why the name could not be used.
14. Name of the county.
15. "This name considered inappropriate." NSHQ Note.
16. Name of neighbouring town.
17. Alternative name suggested by MLA.
18. Alternative name suggested by citizens' committee.
19. In a memo to DOD, 12 Mar 1943, SO STATS wrote: "There is nothing about either of the first two names, of geographical significance. Does 'Hatter's Bay' appeal to you?"
20. Alternative names suggested by the curator of the Perth museum.
21. SO STATS suggested either Lingan or Linganbar.
22. At this time no RN vessel was named Chatham; but there was the RN Dockyard.
23. The Admiralty intended to use this name for a new destroyer.
24. Belgian vessel in RN employ.
25. Approval for use of the name being sought when the requirement for the name ceased.
26. HMS GERALDON could not be located but HMAS GERALTON commissioned in 1942.

Alternative Names Listed by Vessel

Vessel	Town/City, Province	Vessel	Town/City, Province
ABITIBI	Cochrane, ON	NEWTORO	New Toronto, ON (now part of Metro Toronto)
ALGOMA	Algoma Mills, ON		
ALMA	St Joseph D'Alma, QC	NORSYD	North Sydney, NS
ALWINGTON	Portsmouth, ON (now part of Kingston)	NORTHUMBERLAND	Chatham, NB
		ORKNEY	Yorkton, SK
ATHOLL	Campbellton, NB	PENETANG	Penetanguishene, ON
BEACON HILL	Victoria, BC	PESAQUID	Windsor, NS
BORDER CITIES	Windsor, ON	PORTAGE	Portage la Prairie, MB
BUCTOUCHE	Bathurst, NB	POUNDMAKER	North Battleford, SK
CAPE BRETON	Sydney, NS	PRESTONIAN	Preston, ON
CAPILANO	North Vancouver, BC	RANNEY FALLS	Campbellford, ON
CARLPLACE	Carleton Place, ON	ROYALMOUNT	Mount Royal, QC
CHATKENADA	Chatham, ON	RUNNEYMEDE	York township, ON
CHEBOGUE	Yarmouth, NS	SAINT AGATHE	Sainte-Agathe-des-Monts, QC
DAERWOOD	Selkirk, MB	SEA CLIFF	Leamington, ON
DUNVER	Verdun, QC	SHAWINIGAN	Shawinigan Falls, QC
EASTVIEW	Ottawa, ON	SHIPTON	Richmond, QC
FOSTER	Waterloo, ON	ST EDOUARD	Port Alfred, QC
FRONTENAC	Kingston, ON	ST JOSEPH	St Joseph de Grantham, QC
GLENVILLE	Inverness, NS	ST ROMAULD	Farnham, QC
GROU	Pointe Aux Trembles, QC	STE ANNE	Ste Anne de Bellevue, QC
HALLOWELL	Picton, ON	STETTLER	Edmonton, AB
HARDROCK	Geraldton, ON	STONE TOWN	St Marys, ON
HENRYVILLE	Iberville, QC	STORMONT	Cornwall, ON
INCH ARRAN	Dalhousie, NB	STRATHADAM	Newcastle, NB
KALAMALKA	Vernon, BC	SUSSEXVALE	Sussex, NB
KOKANEE	Nelson, BC	THORLOCK	Thorold, ON
LA HAVE	Bridgewater, NS	TISDALE	South Porcupine, ON
LA HULLOISE	Hull, QC	TRENTONIAN	Trenton, ON
LANARK	Perth, ON	VALDORIAN	Val d'Or, QC
LINGANBAR	Dominion, NS	VALLEYFIELD	Salaberry-de-Valleyfield, QC
LIVE OAK	Dunnville, ON	VILLE DE QUEBEC	Québec, QC
MACLEOD	Fort Macleod, AB	WASKESIU	Prince Albert, SK
MALDEN	Amherstburg, NS	WENTWORTH	Dartmouth, NS
MATANE	La Ville De Matane, QC	WEST YORK	Weston, ON
MERRITTONIA	Merritton, ON	WESTBURY	East Angus, QC
MIDDLESEX	London, ON	WULASTOOK	Woodstock, NB

APPENDIX B

Alternative Names, Almost

During the Second World War, the names of some cities and towns were considered to be too long or too similar to other names. Consequently, many had alternative names proposed. Westville, NS, for example, had Drummond, Clare Park and Black Diamond suggested. In any event, after lengthy discussion the original names were employed. Known examples of this practice are:

City/Town	Reason	Notes
Buckingham	HMS	1
Cap-de-la-Madeleine	too long	2
Dolbeau, QC	USS DOLPHIN	3
Fort Frances, ON	ST. FRANCIS	4
Joliette, QC	HMS JULIET	
Jonquière, QC	HMS JONQUIL	
New Glasgow, NS	HMS GLASGOW	
Pointe Claire, QC	ST. CLAIR	
Prince Rupert, BC	PRINCE RUPERT	
Rivière du Loup, QC	RIVIERE DU LOUP	5
Rossland, BC	HMS ROSALIND	
St. Catharines, ON	HMS ST. KATHERINE	
Springhill, NS	HMS SPRINGDALE	
Swansea, ON	HMS SWAN	
Thetford Mines, QC	too long	
Victoriaville, QC	HMS VICTORIAN	6
Westville, NS	not known	
Wallaceburg, ON	HMS WALLACE	

Notes:

1. This was an error. No ship of that name existed. Other names considered were Town of Buckingham, Ville de Buckingham, The Spirit of Buckingham, The Earl C. Hicks, Lièvre Region, Lièvre River, and Papineau (for the county).

2. The name was too long and 'Cap Madeleine' was unacceptable to the town.

3. One alternative name suggested was Ville de Dolbeau. After some discussions, a note in the margin reads "Perhaps DOLPHIN and DOLBEAU are not too similar ..."

4. One alternative name suggested was Rainy River.

5. The name was too long but 'R du Loup' was unacceptable.

6. The name was originally considered to be too long. No vessel named Victorian could be located. The reference is probably to HM Ships VICTORIA and VICTORIOUS. An alternative consideration was Les Bois Francs.

APPENDIX C

Names Selected But Never Used: Second World War

Some twenty-four cities and towns had their names selected for ships but these names were never used for one of the four reasons noted.

1. Two names were assigned but the ships were cancelled: Brampton (Ontario) and Westville (NS)

2. One name was assigned to a hull but the ship was renamed: La Tuque (Québec)

3. Thirteen names received approval but they were never assigned to a ship:

Alexander (Ontario)	Plessisville (Québec)	Rouyn (Québec)
Ingersoll (Ontario)	Pointe Claire (Québec)	St Jerome (Québec)
Listowel (Ontario)	Renfrew (Ontario)	Simcoe (Ontario)
Meaford (Ontario)	Riverside (Ontario)	
Megantic (Québec)	Roberval (Québec)	

4. Approval for use of these eight names was being sought when the requirement for the names ceased:

Amos (Québec)	Grand Prairie (Alberta)	Ste Rose (Québec)
Carman (Manitoba)	(Fort) Macleod (Alberta)	Seaforth (Ontario)
Dolbeau (Québec)	Montmagny (Québec)	

APPENDIX D

Duplicate and Similar Names

Up to 1 Jan 1987, the Canadian navy shared Battle Honours with other Commonwealth navies. (See Chapter 2.) For example, when BONAVENTURE commissioned, her British predecessors had won all the Battle Honours she displayed. Because of this sharing, no two ships in the Commonwealth navies should have used the same name at the same time.

During the Second World War, this non-duplication rule was extended to include similar as well as identical names and in late 1941 the scope was extended to include names used by the USN as well.

Due to our sharing some common heritage, Canada, the USA and the UK employ many of the same names for various geographical features. Because they were originally commissioned during peacetime, many RN and USN vessels shared identical names during the Second World War. Thus among others: HM/US Ships CLEVELAND, MANCHESTER and NORFOLK.

Even for those vessels constructed and named during the Second World War, some duplicate and similar names still appeared in Allied navies. Below is a short, incomplete list of known cases covering the years from 1910. Dates are approximate.

HMCS ACADIA	Sea Cadet camp 1964–SIS
HMCS ACADIAN	patrol boat, 1976–1995
HMCS ANNAPOLIS	destroyer, 1940–45
USS ANNAPOLIS	frigate, 1943–47
HMCS BAYFIELD	minesweeper, 1941–45
USS BAYFIELD	troop transport, Second World War
HMCS BEAVER	armed yacht, 1941–44
HMS BEAVER	base, Humber River, 1939–45
USS BEAVER	submarine tender, 1915–1945
HMCS BURLINGTON	minesweeper, 1940–45
USS BURLINGTON	frigate, 1943–45
HMCS CANADA	patrol vessel, 1915–19
HMS CANADA	battleship, 1914–1920
HMCS COLLINGWOOD	corvette, 1940–45
HMS COLLINGWOOD	base, Fareham, 1939–SIS
HMCS DIANA	depot ship, 1914–15
HMS DIANA	cruiser, 1895–1919
HMCS DISCOVERY	reserve division, 1941–SIS
HMS DISCOVERY	headquarters ship, 1955–SIS

USS DISCOVERER	salvage vessel, Second World War
HMCS DONNACONA	reserve division, 1941–SIS
USS DONNACONA	net tender, circa 1943
HMCS GRENVILLE	tug, 1942–45
HMS GRENVILLE	destroyer, 1943–1970
HMCS HAWKESBURY	corvette, 1944–45
HMAS HAWKESBURY	frigate, 1944–62
HMCS HUNTER	reserve division, 1941–SIS
HMS HUNTER	a. escort carrier, 1942–45
	b. landing ship, 1947–56
	c. patrol craft, 1983–SIS
HMCS MELVILLE	minesweeper, 1941–45
USS MELVILLE	destroyer tender, 1915–45
HMCS NONSUCH	reserve division, 1941–SIS
HMS NONSUCH	a. sloop, cancelled 23 Oct 1945
	b. ex German destroyer, 1947–49
HMCS PEREGRINE	base, 1944–46
HMS PEREGRINE	RNAS, 1945–48
HMCS QUEEN	reserve division, 1941–SIS
HMS QUEEN	escort carrier, 1943–46
HMCS QUEEN CHARLOTTE	reserve division, 1941–46
HMS QUEEN CHARLOTTE	AA Range, 1941–46
HMCS RESTLESS	training ship, 1918–20
HMS RESTLESS	destroyer, 1916–36
HMCS TERRA NOVA	destroyer escort, 1959–1996
HMS TERRA NOVA	icebreaker: named but never built, c. 1964.
HMCS UNICORN	reserve division, 1941–SIS
HMS UNICORN	aircraft carrier, 1941–57
USS UNICORN	submarine, 1945–59

APPENDIX E

Counties and Townships: Alternative Names

During the Second World War the names of some cities and towns could not be used for reasons itemized in Appendix A, and the names of the relevant county or township was employed as an alternative name. Known examples are:

Ship	Named For
BELLECHASSE	St Charles (?), QC
FRONTENAC	Kingston, ON
GLENGARRY*	Glengarry Township, ON
HALLOWELL	Picton, ON
LANARK	Perth, ON
MIDDLESEX	London, ON
NORTHUMBERLAND	Chatham, NB
STORMONT	Cornwall, ON

*This name was approved but never used.

APPENDIX F

Names of Individuals

The nomenclature for the USN states that destroyers are named after individuals. This policy has also seen some submarines and some aircraft carriers named after individuals. In the RN, the names of individuals have been used for battleships and destroyers and at least one submarine. In our naval forces, however, very few of the ships have been named either directly or deliberately for persons.

Where a ship carried the name of an individual, the ships were:

a. either taken over by the navy and retained their original names, e.g. FRENCH, LAURIER, ANDREE DUPREE; or

b. named after a town, city or geographical feature, which had originally been named for an individual, e.g. FRASER, LLOYD GEORGE, MONCTON; or

c. named after another vessel that had originally been named for an individual, e.g. PREVOST and TECUMSEH.

During the Second World War the stated policy was not to name ships after individuals.

Since 1910, by accident, omission or calculation, some nineteen ships are known to have been named directly for individuals. These are:

BURRARD	GROU	ST ANTHONY
CHAMPLAIN (1st & 2nd)	JOLIET	ST CHARLES
CORNWALLIS	LAVALLEE	ST JOHN
DIANA	POUNDMAKER	VANCOUVER (1st)
D'IBERVILLE (1st & 2nd)	QUADRA	WENTWORTH
DONNACONA	RADISSON	—

Of these ships, three — GROU, POUNDMAKER, WENTWORTH — were alternative names for towns and cities during the Second World War. "Viel," another name of an individual, was a name that was proposed but never allocated.

The River class frigate WENTWORTH. Her name was the alternative one for Dartmouth, NS. (FDN Coll.)

APPENDIX G

Ships With Unofficial Names

Seamen have attached names to their ships since the earliest days. All the names listed in this book are official. That is, the Minister of National Defence has authorized a vessel or establishment to commission and carry a certain name. The present RCSC establishments such as ONTARIO have such approval and are thus listed in this volume. Unofficial names are not listed.

Seamen do not appear to favour numbered vessels and as a result, where this occurs, many such vessels receive unauthorized names. Although numbered vessels in the hundreds served during the Second World War, Winston Churchill directed that the numbered submarines in the RN were to receive names. His reason was that it was difficult to ask a man to die for a number. He never expanded his directive to other numbered vessels such as landing craft and motor launches.

In the Second World War, ML Q 060 was built in Orillia, ON. In his book *Sunshine Sketches of a Little Town*, Stephen Leacock turned Orillia into Mariposa and included a steamer, the *Mariposa Belle*. Hence, her first captain called Q 060, HMCS *Mariposa Belle*. She even had a 'badge'.

In Lamb's *The Corvette Navy*, reference is made to HMCS HALO, a shore establishment allegedly located in the clubhouse of the Pictou Golf Club in NS, during the Second World War. No further reference could be located. A telephone conversation with Capt R Donaldson, RCN (Ret'd) in Jan 1994 shed light on the situation. He had talked with Cmdre Little, RCN (Ret'd) who had served in Halo during the war. The name was unofficial, admitted the Commodore, "but we flew the White Ensign."

During the 1980s, several numbered small craft in the Training Group Pacific had unofficial names. There were seven vessels in Sub-Division 2.2 of the west coast training squadron, viz: Badger, YAG 319; Caribou, YAG 314; Cougar, YAG 308; Grizzly, YAG 306; Lynx, YAG 320; Otter, YAG 312; and Racoon, YDT 10. With one exception, all these vessels were named for armed yachts of the Second World War. According to the CO in 1985, Cdr T. Miller, the exception (Badger) was named after Lord Nelson's first command. Actually, HMS LUCY was Nelson's first command.

Note that Racoon was spelled with only one c. The previous vessel had two c's in her name.

CFAV Purveyor, seen each summer in the 1980s at QUADRA, was actually YE 217, an ammunition lighter. Pegasus and Gemini, two Halifax work boats acquired in 1985, are officially YAG 651 and YAG 650 respectively.

The tug PARKSVILLE currently serves on the west coast. On the east coast are her two sisters, MARYSVILLE and MERRICKSVILLE. These two similar names are difficult to distinguish over the local radio net. To avoid confusion, the former is referred to as Parksville.

APPENDIX H

Reserve Divisions

Throughout the years since their formation, the naval reserves have had several titles: RNCVR, RCNVR, RCNR, RCN(R), etc. From Nov 1941, Reserve Divisions have been commissioned and named. The total number in commission at any one time has varied.

Shortly after the unification of the three services in 1968, the naval reserve divisions were officially known as Naval Reserve Units (NRUs). Happily, they now appear once again as HMC Ships.

MALAHAT (Building 91) on Esquimalt Road circa 1950. (Duncan Macphail. PABC 1-02451.)

The following is a list of all reserve units in commission now or in the past:

BRUNSWICKER	DISCOVERY	PATRIOT
CABOT	DONNACONA	PREVOST
CARIBOU	GRIFFON	QUEEN
CARLETON	HALIGONIAN	QUEEN CHARLOTTE
CARTIER	HUNTER	RADISSON
CATARAQUI	JOLIETT	SCOTIAN
CHAMPLAIN	MALAHAT	STAR
CHATHAM	MONTCALM	TECUMSEH
CHIPPAWA	MONTREAL	UNICORN
D'IBERVILLE	NONSUCH	YORK

Notes:

1. PATRIOT was not a reserve division. From 1956—1966, she was the HQ for the reserve divisions.

2. Salaberry was the name allocated for a division scheduled for Salaberry-de-Valleyfield, Québec, in 1990 but she was cancelled before commissioning.

CHATHAM, Prince Rupert with SKIDEGATE in the foreground, 1943. From 1946 this was the reserve division. (FDN Coll.)

Aerial view of CORNWALLIS at her second location on the Annapolis Basin, summer 1943. From 1943 to 1968—and as CFB Cornwallis until 1994—most officers and ratings passed through her gates at least once in their service.

APPENDIX J

Shore Establishments

The following list of commissioned shore establishments does not include radio stations, reserve divisions, or minor non commissioned units such as Debert, NS. The list also excludes Royal Canadian Sea Cadet bases commissioned since 1968. (See Appendix L.)

ACADIA	GANNET	PROTECTOR (I)
AVALON	GIVENCHY	PROTECTOR II
AVALON II	GIVENCHY II	QUADRA
BURRARD	GIVENCHY III	ROYAL ROADS
BYTOWN	GUELPH	ST HYACINTHE
BYTOWN II	HOCHELAGA	SAMBRO
CAPTOR (I)	HOCHELAGA II	SCOTIAN
CAPTOR II	KINGS	SEAGULL
CHALEUR (I)	LANSDOWNE	SHEARWATER (I)
CHALEUR II	MULGRAVE	SHEARWATER II
CHATHAM	NADEN (I)	SHELBURNE
CONESTOGA	NADEN II	SOMERS ISLES
CORNWALLIS	NADEN III	STADACONA (I)
DIANA	NIAGARA	STADACONA II
D'IBERVILLE	NIOBE (I)	STONE FRIGATE
DOMINION	NIOBE II	VENTURE
FORT RAMSEY	PEREGRINE	

APPENDIX K

Radio Stations

Name	Location	Established	Paid Off
First World War—East Coast			
Barrington	Shelburne Co, NS	Jan 1917	Apr 1919
Camperdown	Halifax	19 Aug 1914	
Canso	Guysborough Co, NS		
Cape Race	Newfoundland		
Chedabucto	n/k		
Louisburg	Louisburg, NS		
Point Nelson	n/k		
Saint John	Saint John, NB		
First World War—West Coast			
Alert Bay	Alert Bay, BC	—	Apr 1919
Cape Lazo	n/k		
Dead Tree Point	n/k		
Digby Island	Prince Rupert		
Estevan	Estevan Pt Vancouver Island		
Gonzales Hill	Victoria		
Pachena Point	W coast Vancouver Island		
Point Grey	Vancouver		
Triangle Island	Vancouver Island		

The DF Hut at NRS Harbour Grace, Newfoundland, 1945. (KM Coll.)

Name	Location	Established	Paid Off
Second World War			
Cap d'Espoir	Gaspé Peninsula, QC	Jul 1941	1945?
Coverdale	Coverdale, NB	1941?	
Churchill	Churchill, MB		
Gloucester	near Ottawa	1943	
Gordon Head	Victoria	1942	1945
Goulds (?)	Newfoundland	—	1945?
Harbour Grace	Newfoundland	—	1945?
Lambeth	near London, ON		
Whitehead	Gloucester Co, NS	1940	1947

Goulds, Harbour Grace, and Lambeth were all SN W/T S. Louisburg was a former DOT station taken over, staff and all. Whitehead was a Loran station(?).

Radio Stations, post 1949—Locations

Aklavit	Chimo	Gloucester	Newport Corners
Albro Lake	Churchill	Inuvik	Padloping Island
Aldergrove	Coverdale	Masset	Port Edward
Bermuda	Frobisher Bay	Matsqui	Sumas
Blandford	Gander	Montreal Circle	

Notes:

1. The station at Alert was not an NRS. Established in 1950, its complement was augmented by naval personnel starting in 1961. The station took its name from HMS ALERT which spent the winter of 1875/6 at Cape Sheridan, some eight miles east of the present site.

2. For details on the above stations, see the main entries.

3. Ratings in ALDERGROVE, CHURCHILL, COVERDALE, GLOUCESTER and INUVIK all eventually wore the appropriate cap tally. Ratings in all other NRS wore the tally HMC RADIO STATION.

NRS MASSET in 1953. (RCN E-23198. FDN Coll.)

APPENDIX L

RCSC Establishments since 1968

By an agreement with the then Director of Military Traditions and Heritage (now Directorate of History and Heritage) in NDHQ, Sea Cadet bases may employ the name, badge and Battle Honours but must give them up when the navy requires the name for a vessel.

Names used for Sea Cadet establishments since 1968 include:

ACADIA
GIMLI (?)
MICMAC
ONTARIO
QUADRA
QU'APPELLE
QUEBEC
TILLICUM

RCASC *General Schmidlin* before she became CEDARWOOD. (RCN CN 3588 FDN Coll.)

RCAF rescue boat *Heron*, 13 Dec 1971. (FDN Coll.)

APPENDIX M

Royal Canadian Army Service Corps (RCASC) Vessels

Name	Number	Obtained	Turned Back
Alcelia	Z 56	1940?	
Alfreda			
Anna A	Z 49	25 Nov 1942	20 Jul 1944
Armstrong	—	1940?	
Bernice L	Z 48	—	24 Apr 1944
Beryl	—	1942	
Brigadier Keating	—	1942	
Colonel Benson			
Colonel Holmes	Z 47	1 Nov 1942	23 Apr 1947
Colonel MacDonald			
Colonel Ogilvy	Z 55	1943	23 Apr 1947?
Colonel Peters	Z 35	1 Nov 1942	
Colonel Robertson	—	23 Apr 1947?	
Colonel Roy	Z 45	1942	23 Apr 1947?
Colonel Wadmore	Z 36		
Don III	—	—	23 Apr 1947?
Donvac			
Donvan			
Garland Marie	Z 54	—	22 Sep 1944
General Anderson	Z 27	1 Feb 1942	23 Apr 1947
General Ashton			
General Bigger			
General Burstall			
General Caldwell			
General Cotton	Z 28	1943	23 Apr 1947?
General Drury	—	1943	23 Apr 1947?
General Elking	—	1943	
General Hertzberg	Z 26	21 Feb 1941	
General Kennedy	Z 70		
General Lake	Z 29	1 Nov 1942	
General Page			
General Ross	Z 37		
General Schmidlen	—	1943	26 May 1947
Hickey	Z 52	—	5 Apr 1944
Ivana	Z 50	4 Jul 1944	
Josephine D III	—	1 Nov 1942	

Name	Number	Obtained	Turned Back
Lady Ron	Z 43		
Lella		First World War?	
Motor Boat No 1	Z 58		
Motor Boat No 23	Z 23	1945	
Motor Launch No 25	Z 25	1945	
Naraspur			
Narsapper			
Sapper			
Spring Maid			
Trapper	Z 53	—	11 Aug 1944
Ubique			
Western Girl	Z 57	—	8 Jul 1944

Royal Canadian Air Force Vessels

Name	Number	Obtained	Disposed of
A Catalina			
Amaryllis			
Amorita			
Aristocrat			
Arresteur	B114	Sep 1939	
Atlin	M12		
B.C. Star			
Beaver	B137		
Black Duck	M872	—	1 Apr 1965
Bounty			
Brant			
Cetoma			
Chilco	M10		
Combat	M350	23 Aug 1941	
Detector			
Egret	M925	—	1 Apr 1965
Elaine W	B112		
Eskimo	B367		
Eskimo II			
Evergreen I			
Flamingo	M847	—	1 Apr 1965
G of G 8			
Gannet	M873	—	1 Apr 1965
Guillemot	M849	—	1 Apr 1983
Haida	M206	1944	

Name	Number	Obtained	Disposed of
Heron	M848	—	1 Apr 1965
Huron			
Kiku			
Laurence K Sweeney	B125		
Malahat	—	1946	
Malecite	M231		
Manx	M851	—	1 Apr 1965
Midnight Sun			
Mohawk	B139		
Montagnais	M234		
Newport	M11		
Nicola			
Nimpkish	M535	1944	
Nootka	B105		
OK Service V	B116		
Panda			
Puffin			
Reel Fisher			
Sea Horse	M380		
Sekani	M205		
Shoveller	M200		
Silver Spring			
Snow Prince	M348	12 Sep 1942	
Snowbird II	—	1949	
Songhee	M468	1944	24 Jul 1953
Springtime			
Takuli	M232	1947	
Transporter	M541		
Vega I			
Viki K			
White cliff			
Woodcock			
Work Shop Scow	M159		

Notes:

1. The purpose of these lists is to identify those vessels that served with the RCASC and RCAF. Several of these vessels also served with the navy.

2. On 1 Apr 1965, as part of the impending unification of the three services, the RCN took over the RCAF crash boats, e.g. *Gannet*.

APPENDIX N

Nicknames

These are some of the nicknames given to HMC Ships.

Second World War

ASSINIBOINE	Bones
BADDECK	Bad Deck
BEACON HILL	Leaky Bill
BRANDON	Brand on Bull
BUCTOUCHE	Buck
CHAMBLY	Chambles
Esquimalt (base)	Squibbly
FESTUBERT	Festering Herbert
FREDERICTON	Freddie
Halifax (base)	Slackers
NABOB, HMS	HMCS Canada Dry
QU'APPELLE	Queer Apple
RESTIGOUCHE	Rusty Guts
RIMOUSKI	The Polish Corvette
ST. LAURENT	Sally Rand
SIOUX	S ten U ten
WETASKIWIN	Wet Assed Queen

Post War

ANTIGONISH	Tigonish
ASSINIBOINE	Bones
ATHABASKAN	Athabee; Arthur; B. Ashcan
BONAVENTURE	Bonnie; and later, Pretender
CAP DE LA MADELEINE	The Cap; Mad Cap
CORMORANT	The Love Boat
FREDERICTON	Freddy
JAMES BAY	Jimmy B
JONQUIERE	Queer Boat; Liberace's Yacht
LABRADOR	Great White Bathtub
MAGNIFICENT	Maggie
MICMAC	Old Dobbin
NIPIGON	Nipper
OJIBWA	Oh be joyful
ONTARIO	O Boat; the Big O
RESTIGOUCHE	Rusty Guts
QU'APPELLE	The Fox
QUEBEC	The Big Q
SASKATCHEWAN	Saskabush
ST. LAURENT	Sally Ann

The "Rusty Guts," the first RESTIGOUCHE in Second World War camouflage circa late 1942. (RCN NP-489. FDN Coll.)

APPENDIX O

Vessels of the Fishermen's Reserve

Name	Pennant Number	Notes
ALLAVERDY	Fy 06	
BARKELY SOUND	Fy 23	
BC LADY	Fy 07	
BILLOW	Fy 25	ex Kuraisho, sister to SURF
BLUENOSE	Fy 44	
CAMENITA	Fy 41	
CANCOLIM	Fy 10/P10	
CANFISCO	Fy 17	
CAPE BEALE	Fy 26	
CAPELLA	Fy 39	
CHATHAM S	Fy 47	became SEA WAVE
COMBER	Fy 37	ex CSC II
CREST	Fy 38	ex May
DALEHURST	Fy 35	ex Glendale V
DEPARTURE BAY	Fy 48	
EARLY FIELD	Fy 40	
EHKOLI	Fy 12	
FIFER	Fy 0	
FLORES	Z 25	ex Cancolim II
FOAM	Fy 22	ex LOYAL I
GLENDALE V	Fy 35	became DALEHURST
HOWE SOUND I	Fy 19	
JOAN W II	Fy 34	
JOHANNA	Fy 28	
KUITAN	Fy 14	
LEELO	Fy 15	
LOYAL I	Fy 42	
LOYAL II	Fy 22	became FOAM
MARGARET I	Fy 29	
MARAUDER	FY 03	
MAYAS?	n/k	
MERRY CHASE	Fy 46	
MITCHELL BAY	Fy 05	
MOOLOCK	Fy 16	
MORESBY III	Fy 42	
NENAMOOK	Fy 13	

Name	Pennant Number	Notes
RIPPLE	Z 08	ex BCPP vessel MPL 14
SAKURA	n/k	
SAN TOMAS	Fy 02	
SANTA MARIA	Fy 08	
SEA PRIDE II	Z 126	
SEA WAVE	Fy 47	ex CHATHAM S
SEAFLASH	Fy 45	
SEINER	Fy 32	
SIGNAL	Fy 30	
SKIDEGATE	Fy 20	
SMITH SOUND	Fy 18	
SNOW PRINCE	n/k	
SPRAY	Fy 33?, Z 09	Ex Hatta VII
SPRINGTIME V	Fy 09	
SURF	Fy 24	Ex Araisho, sister of BILLOW
TAKLA	Fy 27	
TALAPUS	Fy 11	
TORDO	Fy 20	
VALDES	Fy 21	
VAN ISLE	Fy 01	
VENCEDOR	Z 21	
WEST COAST	Fy 04	
WESTERN MAID	Fy 36	
ZOARCES	Fy 62	

HMCS TAKLA. (KM Coll.)

Vessels of the Fishermen's Reserve:
Listing by Pennant Number

Pennant Number	Name	Pennant Number	Name
Fy 00	FIFER	Fy 29	MARGARET I
Fy 01	VAN ISLE	Fy 30	SIGNAL
Fy 02	SAN TOMAS	Fy 32	SEINER
Fy 03	MARAUDER	Fy 33?	SPRAY?
Fy 04	WEST COAST	Fy 34	JOAN W II
Fy 05	MITCHELL BAY	Fy 35	DALEHURST
Fy 06	ALLAVERDY	Fy 35	GLENDALE V
Fy 07	BC LADY	Fy 36	WESTERN MAID
Fy 08	SANTA MARIA	Fy 37	COMBER
Fy 09	SPRINGTIME V	Fy 38	CREST
Fy 10/P10	CANCOLIM	Fy 39	CAPELLA
Fy 11	TALAPUS	Fy 40	EARLY FIELD
Fy 12	EHKOLI	Fy 41	CAMENITA
Fy 13	NENAMOOK	Fy 42	MORESBY III
Fy 14	KUITAN	Fy 43	LOYAL I
Fy 15	LEELO	Fy 44	BLUENOSE
Fy 16	MOOLOCK	Fy 45	SEAFLASH
Fy 17	CANFISCO	Fy 46	MERRY CHASE
Fy 18	SMITH SOUND	Fy 47	CHATHAM S
Fy 19	HOWE SOUND I	Fy 47	SEA WAVE
Fy 20	SKIDEGATE	Fy 48	DEPARTURE BAY
Fy 20	TORDO	Fy 62	ZOARCES
Fy 21	VALDES	Z 08	RIPPLE
Fy 22	FOAM	Z 09	SPRAY
Fy 22	LOYAL II	Z 126	SEA PRIDE II
Fy 23	BARKELY SOUND	Z 21	VENCEDOR
Fy 24	SURF	Z 25	FLORES
Fy 25	BILLOW	n/k	MAYAS?
Fy 26	CAPE BEALE	n/k	SAKURA
Fy 27	TAKLA	n/k	SNOW PRINCE
Fy 28	JOHANNA		

APPENDIX P

Government Vessels 1914

The following table is extracted from a list located by Mr Rollie Webb in a miscellaneous collection called the Canadian Naval Service Files in NAC. The title of the document is "Details of Canadian Government Ships excluding dredges, mud hoppers and vessels under 20 tons." The report was prepared by the Department of Naval Service and is numbered 80176-A. Although undated, circumstantial evidence indicates that this version was published late in 1914 or early in 1915.

In this report, no warships are listed for the naval service, only auxiliaries. In addition to the naval auxiliary vessels, ten other government vessels listed here saw naval service for part of their careers. Only named vessels are listed.

Earl Grey and *Montmagny* are listed in the index of the document but not in the main entries. The former spent the month of October 1914 sailing to Russia to be turned over. No details could be found on the latter.

Departmental abbreviations:

Ag = Agriculture; C = Customs; M&D = Militia & Defence; M&F = Marine & Fisheries; NS = Naval Service; PO = Post Office; PW = Public Works; R&W = Railways & Canals.

Name of Vessel	Dept.	Year Built	Displacement (tons)	Guns	Location	Service Employed on	Saw Naval Service
Aberdeen	M&F	1894	1,330	None	Saint John	Light & buoy	Yes
Acadia	NS	1913	1,050	None	Hudson Bay	Hydrographic	—
Agnes	R&W	1913	60	None	Rideau Canal		
Alert	R&W	1886	10	None	Ontario	—	
Alfreda	M&D	1904	270	None	Halifax	—	
Alice	Ag	1907	550	None	Grosse Isle	Quarantine	
Aranmore	M&F	1890	—	None	Halifax	—	
Armstrong	M&D	1901	230	None	Halifax	—	
Bayfield	NS	1889	559	None	Great Lakes	Hydrographic	—
Bellechasse	M&F	1912	576	None	Sorel	—	Yes
Beryl	M&D	1903	45	None	Esquimalt	—	
Bessie Butler	R&W	1907	150	None	Trent Canal	—	
Brant	M&F	1899	—	None	Charlottetown	Light & buoy	Yes

Name of Vessel	Dept.	Year Built	Displacement (tons)	Guns	Location	Service Employed on	Saw Naval Service
Canada	NS	1904	780	2 12pdr 2 3pdr	NS	Fishery	—
Carillon	R&W	1912	100	None	Lachine Canal	—	
Cartier	NS	1910	850	None	St. Lawrence	Hydrographic	—
Champlain	M&F	1904	800	None	Québec	Ferry	
Constance	NS	1891	400	None	PEI	Fishery	—
Curlew	NS	1892	415	None	Bay of Fundy	Fishery	—
Dollard	M&F	1913	—	None	Montréal	—	
Druid	M&F	1902	1,000	None	St Lawrence	Buoy	Yes
Durley Chine	R&W	1913	5,173	None	East Coast	—	
Earl Grey	M&F	—	—	—	—	Ice breaking	Yes
Estevan	M&F	1912	2,100	None	BC	Light & buoy	
Eureka	M&F	1893	—	None	Father Point	Pilot tender	
Frank Perew	R&W	1867	200	None	Lachine Canal	—	
Galiano	NS	1913	850	None	BC	Fishery	—
Grenville	M&F	1914	—	None	St. Lawrence	—	
Gulnare	NS	1893	560	None	NS	Fishery	—
G.W.Yates	R&W	1913	—	None	Hudson Bay	—	
Kathleen	R&W	1907	200	None	Hudson Bay	—	
La Canadienne	NS	1880	500	None	Lake Superior	Hydrographic	—
Lady Evelyn	PO	1901	680	None	Rimouski	Mail tender	Yes
Lady Grey	M&F	1906	1,080	None	St Lawrence	Icebreaker	
Lady Laurier	M&F	1902	1,970	None	Atlantic coast	Light & buoy	
Lambton	M&F	1909	510	None	Great Lakes	Light & buoy	
Lansdowne	M&F	1884	1,3380	None	Bay of Fundy	Light & buoy	Yes
Lillooet	NS	1908	760	None	Pacific Coast	Hydrographic	—
Loretta	R&W	1907	120	None	Rideau Canal	—	
Madge	Ag	1907	310	None	William Head	Quarantine	
Malaspina	NS	1913	850	1 6pdr	BC	Fishery	—
Margaret	C	1913	950	2 6pdr	St Lawrence	Preventive	Yes
Minoca	Ag	1910	275	None	Halifax	Quarantine	
Minto	M&F	1899	2,070	None	Northumberland Strait	Winter mail	
Montcalm	M&F	1904	3,270	None	BC	Ice breaker	

Name of Vessel	Dept.	Year Built	Displacement (tons)	Guns	Location	Service Employed on	Saw Naval Service
Montmagny	M&F	—	—	—	—	—	
Mulgrave	R&W	1893	925	None	Mulgrave	—	
Naden	NS	1913	118	—	Pacific Coast	Hydrographic	—
Neophyte	R&W	1903	—	None	Hudson Bay	—	
Newington	M&F	1889	475	None	St Lawrence	Light & buoy	Yes
Petrel	NS	1892	400	None	NS	Fishery	—
Polana	Ag	1911	410	None	Grosse Isle	Quarantine	
Princess	M&F	1896	850	None	BC	—	
Quadra	M&F	1891	1,260	None	BC	Light & buoy	
Restless	NS	1906	205	None	Prince Rupert	Fishery	—
Rouville	M&F	1906	—	None	St Lawrence	Construction	
Scotia	R&W	1901	2,550	None	Mulgrave	—	
Sheeba	R&W	1912	5,668	None	East Coast	—	
Simcoe	M&F	1909	1,630	None	Great Lakes	Light & buoy	
Speedy	PW	1896	420	None	Maritimes	—	Yes
Stanley	M&F	1888	1,890	None	Atlantic Coast	Light & buoy	
Tyrian	PW	1869	1,300	—	Halifax	Cable ship	
Vigilant	NS	1904	412	None	Lake Erie	Fishery	—

HMCS SPEEDY during the First World War. (KM Coll.)

A former Public Works vessel, LAURENTIAN during the First World War. (KM Coll.)

APPENDIX Q

Other Naval Vessels 1910-1919

In addition to purpose-built warships such as RAINBOW and SHEARWATER, and those vessels listed in Appendix P, the following vessels saw naval service for various lengths of time between 1910 to 1919. Only named vessels are listed.

ALASE
ALASKA
ALBACORE
ALVA AND MAY
AMOS B
ARCADIA
ARTHUR
ARTHUR W
ATLANTA
BALEINE
BARRINGTON
BARTLETT
BECANCOEUR
BERTHIER
BLUE WIND
BOBBIE BURNS
CANSO

CECILIA
C. E. TANNER
CHICKADEE
CHRISTINE
COASTGUARD
CONTRECOEUR
DAVY JONES
DELBERT D
DELIVERANCE
DESCHAILLONS
DIANA
DORET
EGRET
ELIZABETH
ELLEN BERNICE
ETHEL
FALCON

FANTOME
FELICITY
FISPA
FLORENCE
FOAM
FRANK T. COOTE
GLADIATOR
GOPHER
GRAYLING
GRIB
G. S. MAYES
GWENNITH
(HERBERT N. EDWARDS)
HERON WING
HIGHLAND MARY
HOLLY LEAF
ICTHUS

IVY LEAF	MUSQUASH	SHARK
JESSIE	M. W. WEATHERSPOON	SINMAC
JUANITA	NARADA	SPRAY
KARLUK	NEREID	STARLING
KIA ORA	PARAGON	STELLA
LAUREL LEAF	PATHFINDER	STELLA MARIS
LAURENTIAN	PILOT	STORM KING
LAVALTRIE	PREMIER	SWAN
LAVIOLETTE	PRINCE ARTHUR	TANNIS
LILLIAN	PRINCE GEORGE	THISTLE
LILLY	RAMBLER	THREE COUSINS
LORRAINE	ROAMER	TRUSTY
LORTIE RUSSEL	ROANOKE	TUNA
MARGARET A.	ROLLIN E. MASON	ULALLA
HACKETT	ROSE	ULNA
MARTIN J. MARRAM	ROVER	UNA
MAUDE MOSHER	RPS	VALIANT
MEREDITH	RUTH	VIKING
M. E. WHERRY	SABLE I	VINER
MILDRED	SCOTSMAN	VIRGINIA
MINORU	SEAGULL	W. H. LEA
MOHAWK	SEA LARK	WILFRED C
MOTO	SHAMROCK	WILLIAM B. MURRAY

APPENDIX S

CANADIAN-WON BATTLE HONOURS

The following is an unofficial list of all known Battle Honours won by Canadian warships from 1939 to 1991. This list is for named ships only. A name not listed means no honours have been awarded.

The British-won honours from 1588 to 1953 have not been included.

There have been no single ship actions awarded to the Canadian Navy at any time. And there was no award for convoy duties or patrol duties on the western side of the Atlantic during the First World War.

Battle Honours for HM Ships such as PUNCHER, a British ship manned by Canadian naval personnel, are listed. But honours are not listed for HM Ships that carried Canadian names while manned by British naval personnel, e.g. HM Ships BAFFIN, PARRSBORO, and QUALICUM.

This list of awards is extracted from the following records:

1. Admiralty Fleet Order (AFO) 2565/54, 1 Oct 1954.

2. An undated manuscript on Battle Honours for the common Commonwealth list obtained from the Naval Historical Branch, Ministry of Defence, London, by NDHQ/Directorate of History in 1985. Note: there are anomalies in this list, e.g. TROIS RIVIERES is listed as THREE RIVERS; COBOURG as COBURG; etc.; FUNDY, GASPE and others are not listed; and the list disagrees with BRCN 150 as to honours awarded some ships, e.g. FRASER and LA HULLOISE.

3. BRCN 150.

4. NGO 2.06/11. Note: there are anomalies in this list, e.g. THUNDER is awarded ATLANTIC 1941-44, but the AFO does not list her and the Commonwealth list states 1941-42, 1944. In BRCN 150 the award is listed as ATLANTIC 1940-45. Since NIPIGON did not commission until 1941, the NGO seems correct.

5. CANFORGEN 032/94 ADM (PER) 044/94 071700Z JUN 94. Aleutians Battle Honour.

6. CFSO 25/92 Gulf of St Lawrence Battle Honour awarded to Canadian warships.

7. CFSO 5/94 Gulf and Kuwait Battle Honour awarded to Canadian warships.

8. Memo 5400-34 (DHH Heritage Officer) 2 Nov 99 to A/CMS. Amended list of ships awarded the Gulf of St Lawrence Battle Honour.

Many naval reserve divisions rightly continue to display Battle Honours from the common Commonwealth list and will continue to do so until and unless paid off. Only one regular force ship is now entitled to display British-won honours and that is ORIOLE, e.g. DUNKIRK 1940. Reasons for this are explained in Chapter 2.

Battle Honours should be listed and displayed in the order won, which is normally seen by year dates. Where more than one award is listed for a given year, the rule still applies. Due to a lack of time for the necessary research, not all the honours noted below are so listed, e.g. PORT COLBORNE.

Knowledgeable readers may note that many of the ships listed here will probably never have their names used in the Canadian Navy again, e.g. LOCH ALVIE, MEON, TEME, etc. Further, as far as can be determined, the Royal Navy continues to use Canadian-won Battle Honours from the Second World War. This means that during that period Canadian seamen in HMC Ships such as MEON and COLLINGWOOD won Battle Honours for the Royal Navy.

As noted in Chapter 2, the 1988 decision to employ only Canadian-won Battle Honours has been taken. As can be seen by the descriptions written in the Ships Eligible column in Appendix T, however, the award of Battle Honours is at best a subjective matter. Less than four years after AFO 2565 was issued, for example, an Admiralty historian, P.K. Kemp, wrote a memo dated 26 Mar 1958 to his boss Cdr Rowbotham, Head of the Historical Section. To paraphrase the relevant sentence: when British Battle Honours were originally being compiled, some matters did not perhaps receive all the attention they deserved.

And when one nation—Britain, from its own perspective of some four hundred years of battles around the world—decides the awards for another nation—Canada, which can only really look back to 1939—the decisions made must be regarded with some degree of scepticism. Take the award for the Battle of the Atlantic from 1939 to 1945 as one example. The fighting around Britain was divided into several areas; North Sea, English Channel, Biscay. Everything else in the Atlantic north of the equator, including operations in the Caribbean, east coast of the USA, Gulf of St Lawrence and the Irish Sea, were covered by one award.

In the author's opinion, a review of all Canadian naval awards needs to be undertaken from a Canadian perspective. The Gulf of St Lawrence award in 1992, revised in 1999, is an example of such a review. Another is the fact that for Vietnam service in the 1970s, the RAN Naval Board, not the Admiralty, issued a Battle Honour to Australian ships so entitled. Periodically, a review of a given Naval Battle Honour occurs within NDHQ/DHH, which is the reason behind the DHH memo quoted in Record No. 7 above.

HMC Ships and their Battle Honours

AGASSIZ
ATLANTIC 1941–45
GULF OF ST LAWRENCE 1944

ALBERNI
ATLANTIC 1941–44
NORMANDY 1944
NORTH SEA 1944

ALGOMA
ATLANTIC 1941–44
ENGLISH CHANNEL 1945

ALGONQUIN
NORWAY 1944
NORMANDY 1944
ARCTIC 1944–45

AMHERST
ATLANTIC 1941–45
GULF OF ST LAWRENCE 1944

ANNAN
ATLANTIC 1944
NORTH SEA 1944

ANNAPOLIS
ATLANTIC 1941–43

ANTIGONISH
GULF OF ST LAWRENCE 1944
ATLANTIC 1944–45

ARNPRIOR
ATLANTIC 1944–45

ARROWHEAD
ATLANTIC 1941–45
GULF OF ST LAWRENCE 1942, 1944

ARVIDA
ATLANTIC 1941–45

ASBESTOS
ATLANTIC 1944–45

ASSINIBOINE
ATLANTIC 1939–45
BISCAY 1944
ENGLISH CHANNEL 1944–45

ATHABASKAN
ARCTIC 1943–44
ENGLISH CHANNEL 1944
KOREA 1950–53
GULF AND KUWAIT/
GOLFE ET KUWAIT

ATHOLL
ATLANTIC 1944–45

BADDECK
ATLANTIC 1941–45
ENGLISH CHANNEL 1944–45
NORMANDY 1944

BARRIE
ATLANTIC 1941–45
ENGLISH CHANNEL 1942

BATTLEFORD
ATLANTIC 1941–45

BAYFIELD
ATLANTIC 1943–44
NORMANDY 1944

BEACON HILL
ATLANTIC 1944–45
ENGLISH CHANNEL 1944–45

BEAUHARNOIS
ATLANTIC 1944–45

BEAVER
ATLANTIC 1942

BELLEVILLE
ATLANTIC 1945

BITTERSWEET
ATLANTIC 1941–45

BLAIRMORE
ATLANTIC 1943, 1945
NORMANDY 1944

BORDER CITIES
ATLANTIC 1944–45

BOWMANVILLE
ATLANTIC 1944–45

BRANDON
ATLANTIC 1941–45
GULF OF ST LAWRENCE 1944

BRANTFORD
ATLANTIC 1943–44
GULF OF ST LAWRENCE 1942

BROCKVILLE
ATLANTIC 1943–45
GULF OF ST LAWRENCE 1942, 1944

BUCKINGHAM
ATLANTIC 1945

BUCTOUCHE
ATLANTIC 1941–45

BURLINGTON
ATLANTIC 1942–44
GULF OF ST LAWRENCE 1942

CALGARY
ATLANTIC 1942–45
BISCAY 1943
ENGLISH CHANNEL 1944–45
NORMANDY 1944
NORTH SEA 1945

CAMROSE
ATLANTIC 1941–45
GULF OF ST LAWRENCE 1944
NORMANDY 1944
NORTH SEA 1944
ENGLISH CHANNEL 1945

CANSO
ATLANTIC 1944
NORMANDY 1944

CAP DE LA MADELEINE
ATLANTIC 1945

CAPE BRETON
ARCTIC 1944
NORMANDY 1944
ATLANTIC 1944–45

CAPILANO
ATLANTIC 1944–45

CARAQUET
ATLANTIC 1943–44
NORMANDY 1944

CARLPLACE
ATLANTIC 1945

CAYUGA
KOREA 1950–52

CHAMBLY
ATLANTIC 1941–45

CHARLOTTETOWN
ATLANTIC 1942
GULF OF ST LAWRENCE 1942, 1944

CHAUDIERE
ATLANTIC 1944
NORMANDY 1944
BISCAY 1944

CHEBOGUE
ATLANTIC 1944

CHEDABUCTO
ATLANTIC 1942–43
GULF OF ST LAWRENCE 1942

CHICOUTIMI
ATLANTIC 1941–44

CHILLIWACK
ATLANTIC 1941–45

CLAYOQUOT
ATLANTIC 1942, 1944
GULF OF ST LAWRENCE 1942

COATICOOK
ATLANTIC 1944–45
GULF OF ST LAWRENCE 1944

COBALT
ATLANTIC 1941–45

COBOURG
ATLANTIC 1944–45

COLLINGWOOD
ATLANTIC 1941–44

COLUMBIA
ATLANTIC 1940–44

COMOX
ATLANTIC 1940–45

COPPER CLIFF
ATLANTIC 1944–45
NORTH SEA 1944

COWICHAN
ATLANTIC 1941–43
NORMANDY 1944

CRUSADER
KOREA 1952–53

DAUPHIN
ATLANTIC 1941–45

DAWSON
ALEUTIANS 1942–43
ATLANTIC 1944–45
GULF OF ST LAWRENCE 1944

DIGBY
ATLANTIC 1942–44
GULF OF ST LAWRENCE 1942, 1944

DRUMHELLER
ATLANTIC 1941–45
ENGLISH CHANNEL 1944–45
NORMANDY 1944

DRUMMONDVILLE
ATLANTIC 1942–43, 1945
GULF OF ST LAWRENCE 1942

DUNDAS
ATLANTIC 1942–45

DUNVEGAN
ATLANTIC 1941–44

DUNVER
ATLANTIC 1943–45

EASTVIEW
ATLANTIC 1944–45

EDMUNSTON
ATLANTIC 1942–45
BISCAY 1943

ELK
GULF OF ST LAWRENCE 1942

ESQUIMALT
GULF OF ST LAWRENCE 1942
ATLANTIC 1943–44

ETTRICK
ATLANTIC 1943–45
GULF OF ST LAWRENCE 1944

EYEBRIGHT
ATLANTIC 1941–45

FENNEL
ATLANTIC 1941–45

FERGUS
ATLANTIC 1945

FOREST HILL
ATLANTIC 1944

FORT FRANCES
ATLANTIC 1945

FORT WILLIAM
GULF OF ST LAWRENCE 1942
ATLANTIC 1943
NORMANDY 1944

FRASER
ATLANTIC 1939–40

FREDERICTON
ATLANTIC 1942–45

FRENCH
GULF OF ST LAWRENCE 1942

FRONTENAC
ATLANTIC 1944–45

FUNDY
ATLANTIC 1939–45

GALT
ATLANTIC 1941–45

GANANOQUE
ATLANTIC 1942–45
GULF OF ST LAWRENCE 1942

GASPE
ATLANTIC 1939–45

GATINEAU
ATLANTIC 1943–44
NORMANDY 1944

GEORGIAN
ATLANTIC 1941–42, 1944
GULF OF ST LAWRENCE 1942
NORMANDY 1944

GIFFARD
ATLANTIC 1944

GLACE BAY
ATLANTIC 1944–45

GODERICH
ATLANTIC 1942–45

GRANBY
ATLANTIC 1942–44
GULF OF ST LAWRENCE 1942

GRANDMERE
GULF OF ST LAWRENCE 1942
ATLANTIC 1943, 1945

GROU
ARCTIC 1944
ATLANTIC 1944
NORMANDY 1944

GUELPH
ATLANTIC 1944–45

GUYSBOROUGH
ATLANTIC 1943–44
NORMANDY 1944

HAIDA
ARCTIC 1943–45
ENGLISH CHANNEL 1944
BISCAY 1944
NORMANDY 1944
KOREA 1952–53

HALIFAX
ATLANTIC 1942–45

HALLOWELL
ATLANTIC 1944–45

HAMILTON
ATLANTIC 1942–43

HAWKESBURY
ATLANTIC 1944–45

HEPATICA
ATLANTIC 1940–45
GULF OF ST LAWRENCE 1942

HESPELER
ATLANTIC 1944–45

HUMBERSTONE
ATLANTIC 1944–45

HUNTSVILLE
ATLANTIC 1944–45

HURON
ARCTIC 1943–45
ENGLISH CHANNEL 1944
NORMANDY 1944
KOREA 1951–53

HUSKY
ATLANTIC 1940

INGONISH
ATLANTIC 1944
GULF OF ST LAWRENCE 1944

IROQUOIS
ATLANTIC 1943
ARCTIC 1943–45
BISCAY 1943–44
NORWAY 1945
KOREA 1952–53

JOLIETTE
ATLANTIC 1944

JONQUIERE
ATLANTIC 1944

KAMLOOPS
ATLANTIC 1941, 1943–45
GULF OF ST LAWRENCE 1942

KAMSACK
ATLANTIC 1942–45

KAPUSKASING
ATLANTIC 1944–45

KENOGAMI
ATLANTIC 1941–45
GULF OF ST LAWRENCE 1942

KENORA
ATLANTIC 1942–45
GULF OF ST LAWRENCE 1942
NORMANDY 1944

KENTVILLE
GULF OF ST LAWRENCE 1942
ATLANTIC 1944–45

KINCARDINE
ATLANTIC 1944–45

KITCHENER
ATLANTIC 1942–43
GULF OF ST LAWRENCE 1942
ENGLISH CHANNEL 1944–45
NORMANDY 1944

KOKANEE
ATLANTIC 1944–45
GULF OF ST LAWRENCE 1944

KOOTENAY
ATLANTIC 1943–45
NORMANDY 1944
ENGLISH CHANNEL 1944
BISCAY 1944

LACHINE
ATLANTIC 1942–45
GULF OF ST LAWRENCE 1942

LACHUTE
ATLANTIC 1945

LA HULLOISE
ATLANTIC 1945
NORTH SEA 1945

LANARK
ATLANTIC 1944–45

LA MALBAIE
ATLANTIC 1942–45
GULF OF ST LAWRENCE 1942, 1944

LASALLE
GULF OF ST LAWRENCE 1944
ATLANTIC 1945

LAUZON
ATLANTIC 1944–45

LEAMINGTON
ARCTIC 1942
ATLANTIC 1944–45

LEASIDE
ATLANTIC 1944–45

LETHBRIDGE
ATLANTIC 1941–45
GULF OF ST LAWRENCE 1942, 1944

LEVIS
ATLANTIC 1941, 1944–45
GULF OF ST LAWRENCE 1944

LINDSAY
ATLANTIC 1944–45
ENGLISH CHANNEL 1944
NORMANDY 1944

LOCH ACHANALT
ENGLISH CHANNEL 1945

LOCH ALVIE
ARCTIC 1944–45
ENGLISH CHANNEL 1945

LONG BRANCH
ATLANTIC 1944–45

LOCKEPORT
GULF OF ST LAWRENCE 1944

LONGUEUIL
ATLANTIC 1944–45

LOUISBURG
ATLANTIC 1941–42, 1944–45
ENGLISH CHANNEL 1944–45
NORMANDY 1944

LUNENBURG
ATLANTIC 1942–45
GULF OF ST LAWRENCE 1942
NORTH AFRICA 1942–3
ENGLISH CHANNEL 1944
NORMANDY 1944

MAGOG
GULF OF ST LAWRENCE 1944

MAHONE
ATLANTIC 1942, 1944–45

MALPEQUE
ATLANTIC 1941–42
NORMANDY 1944

MARGAREE
ATLANTIC 1940

MATANE
ATLANTIC 1944
NORMANDY 1944
ARCTIC 1945

MATAPEDIA
ATLANTIC 1941–45
GULF OF ST LAWRENCE 1944

MAYFLOWER
ATLANTIC 1941–43
NORMANDY 1944
ENGLISH CHANNEL 1945

MEDICINE HAT
ATLANTIC 1943
GULF OF ST LAWRENCE 1944

MEON
ATLANTIC 1944–45
GULF OF ST LAWRENCE 1944
ENGLISH CHANNEL 1944
NORMANDY 1944

MELVILLE
GULF OF ST LAWRENCE 1944

MERRITTONIA
ATLANTIC 1945

MIDDLESEX
ATLANTIC 1944–45

MIDLAND
GULF OF ST LAWRENCE 1944

MILLTOWN
ATLANTIC 1942–44
GULF OF ST LAWRENCE 1942
NORMANDY 1944

MIMICO
NORMANDY 1944
ATLANTIC 1945
ENGLISH CHANNEL 1945

MINAS
ATLANTIC 1941–44
NORMANDY 1944

MONCTON
ATLANTIC 1942–43

MONNOW
ARCTIC 1944
ATLANTIC 1944–45
NORTH SEA 1945

MONTREAL
ATLANTIC 1944–45

MOOSE JAW
ATLANTIC 1941–43
ENGLISH CHANNEL 1944–45
NORMANDY 1944

MORDEN
ATLANTIC 1941–45

MULGRAVE
GULF OF ST LAWRENCE 1942
ATLANTIC 1943–44
NORMANDY 1944

NANAIMO
ATLANTIC 1941–44
GULF OF ST LAWRENCE 1944

NAPANEE
ATLANTIC 1941–45

NENE
ARCTIC 1944–45
ATLANTIC 1944
NORTH SEA 1945

NEW GLASGOW
ATLANTIC 1944–45

NEW WESTMINSTER
ATLANTIC 1942–45

NEW WATERFORD
ATLANTIC 1944

NIAGARA
ATLANTIC 1940–44

NIPIGON
ATLANTIC 1941–45
GULF OF ST LAWRENCE 1942, 1944

NOOTKA
KOREA 1951–52

NORANDA
ATLANTIC 1943–45
GULF OF ST LAWRENCE 1942

NORSYD
ATLANTIC 1944–45
GULF OF ST LAWRENCE 1944

NORTH BAY
ATLANTIC 1944–45

OAKVILLE
ATLANTIC 1942–45

ORANGEVILLE
ATLANTIC 1944–45

ORILLIA
ATLANTIC 1941–45

ORKNEY
GULF OF ST LAWRENCE 1944

OSHAWA
ATLANTIC 1944–45

OTTAWA
ATLANTIC 1939–45
NORMANDY 1944
ENGLISH CHANNEL 1944
BISCAY 1944

OUTREMONT
ATLANTIC 1944
ARCTIC 1944
NORMANDY 1944

OWEN SOUND
ATLANTIC 1944–45

PARRSBORO
ENGLISH CHANNEL 1942
ATLANTIC 1943
NORMANDY 1944

PARRY SOUND
ATLANTIC 1944–45

PENETANG
ATLANTIC 1945

PETERBOROUGH
ATLANTIC 1944–45

PETROLIA
ATLANTIC 1944–45

PICTOU
ATLANTIC 1941–45

PORT ARTHUR
ATLANTIC 1942–44
GULF OF ST LAWRENCE 1942
MEDITERRANEAN 1943
NORMANDY 1944
ENGLISH CHANNEL 1945

PORT COLBORNE
ARCTIC 1944
ATLANTIC 1944–45
ENGLISH CHANNEL 1944
NORMANDY 1944
NORTH SEA 1945

PORT HOPE
GULF OF ST LAWRENCE 1942
ATLANTIC 1943–45

PORTAGE
ATLANTIC 1944–45

POUNDMAKER
ATLANTIC 1944–45

PRESCOTT
ATLANTIC 1941–45
NORTH AFRICA 1942–3
ENGLISH CHANNEL 1944–45
GULF OF ST LAWRENCE 1944
NORMANDY 1944

PRINCE DAVID
ATLANTIC 1941
ALEUTIANS 1942
AEGEAN 1943–4
NORMANDY 1944
SOUTH FRANCE 1944

PRINCE HENRY
ALEUTIANS 1942
AEGEAN 1943–4
SOUTH FRANCE 1944

PRINCE ROBERT
ALEUTIANS 1942
ATLANTIC 1943–44
ENGLISH CHANNEL 1944

PRINCE RUPERT
ATLANTIC 1944

PROTECTEUR
GOLF AND KUWAIT/GOLFE ET KUWAIT

PUNCHER, HMS
ATLANTIC 1944

QU'APPELLE
ATLANTIC 1944
NORMANDY 1944
BISCAY 1944

QUESNEL
ATLANTIC 1942–45
GULF OF ST LAWRENCE 1944

QUINTE
ATLANTIC 1941–42

RACCOON
GULF OF ST LAWRENCE 1942

RED DEER
ATLANTIC 1942–45

REGINA
ATLANTIC 1942–44
GULF OF ST LAWRENCE 1942
MEDITERRANEAN 1943
ENGLISH CHANNEL 1944
NORMANDY 1944

REINDEER
ATLANTIC 1940
GULF OF ST LAWRENCE 1942

RESTIGOUCHE
ATLANTIC 1939–45
NORTH SEA 1940
MEDITERRANEAN 1943
NORMANDY 1944
BISCAY 1944

RIMOUSKI
ATLANTIC 1942–45
ENGLISH CHANNEL 1944–45
NORMANDY 1944

RIVIERE DU LOUP
ATLANTIC 1944–45
GULF OF ST LAWRENCE 1944

ROCKCLIFFE
ATLANTIC 1945

ROSTHERN
ATLANTIC 1941–45

RUNNEYMEDE
ATLANTIC 1944–45

SACKVILLE
ATLANTIC 1942–44

SAGUENAY
ATLANTIC 1939–42

ST BONIFACE
ATLANTIC 1944–45

ST CATHARINES
ATLANTIC 1943–44

ST CLAIR
ATLANTIC 1943–44

ST CROIX
ATLANTIC 1940–43

ST FRANCIS
ATLANTIC 1941–43

ST LAMBERT
ATLANTIC 1944–45

ST LAURENT
ATLANTIC 1939–45
NORMANDY 1944

SAINT JOHN
ARCTIC 1944
ATLANTIC 1944
ENGLISH CHANNEL 1944
NORMANDY 1944
NORTH SEA 1945

ST PIERRE
ARCTIC 1945
ATLANTIC 1945

ST STEPHEN
ATLANTIC 1944–45

ST THOMAS
ATLANTIC 1944–45

STE THERESE
GULF OF ST LAWRENCE 1944
ATLANTIC 1945
NORTH SEA 1945

SARNIA
ATLANTIC 1942–43
GULF OF ST LAWRENCE 1942

SASKATCHEWAN
ATLANTIC 1943–44
NORMANDY 1944
BISCAY 1944

SASKATOON
ATLANTIC 1942–45

SAULT STE MARIE
ATLANTIC 1944–45

SHAWINIGAN
ATLANTIC 1942–44
GULF OF ST LAWRENCE 1942, 1944

SHEDIAC
ATLANTIC 1941–44

SHERBROOKE
ATLANTIC 1941–45

SIOUX
NORMANDY 1944
ARCTIC 1944–45
ATLANTIC 1945
KOREA 1950–52

SKEENA
ATLANTIC 1939–44
NORMANDY 1944
BISCAY 1944

SMITHS FALLS
ATLANTIC 1945

SNOWBERRY
ATLANTIC 1941–44
BISCAY 1943
GULF OF ST LAWRENCE 1944
ENGLISH CHANNEL 1945

SOREL
ATLANTIC 1941–45
NORTH SEA 1942

SPIKENARD
ATLANTIC 1941–42

SPRINGHILL
GULF OF ST LAWRENCE 1944

STETTLER
GULF OF ST LAWRENCE 1944

STONE TOWN
ATLANTIC 1944–45

STORMONT
ARCTIC 1944
ATLANTIC 1944–45
ENGLISH CHANNEL 1944
NORMANDY 1944

STRATFORD
ATLANTIC 1942–44
GULF OF ST LAWRENCE 1942

STRATHADAM
ATLANTIC 1945

STRATHROY
ATLANTIC 1945

SUDBURY
ATLANTIC 1941–44

SUMMERSIDE
ATLANTIC 1941–44
GULF OF ST LAWRENCE 1942, 1944
ENGLISH CHANNEL 1944–45
NORMANDY 1944

SUSSEXVALE
ATLANTIC 1945
ENGLISH CHANNEL 1945

SWANSEA
ATLANTIC 1943–44
NORMANDY 1944
ENGLISH CHANNEL 1944

SWIFT CURRENT
ATLANTIC 1943–44
GULF OF ST LAWRENCE 1944

TERRA NOVA
GULF AND KUWAIT/GOLFE
ET KUWAIT

TEME
NORMANDY 1944

THE PAS
ATLANTIC 1942–33

THETFORD MINES
GULF OF ST LAWRENCE 1944
ATLANTIC 1945
NORTH SEA 1945

THORLOCK
ATLANTIC 1945

THUNDER
ATLANTIC 1941–44
NORMANDY 1944
ENGLISH CHANNEL 1944–45

TILLSONBURG
ATLANTIC 1944–45

TIMMINS
ATLANTIC 1942–45

TORONTO
GULF OF ST LAWRENCE 1944

TRAIL
ATLANTIC 1941–45
GULF OF ST LAWRENCE 1942

TRANSCONA
ATLANTIC 1943–45

TRENTONIAN
ATLANTIC 1944
ENGLISH CHANNEL 1944–45
NORMANDY 1944

TRILLIUM
ATLANTIC 1940–45

TROIS RIVIERES
ATLANTIC 1942–43
GULF OF ST LAWRENCE 1942, 1944

TRURO
ATLANTIC 1942–45
GULF OF ST LAWRENCE 1942, 1944

UGANDA
OKINAWA 1945

UNGAVA
ATLANTIC 1941–45
GULF OF ST LAWRENCE 1944

VALLEYFIELD
ATLANTIC 1944

VANCOUVER
ALEUTIANS 1942–43
ATLANTIC 1944–45

VEGREVILLE
GULF OF ST LAWRENCE 1942
ATLANTIC 1944

VICTORIAVILLE
ATLANTIC 1945

VILLE DE QUEBEC
ATLANTIC 1942–44
GULF OF ST LAWRENCE 1942
MEDITERRANEAN 1943
ENGLISH CHANNEL 1944–45

VISON
GULF OF ST LAWRENCE 1942

WALLACEBURG
ATLANTIC 1944–45

WASAGA
ATLANTIC 1944
NORMANDY 1944

WASKESIU
ATLANTIC 1943–45
ARCTIC 1944
NORMANDY 1944

WENTWORTH
ATLANTIC 1944–45

WEST YORK
ATLANTIC 1945

WESTMOUNT
  GULF OF ST LAWRENCE 1942
  ATLANTIC 1944

WETASKIWIN
  ATLANTIC 1941–45
  GULF OF ST LAWRENCE 1944

WEYBURN
  ATLANTIC 1942
  GULF OF ST LAWRENCE 1942
  NORTH AFRICA 1942–43

WINDFLOWER
  ATLANTIC 1941

WINNIPEG
  ATLANTIC 1943–45

WHITETHROAT
  ATLANTIC 1945

WOODSTOCK
  ATLANTIC 1942–44
  GULF OF ST LAWRENCE 1942
  NORTH AFRICA 1942–3
  ENGLISH CHANNEL 1944
  NORMANDY 1944

APPENDIX T

SECOND WORLD WAR & KOREA: BATTLE HONOUR PARAMETERS

This information has been extracted mainly from Admiralty Fleet Order 2565/64, 1 Oct 1954, "Battle Honours for HM Ships and Fleet Air Arm Squadrons" which included RCN ships.

Selected Battle Honours from the common Commonwealth list pertaining to the RCN:

Area Battle Honour	Years	Area Limits	Ships Eligible
ATLANTIC	1939–45	The North Atlantic, from the Equator to the Arctic Circle.	All ships and submarines which were employed as escorts to ocean convoys in the North Atlantic, and also those ships of Support Groups which took part in a successful action.
BISCAY	1940–45	Between the latitudes of Ushant and Cape Ortegal from 12W to the coast of France	Ships and submarines which were employed on patrol duty in the area and took part in a successful action. The interception and sinking of enemy blockade runners is not a qualification for the award.

Area Battle Honour	Years	Area Limits	Ships Eligible
NORTH SEA	1939–45	The North Sea and all waters to the eastward, between Southend and the Shetland Islands, except coastal waters of Norway.	All ships which were employed as escorts to coastal convoys on the East Coast of the UK. Also ships and submarines which were employed on patrol duty in the area and took part in a successful action.
ENGLISH CHANNEL	1939–45	The Channel and all waters on the South Coast of Britain between Southend and Bristol, the western limit being a line drawn from Ushant to the Scilly Islands, and thence to the North Coast of Cornwall.	All ships which were employed as escorts to Channel coastal convoys, and also other ships and submarines which took part in a successful action in the area. Successes achieved in connection with Operation Neptune are recognized by NORMANDY.
NORWAY	1940–45	The coastal waters of Norway, as far north as the latitude of Tromso.	All ships and submarines which were engaged in the Norway operations from 8 April to 8 June 1940, and also those which took part in a successful action in these waters at later dates. Recognition of Fleet Air Arm attacks, such as those on *Tirpitz*, is normally restricted to the carriers and air squadrons concerned; the covering escorts on those occasions are not eligible for the award.
ARCTIC	1941–45	Within the Arctic Circle, except for the coastal waters of Norway to the southward of Tromso.	All ships, including the covering forces which were employed as escorts to or in support of the convoys running to and from North Russia; also those ships and submarines which operated in the area and took part in a successful action.

Area Battle Honour	Years	Area Limits	Ships Eligible
MEDITER-RANEAN	1940–45	The whole of the Mediterranean, the western limit being a line joining Cape Spartel and Cape Trafalgar.	All ships and submarines which took part in successful actions that are not covered by any of the named Battle Honours for area. That is to say, the destruction of an enemy ship or submarine which was effected during and in connection with a recognised campaign, e.g. SICILY 1943, is regarded as an incidental item of the campaign, and not as qualifying for a separate award. If, however, the success was unconnected with any named operation for which a Battle Honour is granted, then it will qualify for the general award of MEDITERRANEAN with the year date(s). Minor bombardments will also qualify for this award.
AEGEAN	1943–44	All waters of the Aegean Archipelago between 35 to 42 N and 22 to 30 E.	Ships and vessels which were engaged with the enemy in the area between 7 Sep and 28 Nov 1943, and also during 1944.
OKINAWA	1945	The Far East.	All ships and submarines which are mentioned in the published dispatch as having taken part in Operation Iceberg.
KOREA	1950–53	Not known	All ships under United Nations command which took part in operations against Communist forces in Korea between 2 July 1950 and 27 July 1953

Second World War Fleet Actions, Campaigns, etc.

Action/Campaign	Dates
SICILY 1943	10 July–17 August 1943
NORTH AFRICA 1942–43	8 November 1942–20 February 1943
NORMANDY 1944	6 June–3 July 1944
SOUTH FRANCE 1944	1–27 August 1944

APPENDIX U

MARCORD 10-2, PARTIAL

This is an extract of the relevant four of eleven pages of the MARCORD (Maritime Command Orders), as updated and promulgated in 1999.

MARCORD 10-2

VOLUME 1

OPI: N33

MARITIME COMMAND ORDERS
SHIPS' STANDARD IDENTIFICATION SYSTEM

PURPOSE

1. This order sets out the policy and procedures for the identification and naming of Her Majesty's Canadian Ships (HMC Ships), Canadian Forces Auxiliary Vessels (CFAVs), Yardcraft and Naval Reserve Divisions (NRDs).

SCOPE

2. The identification system described in this order covers all military and civilian manned vessels operated by the Canadian Forces (CF) and the Department of National Defence (DND).

DEFINITIONS

3. The terms used in the identification system are as follows:

   a. **SHIP TYPE** means a category of ship which conforms to a stated purpose, size, role or capability (destroyer);

   b. **SHIP CLASS** means a group of ships built to a standard design. The ships of the class will normally be identified by the name of the lead ship of the class (IROQUOIS);

   c. **NATO STANDARD SHIP DESIGNATOR** means a functional designator consisting of not more than five letters specific to the role or capabilities of a vessel (DDH). The details of this system are contained in STANAG 1166 (Standard Ship Designator System);

   d. **HULL NUMBER** means the number used to identify individual ships in a class. It will usually be of three digits and will be assigned sequentially based on keel laying dates (280);

e. **IDENTIFIERS** means the combination of the NATO Standard Ship Designator and the hull number assigned to the vessel (DDH 280); and

f. **OFFICIAL NAME** means the ship name approved by the Minister (HMCS IROQUOIS).

IDENTIFICATION PROCEDURES

4. All DND vessels shall be assigned NATO identifiers and, where appropriate, official names. All HMC Ships and NRDs shall be named. Auxiliary vessels that proceed to sea in the normal course of their duties shall also be named. Harbour, yard or landing craft and other such vessels may also receive names. All DND ships are preceded by a title, usually abbreviated:

a. HMCS for warships and NRDs; and

b. CFAV for auxiliaries.

5. Current official names and ship identifiers are listed in Appendix A. Identification of ships in the CF inventory will be in accordance with the following procedures:

a. IDENTIFIERS. Vessels will be assigned a NATO Standard Ship Designator and a hull number. The combination of designator and hull number is to produce an identifier which is to be unique within NATO. Identifier assignment is controlled by MARCOMHQ/N3 1-3 SSO FRC (Fleet Replacement Coordination); and

b. OFFICIAL NAMES. It is the responsibility of the Acquisition Project Director (APD) to initiate the identification process by informing SSO FRC of the type and number of vessels, purposes, size and the expected date of acquisition. SSO FRC will then solicit name proposals and convene the Ships' Names Committee (SNC) to review the proposals and make recommendations to the senior naval staff. Selected names will be staffed via the Maritime Commander and the Chief of the Defence Staff for endorsement, to the Minister of National Defence for approval.

6. Guidelines for name proposals are provided in Annex B.

SHIPS' NAMES COMMITTEE

7. The SNC will be under the chairmanship of Marcom HQ N3 1-3 SSO FRC. Any other interested group or person may be asked to join.

8. The purpose of this committee is to:

a. produce name proposals or evaluate suggestions and proposals put forward by interested parties for ships' names for all warships, auxiliaries, yardcraft and NRDs and other installations or facilities. The names of purchased or acquired vessels are also to be evaluated and, if found to be unsuitable, a recommendation on appropriate names is to be made. Guidance for warship and auxiliary vessel names is set out in Annex B;

b. evaluate proposals for official badges and mottos and make a recommendation on the selection of a final choice for Command endorsement; and

c. provide advice and guidance to the senior naval staff on any naming problems that may arise.

9. Lineages and battle honours associated with ships' names should be solicited from the Directorate of Military Traditions and History (DMTH) in NDHQ.

(OPI MARCOMHQ N31-3 SSO FRC)

Issued 1996

ORIGINAL

ANNEX B

VOLUME 1

GUIDELINES FOR OFFICIAL NAME PROPOSALS

I.   The following principles should be observed for class names:

a. Warships and Large Auxiliaries. Each class will normally be named after the leadship [sic] in that class (HALIFAX).

b. Small auxiliaries and yardcraft. Each class shall have either a descriptive or summary class name based on:

(1) the group of names themselves (Saint Class tugs);

(2) a syllable common to each name (Ville Class tugs); or

(3) a common first letter.

NOMENCLATURE

2. Although there have been many exceptions, the historical nomenclature trends for ships have been as follows:

a. aircraft carriers have been named after islands;

b. cruisers have been named after provinces;

c. destroyers have been named for rivers, native peoples or native language groupings;

d. frigates have been named for cities and towns;

e. minesweepers have been named for bays or coastal formations such as straits, basins, sounds, harbours or estuaries;

f. conventional submarines have been named for fish or other marine creatures, using local or common names where feasible;

g. replenishment vessels have been given names that describe or depict their roles;

h. maintenance vessels have been named for capes or peninsulas;

i. large auxiliaries have had functional names;

j. small auxiliaries and yardcraft have been named for smaller communities such as hamlets and dispersed villages; and

k. NRDs have been named after an historical vessel or historical figure that was connected with and exercised an influence upon the general area that the division serves.

3. In general, names proposed for HMC Ships and CFAVs should:

a. be immediately recognizable as Canadian;

b. sound pleasing to the ear;

c. be easy to pronounce;

d. not be liable to ridicule;

e. be easily distinguishable in both written and spoken form, from the names of other HMC Ships, other ships likely to be encountered and CF bases and stations;

f. be relatively short, less than 14 letters and space;

g. be appropriate to the type and size of ship. It is desirable that each type of ship be distinguishable by the names within that type;

h. where possible, have an historical or traditional past or connotations; and

i. where practicable, provide geographic and linguistic balance throughout a class.

4. In peacetime, it is not advisable to reuse the name of a ship lost or paid off for a considerable period of time.

5. Except for NRDs, names of persons or families are not used for HMC Ships, although ships may be named for geographical features, towns, etc, that are named for persons.

6. A ship purchased or acquired that already possesses a name, should have her original name submitted for an evaluation by the SNC. A recommendation shall then be forwarded to the senior naval staff as to whether or not the

original name should be retained. If not, suitable alternate names will be suggested by the Committee.

7. When submitting names to the SNC, the above guidelines should be taken into account when initiating a proposal.

Issued 1996

Some naval vessels live on: the former harbour craft EDNORINA at the fisherman's wharf, Victoria, 20 Aug 1994. (G Wragg. KM Coll.)

West coast ships returning from Australia 16 May 1978. On the right of the formation is KOOTENAY and on her left are TERRA NOVA, RESTIGOUCHE, PROVIDER, YUKON, SASKATCHEWAN and QU'APPELLE.

ABBREVIATIONS AND EXPRESSIONS

(A)	Atlantic Coast
A/	Assistant or Acting
A/A	Anti-aircraft
A/COPR	A/Chief of Operational Readiness, CFHQ
A/S	Anti-submarine
ACNS	Assistant Chief of the Naval Staff, NSHQ Ottawa
Admiralty	Royal Navy Headquarters, London, England
ASW	Anti-submarine Warfare
B	Indicates that an official Canadian badge has been devised.
B*	Badge, British. Indicates the ship had an official RN badge.
BATM	British Admiralty Technical Mission, Ottawa, Second World War.
BCPA	British Columbia Provincial Archives
BCPP	British Columbia Provincial Police
bldg	building
BRCN	Book of Reference, Canadian Navy
CANGEN	CF General message
CCCS	Captain (later Commodore) Commanding Canadian Ships and Establishments in the UK
CCNO	Canadian Confidential Naval Orders
CDS	Chief of the Defence Staff, CFHQ/NDHQ
CF	Canadian Forces
CFAO	CF Administrative Orders
CFAV	Canadian Forces Auxiliary Vessel
CFB	Canadian Forces Base
CFHQ	Canadian Forces Headquarters, Ottawa
CFP	Canadian Forces Publication
CFS	Canadian Forces Station
CFSO	Canadian Forces Supplemental Order
CGS	Canadian Government Ship (term used circa 1867–1939)

CinC	Commander in Chief
circa	about the year; used to indicate an approximate date
CMDO	Chief, Maritime Doctrine and Operations, NDHQ
CMS	Chief of the Maritime Staff, NDHQ
CN	Canadian Navy—used only in reference to contracts for vessel, e.g. CN 506
CNAV	Canadian Naval Auxiliary Vessel
CNS	Chief of the Naval Staff
CNTS(S)	Chief Naval Technical Services (Ships), NSHQ
CO	Commanding Officer
Co	Company or County
COAC	Commanding Officer Atlantic Coast
com'd	commissioned
COND	Commanding Officer, Naval Divisions
COPC	Commanding Officer Pacific Coast
COPR	Chief of Operational Readiness, CFHQ
CORD	Commanding Officer, Reserve Divisions
CPF	Canadian Patrol Frigate
CWAC	Canadian Women's Army Corps
D Hist	Directorate of History, NDHQ
D OPS	Director of Operations, CFHQ
D OPS(M)	Director of Operations (Maritime), CFHQ
D Sea	not known
D/MND	Deputy Minister of National Defence
DC or D Cer	Directorate of Ceremonial, NDHQ
Dept	Department
DG Ships	Director General Ships
DGFA	Director General of Fleet Accounting, NSHQ
DGMDO	Director General Maritime Doctrine and Operations, NDHQ
DGMF	Director General of Maritime Forces(?), CFHQ
DHH	Directorate of History and Heritage, NDHQ
DMOPR	Director Maritime Operations, Plans and Reserves, NDHQ
DMTH	Directorate of Military Traditions and Heritage, NDHQ
DN COMM	Director Naval Communications, NSHQ
DN Inf	Director Naval Information Services, NSHQ
DND	Department of National Defence
DNP	Director of Naval Personnel, NSHQ
DNPO	Director Naval Plans & Operations, NSHQ
DOD	Director Operations Division, NSHQ
DOT	Department of Transportation
DPW	Department of Public Works

DRB	Defence Research Board	LF	long foc'sle (referring to a Corvette)
DS DIV	Director Signals Division, NSHQ	M/S	Minesweeper
DSS	Director of Special Services, NSHQ, Second World War	MARCOM	Maritime Command
		MARCORD	Maritime Command Order
est'd	established	MARLANT	Maritime Command, Atlantic
F.R.	Fishermen's Reserve		
FAA	Fleet Air Arm	MARPAC	Maritime Command, Pacific
FOAC	Flag Officer Atlantic Coast	MB	Motor Boat
FOIC	Flag Officer in Charge	MCDV	Maritime Coastal Defence Vessel, the Kingston class.
FOPC	Flag Officer Pacific Coast		
Fr	French	MND	Minister of Marine & Fisheries and of the Naval Service, 1910–1921;
Geog	geographical		
gov't	Government		
GV	Gate Vessel		Minister of National Defence, 1921–1940;
HC	Harbour craft		
HDPC	Harbour defence patrol craft		Minister of National Defence for Naval Services, 1940–46;
HFDF	High Frequency Direction Finding		
HMAS	His/Her Majesty's Australian Ship		Minister of National Defence, 1946–present
		ML	Motor Launch
HMC NRS	His/Her Majesty's Canadian Naval Radio Station	MTB	Motor Torpedo Boat
		MV	Motor Vessel
HMCS	His/Her Majesty's Canadian Ship	N Sec't	naval secretary
		N*	on entering naval service, vessel retained original name
HMIS	His/Her Majesty's Indian Ship		
HMNZS	His/Her Majesty's New Zealand Ship	N.O.	Naval Monthly/Routine/General Orders, circa 1930–1949
HMS	His/Her Majesty's Ship		
HPC	Harbour patrol craft	n/k	not known
HQ	Headquarters	NCSM	Navire canadien de sa Majesté

NDHQ	National Defence Headquarters, Ottawa
NOIC	Naval Officer in Charge
NRS	Naval Radio Station
NSHQ	Naval Service Headquarters, Ottawa
NW/TS	Naval Wireless/Telegraphy Station
o/c	on completion
OIC	Officer in Charge
(P)	Pacific Coast
pd. no.	pennant number
PMO	Project Management Office
PNO	Principal Naval Overseer
PV	Patrol Vessel
RCAF	Royal Canadian Air Force
RCASC	Royal Canadian Army Service Corps
RCN	Royal Canadian Navy
RCNR	Royal Canadian Naval Reserve
RCNVR	Royal Canadian Naval Volunteer Reserve
RCSC	Royal Canadian Sea Cadets
Ret'd	Retired
RN	Royal Navy
RNAS	Royal Naval Air Service
RNCAS	Royal Naval Canadian Air Service
RNCVR	Royal Naval Canadian Volunteer Reserve
RNethN	Royal Netherlands Navy
RNorN	Royal Norwegian Navy
RNR	Royal Naval Reserve
SB	Special Branch
SCNO	Senior Canadian Naval Officer
Sec't	secretary
SF	short foc'sle (referring to a corvette)
Ship	a vessel or establishment in commission
[sic]	thus used, e.g. word or phrase was used in the manner indicated
SIS	still in service
SNC	Ships' Names Committee, 1987–1995
SNO	Senior Naval Officer
SNOIC	Senior Naval Officer in Charge
SO STATS	Staff Officer Statistics, NSHQ
SSO	Senior Staff Officer
TE	Training Establishment
TRUMP	Tribal Class Modernization & Update Project, 1985–96 (for the Iroquois Class)
USN	United States Navy
USS	United States Ship
VCDS	Vice Chief of the Defence Staff, CFHQ/NDHQ
VCNS	Vice Chief of the Naval Staff, NSHQ
W/T	Wireless/Telegraphy
WRCNS	Women's Royal Canadian Naval Service (pronounced "wrens")
YFP	yard craft

Bibliography

Published Sources: Books

Alden, John D. *Flush Decks and Four Pipes*. Annapolis, Maryland: US Naval Institute, 1965.

Arbuckle, Lt(N) Graeme. *Customs and Traditions of the Canadian Navy*. Halifax: Nimbus Publishing, 1985.

Arbuckle, Lt(N) Graeme. *Badges of the Canadian Navy*. Halifax: Nimbus Publishing, 1987.

Armstrong, G.H. *The Origin and Meaning of Place Names in Canada*. Toronto: Macmillan, 1972.

Atlas and Gazetteer of Canada. Ottawa: Queen's Printer, 1969.

Badges of the Canadian Forces. CFP 267. Ottawa, Department of National Defence, 1976.

Battle Honours for H.M. Ships and Fleet Air Arm Squadrons. Admiralty Fleet Order 2565/54, 1 Oct 1954.

Boutilier, James A, Ed. *RCN in Retrospect, 1910-1968*. Vancouver: University of British Columbia Press, 1982.

Brice, Martin H. *The Tribals, Biography of a Destroyer Class*. London: Ian Allan, 1971.

Canadian Navy List. Ottawa: King's/Queen's Printer. Various editions.

Ceremonial Manual—HMC Ships. Maritime Command, 1 Aug 1984.

CF Administrative Order 36-7, Annex B. Class Designators, Type Indicator and Hull Number of HMC Ships. 15/81, and subsequent editions.

Confidential Canadian Navy Orders. Ottawa: King's Printer. Various editions.

e O class submarines in Bedford Basin in the 1990's.

Colledge, J.J. *Ships of the Royal Navy: An Historical Index*, Volumes 1 & 2. Newton Abbott, Devon: David & Charles, 1969 - 1970.

Colledge. J.J. *Ships of the Royal Navy: The Complete Record*, Volumes 1 and 2. London: Greenhill Books, 1987.

Conway's All the World's Warship's, 1860-1905. New York: Mayflower Books Inc., 1979.

Corbet, E. *Calgary's Stone Frigate*. Century Calgary Publications, 1975.

Cunningham, Viscount. *A Sailor's Odyssey*. London: Hutchinson, 1952.

Ditmar, F.J., & J.J. Colledge, *British Warships, 1914-1969*. London: Ian Allan, 1972.

Elliott, Peter. *Allied Escort Ships of World War II*. London: Eyre & Spottiswoode, 1963.

Essex, James B. *Victory in the St. Lawrence*. Erin, Ont: Boston Mills Press, 1984.

Flags, Ensigns, Colours, Pennants and Honours for the Canadian Forces, CFP 200. Ottawa: Department of National Defence, 1980.

From White Caps to Contrails. 1981.

Gazetteer of Canada. Ottawa: Energy, Mines & Resources Canada, various volumes, 1966-1974.

Gregory, Walter. *Memories of HMCS TRENTONIAN*. 1979.

Hadley, Michael L. *U-Boats Against Canada*. Kingston: Queen's University Press, 1985.

Harder, Kelsie B. *Illustrated Dictionary of Place Names*. New York: Van Nostrand Reinhold Co.

Hodges, Peter. *Tribal Class Destroyers*. London: Altmark Publishing Co., 1971.

Honours, Flags and Heritage Structure of the Canadian Forces, CFP A-AD-200-000/AG-00, Chapter 3. Ottawa: Department of National Defence, to be published in the year 2000.

Huntford, Roland. *Scott and Amunsen*. London: Hodder & Stoughton, 1979.

Jane's Fighting Ships. London: Sampson Low, Maiston & Co. Ltd., various editions.

Johnston, J.R. "Canadian U-Boat Commander." *Salty Dips*, Vol 2. Ottawa: Naval Officers' Association, 1985.

Kealy, J.D.F. and E.C. Russel, *History of Canadian Naval Aviation*. Ottawa: Queen's Printer, 1965.

Lamb, James B. *The Corvette Navy*. Scarborough: Macmillan, 1977.

Lawrence, Hal. *A Bloody War*. Scarborough: Macmillan, 1979.

Lawrence, Hal. *Tales of the North Atlantic*. Toronto: McClelland & Stewart, 1985.

Lay, RAdm H.N. *Memoirs of a Mariner*. Stittsville, Ontario: Canada's Wings, 1982.

Lenton, H.T. *British Escort Ships*. W.W.2 Fact Files. London: MacDonald and Jane's, 1974.

Lenton, H.T., & J.J. Colledge, "British and Dominion Fleet Losses." *Warship Losses of World War II*. London: Ian Allan, 1964.

Lenton, H.T., & J.J. Colledge, *Warships of World War II*. 2nd Edition. London: Ian Allan, 1973.

Longstaff, Maj F.V. *HMCS NADEN Naval Barracks*. Victoria: Saanich Peninsular & Gulf Islands Review, 1957.

Longstaff, Maj F.V. *The Esquimalt Naval Base*. Vancouver: Clarke & Stuart Co. Ltd., 1942.

Lynch, Mack, ed. *Salty Dips*, Volumes I, II & III. Ottawa: Love Printing, 1983, 1986?, 1988.

Lynch, Thomas G. *Canada's Flowers*. Halifax: Nimbus Publishing, 1981.

Lynch, Thomas G. *The Flying 400*. Halifax: Nimbus Publishing, 1983.

Lynch, Thomas G., ed. *Fading Memories: Canadian Sailors and the Battle of the Atlantic*. Halifax: The Atlantic Chief and Petty Officers Association, 1993.

Lynch, Thomas G. and James B. Lamb, *Gunshield Graffiti*. Halifax: Nimbus Publishing, 1984.

Macdonald, W.B. *At Sea and by Land, The Reminiscences of William Balfour Macdonald, RN*. Victoria: Sono Nis Press, 1983. Edited by S W Jackman.

Macpherson, K. *Canada's Fighting Ships*. Toronto: Samuel Stevens, Hakkert & Co., 1975.

Macpherson, K., & J. Burgess, *The Ships of Canada's Naval Forces 1910-1981*. Toronto: Collins, 1981.

Manning, Capt T.D., and Cdr C.F. Walker, *British Warship Names*. London: Putnam, 1959.

Manning, T.D. *The British Destroyer*. London: Putnam, 1951.

Manual of Customs and Traditions for the Canadian Navy. Victoria: Naval Officer Training Centre, 1981.

March, Edgar J. *British Destroyers, 1892-1953*. London: Seeley, Service & Co. Ltd., 1966.

McKee, Fraser. *The Armed Yachts of Canada*. Toronto: The Boston Mills Press, 1983.

McKee, Cdr (NR) Fraser M. *Volunteers for Sea Service*. Toronto: Houstons Standard Publications, 1973.

Milner, M. *Canada's Navy: The First Century*. Toronto: University of Toronto Press, 1999.

Milner, M. *HMCS Sackville, 1941-1985*. Halifax: Canadian Naval Memorial Trust, 1995.

Milner, M. *North Atlantic Run*. Toronto: University of Toronto Press, 1985.

Naval General Orders. Ottawa: King's/Queen's Printer. Various editions.

Naval Monthly Orders. Ottawa: King's Printer. Various editions.

Naval Routine Orders. Ottawa: King's Printer. Various editions.

Naval Service File Directory and Manual. BRCN 201, First Edition. Naval Headquarters, 1 Dec 1945.

Nelson, Lt. Col, F.D.H. and Dr. N.E. Oliver, *CFB Esquimalt, Military Heritage*. Esquimalt: Queen's Printer (?), 1982.

Particulars of Canadian War Vessels. C.B.(CAN) 0808 (January 1944). Ottawa: NSHQ, Jan 1944.

Paying Off of Ships. *Maritime Command Orders*, Volume 1, MARCORD 40-1.

Peck, Capt Donald. "The Gumboot Navy," in White, E (ed.), *Raincoast Chronicles Six/Ten*. Madeira Park, BC: Harbour Publishing, 1983.

Popp, Carol. *The Gumboot Navy*. Lanztville, BC: Oolichan Books, 1988.

Preston, Antony. *V and W Class Destroyers, 1917-1945*. London: Macdonald, 1971.

Raven, A., and Roberts, J. *British Cruisers of World War Two*. London(?): Naval Institute, 1980.

Report of the Department of National Defence of Canada (for various years). Ottawa: King's Printer.

Royal Canadian Navy Badges, Battle Honours, Mottoes. BRCN 150, Volumes 1 to 4. Ottawa: Naval Headquarters, 1964.

Royal Canadian Navy, Particulars of Canadian War Vessels. CBCN 8203. Ottawa: Naval Headquarters, 1 Mar 1963.

Russell, E.C. *Customs and Traditions of the Canadian Armed Forces*. Ottawa: Deneau Publishing, 1981.

Schull, Joseph. *The Far Distant Ships*. Ottawa: Department of National Defence, 1952.

Smith, Peter C. *Royal Navy Ship's Badges*. St Ives: Balfour Books, 1974.

Stuart, J.T. *Halifax's Citizen Naval Force*. 3 Jan 1984.

Summary of British Warships, BR642B. London: Admiralty, Jan 1944.

Swain, LCdr Hector. *History of the Naval Reserves in Newfoundland.* St John's: Provincial Archivist, 1975.

The Canadian Navy List. Ottawa: King's/Queen's Printer. Various years, 1914-1966.

"The HMCS Montcalm Story." Undated but circa 1956.

The Queen's Regulations and Orders for the Royal Canadian Navy. Vols I, II and III. Ottawa: Queen's Printer, 1952.

The Royal Military College of Canada Review. Kingston: RMC, June 1940.

The Stone Frigate 1914. Kingston: Royal Military College. *1941 Yearbook.*

Thomas, David A. *A Companion to the Royal Navy.* London: Harrap, 1988.

Thornton, J.M. *HMCS Discovery and Deadman's Island.* circa 1975.

Thorton, J.M. *The Big 'U'.* Vancouver, J.M. Thorton, 1983.

Tucker, Gilbert N. *The Naval Service of Canada* (2 Vols). Ottawa: Minister of National Defence, 1952.

Warner, Oliver. *Battle Honours of the Royal Navy.* London: George Philip & Son Ltd., 1956.

Warrilow, Betty. "NABOB, The First Canadian-Manned Aircraft Carrier." Owen Sound: Escort Carriers Association, 1989.

Weightman, A.E. *Heraldry in the Royal Navy.* Aldershot: Gale & Polder, 1957.

Welcome Aboard. Second Division, Canadian Training Squadron. Pamphlet, circa 1983.

Wilkinson, B.J., T.P. Stopford, and D. Taylor, *The A to Z of Royal Naval Ships' Badges 1919 - 1989.* Volumes 1 and 2. Orpington, Kent: Neptune Books, 1987 & 1989.

Young, John. *A Dictionary of Ships of the Royal Navy of the Second World War.* Cambridge, England: Patrick Stephens, 1975.

Published Sources - Periodicals

CF Communications System *Intercom*
  "CFS Mill Cove," Feb 1966
  "CFS Gloucester," Sep 1966
  "HMCS ALDERGROVE," Jun 1966.
Communications & Electronics *Newsletter*
  "CFS Masset," Sgt W.J. Wilson. 1976/2
  "Gander, Newfoundland and CFB Gander," CWO D. Cox. 1975/2.
Royal Canadian Navy Monthly Review—various articles but in particular:
  "Gaspé: The Story of a Base," Apr 1943, No. 16, p 12.

"HMCS BRUNSWICKER," Mar 1948, p 32-36.

"HMCS CARLETON," Apr 1948, p 34-38.

"HMCS GRIFFON," Jan-Feb 1948, p 46-50.

"HMCS QUEEN," May 1948, p 38-41.

"Insignia Descriptions," Sep 1942, No. 9, p 61-3.

"Practice of Naming Ships," Jan 1943, No. 13, p 56.

"RCN Insignia," Sep 1942, No. 9, p 59-60.

"RCN Insignia," Oct 1942, No. 10, p 7-8.

"Ships' Badges—Their Origin and Use," Jul 1942, No. 7, p 16-22.

The Bulletin, the newsletter of the Esquimalt Chief and Petty Officers' Association, various editions.

"Early Corvette Names," June 1998. LCdr D J Freeman (Ret'd).

"Canadian Warship Nomenclature," parts 1 and 2, Oct 1996 and May 1997. LCdr D J Freeman (Ret'd).

"HMCS BEACON HILL, Victoria's Own Warship," Aug/Sep1998. LCdr D J Freeman (Ret'd).

The Crowsnest—various articles but in particular:

"A Badge Comes Home," Anonymous. Feb 1961, p 5-8.

"A Home of Her Own for HMCS QUEEN," Anonymous. Aug 1955, p 20.

"A Letter from the Queen," Naval Historical Section. Oct 1964, p 14-16.

"A Navy for Canada," Cdr Robert A. Grosskurth. May-June 1960, p 26-29.

"A New Ship Commissions," Anonymous. Dec 1952, p 15.

"A Query about the Rainbow," Anonymous. Oct 1959, p 24.

"Badges and Battle Honours," E.C. Russell. Jun 1965, p 22-24.

"Barber Pole Sails Again," Anonymous. Apr 1962, p 4.

"Funnel Markings," Anonymous. Mar 1956.

"Heraldry on the High Seas," P.C. Apr 1956, p 13-15.

"HMCS BONAVENTURE Joins the Fleet," Anonymous. Feb 1957, p 4-7.

"HMCS NIAGARA," Anonymous. Nov 1952, p 4-6.

"Mottoes," Ph.Ch. Aug 1958, p 8-10.

"Naval Divisions Reduced to 16," Anonymous. Jan 1965.

"New Headquarters for PREVOST," Anonymous. Dec 1957.

"Niobe in the Valley," R.M.S. Sep 1960, p 11-13.

"Official Badges for RCN," Anonymous. Dec 1948, p 6-7; Feb 1949, p 32; Mar 1949, p 25; Apr 1949, p25; May 1949, p 29; Jun 1949, p 24; Jul 1949, p11; Aug

1949, p 23; Oct 1949, p 32; Nov 1949, p 35; Dec 1949, p 23; May 1950, p 32.

"Ojibwa's Badge," Anonymous. Mar - Apr 1965, p 30.

"Origins of Canadian Naval Law," Lt Cdr A.D. Taylor. Apr 1958, p 21-22.

"RCN Custodian of Fort Pepperrell," Anonymous. Oct 1961, p 13.

"Sailors in Eskimo Land," Anonymous. Jun 1955.

"Symbols and Ships," Lt Cdr (SB) Alan B. Beddoe. Aug 1961, p 5-9.

"The Big Cheese Deal," Anonymous. Feb 1957, p 7.

"The Commissioning of HMCS CARIBOU," Anonymous. Oct 1953, p 8-9.

"The Comox Story," Naval Historical Section. Mar 1958, p 12-17.

"The Cook, a Mighty Man was He," E.C. Russell. Jan 1960, p 19.

"The Corner Brook Navy," Anonymous. Sep 1962, p 10.

"The Days of the RNCVR," Lt(SB) P. Ward, Apr 1962, p 16-18.

"The Frigate Story." Anonymous. Apr 1962, p 33-34.

"The Invasion of Padloping Island," Anonymous. Feb 1954, p 18.

"The Padre and the Pigs," Anonymous. Dec 1961, p 10.

"The RCNR's New Outlook," Anonymous. Apr 1963, p 10.

"The Short But Useful Life of HMCS NIOBE II," Anonymous. Feb 1957, p 7-8.

"Weepers Jeepers! Lookit the Names They Give Our Sweepers," R.G.C. Mar 1956, p 8.

"Whence the Funnel's Maple Leaf," Anonymous. Jun 1957, p 15-16.

"Who Did Paint the First Maple Leaf," A.J. Bell. Sep 1957, p 27.

Other Periodicals

Anonymous. "It's a Fact—Blue Boat." *The Dockyard News*. Esquimalt, 25 Nov 1959.

Freeman, D J, LCdr (Ret'd). "Canadian Warship Names." *Starshell*, the national publication of The Naval Officers' Association of Canada, Spring 1997, published without permission of the author.

JAF. "ffoulkes' ffine designs." *Navy News*, Portsmouth, England. March 1997, page 20.

Jordon, Mabel E. "HMC Dockyard, Esquimalt." *Canadian Geographic Journal*. Ottawa: Canadian Geographic Society, Apr 1955.

Jordon, Mabel E. "Royal Roads Services College." *Canadian Geographical Journal*. Ottawa: Canadian Geographic Society, Jun 1954.

Keenleyside, Hugh. "The Great Yacht Plot." *Weekend Magazine*. Montréal, 23 Mar 1974.

Manning, T.D. "Type Names." *The Navy*, Nov 1958, p 323.

Milner, Marc. "HMCS SOMERS ISLES." *Canadian Defence Quarterly*, Vol 14, No 3, Winter 1984/85.

Sayer, VAdm Sir Guy. "The Naming of H.M. Ships." *Nautical Magazine*, Apr 1963, p 198-202.

Stubbs, Dorothy I. "HMCS QUADRA." *North Island Advertiser*. Courtenay, BC. 30 Jul 1977.

Whyard, Sub-Lieut Florence, W.R.C.N.S. "His Majesty's Canadian Ship CONESTOGA." *Canadian Geographical Journal*. Ottawa: Canadian Geographic Society, April 1945.

Unpublished Sources

Directorate of Auxiliary Vessels, NDHQ Ottawa:

"Alphabetical list of HMC local craft," 1 Nov 1945

"Canadian Forces Auxiliary vessels and yard craft," 19 Jan 1984

"Disposition of HMC local craft—east coast," 1 Apr 1945

"Vessels removed from list during Oct 1945"

Kilgour, Robert W. "A History of Canadian Naval Auxiliary Vessels," 1967.

Directorate of History and Heritage, NDHQ Ottawa:

"A Brief History of the Name Hochelaga in the Royal Canadian Navy." Ottawa: Naval Historical Section. 26 Jul 1955.

"Brief History of HMCS ORIOLE." 11 Apr 1974 (ORIOLE file).

"Esquimalt Naval Base." 24 Mar 1960.

Files:

Brief Histories of HMC Ships

Individual Reserve Divisions

Individual Ships

Individual Shore Establishments

Miscellaneous Lists & Correspondence with respect to Naming of HMC Ships

Naming of HMC Ships, Volumes 1 to 6

Royal Navy Ships on Loan to RCN

Ship's Names, NS 8000-5, Volumes 1 and 2

"HMCS VENTURE and her namesakes, 1787-1977"

"Launching, Naming and Commissioning Ceremonies." Lt(N) John Eden, circa 1974.

"Notes on the History of HMCS GIVENCHY." Ottawa: Office of the naval historian, 6 Aug 1954 (GIVENCHY file).

"Pennant List of the Canadian Fleet." 3 May 1974.

"Pennant Numbers of HMC Ships 1910-1949." 27 Apr 1971.

"RCN Shore Establishments on the Canadian East Coast 1910-1919." Ottawa: Naval Historical Section, 1961 (GUELPH I file).

Naval Board Minutes, to 1968.

Naval Staff Minutes, to 1968.

Directorate of Information, NDHQ Ottawa:
> Base Files:
> > CFB Alert
> > Dartmouth, NS
> > HMCS BYTOWN
> > HMCS D'IBERVILLE
> > HMCS HOCHELAGA
> > HMCS NADEN
> > HMCS STADACONA, RCN BARRACKS
> > HMCS QUEEN
> > HMCS VENTURE
> Ship Files:
> > CNAV Quest, 14 Aug 1969
> > HMCS MAGNIFICENT
> > HMCS ORIOLE, Feb 1972
> > HMCS QUEBEC
> > RAINBOW AND NIOBE, 24 Mar 1960

Office of Public Affairs:
> List of Ship's Bells, Revision 4, Jun 1983, NDHQ/DSRO 4.

Maritime Command Museum, Admiralty House, Halifax:
> "List of Ships of the RCN, 1910-1965," HP 164/65.

Canadian Forces School of Communications and Electronics Museum, CFB Kingston:
> "AKLAVIK (INUVIK) 1925-1959, Station Scrap Book"
> "Information book, HMCS COVERDALE, 1949-1971"
> "Information book, HMCS GLOUCESTER, 1943-1972"
> "Information book, NRS BERMUDA, 1963-"
> "Information book, NRS GANDER"
> "Information book, NRS INUVIK, Mar 1960 -"

Royal Military College Library, Kingston, Ontario:
> Ogle, LCdr D. "The Creation of Canadian Naval Aviation in World War II." An essay for War Studies 500 at the Royal Military College, April 1981.

Ogle, LCdr D. "The Politics of Walter Hose." An essay for War Studies at the Royal Military College, 21 Oct 1975.

Public Archives, Ottawa:

British Admiralty Technical Mission, RG 24 5619, NSS 30-1-3.

Flags to be Flown on Land, RG 24 5589, NSS 9-2-2.

General Data and Conditions Relative to Flags, RG 24 5588, NSS 9-2-2.

HMC Patrol Vessels, RG 24 5654 to 5666, NS 58-1-1 to 58-215-1.

Naming of Ships, RG 24 3988 to 90, NS 1057-1-5, Volumes 1 to 6.

Names for New Construction, RG 83-84/167 Navy 3539, NSC 8000-5, Volume 3.

Naval Council Minutes, RG 24 4044, NSS 1078-3-4, Volume 1.

Naval Establishments:

–Pictou RG 24 5606, NSS 40-9-2

–St John's RG 24 5637, NS 40-21-2.

Prince Class Liners, RG 24 5608, NSS 29-26-1.

RCSC Camps, RG 24 D1, NSS 1000-173/49, Vol 1 to 4.

Ships Requisitioned, 1938-1942 RG 24 5593 to 5595, NS 20-14-1, etc.

Work-up Bases, RG 24 4034, NSS 1070-2-2.

National Defence Records Management, NDHQ Ottawa:

Naming of Buildings, Units, Locations, Ships and Aircraft. NDHQ 1000-5.

Other:

Renaming Ceremony (HMS VICTORY) booklet, 1 Aug 1974.

Commonwealth Naval Shore Establishments, c. 1850-1988. LCdr David J Freeman, CF, 1988.

Interviews

J. MacNelly, former Lt(SB) RCNVR, Toronto, 27 May 1985.

D. Kealy, Directorate of History, Ottawa, 4 May 1984.

Lt Cdr R. Notley, RN (Ret'd), Victoria, BC, 29 Sep 1995.

A/Capt Alfred C Wurtele, RCN (Ret'd), Victoria, BC, 8 June 1998.

Adm J R Anderson, CF (Ret'd), North Saanich, BC, 6 Jan 2000.

Index

General Index

The third VANCOUVER (on far side) and the second TORONTO in 1993. PRESERVER is in the background.
(Cpl W Marcoux, CF SWC93-381-1. NPA)

Index of Ships

NONSUCH 157
NORHAM CASTLE 122
ONYX 168
PARRSBORO 127
PASLEY 140
PATRIOT 117
PATRICIAN 117
PINCHER 141
PUNCHER 62, 124, 127, 141
QUALICUM 127
QUEBEC 36, 139-40
QUEEN ELIZABETH 145
QUEEN 141, 145
QUEENBOROUGH 140
RAINBOW 21
RIBBLE 62, 132
SEABORN 171
SEABORN II 130
SHEARWATER 125
SHIPPIGAN 127
SNOWBERRY 133
SPIKENARD 133
TADOUSSAC 127
TEME 132
TORBAY 119
TORREADOR 117, 119
TOWER 51
TRILLIUM 133
UGANDA 122
UNICORN 30

VANCOUVER 117
VICTORIA 144
VICTORY 33, 52-3, 152
VIMY 117
VIXEN 122
WARRIOR 56, 157
WARSPITE 60
WEDGEPORT 127
WHITBY 62
WINDFLOWER 133
WOLFE 150, 157

Other ships

Acadia, CGS 27
Acadian, RCMP 147
Advocate 118
ALABAMA, USS 70
Albacore 26
BURRFISH, USS 103
Canada, CGS 26, 41
Columbia 119
Cygnus, RCMP 158
DALHOUSIE, HMIS 99
Diana 41
DRUMMOND (Argentine) 150
Earl Grey, CGS 27
Emerillon 155
French, RCMP 158
GAMBIA, HMNZS 123

General Schmidlin 170
Gulnare 26
HAWKSBURY, HMAS 62
Helena 41
Irvine, RCMP 158
JUNEAU, USS 69
Laurentian, DOT 150
LAWRENCE, HMIS 150
Lord Kelvin 28
LOS ANGELES, USS 70
Lusitania 71
MacBrien, RCMP 158
Macleod, RCMP 158
Margaret, CGS 26
MELVILLE, HMAS 62
Oracle 32-3, 149, 153
Oriole IV 169
Restico 149
Queen Elizabeth, RMS 145
Queen Mary, RMS 75
Tarantula 118
Terra Nova 42
Titanic 71
Victoria, RCMP 158
Winchester 118

Index of Cities, Towns, Place and other names